TOURISM ECOLABELLING
Certification and Promotion of Sustainable Management

To Julie and Carina

TOURISM ECOLABELLING
Certification and Promotion of Sustainable Management

Edited by

X. FONT

Centre for the Study of Small Tourism and Hospitality Firms
School of Tourism and Hospitality Management
Leeds Metropolitan University
Leeds
UK

and

R.C. BUCKLEY

International Centre for Ecotourism Research
School of Environmental and Applied Science
Griffith University
Gold Coast
Australia

CABI *Publishing*

CABI *Publishing* is a division of CAB *International*

CABI Publishing
CAB International
Wallingford
Oxon OX10 8DE
UK

CABI Publishing
10E 40th Street
Suite 3203
New York, NY 10016
USA

Tel: +44 (0)1491 832111
Fax: +44 (0)1491 833508
Email: cabi@cabi.org
Web site: http://www.cabi.org

Tel: +1 212 481 7018
Fax: +1 212 686 7993
Email: cabi-nao@cabi.org

A catalogue record for this book is available from the British Library, London, UK.

Library of Congress Cataloging-in-Publication Data

Tourism ecolabelling: certification and promotion of sustainable management / edited by X. Font and R.C. Buckley
     p.   cm.
  Includes bibliographical references and index.
  ISBN 0-85199-506-3 (alk. paper)
  1. Ecotourism--Certification. 2. Eco-labeling. I. Font, Xavier. II. Buckley, Ralf.
  G155.A1 T5917 2001
  338.4'791--dc21   00-057975

ISBN 0 85199 506 3

Typeset by AMA DataSet Ltd, UK
Printed and bound in the UK by Biddles Ltd, Guildford and King's Lynn

Contents

v

Part IV. Information Sources

Contributors

Professor Ralf Buckley is Director, Nature and Adventure Tourism for the Cooperative Research Centre for Sustainable Tourism, and Chair in Ecotourism at Griffith University. He is currently co-director of the CRC Tourism/Tourism Council Australia 'Green Leaders Initiative' on Best Practice Environmental Management in Tourism, and leader of the new CRC Tourism 'Nature Tourism Initiative'. He has written over 150 articles in science, management and tourism journals, seven books, and over 100 consultant reports; and has carried out consultant and research projects in over 40 countries worldwide. Griffith University PMB 50 Gold Coast Qld 9726, Australia (R.Buckley@mailbox.gu. edu.au).

Dr Dimitrios Diamantis is Lecturer in tourism and responsible for research and development in Les Roches Management School in Switzerland. Prior to this, he worked in the International Centre for Tourism and Hospitality Research in Bournemouth University, UK, as a researcher for the Millennium Vision Policy for the World Travel and Tourism Council (WTTC). Alongside his research activities he teaches graduate and postgraduate students as well as coordinating a discussion group for the development of tourism in UNESCO's biosphere reserves. He has a degree in Hotel Management from South-Bank University, a Masters in Tourism Marketing from Surrey University, a Diploma in Marketing from the Chartered Institute of Marketing (CIM) and a PhD from Bournemouth University. Tourism and Hospitality Research Center, Swiss Hotel Association, Les Roches Management School, CH-3975 Bluche-Crans-Montana, Valais, Switzerland (d_diamantis@hotmail.com).

Attina Dominé studies geography, economics and journalism at the Free University Berlin with the main emphasis on social and economic geography. As a research assistant at Ecologic her work focuses on tourism and the environment. Ecologic, Pfalzburger Strasse 43-44, 10717 Berlin, Germany (domine@ecologic.de).

Megan Epler Wood is the founder and President of The International Ecotourism Society (TIES), an international NGO with 1700 members in 70 countries. She teaches annual international workshops for The George Washington University on ecotourism planning, management and destination development. She has led stakeholder meetings, forums, conferences and workshops in Latin America, the Caribbean, Africa and Asia on key issues relating to the development of responsible ecotourism. She was the facilitator and editor for the development of the TES *Ecotourism Guidelines for Nature Tour Operators* in 1993 and editor and author for the TES text, *Ecotourism: a Guide for Planners and Managers*, Vol. 2 in 1998. She developed the 'Your Travel Choice Makes a Difference' campaign to increase global ecotourism awareness via a website, advertising and a consumer guide in 1999. TIES, PO Box 668, Burlington, VT 05402, USA (http://www. ecotourism.org/, ecomail@ecotourism.org).

Xavier Font is Senior Lecturer in Tourism Management at Leeds Metropolitan University. His research focuses on marketing and management of rural tourism and outdoor recreation, and he has co-authored and co-written three books in English and Spanish (*Forest Tourism and Recreation, Environmental Management for Rural Tourism and Recreation* and *Marketing de destinos turísticos: análisis y desarrollo*). Formerly he was project officer for Tourfor, a EU LIFE project developing proposals for a European ecolabel. He is currently a member of the PAN Parks Advisory Board. Leeds Metropolitan University, Calverley St, Leeds LS1 3HE, UK (X.Font@lmu.ac.uk).

Lesley Forsyth is a graduate in international tourism management from Leeds Metropolitan University. After her studies, she carried out research on behalf of the editors for the completion of this book's directory. She has worked on placement at the Northumbria Tourist Board, and undertaken primary research on the branding of tourist destinations, with reference to Hadrian's Wall World Heritage Site, England. Leeds Metropolitan University, Calverley St, Leeds LS1 3HE, UK.

Ute Haak (Dipl.-Ing) studied landscape planning in Hannover and is a graduate in engineering. She is a project employee of the Academy for Environmental Research and Education in Europe. In 1997 she received a diploma for her research on ecolabels in tourism. She is a member of the working group 'leisure time, sports, tourism' of the

Federation for the Protection of the Environment and Nature (Bund für Umwelt und Naturschutz Deutschland, BUND). Akademie für Umweltforschung und -bildung in Europa, AUbE, August-Bebel-Str 16-18 33602, Bielefeld, Germany (Akademie-fuer-Umwelt@t-online.de).

Eva Haas (Dipl.-Betriebswirtin) studied business economics in Worms (FH/technical college) and is a graduate in tourism. She is a project employee of Ecotrans, the European Network for Sustainable Development in Tourism. Since 1998 she has worked in the project ECO-TIP (European Commission co-financed), the leading information system on ecolabels and best practice examples for sustainability in tourism. Since 1999 she has been a member of the European ECO-TIP management group and is responsible for its database, website and ecolabels. Furthermore she works in the project Federal Competition for Children and Youth Travel (TopTeamNaTour) on the working group Youth Travel with Insight (Arbeitsgemeinschaft Jugendreisen mit Einsicht). ECOTRANS e.V., Berliner Promenade 7, D-66111 Saarbrücken, Germany (http://www.ecotrans.org/, Ecotrans@t-online.de).

Elizabeth Halpenny is the former Projects Director of The International Ecotourism Society. During her time at the Society she co-developed new training programmes and curricula focused on various facets of the ecotourism field including ecotourism services, facilities, planning and management, as well as specialized courses in community participation and marine ecotourism. Ms Halpenny also managed the Society's newly completed marine initiative, a project focused on the development of guidelines and collection of best practices for small-scale, low-impact tourism activities in coastal areas. Two of her final projects at TIES included the coordination of a meeting on international development policy and ecotourism, and a study of ecolodges finance. She has worked in Indonesia, Kenya and the Caribbean, and travelled throughout Central America and Europe examining nature and cultural tourism trends and products. R.R.#2 Almonte, Ontario K0A 1A0, Canada (ehalpenny@sympatico.ca).

Herbert Hamele is the President of Ecotrans, a European network of experts and organizations in tourism, environment and regional development, which is seeking to promote good practice in the field of sustainable tourism. Ecotrans was established in 1993 and has NGO members in nine European countries. Ecotrans is host to one of the strongest databases on tourism ecolabels in Europe, and is actively involved in the feasibility study for a single European ecolabel. ECOTRANS e.V., Berliner Promenade 7, D-66111 Saarbrücken, Germany (http://www.ecotrans.org/, Ecotrans@t-online.de).

Walter Kahlenborn holds a degree in business engineering and one in philosophy and history. In 1996 he started to work with Ecologic, Centre for International and European Environmental Research. His work focuses on the integration of environmental concerns in different sector policies. As a Senior Fellow he is responsible for all Ecologic projects concerning tourism and the environment. In this role, he coordinated projects analysing the interface of tourism policy and environmental policy in Germany and globalization and tourism for the German Parliament. The results of both projects were published in book form recently. Ecologic, Pfalzburger Strasse 43-44, 10717 Berlin, Germany (kahlenborn@berlin.snafu.de).

Dr Claudia Lübbert is Assistant Professor at the Institut of Economic Geography, University of Munich. Her main research fields are quality and environmental management in tourism, and she has expertise as a project manager in tourism. University of Munich (LMU), Institute of Economic Geography, Geschwister-Scholl-Platz 1, Munich, Germany (luebbert@bwl.uni-muenchen.de).

Dr Tanja Mihalič is Associate Professor of Tourism Economics and Management at the Faculty of Economics, University of Ljubljana. Her current research interests include environmental economics, tourism competitiveness and tourism policy; her practical work is related to environmental labelling in the tourism and hospitality industry. Kardeljeva pl. 17, 1000 Ljubljana, Slovenia (Tanja.Mihalic@uni.-lj.si).

Vinod Sasidharan is a PhD candidate and instructor in leisure studies at the School of Hotel, Restaurant, and Recreation Management, The Pennsylvania State University. His primary research focus includes sustainability issues in tourism planning and management and urban recreational resource planning and management. He has published papers in the areas of sustainable development of coastal and marine tourism resources; recreation and tourism trends in response to El Niño and global climatic change; influence of tourism and recreation on forest succession; and incorporating urban wildlife and environmental values of ethnic minorities in urban park interpretation. School of Hotel, Restaurant, and Recreation Management, The Pennsylvania State University, 201 Mateer Building, University Park, PA 16802, USA (vxs18@psu.edu).

Dr Richard Sharpley is Senior Lecturer in travel and tourism at the University of Northumbria at Newcastle. His main research interests include the sociology of tourism, focusing in particular on the consumption of tourism, rural tourism, and tourism and development issues. He has written a number of articles and text books, including

Tourism and Leisure in the Countryside and *Tourism, Tourists and Society*, both now in their second edition. University of Northumbria at Newcastle, Division of Travel and Tourism, Longhirst Campus, Longhirst, Morpeth, Northumberland NE61 3LL, UK (richard. sharpley@unn.ac.uk).

Rolf Spittler (Dipl.-Geogr.) has been the Manager of the Academy for Environmental Research and Education in Europe since 1996. He studied geography, specializing in landscape ecology, in Münster. His work at the academy focuses on leisure time and tourism, consultancy project work and education on nature protection, evaluation of intervention concerning planning of infrastructure, development of environmentally compatible alternatives for location and use. Since 1997 he has also been leader of the landscape planning office NEULAND-Westfalen. Since 1993 he has been honorary speaker of the working group on leisure time, sports, tourism of the Federation for the Protection of the Environment and Nature (Bund für Umwelt und Naturschutz Deutschland, BUND). He is also a member of the community of the Association for Ecological Tourism in Europe (Ökologischer Tourismus in Europa, ÖTE). Akademie für Umweltforschung und -bildung in Europa, AUbE, August-Bebel-Str 16-18, 33602 Bielefeld, Germany (Akademie-fuer-Umwelt@t-online.de).

Kirsty Thorpe is a graduate in tourism management from Leeds Metropolitan University. After her studies, she carried out research on behalf of the editors for the completion of this book's directory. Previously, she undertook primary research on the analysis of heritage interpretation and its effects on residents in York, England. Leeds Metropolitan University, Calverley St, Leeds LS1 3HE, UK.

Professor John Tribe is Head of Research in the Faculty of Leisure and Tourism at Buckinghamshire Chilterns University College, UK. He has published books in leisure and tourism on economics, strategy, environmental management and forest management. He was director of a European Union research project (Tourfor) investigating the use of environmental management systems to encourage sustainable recreation uses in forests, and he is currently directing a tourism education project in Moldova. Faculty of Leisure and Tourism, Buckinghamshire Chilterns University College, High Wycombe HP11 2JZ, UK (john.tribe@bcuc.ac.uk).

John Westlake is Professor in Tourism and Deputy Head of the International Centre for Tourism and Hospitality Research in Bournemouth University. He is a planner and geographer by background and previously worked in central government and in the University of

Surrey in the UK. He has acted as consultant on training activities in many countries on behalf of many international organizations. International Centre for Tourism and Hospitality Research, Bournemouth University, PO Box 2816, Poole BH12 5YT, UK (jwestlak@bournemouth.ac.uk).

Pamela Wight is President of Pam Wight & Associates, an international consultancy specializing in sustainable tourism. Projects involve environmental and resource planning, impact management, public participation, protected areas and conservation planning, community development and capacity building, and feasibility studies and development planning. She has been involved in consulting since 1974, and spent 7 years with the province of Alberta's Ministry of Economic Development and Tourism, involved in ecotourism projects, land use planning, and Canada's first 'green tourism' initiative. Pam's focus is on attempting to provide practical applications for cutting edge theory, providing approaches to making projects work in real-world situations. Her voluntary work includes participating in college and government committees, The International Ecotourism Society's Advisory Board, and authoring numerous publications. Pam Wight & Associates, 14715-82 Ave, Edmonton, Alberta, Canada, T5R 3R7 (pamwight@superiway.net).

Foreword

The tourism industry plays a major economic role in many countries, and can make significant contributions to environmental protection as well as socio-economic development. But through its own activities, which can result in high levels of resource consumption, and of pollution and waste, tourism may also lead to adverse environmental impacts. At the same time, beaches and mountains, rivers, forests and biodiversity make the environment a basic resource upon which the tourism industry depends to thrive and grow. It therefore makes good business sense for the tourism industry to operate in an environmentally sound manner.

Ecolabels in tourism and other sectors act as incentives to encourage businesses to achieve significant improvements in their environmental performance. They are one of the many voluntary instruments that can provide an effective complement to formal regulation by national authorities. Credible ecolabels promote sustainable consumption patterns by providing concise and accurate information to consumers to help them identify those products and services which incorporate a good level of environmental performance.

Well-designed ecolabel schemes also provide an indirect source of guidance, through the criteria, evaluation and monitoring procedures that each scheme adopts, to help enterprises improve their environmental practices. These assist enterprises to identify critical issues that they need to address, and to select the most effective corrective and preventive actions, as well as providing external assessment for the year-on-year improvements that enterprises seek to achieve. This can be of particular assistance to small and medium-sized enterprises. Gaining an ecolabel can also enhance the commercial image of a business, and can facilitate relationships with other stakeholders.

However, ecolabels will only be effective in promoting sound levels of environmental performance if they are credible to consumers, to national regulatory authorities, to environmental specialists, to international, national, local and civil society organizations, as well as to businesses themselves. Only if they have sound criteria backed by sound evaluation and monitoring procedures that are transparent and open to public scrutiny, will ecolabels contribute to effective environmental management. Without these, an ecolabel is simply a marketing tool that could mislead consumers by implying a level of environmental performance in the absence of proper measurement of standards achieved.

The United Nations Environment Programme strongly supports the use of effective voluntary instruments of all types as tools to encourage long-term commitments and improvements that go beyond minimum standards set in regulations. UNEP's work, which includes assessments of Codes of Conduct[1] and Ecolabels[2] in the tourism sector is helping to increase understanding of voluntary instruments and to facilitate their use.

Based on UNEP's experience, key factors for the credibility of voluntary initiatives, including ecolabels, are that:

• all stakeholders participate in their development;
• their criteria are based on sustainable development, including environmental protection and social factors, and take into account best available technology;
• they provide businesses with a significant but achievable challenge that leads to real and continuous performance improvements;
• technical support is available to businesses that wish to implement the criteria;
• information about the actual performance of participating enterprises is publicly reported;
• they are supervised by independent, not-for-profit organizations.

UNEP, in cooperation with UNESCO and the World Tourism Organization, is also supporting the Tour Operators' Initiative for Sustainable Tourism Development. Although it is not an ecolabel, the Tour Operators' Initiative is based on similar elements and overall objectives. Tour operator members of the Initiative commit themselves to adopting the principles of, and best practices for, sustainable development in their own operations and in their relations with their business partners. They also commit to preparing a corporate policy for their implementation of sustainable development and to reporting regularly on their progress.

As this book demonstrates, the potential of ecolabels is recognized by many different groups of stakeholders. The growing number of

---

1   UNEP (1995) *Environmental Codes of Conduct for Tourism*. UNEP, Paris.
2   UNEP (1998) *Ecolabels in the Tourism Industry*. UNEP, Paris.

ecolabels in tourism raises questions on how to set clear standards for the design and implementation of ecolabels themselves, and how to ensure that they are used appropriately as an instrument for raising performance standards. In all circumstances, one of the essential tests of an ecolabel is whether it leads to the good long-term environmental management that is a fundamental condition for sustainability in the production of goods and the delivery of services.

The need for better understanding of voluntary initiatives, including ecolabels, and for assessment of their effectiveness as tools for performance and quality improvement, has been highlighted by UNEP, the UN Commission on Sustainable Development and other international bodies. It is vital to distinguish those ecolabels and other initiatives that are effective in generating real benefits for environmental protection and sustainable development, from those that are ineffective or misleading in their claims. In its review of progress and assessment of future trends, this book makes a significant contribution to our understanding of ecolabels and their application in tourism. I welcome it wholeheartedly.

Jacqueline Aloisi de Larderel
Director, Division of Technology, Industry and Economics
United Nations Environment Programme
Paris, July 2000

Preface

This book on ecolabels and certification schemes in the tourism industry represents a major contribution to the achievement of a higher level of sustainability in tourism. The book describes in detail over 70 of such schemes currently applied in a wide spectrum of countries, mostly developed societies of the northern hemisphere, plus Australia. It also suggests ways for widening the applicability and hence validity of these ecolabels and certification systems.

The subject of ecolabels in tourism has been increasingly attracting the attention of tourism policymakers at the international, national and local levels, as well as within the tourism industry. For public sector officials, ecolabels are envisaged as a possible mechanism for encouraging sustainable practices in the tourism industry without resorting to official regulatory frameworks and burdensome bureaucratic control and inspection procedures; the latter, however, may still be necessary to validate the rather large number of ecolabels currently in application. In the private sector, ecolabels are predominantly seen as a marketing and promotional tool to provide guarantees to the consumer that the product and services that a company sells are 'sustainable', or at least that the firm is committed to improving its environmental sustainability.

There is a need for a higher degree of convergence between public sector interest in ecolabels and private sector motivation for adopting ecolabels or similar schemes. In other words, ecolabels and voluntary schemes in tourism should serve to stimulate the continuous introduction of sustainable practices by tourism companies of all sizes and in all subsectors of the industry. Therefore, with the help of this book, efforts can and should be made to make these schemes more efficient by setting up increasingly stringent criteria for granting labels, by making these criteria as universal as possible so that labels can be easily recognized by domestic and international tourists at any destination, and by improving their monitoring and verification processes.

This is also a timely publication, since many countries, local authorities, non-government organizations and private organizations are considering the introduction of new ecolabels, voluntary initiatives or certification schemes related to sustainability in their tourism operations. A careful analysis of the positive and negative aspects of existing schemes will help them to devise the most suitable one for their local conditions, thus reducing the natural learning and trial-and-error period typical of these relatively new certification arrangements.

The publication of this book coincides with an effort currently being made by the World Tourism Organization in the framework of its programme of work in the field of sustainable development of tourism. As recommended by the UN Commission on Sustainable Development at its 7th session, WTO is trying to assess the effectiveness of voluntary initiatives in tourism, in terms of their actual contribution to the long-term sustainability of the sector, and to identify the factors that make some voluntary schemes more efficient than others. This book already provides an excellent basis for such an evaluation.

Eugenio Yunis
Chief, Sustainable Development of Tourism
World Tourism Organization
Madrid, July 2000

Acknowledgements

The authors acknowledge the support received from a variety of individuals and institutions without which this book would not have been completed. The idea for this book arose during work at Buckinghamshire Chilterns University College on an ecolabelling project for the European Commission with John Tribe, Head of Research and friend; we are in debt to him for his guidance and mentorship.

From Leeds Metropolitan University, we thank in particular Rhodri Thomas, Principal Lecturer in Research, and Vicky Harris, Head of School, for the support in time and resources given to write this book. Special thanks are due to Kirsty Thorpe and Lesley Forsyth, graduates in tourism management at Leeds Metropolitan University, for their hard work in collecting and compiling data for the directory of ecolabels. We should also thank Dirk-Abe Schaafsma and Nicola Rincknowotny for the translation of material from German to English.

A wide number of institutions have been instrumental in the provision of information for this book. The authors would like to thank Herbert Hamele, from Ecotrans, and Manfred Pils, from Naturfreunde Internationale, for their support in providing data on tourism ecolabels. The authors would also like to thank Jacqueline Aloisi de Larderel, from the United Nations Environment Programme (Industry and Environment) for writing the foreword to this book and Eugenio Yunis, from the World Tourism Organization, for writing the preface.

Finally we would like to express our thanks for the help and support of Tim Hardwick from CAB *International*.

Xavier Font and Ralf Buckley
Leeds and Queensland, February 2001

xxi

Chapter 1

Regulating the Green Message: the Players in Ecolabelling
XAVIER FONT

Introduction

Green sells. Moving away from mass tourism, postmodern travellers want to believe that their use of tourism facilities and their presence in tourist destinations will not damage the resources they visit and embrace the promises offered by tourism companies. The development of direct selling, the increase in specialist tour operators and the consolidation of independent travel has provided the platform for tourism consumers to look for alternative holiday concepts. Environmental concerns among the public and a growing number of consumers willing to choose greener products has made the environment one of the key tools to gain competitive advantage, and a common element of tourism's segmenting, targeting and positioning strategies. Small group sizes and the opening of new tourist destinations allow high spenders to buy the green dream, sold by an increasing number of operators promoting themselves as environmentally friendly, sustainable, green, ecological, soft, natural, rural . . ..

The increasing number of green marketing claims in tourism has raised many eyebrows, and one basic question: are there any methods to ensure the validity of such claims? Systems to regulate environmental promotion vary across borders, ranging from legislation to industry self-regulation to voluntary codes of practice (Polonsky, 1995; DoE, 1997; Leubuscher et al., 1998). Table 1.1 shows the effectiveness of green claim control regimes across members of the European Union, showing a direct relationship between those countries where the environment is considered of importance and where systems enforce good practice. The effectiveness of methods to control green claims made by companies has a direct impact on the public's confidence in the green message, since most consumers have a low comprehension of the green

© CAB International 2001. Tourism Ecolabelling
(eds X. Font and R.C. Buckley)

Table 1.1. The effectiveness of green claim control regimes in Europe (Leubuscher et al., 1998).

Member state	Access to complaints procedures (public/ self-regulation)	Level of activity in green complaints (public/self regulation)	Effect on claims, excluding on pack claims	Consumer information
Austria	Good	None	*	Average +
Belgium		None/significant	*	Average/ poor
Denmark	Good	Very active	**	Very active
Finland	Excellent	Active	**	Active
France	Good/good	Limited	*	?
Germany	Good/good	Active	**	Active
Greece	Fair/fair	None/none		Poor
Ireland		None		Poor
Italy	Fair/good	Limited	*	Poor
Luxembourg				?
Netherlands	Excellent	Very active	**	Active
Portugal	Fair	None		Poor
Spain	Fair	None	—	Poor
Sweden	Excellent	Very active	**	Very active
United Kingdom	Fair/good	Active	*	Average

jargon and a sceptical view of claims made, despite thinking that they ought to buy green when possible.

There has been a proliferation of green marketing terms used to sell physical goods; supermarket shelves are full of products with environmental claims on their packs, the most important area for regulation (NCC, 1996a; Leubuscher et al., 1998). Some frequently used but hard to verify green marketing terms are atmosphere-friendly, bio-degradable, compostable, dioxin-free, earth-friendly, energy friendly, fresh, green, natural and so on (Wasik, 1996). Since outright false environmental claims have been controlled by advertising standards organizations, companies are moving towards the promotion of subliminal green corporate images.

Yet the move towards using the environment to sell tourism products has been less obvious, partly because the environmental setting of resorts and tourism facilities has always been part of the product itself. For this reason the use of environmental terms in tourism marketing is more subtle, or at least more acceptable in the eyes of the consumer. If in physical goods the green showcase is the product's packaging, in tourism the green message comes across in brochures, advertisements and Internet pages. Green claims in tourism are also harder to verify, due to the intangible, perishable, inseparable and heterogeneous nature of the products. Furthermore, they are also harder to regulate, since a large number of them refer to the quality of the environment at the destination, rather than to the impact made by the tourism company. Voluntary guidelines to meet ecotourism principles mean few operators will comply (Sirakaya and McLellan, 1998) and only about half of the product and management claims in the World Congress of Adventure Travel and Ecotourism were supported by factual details (Buckley and Clough, 1997).

Considering the ethics of tourism development, Wheeler states that 'there is a need to change the nature of the product claims by increasing specificity about where the environmental benefit in the product or service lies; increasing precision in terminology accompanied by definitional support; and increasing specificity in product benefits' (1998: 1). The development of ecolabels in the tourism industry responds to the need to regulate the green message by identifying those tourism organizations that actively promote tourism that does not damage the environment (Mihalic, 1996, 1999). The United Nations Environment Programme states that ecolabels are 'one of the most promising voluntary approaches . . . to attain high environmental standards' (1998: 1). Ecolabels are methods to standardize the promotion of environmental claims by following compliance to set criteria, generally based on third party, impartial verification, usually by governments or non-profit organizations.

A wide range of ecolabels in tourism, hospitality and land management have been introduced during the last decade, most of them run at sub-national level. Most of these are subsidized and in most cases they have not reached the expected level of public interest or industry take up. At present these are very much operating independently of complementary environmental initiatives and programmes. Although ecolabels can recognize good practice, the introduction of verification systems needs to go hand-in-hand with the regulation of claims outside verification, since these undermine the 'official' ecolabels. Looking back at Table 1.1, it is not surprising that the stronger ecolabels are in those countries with tougher environmental legislation and effective methods to implement it. Failure to control green claims puts at a disadvantage the operator that seriously attempts to address the environmental impacts it causes.

Book Rationale and Overview of Chapters

For the purpose of this book, ecolabels will be viewed as marketing tools to promote good environmental performance. The boundaries between labels and awards are quite blurred in tourism, since there are several labels given to a small number of applicants, and tourists do not always distinguish between them. This text will examine how these are managed, rather than the scientific issues behind the environmental testing of criteria. Ecolabels do not only relate to ecotourism operators, but to any tourism company that uses the environment as part of its marketing strategy or that looks for external recognition for its environmental performance. This book will review the progress made to date by ecolabels in helping to control misleading claims in tourism marketing by providing state-of-the-art information and expertise from a variety of countries actively working on management of environmental impacts of tourism. Only ecolabels specific to the tourism industry will be reviewed, as there is a current gap in the literature. Therefore, this book will not focus on the work done by the International Standardization Office (ISO) in setting up the ISO 14000 series standards; there are numerous publications specifically dealing with these (see for example Tibor and Feldman, 1996; Sayre, 1996; Johnson, 1997; Sheldon, 1997).

The book is divided into an introductory section and four parts, from a broader to a more specific level. The two introductory chapters overview the players (Chapter 1) and issues (Chapter 2) in ecolabelling, as a means to provide a framework for the rest of the book.

Part I contextualizes tourism ecolabels by considering their relationship with sustainable tourism and ecotourism (Chapter 3) and the impact of ecolabels in holiday consumption (Chapters 4, 5 and 6). Chapter 4 links consumer behaviour theories to the consumption of tourism and the impacts of ecolabels. This is followed by an analysis of the implications of the environmental behaviour of tourists towards destinations and tourism products (Chapter 5). As a last contribution in this section, Chapter 6 presents some up-to-date market research carried out in Germany.

Part II takes a more practical approach. Two chapters review the process of developing an ecolabel (Chapter 7) and the pitfalls in their development and implementation (Chapter 8). The rest of this section is devoted to the progress made in developing ecolabels, first looking at ecotourism labels internationally (Chapter 9) and then specific quality labels in Australia (Chapter 10), Canada (Chapter 11) and Europe (Chapter 12), with clear contrasts across their development stages and expected outcomes.

Part III of the book reviews recent changes in ecolabels and their current developments (Chapter 13), and compares the quality of tourism ecolabels based on their criteria, management, performance and validity (Chapter 14). These two chapters raise issues of the validity of small labels, and how stronger, broader labels can do a better job of promoting sustainable tourism, which is then picked up in Chapter 15 when considering the advantages and disadvantages of internationalizing labelling schemes. The book is concluded by reviewing the contribution made to the literature and the issues arising from the research, and suggesting methods for the development of tourism ecolabels (Chapter 16).

Part IV presents a directory of current ecolabels, with useful addresses and comments on the labels, criteria, management and industry take up, which underpin a variety of chapters in this book. This directory was compiled at Leeds Metropolitan University with support from Ecotrans (2000) and Naturfreunde Internationale (2000), among other sources.

The rest of this chapter reviews the key players in tourism ecolabels, as shown in Fig. 1.1, and links across other chapters in the book.

The Tourism Market

The growth of the demand for and supply of ecotourism and the reported generic interest of the public for environmental issues in the

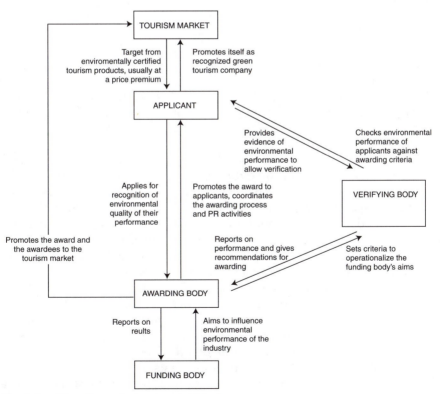

Fig. 1.1. The players in tourism ecolabels.

last decade has been used to justify the potential role of environmental considerations in purchasing holidays. 'The consumer's potential contribution to improved environmental performance is now internationally recognized' (Leubuscher *et al.*, 1998: 4) yet the conversion from potential to actual green purchases is lower than claimed (NCC, 1996b; Wong *et al.*, 1996), partly due to a lack of understanding of the role of the environment against other considerations in holiday choice, such as price, availability, adequacy, quality and so on (Manfredo, 1992). Wong *et al.* state that 'in absence of clarity of green products' environmental benefits, product performance and other attributes, not green benefits, remain the main determinants of product preference and choice' (1996: 263). Chapter 4 reviews the consumer behaviour context of ecolabelling in an effort to identify the 'green tourist' among consumption practices, and hence to provide the basis for the more effective design and targeting of ecolabels.

The importance of the environment as part of a holiday destination means that tourists may look for ecolabels to ensure their destination has a clean, pleasant surrounding. Quite a few of the tourism ecolabels overlap with health concerns, such as the Blue Flag, testing bathing water quality. Fewer tourists will be concerned enough to go beyond this, and to consider labels proving good environmental practices or environmental improvement, although both may be related. Yet reported environmental concerns referring to destination cleanliness can be interpreted out of context to justify the development of ecolabelling initiatives which will be incidental to the tourist. Understanding the consumer's environmental behaviour will provide the ecolabel organizer with the tools to sharpen their marketing strategies to ensure that tourists are aware of how good environmental practice benefits them as individuals.

Chapter 5 shows how the market mechanism can be routed towards environmental protection, preservation and even towards the upgrading of already degraded environments through various kinds of environmental labelling. The market functioning of ecolabelling is explained by environmental behaviour theories, arguing that all categories of environmental labelling in tourism are not equally effective in attracting tourist demand and distinguishes between eco-, environmental quality and quasi labels.

The development of ecolabels has been mostly a top-down approach, recognizing the industry's need to clean up its act and introducing methods to do so, both in the tourism industry as well as other sectors such as manufacturing and forestry (Font and Tribe, 2001). Yet even in Germany, considered to be one of the countries with most established environmental seals of quality in tourism, Lübbert considers that these have not been very successful. One of the suggested reasons is that limited market research has been carried out to test the validity of ecolabels. In Chapter 6, Lübbert shows the German market expectations of an ecolabel for the tourism industry: a credible awarding and controlling body, information, point of reference, comparability of products and spatial areas, relevant award criteria and quality criteria. Lübbert then draws conclusions from the implications of market research in the development of ecolabels.

The Funding Body

Funding bodies are the organizations that pay for a large part of the costs of development or management of an ecolabel. Funding bodies tend to be governmental or non-profit organizations, and in a smaller number of cases, industry associations or tourism companies. The current trend is to include both public bodies and non-governmental organizations (NGOs) to guarantee credibility and transparency of the label, while also engaging industry associations and large tourism companies to ensure the industry commitment to applying for the label, and therefore the long-term survival of the label. Tourism ecolabels are run at a loss; very few can finance themselves through the costs of application, hence the importance of funding bodies. In general, a large percentage of the label's costs (usually fixed costs) are met via contributions in kind, such as office space and the payment of salaries, while the price of applications only pays for the verification process. This is likely to change in the near future, since the majority of labels have been running for less than 10 years, and funding bodies will soon ask for greater independence and self-sufficiency from the awarding bodies.

The success of a tourism ecolabel needs to be assessed against the objectives of the funding body, broadly: (i) the improvement of environmental performance of the industry; and (ii) the benefits of associating the funding body with 'good causes'. In the first case, the ecolabel will be run from a resource-based point of view, with strong management and verifying criteria, but limited customer projection. In the second case, the award will be run as a glamorous public relations exercise to ensure that the funding body benefits from a green image. This will certainly reach the potential tourism market, but the funding body is more likely to be remembered than the awardees.

Several chapters in this volume consider the position and role of funding agencies. Chapter 7 reviews the role of the funding agency in the development of a label, and Chapter 8 pinpoints some of the pitfalls of ecolabelling arising from the funding body's actions and position. Chapter 9 reviews ecotourism certification programmes, which to date have been launched by governments and NGOs, often with inadequate support from industry. Chapters 10, 11 and 12 consider the actions taken by funding bodies in Australia, Canada and Europe. Chapter 13 outlines the state-of-the-art in ecolabels, and therefore focuses on what funding bodies have done in the recent past and aim to do in the near future.

The Ecolabel and its Awarding Body

The 1990s were years of major growth in the number of tourism ecolabels. The directory in this book collects a sample of them, as a showcase of the gaps and overlaps in the current systems. For small ecolabels the funding and awarding body are the same organization, and therefore what we call here the awarding body will be the operational arm of the funding body. Yet, the most powerful and useful approaches to ecolabelling must be third party seals of approval (Welford, 1995), involving outsourcing the task to an independent body that receives an annual grant in aid.

Ecolabels can be classified in many different ways, but in general they show a concentration on developed countries. Different approaches have been taken in different countries, and this book presents views from Australia, Canada and Europe as three examples (Chapters 10, 11 and 12). Australia is unique in its development of the Nature and Ecotourism Accreditation Programme (NEAP), one of the strongest programmes certifying tour operators. North America is rather reluctant to introduce ecolabels as a whole and few programmes can be found; this book presents the Canadian experience in developing a best practice resource that can be easily used as the basis for a manual and set of criteria for a strong ecolabel. Finally, Europe has the largest number of labels, mostly around Germany, Austria and Scandinavia, overlapping in some cases, and rather confusing to the potential tourist. Issues in relation to economies of scale arise here, and the consideration of streamlining ecolabels comes across several difficulties.

This book reviews some of the major ecolabels in tourism, from different perspectives. Chapter 14 makes comparisons between European labels, considering their criteria, management, focus and outcomes. Chapter 13 reviews the changes that have taken place in the past 3 years, highlighting which labels are thriving and which are fading out. These analyses are underpinned by the directory of ecolabels in Part 4 of the book, the result of up-to-date primary research based on work from Ecotrans (2000), Naturfreunde Internationale (2000), UNEP (1998) and qualitative sources of enquiry.

Despite all the national efforts, the tourism ecolabels' marketplace is international, and it therefore calls for across-country measures. Chapter 15 focuses on the reasons why ecolabels will internationalize, such as economic globalization, the economic advantages of international labels, the growing interest of international bodies in the tourism sector, and consumer needs, and also the consequences of internationalizing labels, such as the adaptation of criteria to regional conditions, bureaucratization of top-heavy labels, and potential misuses. The conclusion of this chapter is, however, positive towards the internationalization process, considering that it will encourage transparency, clarity, public awareness and trust, greater industry interest and ability to operate in countries without national schemes. Recommendations are given to national environmental policy makers to benefit from the trend of internationalization. Chapter 9 also considers the need for internationalization of ecolabels, asking the international community for methods to support local ecotourism certification programmes with a credible international framework and funding.

An awarding body may target many different sectors of the industry, basically differentiated between providers of tourism products (such as hotels, airlines, attractions and destinations) and distribution channels (travel agents and tour operators). It has to be noted that there are also many more labels specific to accommodation providers than to other types of tourism organizations, and there is a significant lack of schemes for destinations and travel agents (UNEP, 1998). This is caused by the difficulty to verify and certify certain tourism operations. In the case of tourism products, it is easier for the company to verify its environmental performance because the company being examined has control over the delivery of its products, and a good part of its purchases can be geared towards products already certified as green (fuel, food, timber, etc.), therefore keeping the chain of custody. This is why accommodation providers can easily be targeted for environmental improvement (see also Chapter 9). However, a limited number of these providers will be able to reach their prospective customers with their green image and make a difference in their purchasing behaviour. In the case of distribution channels such as travel agents and tour operators, these do have the mechanisms to communicate with the potential environmentally conscious market, yet it is very hard for a tour operator to ensure that its packages, often run by local operators, meet the green claims, and even harder for a travel agent due to its broader product portfolio. The lack of control from these distribution channels makes it very costly for an environmental certification process, and therefore requires a much greater commitment from the tourism operator. Also for a tour operator to be environmentally conscious, it needs to find like-minded providers, limiting its choice and potentially making its product less competitive. The next few years should see an increase in the certification of distributing channels when there are enough holiday product components certified, and hopefully this will fuel an increase in customer awareness.

The projected growth of tourism ecolabels calls for an in-depth study of the process. Chapter 7 considers developing an ecolabel in three phases, plus project management tasks. The first phase consists of positioning the concept of an ecolabel among other environmental promotion tools and planning the ecolabel by considering the stakeholders to be included. The second stage involves developing the criteria to be used, the methods of verification and the tools to be made available to potential awardees, as well as consulting both with potential sites and stakeholders and piloting the guidelines written to help applicants. In the third stage the process is wrapped up by focusing on the proposals for managing the ecolabel, such as funding, alternative methods of running it and associated costs, bodies willing to endorse the label, and finally to market the proposals to sites and stakeholders to increase the interest in the ecolabel before handing over the proposals to the funding body.

It is necessary to be aware not only of the process, but also of the potential pitfalls of developing an ecolabel. Chapter 8 looks at these issues in detail, reviewing various stages of the ecolabelling process following the phases outlined in Chapter 7. The most common pitfalls are the economies of scale required to make an ecolabel work; under financial and management pressure, the ecolabel may give in to the preponderant influence of profit-seeking private sectors and the need to relax standards.

The Verifying Agency

The awarding body will have prepared a list of criteria to verify the tourism company's performance and management, and a briefing for a verifying agency to undertake this task. The verifying body has the difficult task of operationalizing these criteria, which are too often the result of compromises, showing their weaknesses at this stage.

Increasing interest in the sustainability of tourism products and providers has raised the question of which indicators can be used to determine sustainability and which methods are available to encourage the production and consumption of sustainable tourism products. Environmental codes of conduct have been developed, but the difficulty comes in the verification performance and management in the service industry. Environmental indicators and management systems were developed for manufacturing first, and later on acknowledged in tourism (see for example Ding and Pigram, 1995; Diamantis, 1998), although only the larger tourism companies will have the means to implement fully fledged environmental management systems, owing to their cost and the economies of scale involved. This leaves most tourism companies in the sticky position of having to justify the environmental soundness of their operations with limited means; even when they may be more responsible than larger companies they do not have the backing to prove it. Tourism ecolabels have responded by keeping their criteria to simple facts, mostly verified through site visits and little paperwork, although some recent labels are demanding stricter environmental management structures. This is one of the key issues that will determine the future shape and content of ecolabels.

It is also at the verification stage that differences between applicants become clearer. Some applicants will operate in new tourist destinations opening up to tourism by using their ecological and wildlife qualities to attract tourists. As a criticism to this approach, Wheeler states that

> the green concept allows the tourist industry to improve its own image while in reality continuing its familiar short term commercial profits strategy. The industry is happy because it can legitimately open up new areas for the more discerning (and expensive) range of the market, and tourists can enjoy the holiday they want with a clear conscience.
>
> (Wheeler, 1998: 7)

Yet, other applicants will be tourism operations that make efforts to reduce environmental impacts by, for example, implementing environmental management systems. This will help the overall tourism industry to become greener, but it also means that any kind of destination or operation can be awarded as being green, just on the basis that they are making an effort, despite potentially still having a worse environmental performance than others. In this case, destinations such as Benidorm in Spain, attracting over 4 million visitors per year and one of the key mass market destinations in the Mediterranean, should be awarded for their obvious efforts to improve their environmental performance. The criteria will vary according to the target of the ecolabel, and the verification will have to be adapted. Chapters 5 and 6 consider the implications from the market point of view.

The Applicant and the Tourism Industry

Tourism companies have many reasons to want to be seen to be environmentally respectful. Not only does it sell to prospective customers, but it is also beneficial for a company when dealing with the public sector, non-profit organizations, traders and company employees, as seen in Table 1.2 (Ledgerwood and Street, 1993; Post and Altman, 1994; Miller and Szekely, 1996; Tsai and Child, 1997; Hartman and Stafford, 1997; Menon and Menon, 1997). First of all, companies might want to preserve environmental resources, and influence others in this practice. Second, tourism companies may want to be seen to be environmentally friendly to gain corporate advantage through enhanced image. Third, companies may want to make savings or increase revenues from

Table 1.2. Benefits of green management and marketing (Font, 2001).

| Aims | Target markets | | | | |
	Organization itself	Traders	Non-profit organizations	Public sector	Customers
Resources preservation	Staff awareness	Ability to influence	Expert input to product design	Leadership	Managed consumption through education
Corporate advantage through image	Good staff relations	Access new suppliers Access to capital	Product endorsement	Status/PR Input in planning policies	Promotion Access to new markets
Financial benefits	Eco-savings	Reduced insurance Recycling revenues	Indirectly, through image reinforcement	Funding opportunity Penalty avoidance Possible tax incentives	Increase in usage prices

environmental practices and a green image, ranging from incentives to higher selling prices to cost savings (Font, 2001).

Many of the benefits mentioned in Table 1.2 come from green marketing, rather than green management, hence the temptation of promoting tourism products with references to unspoilt nature where this is consumed, but not protected, through tourism. Although none of the chapters in the book deals specifically with the industry's response to ecolabels, this is considered throughout as part of the current take up (Directory), industry's contribution to the development of labels (Chapter 7), their role in promoting sustainable tourism (Chapter 3) and their responsibility in the pitfalls of ecolabels (Chapter 8), to give some examples.

Different industries will use the environment in their marketing strategies at different times, depending on the availability of other sources of competitiveness, competitors' pressure and consumer pressure. The strategic use of the environment as a marketing tool has been broadly adapted to tourism, shown in the seven profiles listed below, and mapped out in Fig. 1.2 considering the importance they give to their environmental performance through green management against their use of the environment in their promotion through green marketing (Roome, 1992; Steger, 1993; Gummesson, 1994; Jose, 1996; Menon and Menon, 1997; Azzone *et al.*, 1997; Schaefer and Harvey, 1998). One of the key arguments for using award schemes behind

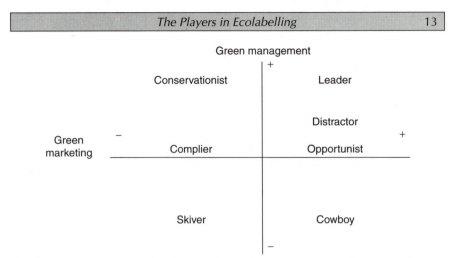

Fig. 1.2. Corporate attitudes towards the environment. (Source: Font, 2001.)

environmental achievements and claims is to ensure that only companies with good environmental management engage in green marketing (Font, 2001).

- *The conservationists*. Companies internalizing environmental costs on a continuous improvement basis. These companies understand the green path as a continuous improvement path, rather than a fixed state. Their management systems incorporate environmental issues, and they set themselves increasing targets higher than governmental regulations, yet they do not use their environmental performance to promote themselves, often because this would generate additional unwanted demand.
- *The leaders*. Those companies that will have environmental standards as high as the conservationist companies, and will also use their environmental performance as a promotional tool. These will be companies using competitive edge environmental management with a marketing focus, i.e. they will be 'enviropreneurial' companies.
- *The distractors*. Companies that will take the 'can do' approach rather than the 'should do'. These companies will want to be seen as green, and will focus on issues that they can easily deal with as their environmental flagship.
- *The compliers*. These are companies that comply with current legislation as a hurdle to tourism development. Environment is not a priority, and it will have few implications for management.
- *The opportunists*. Companies that use environmental claims for marketing purposes, with little change in their resource planning and management. These companies will comply with the basic

environmental legislation and will have institutionalized environmental concerns via mission statements and broad aims. These will
be presented to society via promotion, but with little background.

- *The skivers.* Opportunity-driven companies that, in the name
  of economic profits, will deny their most basic responsibilities
  to the environment. These companies do not comply with all
  environmental legislation and try to not draw attention to the
  environment around their organization.
- *The cowboys.* Similar to the skivers, but these companies promote
  their tourism products as being nature-based without being
  respectful to the resources used. This can be easier in tourism
  than other sectors due to differences between the tourist destination and the tourists' origin caused by the distance and the legal
  frameworks.

Conclusions: Ecolabels and the Environment

Most ecolabels in tourism, hospitality and destinations are run as
public relations exercises for funding bodies to show that they are
doing their bit, and for applicants to seek industry recognition. Few
ecolabels are market driven, because although there is an increase in
interest in environmental issues, these still play a relatively small
role in the consumer decision making process, after price, availability
and convenience, among other determinants. After an initial hype of
supposed green consumerism, green consumers are fewer than first
thought (NCC, 1996b; Diamantis and Ladkin, 1999; see also Chapter
4). Yet the environment must sell to some consumers, since it is
increasingly used by companies as a source of competitive advantage,
and carefully planned ecolabels have a latent market.

The question one needs to ask at the end of the day is: what do
ecolabels mean to the environment? Most ecolabels mention the
protection of environmental resources as their objective, yet little
evidence is available on whether these objectives are met, and the
intentions of expansion (both geographically and through market
penetration) of awarding agencies cannot be taken as proof of success
on their own. Advocates of tourism ecolabels will emphasize that these
minimize the damage, a more realistic aim than avoiding it, yet critics
say that the certification of tourism products is endorsing the use of
fragile natural resources.

Can ecolabels encourage sustainable tourism and ecotourism? This
is indeed the case, although with exceptions. Economies of scale and
scope in certification programmes, as well as the ability of non-certified
products to confuse potential consumers, limit the validity of ecolabelling programmes (see Chapter 3). In the case of ecotourism, this is

even more of a challenge due to the difficulty in measuring sustainable development goals established for the ecotourism industry (see Chapter 9). While green standards for the mainstream tourism industry tend to rely on the measurable reduction of energy and waste, ecotourism standards go well beyond questions of eco-efficiency. Existing ecotourism certification programmes are more responsive to national and local stakeholder concerns than international programmes, and more likely to check on how ecotourism companies contribute to conservation of protected areas and what mechanisms are in place to ensure benefits reach local people.

Besides labelling tourism and ecotourism operators, there are several labels that focus on testing a particular aspect of their operations, such as the paper they print their brochures on, which are then used to promote the operator as green. Although this in itself does not cause any harm, it is unethical to promote the product as environmentally friendly just on the basis of the certification of one single attribute, and it confuses consumers.

This initial review of the players in tourism ecolabelling aims to raise some major issues that tourism ecolabelling programmes need to address. These will be further examined in Chapter 2, and dealt with in more detail in the rest of this book.

References

Azzone, G., Bertelè, U. and Noci, G. (1997) At last we are creating environmental strategies which work. *Long Range Planning* 30(4), 562–571.

Buckley, R.C. and Clough, E. (1997) Who is selling ecotourism to whom? *Annals of Tourism Research* 24, 479–480.

DoE (1996) *Green Claims Code of Practice: a Consultation Paper*. Department of the Environment, London.

DoE (1997) *A Strategy on Environmental Information about Products for Consumers in the UK*. Department of the Environment, London.

Diamantis, D. (1998) Environmental auditing: a tool in ecotourism development. *Eco-Managment and Auditing Journal* 5(1), 15–21.

Diamantis, D. and Ladkin, A. (1999) 'Green' strategies in the tourism and hospitality industries. In: Vellas, F. and Bécherel, L. (eds) *The International Marketing of Travel and Tourism: a Strategic Approach*. Macmillan, London, pp. 121–144.

Ding, P. and Pigram, J. (1995) Environmental audits: an emerging concept in sustainable tourism development. *Journal of Tourism Studies* 6(2), 2–10.

Ecotrans (2000) Eco-Tip page: Ecolabels and awards in tourism in Europe, http://www.eco-tip.org/Eco-labels/ecolabels.htm, last updated 27 January, 2000, viewed June 2000.

Font, X. (2001) Green marketing and management in tourism and hospitality firms. *Journal of Sustainable Tourism* (in press).

Font, X. and Tribe, J. (2001) Promoting green tourism: the future of environ-
   mental awards. *International Journal of Tourism Research* 3(1), 1–13.
Gummesson, E. (1994) Service management: an evaluation and the future.
   International Journal of Service Industry and Management 5(1), 77–96.
Hartman, C. and Stafford, E. (1997) Green alliances: building new business
   with environmental groups. *Long Range Planning* 30(2), 184–196.
Johnson, P. (1997) *ISO 14000: The Business Manager's Complete Guide to
   Environmental Management.* John Wiley & Sons, New York.
Jose, P. (1996) Corporate strategy and the environment: a portfolio approach.
   Long Range Planning, 9(4), 462–472.
Ledgerwood, G. and Street, E. (1993) Corporate strategy and environmental
   sustainability: establishing an environmental market ethos to gain
   competitive advantage. *Greener Management International* 3, 41–49.
Leubuscher, S., Hager, W., Wattiez, C., Mombrù, J. and Liaska, E. (1998) *Study
   on Verification and Control of Environmental Product Claims.* Prepared for
   the European Commission DG Health and Consumer Protection, Prospect
   C&S, Brussels.
Manfredo, M. (1992) *Influencing Human Behaviour: Theory and Applications
   in Recreation, Tourism and Natural Resources Management.* Sagamore,
   Champaign, Illinois.
Menon, A. and Menon, A. (1997) Enviropreneurial marketing strategy: the
   emergence of corporate environmentalism as market strategy. *Journal of
   Marketing* 61(1), 51–67.
Mihalic, T. (1996) Ecological labelling in tourism. In Briuglio, L., Archer, B.,
   Jafari, J. and Wall, G. (eds) *Sustainable Tourism in Islands and Small
   States: Issues and Policies.* Pinter, New York, pp. 197–205.
Mihalic, T. (1999) Equity in outgoing tourism through tourist certificates.
   International Journal of Contemporary Hospitality Management 11(2/3),
   128–131.
Miller, J. and Szekely, F. (1996) What is green? *European Management Journal*
   13(3), 322–333.
Naturfreunde Internationale (2000) Eco-Tours page: environmental seals and
   awards, http://www.eco-tour.org/information_en.html, last updated 3
   June, 2000, viewed June 2000.
NCC (1996a) *Green Claims: a Consumer Investigation into Marketing Claims
   about the Environment.* National Consumer Council, London.
NCC (1996b) *Shades of Green: Consumer's Attitudes to Green Shopping.*
   National Consumer Council, London.
Ottman, J. (1996) Suggestions for environmental labeling. *Marketing News* 3
   June, 13.
Peattie, K., and Charter, M. (1994) Green marketing. In Baker, M. (ed.) *The
   Marketing Book.* London, Butterworth-Heinemann, pp. 691–712.
Polonsky, M. (1995) Cleaning green marketing claims: a practical checklist. In
   Polonsky, M. and Mintu-Wimsatt, A. (eds) *Environmental Marketing:
   Strategies, Practice, Theory and Research.* The Haworth Press, New York.
Post, J. and Altman, B. (1994) Managing the environmental change process:
   barriers and opportunities. *Journal of Organizational Change Management*
   7(4) 64–81.

Roome, N. (1992) Developing environmental management strategies. *Business Strategy and the Environment*, 1(1), 11–24.

Sayre, D. (1996) *Inside ISO 14000: the Competitive Advantage of Environmental Management*. St Lucie Press, Boca Raton, Florida.

Scace, R., Grifone, E. and Usher, R. (1992) *Ecotourism in Canada*. Canadian Environmental Advisory Council, Supply and Services Canada, Ottawa.

Schaefer, A. and Harvey, B. (1998) Stage models of corporate 'greening': a critical evaluation. *Business Strategy and the Environment* 7, 109–123.

Sheldon, C. (ed.) (1997) *ISO 14001 and Beyond: Environmental Management Systems in the Real World*. Greenleaf Publishing, Sheffield, UK.

Sirakaya, E. and McLellan, R. (1998) Modelling tour operator's voluntary compliance with ecotourism principles: a behavioural approach. *Journal of Travel Research* 36, 42–55.

Steger, U. (1993) The greening of the board room: how German companies are dealing with environmental issues. In: Fisher, K. and Schot, J. (eds) *Environmental Strategies for Industry*. Island Press, Washington, DC.

Tibor, T. and Feldman, I. (eds) (1996) *Implementing ISO 14000: a Practical, Comprehensive Guide to the ISO 14000 Environmental Management Standards*. Irwin Professional Publishing, New York.

Tsai, T. and Child, J. (1997) Strategic responses of multinational corporations to environmental demands. *Journal of General Management* 23(1), 1–22.

UNEP (1998) *Ecolabels in the Tourism Industry*. United Nations Environmental Programme, Paris.

Wasik, J. (1996) *Green Marketing and Management: a Global Perspective*. Blackwell, Cambridge, Massachusetts.

Welford, R. (1995) *Environmental Strategy and Sustainable Development: the Corporate Challenge for the 21st Century*. Routledge, London.

Wheeler, M. (1998) Tourism marketing ethics: an introduction, *The Virtual Conference in Ethics of Tourism*, http://www.mcb.co.uk/services/conferen/jan98/eit/paper2-1.htm

Wight, P. (1994) Environmentally responsible marketing of tourism. In: Cater, E. and Lowman, G. (eds) *Ecotourism: a Sustainable Option?* John Wiley & Sons, Chichester, pp. 39–53.

Wong, V., Turner, W. and Stoneman, P. (1996) Marketing strategies and market prospects for environmentally-friendly consumer products. *British Journal of Management* 7(3), 263–281.

Chapter 2

Major Issues in Tourism Ecolabelling

RALF C. BUCKLEY

Introduction

The aim of this chapter is to introduce the major issues in tourism ecolabelling that are examined throughout the book. It complements Chapter 1 by considering the background to ecolabels, what they are and what they are meant to do, and the differences between quality and performance labels, and labels for destinations and organizations. The chapter also focuses on issues important to the individual environmentally aware tourist: the technical content of the label, its recognition and reliability, the level of maturity and penetration, thresholds and tiers. The chapter then critically analyses the current use and context of ecolabels in tourism, emphasizing equity and effectiveness issues, the relation between environmental legislation and the additional quality that an ecolabel should require, and how this links to designing an ecolabel and establishing benchmarks. Finally it considers how these issues will affect attempts to internationalize tourism ecolabels, within the context of international trade law relating to ecolabels more generally.

Understanding Ecolabels in Tourism

To be meaningful to a consumer, an ecolabel must be part of an ecolabel scheme, administered by a reputable organization. Without this back-up, an ecolabel is just a marketing hook, and largely meaningless: the term 'ecotour' can itself be a prime example. Like any form of quality label, an ecolabel must have defined and transparent criteria for use, and effective means to prevent abuse (see Chapters 6 and 13). This can be achieved through national or international standards organizations, with the potential to prosecute for misuse under fair-trading legislation. Or it can be achieved through certification or accreditation schemes, either public or private, with expulsion and negative publicity as a deterrent for misuse. Various examples can be found in the directory at the end of this book.

Note that environmental award schemes would not generally be considered as ecolabels, because an ecolabel should be available to any applicant which meets predefined threshold criteria, whereas an award is only available to a small number of applicants, selected by a competitive ranking. Many of the arguments in this book, however, also apply to awards, and the directory lists some established awards as well as labels.

An ecolabel is primarily a tool in consumer choice. How much weight consumers give it will depend on: (i) how much the consumers care about the environment; and (ii) how much real environmental difference they think there is between labelled and unlabelled products. Consumer confidence in any ecolabel is likely to be increased if government bodies also rely on it: for example if land management agencies or tourism promotion bodies give preference to ecolabelled products (see Chapters 4 and 5).

Quality and Performance Labels

Tourism ecolabels may be considered in two main categories: environmental quality labels for tourism destinations and environmental performance labels for tourism providers (see Chapter 5). Only one or two labels cross over these categories.

The Blue Flag label for clean beaches in Europe, and more recently for marinas, is perhaps the best-known example of a destination quality ecolabel. The Australian National Ecotourism Accreditation Programme (NEAP), is a well-known example of an operator performance ecolabel. The scheme operated by the German company Turistik Union International (TUI) covers both destinations and operators, as does Green Globe 21, revised from the Green Globe scheme originated by the World Travel and Tourism Council (see the directory).

There has been little research to determine how different consumers respond to tourism ecolabels of various types (see Chapter 6). In practice, destination quality and operator performance are unlikely to be independent. An environmentally concerned tourist is more likely to take care selecting an environmentally concerned tour operator to take them to a pristine wilderness, than to take them to a polluted city.

Technical Content and Consumer Reactions

Geographic scope and technical detail vary enormously between different tourism ecolabel schemes. Green Globe 21 aims to cover all forms of tourism worldwide, but the level of technical detail is currently very low. So the brand is recognizable to consumers but the information it conveys is rather minimal. Some of the smaller European ecolabels cover only a single style of accommodation in a single municipality. The information may be detailed, but very few tourists can use it (see directory examples).

Environmentally knowledgeable tourists will probably only pay attention to ecolabels with detailed and transparent criteria and an effective audit procedure. Tourists with a broad environmental concern but little technical knowledge may pay more attention to a well-known brand name, irrespective of technical back-up. However, consumers routinely differentiate between products on the basis of almost hair-splitting criteria, such as the chunkiness of peanut butter or the precise print pattern on a bikini or shorts. They could make equally fine choices between tourism products on environmental grounds, if they think it is important. We do not yet know if they do. Ecolabels for manufactured consumer products have survived and succeeded, however, from biodegradable detergent to dolphin-friendly tuna, unpackaged cosmetics to sustainably cut timber. This suggests that enough consumers will pay a premium or give preference to ecolabelled products to make them valuable for retailers and manufacturers. Ecolabels in tourism have now existed for long enough that it would be quite feasible to test consumer reaction and response.

Recognition and Reliability

An ideal tourism ecolabel scheme would appear to need a global brand name and audit process, local implementation, detailed technical criteria for different types of tourism activity or service, multiple labelling levels, and high transparency and public accessibility of information. In practice, broad scope, both geographic and sectoral, currently seems to conflict with technical substance and transparency (see Chapter 9). Broad schemes such as Green Globe 21 seem to have rather vague criteria and lax entry requirements in order to be acceptable to industry and government worldwide; but the downside is that for well-informed consumers from developed nations, such a label may not contribute effectively to consumer choice. Experience in other retail sectors suggests that consumers, and consumer protection organizations, want labels with both guts and teeth: substantive technical criteria, and transparent and effective audit and enforcement. Once consumers have paid a premium price for an ecolabelled product, they want it to mean something, and they are likely to lobby governments for legislation if they feel they are being duped. Equally, of course, if an ecolabel really does have guts and teeth, providers will only adopt it if they are satisfied that it yields a market advantage which outweighs its costs.

Maturity and Penetration

For consumers to take account of tourism ecolabels in purchasing decisions, the label needs to differentiate clearly and reliably between products with high and low environmental performance or quality. To do this, an ecolabel scheme needs not only guts and teeth but also maturity and penetration: consumers need confidence that every product in the sector has been considered for ecolabelling and either accepted or rejected, so that the absence of a label means as much as its presence. If unlabelled products are often just as good as labelled ones, consumers are unlikely to rely on the label. Indeed, to give full credence to an ecolabel, consumers need to see that there are routine re-evaluations of all potential products, with some being granted the label and others losing it at each iteration.

Thresholds and Tiers

If the label has only a single tier, this implies that the cut-off threshold for the ecolabel should be neither so high that very few products earn the label, nor so low that almost all products can earn it. If very few products earn the label, it may still be meaningful – as with some of the quality labels for luxury hotels – but few consumers can use it in purchasing decisions. Similarly, if almost all products earn the label, it may still be meaningful as a basic screening criterion for almost all consumers – as with, say, professional qualifications for an accountant – but it will not influence many purchasing decisions. So the technical criteria for an ecolabel may need to change over time, if the overall level of environmental performance in the sector evolves. Alternatively, a multi-tier ecolabel can incorporate a basic entry level, a mid-level which is the main one used by consumers, and a top level to recognize the highest performers, as in the 2000 version of the Australian National Ecotourism Accreditation Programme (NEAP II) (see Chapter 11).

Who Uses Ecolabels and What For?

Current tourism ecolabel schemes suffer from lack of penetration and discrimination. As yet, there is apparently no systematic difference in environmental performance between tourism products which do have ecolabels and those which do not. It seems that many tourism operators see ecolabels as marketing schemes from which they would gain no particular advantage. This may change if members of current tourism ecolabel schemes succeed in their efforts to have the label adopted as either mandatory or preferential criteria for licensing in national parks. On the one hand, it would be valuable for land managers to have an independent evaluation of the environmental performance of different operators as a screening mechanism in issuing permits. On the other hand, if the evaluation scheme is run by the same tour operators who are applying for the permits, then clearly it will not be independent! (see Chapter 14). The potential adoption of a privately run industry ecolabel by public land management agencies illustrates that ecolabels can be used as instruments of government policy as well as mechanisms for consumer choice. From a policy perspective, ecolabels raise issues of equity, effectiveness and compatibility with other instruments (see Chapter 15).

Equity and Effectiveness

Equity issues arise if there are significant differences in environmental impacts between ecolabelled and unlabelled tourism products in the same area, and the products with better environmental performance are more expensive. If only some tourists will pay the price premiums for more environmentally friendly tourism products, the overall environmental quality in the destination area will be lower than if all tourists pay this premium. Purchasers of ecolabelled products get less environmental benefit than they have paid for, and purchasers of unlabelled products get more than they have paid for. Hence the former are subsidizing the latter. Since the purchase of an ecolabelled product is a private consumer decision, the subsidy is not only inequitable, but requires a measure of altruism.

Indeed, the commercial survival of ecolabelled products in other industry sectors, notably among highly price-competitive retail manufactured goods, foods and consumer products, shows that many consumers are sufficiently concerned about the environment that they will pay to protect it even if they have to subsidize less-concerned citizens in the process. For the tourism sector, however, where ecolabels currently have low penetration, low reliability, low consumer recognition, and considerable uncertainty in environmental outcomes, ecolabels alone are unlikely to be effective instruments of environmental policy.

Tourism ecolabels may, however, be an effective component of a policy bundle or pyramid (Gunningham *et al.*, 1998), if they are coupled with environmental regulations which set a basic threshold for environmental performance which all tourism products must meet, with ecolabelled products providing an optional best-practice add-on for a small extra charge.

Legislative Base and Ecolabel Add-on

In practice, environmental legislation in all industry sectors differs enormously between different countries and jurisdictions in regard to issues such as sewage treatment, waste discharge, energy efficiency, atmospheric emissions, noise, recycling, national parks, endangered species, environmental impact assessment, environmental management systems, and so on. There are equally significant differences in legislation that are not specifically related to the environment, but have environmental implications: for example in regard to building regulations, boat and vehicle licensing, development planning, fisheries, forestry and foreshores. In addition, some countries and states have specific legislation covering particular types of tourist activity, such as whale-watching. Finally, legal frameworks for liability, insurance, professional certification, etc., can also have a major influence on the practical conduct of tour operations.

What this means for tourism ecolabels is that particular aspects of environmental performance which one country incorporates into an ecolabel scheme, may already be required by law in another country. If a global tourism ecolabel required the same absolute standard of environmental performance from companies in all countries, then the differential between ecolabelled and unlabelled products would be much greater in some countries than others. On the other hand, if a global ecolabel scheme simply required the same differential improvement in environmental performance between unlabelled and ecolabelled products, then an ecolabelled product in one country might well have a lower actual standard of environmental performance than an unlabelled product in another country (see Chapter 15). The question is: which means more to the consumer, or what does the consumer expect? Do they choose the destination country first, and then use an ecolabel to look for an operator with above-average environmental performance? Or do they expect that an ecolabelled product should meet some basic environmental standards anywhere in the world? Or is it a combination of these factors? Similar considerations apply to purely national ecolabels, if they are used in purchasing decisions by international travellers. Three chapters in this volume are dedicated to understanding consumer behaviour in relation to tourism ecolabels (see Chapters 4, 5 and 6).

Ecolabel Design and Benchmarks

Tourism ecolabels may be constructed in many different ways, and we do not know what consumers pay most attention to. For example, ecolabels may be based either on inputs or outputs: environmental technology adopted, or environmental impacts produced. They may involve qualitative or quantitative criteria: adoption of a recycling programme, or proportion of materials recycled. They may use aggregate or proportional measures: energy consumed in total, or per capita. They may use absolute or relative measures; and they may require either actual demonstrated environmental performance, or merely a commitment to improvement (see Chapters 7, 8 and 14).

For consumers to interpret any of these, they need benchmarks against which to compare. This in turn requires routine reporting of corporate environmental performance, as currently required in some jurisdictions but not many. At the very least, it needs guidelines for best practice, something which consumers and corporations can use to judge existing environmental performance and plan improvements. The Canadian example is very useful in this case (see Chapter 10).

Ecolabels and International Trade

International differences between tourism ecolabels may possibly also have implications under international trade law. Currently, member countries of the World Trade Organization can apply product standards to imports, including environmental product standards, but not process standards. This means that they can discriminate between products, for example through bans or differential duties, on the basis of environmental characteristics of the product itself or the way it is used (e.g. energy efficiency), but not on the way it is produced (e.g. disposal of manufacturing wastes). Producers, however, both domestic and exporting, are allowed to provide this information in the form of an ecolabel, so that individual consumers may take it into account in purchasing decisions. For example, a country cannot ban the import of unsustainably logged timber, but consumers may choose not to buy timber unless it is certified as sustainably harvested.

In industry sectors which export goods or resources from less to more developed nations, the trade ban on environmental process standards is a major barrier to improved environmental legislation. It allows companies to extract resources in less developed countries (LDCs) with little heed for environmental impacts; and companies in developed countries to lobby against domestic environmental laws on the grounds of unfair competition from imports. Under these circumstances, concern by consumers in importing nations, over environmental impacts in exporting LDCs, provides direct consumer support for ecolabels (see Chapter 15).

In tourism, however, the situation is somewhat different. Economically, tourism is an export from less to more developed nations, but the product is consumed in the less developed nations where it is produced: product and process are inseparable. Environmental laws in destination nations apply to domestic and international tour operators alike. Strong environmental laws in either originating or destination countries do not place tour companies at any competitive disadvantage. In fact, by reducing impacts from other sectors they benefit tourism. So unlike other sectors, it makes better sense for the tourism industry to lobby for effective environmental legislation than to pursue ecolabel schemes as a substitute. Indeed, it seems that ecolabels in tourism may well be aimed as much at regulators as its primary consumers. In Australia, for example, companies with accreditation under the Nature and Ecotourism Accreditation Programme are attempting to gain preferential treatment for operating licences in national parks, which are becoming highly valuable business commodities in the tourism industry.

Conclusions

This chapter has provided an overview of some of the major issues affecting the planning, management, marketing and development of tourism ecolabels. This is by no means exhaustive but it reflects the current discussions between the tourism industry, environmental organizations and governmental bodies. The issues mentioned are analysed further, from different perspectives, in subsequent chapters of this book.

Reference

Gunningham, N., Grabosky, P. and Sinclair, D. (1998) *Smart Regulation: Designing Environmental Policy*, Oxford Socio-Legal Studies. Clarendon Press, Oxford.

Chapter 3

Ecolabelling in the Context of Sustainable Tourism and Ecotourism

DIMITRIOS DIAMANTIS AND JOHN WESTLAKE

Introduction

The purpose of the ecolabelling and/or certifications schemes in tourism is to highlight the best practices for products and services. Such schemes aim to ensure that different components of the tourism industry from both the demand and the supply elements are conducting their practices with fewer negative impacts on the environment, on society and on the economy. Due to the enormous size of the tourism industry, such schemes have been initiated in the most benign forms of tourism, especially ecotourism and rural products. A wide range of tourism, hospitality and recreational land management operations have appeared in the 1990s, a selection of which can be found in the directory at the end of this book. In addition to sector-specific awards, the International Standard Organization (ISO) and the Eco Management and Auditing Scheme (EMAS) also provide generic certification schemes based on the application of an environmental management system. In any case, tourism companies and destinations can apply either for specific certification schemes or more generic ones, such as EMAS, all depending on the size of their business, the types of products and their financial situation.

It would appear then, that ecolabelling and certification schemes in tourism have been operationalized to ensure more sustainable management or sustainable consumption in tourism practices. In many instances, however, entrepreneurs in the tourism industry are claiming that they practise sustainability, even before they open for business. It is tempting to argue further that, as there is a lot of discussion revolving around the true meaning of sustainability and ecotourism, such ecolabelling schemes will not be practising sustainability successfully.

© CAB *International* 2001. *Tourism Ecolabelling*
(eds X. Font and R.C. Buckley)

This chapter discusses the concept of ecolabelling in the context of sustainability and ecotourism. It outlines the limitation of the current practices of sustainability in tourism and discusses the view of creating certain ecolabelling schemes based on the four types of sustainability in tourism destinations. In addition, the chapter details the position and links between sustainable and ecotourism products as well as the limitations of creating an ecolabelling scheme for ecotourism. It progresses to an examination of ecotourism definitions, where the view of defining ecotourism on the basis of different trade-off scenarios will be noted. Next, it examines certain ecolabelling frameworks based on ecotourism trade-off definitions as well as the possibilities of creating such schemes based on environmental management techniques. The chapter concludes with certain suggestions for how ecolabelling schemes could be formulated in tourism destinations.

Sustainability in Tourism

Within the sustainability agenda in tourism, there are a variety of terms, definitions and management models that have created confusion with regard to the effectiveness of sustainable practices in this sector. For instance, sustainable tourism is regularly regarded as part of sustainable tourism development or as a form of tourism which entails all the alternative tourism products (Inskeep, 1991; WTO, 1993, 1995; Lane, 1994; Cater, 1995; Hunter, 1995a,b, 1997; Orams, 1995a,b; Wahab, 1997; Goodall and Stabler, 1997; Nepal, 1997; Wall, 1997; Mowforth and Munt, 1998: 105–111). Theoretically speaking, the evolution of these two terms has made it difficult to clarify whether there are in fact two distinct concepts or just one, which encompasses the other. Although the initial difference between these two concepts is derived explicitly from the development perspective (Wall, 1997), other researchers regard sustainable tourism as a product and have drawn comparisons with mass forms of tourism (Lane, 1994; Godfrey, 1996).

As a result, a number of limitations have arisen concerning the general search for sustainable development within tourism. Firstly, the issue of geographical equity, in that whether the focus is specifically on the destinations or on a particular tourist resort, it has to take into consideration the implication of such equity issues in a general geographical context (Hunter, 1995b). Secondly, sustainable tourism development also has to abort the notion of 'single-sector tourism development planning' (Hunter, 1995b: 162; Wall, 1997). Here, the concern is that this development is extremely tourism-centric rather than mutual sustainability-centric (Hunter, 1995b; Collins, 1996; Wall,

1997). Thirdly, is the issue of resources utilization and usage. This issue initially entails views that sustainable tourism development should 'preserve the tourism's future seed corn' (Lane, 1994: 104; Hunter, 1995b). Again, the issue that arises is that sustainable tourism development should aim to contribute to preserving all the resources, and not only those used by tourism development (Hunter, 1995b; Collins, 1996).

As a result of these limitations, the question that comes to mind is whether or not current ecolabelling schemes address these issues. At the moment, ecolabelling schemes seem to accept certain indicators that guarantee sustainability and ignore all three issues. So in an ideal research setting, ecolabelling schemes with regard to sustainability should adopt certain trade-off scenarios based on the philosophy of the types of sustainability in order to address better the sustainability issues.

Types of Sustainability and Ecolabelling

Current sustainable development practices claim to be related to issues of geographical equity, tourism development planning, resource utilization and usage (Hunter, 1995b; Collins, 1996). Each of these factors suggests that tourism sustainable practices have to be embodied with certain trade-off scenarios (Wall, 1997: 45), or trade-off tourism (Collins, 1996), or with the view to reflect its multidimensional characteristics (Wahab, 1997: 137). In particular it has been suggested that there are four different approaches to sustainable development based on the four types of sustainability, which are also in themselves trade-off scenarios and not tourism centric (Hunter, 1997: 860–863) (see Table 3.1). As a result, ecolabelling schemes could be adapted to coincide with different types of sustainability:

1. *Very weak*: ecolabelling schemes that aim to preserve the current practices of the tourism products and services.
2. *Weak*: ecolabelling schemes that aim to preserve only the new forms of development in the destination or surrounding areas.
3. *Strong*: ecolabelling schemes that aim to apply an environmental management system in the destination and services.
4. *Very strong*: ecolabelling schemes that aim for the absolute preservation of tourism products and services.

For example, in a very strong scenario of ecolabelling, the life cycle assessment (LCA) methodology can provide the foundation of the scheme. As a result, LCA components could be applied:

Table 3.1. Types of sustainability within tourism (Westlake and Diamantis, 1998).

Types	Characteristics
Very weak Tourism imperative scenario	Status: Tourism in its early stages Criteria: Tourism activities do not generate more degradation Benefits: Tourism is an alternative form of development Creates more employment Increases environmental protection Costs: Creates certain antagonistic impacts
Weak Product-led tourism scenario	Status: Tourism is developed Criteria: Sustain tourism activities and develop new products Benefits: Improvement of the local economy and employment Assist preservation practices of surrounding destinations Expansion and diversification of tourism planning Costs: Conserve only existing infrastructure and products
Strong Environmental-led tourism scenario	Status: Tourism in its early stages Criteria: Environmental management utilization Benefits: Environmental quality Economic and employment growth Specialized tourism destination Costs: Only in circumstances lacking focus and commitment
Very strong Neotenous tourism scenario	Status: Tourism in its exploitation and involvement stages Criteria: Absolute preservation of resources Benefits: Protection of renewable and non-renewable resources Long-term environmental attractiveness Costs: Tourism growth is limited Tourism development is abolished to minimize generation of negative environmental impacts Tourism development is sacrificed in cases where other sectors employ better environmental practices

1. *Inventory* of the different products at the destination and the gathering of data relating to the material and energy inputs of the different products.

2. *Impact analysis*: establishment of the environmental, economic, social and cultural impacts of each of the different products examined in the inventory assessment.

3. *Impact assessment*: the classification, characterization and valuation of the different impacts.

4. *Improvement*: a formal and systematic appraisal of the product's impact over a period of time.

The advantages of selecting such techniques to provide the foundations of an ecolabelling scheme lie in the measurement of the different impacts over the life span of the destinations' products and services.

The disadvantages with applying the LCA lie in the complexity of the issues involved and the elements that ought to be included in such an assessment and the consistency of different environmental values.

Clearly, although these four different types of ecolabelling with regard to sustainability present an ideal situation, they do provide a number of alternatives for tourism managers. If one considers the question of why ecolabelling schemes could apply only to ecotourism and benign forms of tourism and not to mass tourism products, such types of ecolabelling could overcome these problems. This suggests that if a destination is providing mass tourism products but new forms of development are occurring in such destinations, the weak type of ecolabelling only should be applied for such new forms of development. In addition if a destination is providing mass tourism products, it can apply the very weak type of ecolabelling in that it can preserve only some of the current mass tourism practices. Further, the strong and very strong types of sustainability can be applied in all the destinations regardless of whether they have mass tourism or ecotourism products, but it is more likely that these certification schemes are most suited for ecotourism destinations. This is because both strong and very strong types of ecolabelling are aiming to apply strict environmental management schemes, a scenario that is not suitable to the current status of many mass tourism destinations. For ecotourism-related products and services, however, ecolabelling schemes have to coincide with the definitions of ecotourism. Based on a similar trade-off scenario philosophy certain types of ecolabelling can be recommended only for ecotourism practices.

Ecotourism

The popular appearance of ecotourism in the late 1980s was treated as a panacea to all tourism-related problems in the destination areas. Its popularity claimed to be associated with (Boo, 1990, 1991a,b, 1992, 1993; Ceballos-Lascurain, 1991a,b, 1993a,b, 1996; Hvenegaard, 1994: 25; Blamey, 1995a,b; Orams, 1995a; Dowling, 1996; Lindberg and McKercher, 1997; Diamantis, 1998a,b, 1999):

- a general search for the natural attractions during a holiday;
- an eagerness to achieve sustainable development by any means;
- potential employment opportunities in natural areas; and
- a shift towards planning in protected areas.

This popularity has also been translated into increased visits for ecotourism-related purposes, claimed to account for around 20% of total tourism arrivals (WTO, 1998). There are, however, a number of pitfalls, most of which are associated with the position of ecotourism and its similarities to other 'green' tourism products.

Ecotourism is treated both as a sub-component of alternative tourism and as natural-based tourism, mainly part of the concept of sustainability. In addition, other forms of sustainable tourism have claimed to have similarities to ecotourism as well as being part of both nature-based travel and alternative tourism. On the other end of the spectrum, both mass tourism and other forms of tourism such as events/festivals, conferences and business tourism, are searching for sustainability in their practices and as such are placed outside the sustainability borders.

Ecotourism characteristics are the opposite of those of mass tourism especially the experiential aspects of both concepts. For instance, the ecotourism product is not commodified whereas the mass tourism product is. The ecotourism activities depend on the natural and cultural environment whereas mass tourism activities depend on the built environment (Jaakson, 1997). Finally, certain types of alternative, nature-based, ecotourism, and sustainable forms of tourism which have practised unsustainable principles are situated outside the borders of sustainability and have been re-positioned with other tourism products which are searching for sustainable practices.

For the purpose of this chapter, this conceptual position of ecotourism within the tourism product spectrum suggests that if one considers developing a certification process for ecotourism it has to take into account the similarity of ecotourism to other forms of alternative tourism. This suggests that if a certification process is well developed for ecotourism products and services, it could well be applied for other forms of sustainable tourism, such as farm and rural tourism. At the moment, however, certain certification practices for ecotourism products and services do not address these issues, as they tend to assess only ecotourism-related practices.

As such, the challenge of creating a certification process (ecolabelling) for ecotourism could be classified into three categories. First, that of clarifying any limitations of the definitional perspective of ecotourism and creating ecolabel programmes based on overcoming such limitations. Second, ensuring ecolabelling programmes guarantee the sustainability of ecotourism products. Third, assessing whether current ecolabelling practices for ecotourism can be applied to other green products of tourism, especially farm and rural tourism.

Definitions of Ecotourism and Ecolabelling

Looking at the definitions of ecotourism, most of them lack a focus over their components. Orams (1995a) suggests that most ecotourism definitions lie between the passive position (i.e. concentrates solely on ecotourism development, not enhancing the antagonistic impacts or the ecotourists' need to be satisfied) and the active position (i.e. actions of protecting the environment and the behavioural intentions of eco-tourists). Alternatively, ecotourism has been classified based on three criteria (Wall, 1994: 5): the characteristics of the destinations; the motivations of its participants; and the organizational characteristics of the ecotourism trip.

More specifically, ecotourism was first defined as

> traveling to relatively undisturbed or uncontaminated natural areas with the specific objective of studying, admiring, and enjoying the scenery and its wild plants and animals, as well as any existing cultural manifesta-tions (both past and present) found in these areas
> (Ceballos-Lascurain, 1987: 14, 1991a,b, 1993a,b, 1996).

In a similar vein, other researchers elaborated this definition by emphasizing certain aspects of it. For example:

- Ziffer (1989) highlighted *the conservation, natural-based, economic and cultural* components of ecotourism;
- Boo (1991b) viewed ecotourism not only from the *natural and conservation components*, but also the *economic and educational elements*;
- Forestry Tasmania (1994) emphasized the *nature-based, educa-tional, social and sustainability* components of ecotourism by distinguishing between ecotourism and nature-based tourism;
- Blamey's dimensions of ecotourism included four main components: *nature-based, environmentally educated, sustainably managed and distance/time* (Blamey, 1995a,b, 1997);
- Boyd's and Butler's definition emphasized the *natural-based, conservation and social* components of the concept in the case of Northern Ontario, with an emphasis on the minimization of the impacts of ecotourism over existing resource uses in the destination (1993, 1996a,b); and
- Lindberg's and McKercher's definition highlights the *natural-based and sustainability* components of ecotourism (1997).

A comparison of these definitions indicates that ecotourism tends to have three main components: *natural based, educational* and *sustainable management*, which includes economic, social, cultural and ethical issues. Although these themes are more or less clear (Diamantis, 1999), limitations arise in attempts to express all these components by a single definition in all circumstances and all ecotourism research settings. It seems that it is better to operationalize the concepts based on trade-off scenarios of its themes, rather than trying to explore it from a specific standpoint.

Looking at the trade-off definitions of ecotourism, four different definitional approaches can be devised ranging from very weak to very strong (see Table 3.2):

- *Very weak*: the core emphasis could be given to the natural-based component. For example, a definition of ecotourism could be implied on the basis of ecotourism practices in both protected and non-protected areas.
- *Weak*: the core emphasis could be mainly on the natural-based component and to a lesser degree on the educational and sustainability components. Here, a definition of ecotourism could stress the basis of ecotourism practices in both protected and non-protected areas, which generates a low level of education/ conservation/economic/social/cultural benefits to the destination.
- *Strong*: all three elements should be considered equally. For instance, a definition of ecotourism could stress the basis of ecotourism practices in both protected and non-protected areas, which generates a high level of education/conservation/ economic/social/cultural benefits to the destination.
- *Very strong*: all three elements should be equally considered but with less emphasis on the economic aspects of ecotourism. In this case, a definition of ecotourism could stress the basis of ecotourism practices in both protected and non-protected areas, which generates a high level of education/conservation/social/cultural benefits and a low level of economic rewards to the destination.

Table 3.2.   Trade-off definitions of ecotourism.

Definition	Elements
Very weak	Main emphasis:
	Natural-based component: protected and non-protected areas
Weak	Main emphasis:
	Natural-based component: protected and non-protected areas
	Less emphasis:
	Educational component: interpretation and training programmes
	Sustainability component: economic and/or social-cultural elements
Strong	Main emphasis:
	Natural-based component: protected and non-protected areas
	Educational component: interpretation and training programmes
	Sustainability component: equal emphasis on economic and social-cultural elements
Very strong	Main emphasis:
	Natural-based component: protected and non-protected areas
	Educational component: interpretation and training programmes
	Sustainability component: emphasis on social-cultural elements rather than on economic elements

The benefit of creating these kinds of definitions is that they coincide with the different types of sustainability (Hunter, 1997; Westlake and Diamantis, 1998) as well as avoiding an examination of the concept of ecotourism from a specific perspective such as economic, social, cultural and conservation. Inevitably, these views highlight another dilemma: that of the effective application of these definitions especially over the issues of ecolabelling and acceleration schemes. In other words, the question that comes to mind is that in an ideal research setting ecolabelling schemes have to reflect the different trade-off scenarios of ecotourism. Here, four different schemes can be created:

1. *Very weak*: ecolabelling scheme that deals only with the management of different products in the protected and non-protected areas.
2. *Weak*: ecolabelling scheme with a main emphasis on the natural-based component of ecotourism and less emphasis on the educational and sustainability aspects.
3. *Strong*: ecolabelling scheme that assesses the natural-based, educational and sustainability components of ecotourism.
4. *Very strong*: ecolabelling scheme that assesses all three components of ecotourism but does not deal with the economic aspects of the ecotourism products.

These different scenarios with regard to ecotourism, present an alternative way of thinking in terms of matching the definitional limitations of ecotourism with the needs of the different ecotourism destinations. If one considers that there is no international system of ecotourism certification (see Chapter 9) as well as that this agenda on ecolabelling on ecotourism is just starting to emerge, these four different scenarios for ecotourism ecolabelling could be applicable in different settings. A key element of their success, however, is that they should be accompanied by an appropriate selection of indicators as well as the support of the different stakeholders and local communities.

Ecolabelling in the Context of Sustainability and Ecotourism

If practising an ecolabelling scheme in the context of sustainability and ecotourism is a formidable challenge, the task takes on an additional dimension when set against the different types of sustainability and the different types of ecotourism definitions. Here, different ecolabelling schemes can be created ranging from the very weak to the very strong, all depending upon the setting in which they are applied. In addition, for each of these scenarios, ecolabelling schemes need to be accompanied by the use of certain indicators. Sustainability and ecotourism indicators are the instrumental tools to measure environmental performance, and for the tourism perspective the World

Tourism Organization (1995) has initiated some work on indicators methodology. At the moment indicators to measure sustainability and ecotourism practices can either look at the environmental, economic, social and management agenda of the destination and products or can be divided into core indicators (i.e. planning process, consumer satisfaction) and site-specific elements (i.e. environmental, social) (WTO, 1995).

When it comes to selecting certain indicators to practise eco-labelling schemes in selected regions, then the situation becomes very problematic. If one considers applying the four types of ecolabelling for sustainability or ecotourism, certain indicators to measure the environmental or ecotourism performance need to be selected. As a result, before an ecolabelling scheme is attempted, certain environmental indicators need to be selected to fit each of these scenarios. Thus the following steps can be considered in creating an ecolabelling scheme (see Chapters 7 and 8).

1. Select an ecolabelling scenario for sustainability and/or ecotourism purposes;
2. Select certain indicators to fit that scenario (i.e. very strong ecotourism scenario: select certain environmental, social, management indicators but not economic indicators);
3. Conduct research in the destination or on the product to see the applicability of the selected indicators;
4. Consult a number of stakeholders to obtain their views and develop a list of new indicators;
5. Summarize the key concept of the ecolabelling programme;
6. Consult a number of stakeholders to obtain their views on that programme;
7. Consult an independent verifier to acknowledge the ecolabelling scenario; and
8. Develop a feedback process.

However, at present, due to the lack of research in the field of eco-labelling, these different schemes on either sustainability or ecotourism practices are very difficult to operate in tourism destinations. One of the most obvious goals, however, in creating a successful ecolabelling scheme is that of the participation of different stakeholders and communities in the decision process. Only under such circumstances will an ecolabelling scheme become operational in the setting in which it is applied and avoid the risk of becoming impractical and inconsistent.

Conclusion

This chapter has articulated an agenda for discussion on the conceptual approaches of ecolabelling for sustainability and ecotourism purposes. The current practices of sustainable tourism and ecotourism have inherent weaknesses, most of which were raised from the lack of agreement over the definitional perspective. It seems that it is worthwhile defining and managing sustainability and ecotourism based on trade-off scenarios rather than from a specific standpoint. In this respect different types of ecolabelling have been suggested with regard to sustainability, and four different definitions of ecotourism have been introduced ranging from very weak to very strong, depending upon the setting and the standpoint of the examined concept.

Thereafter, within the agenda of ecotourism there are also the issues of accreditation and certification for the best practices within an ecolabelling scheme. Traditionally the elements were included in an ecolabelling scheme and were very general, which inevitably made them impractical in many destinations. In avoiding such circumstances, four different ecolabelling schemes could be created based on the trade-off definitions of ecotourism in a way that can become practical in the setting in which they applied. Then, the challenge of creating an ecolabelling scheme or schemes for ecotourism products and services only still remains intact, if one considers the numerous similarities between ecotourism and other green products such as rural tourism. Here, there is a need for clear guidelines on what an ecolabelling scheme for green products similar to ecotourism will look like as well as how they will best represent the true meaning of sustainability. Clearly, the process of making ecotourism and sustainability into rigorous concepts requires research which will confront trade-off definitions as well as management approaches that espouse the types of sustainability and the participation of the different stakeholders in the decision process. A failure to do this will inevitably confirm that ecotourism is a buzzword phenomenon and that sustainability is an impractical concept, and ecolabelling schemes could misjudge the best practices in tourism destinations.

References

Blamey, R.K. (1995a) *The Nature of Ecotourism*. Bureau of Tourism Research, Canberra, Australia.

Blamey, R.K. (1995b) The elusive market profile: operationalising ecotourism. Paper presented at the Geography of Sustainable Tourism Conference, University of Canberra, ACT, Australia, September.

Boo, E. (1990) *Ecotourism: the Potential and Pitfalls*, vols 1 and 2. World Wide Fund for Nature, Washington, DC.

Boo, E. (1991a) Ecotourism: a tool for conservation and development. In: Kusler, J.A. (compiler) *Ecotourism and Resource Conservation, a Collection of Papers*, vol. 1. Omnipress, Madison, Wisconsin, pp. 54–60.

Boo, E. (1991b) Planning for ecotourism. *Parks* 2(3), 4–8.

Boo, E. (1992) *The Ecotourism Boom: Planning for Development and Management*, WHN technical paper series, Paper 2. WWF, Washington, DC.

Boo, E. (1993) Ecotourism planning for protected areas. In: Lindberg, K. and Hawkins, D.E. (eds) *Ecotourism: Guide for Planners and Managers*. The Ecotourism Society, North Bennington, Vermont, pp. 15–31.

Boyd, S.W. and Butler, R.W. (1993) *Review of the Development of Ecotourism with Respect to Identifying Criteria for Ecotourism for Northern Ontario*, Report for Department of Natural Resources/Forestry. Ministry of Natural Resources, Sault Ste Marie, Ontario, Canada.

Boyd, S.W. and Butler, R.W. (1996a) Seeing the forest through the trees using geographical information systems to identify potential ecotourism sites in Northern Ontario, Canada. In: Harrison, L.C. and Husbands, W. (eds) *Practicing Responsible Tourism: International Case Studies in Tourism Planning, Policy and Development*. John Wiley & Sons, Chichester, UK, pp. 380–403.

Boyd, S.W. and Butler, R.W. (1996b) Managing ecotourism: an opportunity spectrum approach. *Tourism Management* 17(8), 557–566.

Cater, E. (1995) Environmental contradictions in sustainable tourism. *The Geographical Journal* 161(1), 21–28.

Ceballos-Lascurain, H. (1987) The future of ecotourism. *Mexico Journal* (January), 13–14.

Ceballos-Lascurain, H. (1991a) Tourism, ecotourism, and protected areas. In: Kusler, J.A. (compiler) *Ecotourism and Resource Conservation, a Collection of Papers* vol. 1. Omnipress, Madison, Wisconsin, pp. 24–30.

Ceballos-Lascurain, H. (1991b) Tourism, ecotourism and protected areas. *Parks* 2(3), 31–35.

Ceballos-Lascurain, H. (1993a) Ecotourism as a worldwide phenomenon. In: Lindberg, K. and Hawkins, D.E. (eds) *Ecotourism: Guide for Planners and Managers*. The Ecotourism Society, North Bennington, Vermont, pp. 12–14.

Ceballos-Lascurain, H. (1993b) Overview on ecotourism around the world: IUCN's ecotourism program. In: *Proceedings of 1993 World Congress on Adventure Travel and Eco-tourism, Brazil*. The Adventure Travel Society, Englewood Cliffs, New Jersey, pp. 219–222.

Ceballos-Lascurain, H. (1996) *Tourism, Ecotourism, and Protected areas*. IUCN, Gland, Switzerland.

Collins, A. (1996) *The Limits of Tourism as an Engine of Sustainable Development*, Discussion Paper No. 82. Department of Economics, University of Portsmouth, Portsmouth, UK.

Diamantis, D. (1998) Consumer behaviour and ecotourism products. *Annals of Tourism Research* 25(2), 515–518.

Diamantis, D. (1999) *The Concept of Ecotourism: Definitions and Components.* Report for the Center International de Recherches et d'Etudes Touristiques, Planning and Development Series, vol. 19. CIRET, France.

Dowling, R.K. (1996) Ecotourism: the rising star in Australia tourism. In: *Strategic Alliances: Ecotourism Partnerships in Practice Conference Proceedings.* The Ecotourism Association of Australia, Red Hill, Australia, pp. 19–24.

Forestry Tasmania (1994) *Guided Nature-Based Tourism in Tasmania's Forests: Trends, Constraints and Implications.* Forestry Tasmania, Hobart, Australia.

Godfrey, K.B. (1996) Towards sustainability? Tourism in the Republic of Cyprus. In: Harrison, L.C. and Husbands, W. (eds) *Practicing Responsible Tourism: International Case Studies in Tourism Planning, Policy and Development.* John Wiley & Sons, Chichester, UK, pp. 58–79.

Goodall, B. and Stabler, M.J. (1997) Principles influencing the determination of environmental standards for sustainable tourism. In: Stabler, M.J. (ed.) *Tourism and Sustainability: From Principles To Practice.* CAB International, Wallingford, UK, pp. 279–304.

Hunter, C. (1995a) Key concepts for tourism and the environment. In: Hunter, C. and Green, H. (eds) *Tourism and the Environment: a Sustainable Relationship?* Routledge, London, pp. 52–92.

Hunter, C. (1995b) On the need to re-conceptualize sustainable tourism development. *Journal of Sustainable Tourism* 3(3), 155–165.

Hunter, C. (1997) Sustainable tourism as an adaptive paradigm. *Annals of Tourism Research* 24(4), 850–867.

Hvenegaard, G.T. (1994) Ecotourism: a status report and conceptual framework. *The Journal of Tourism Studies* 5(2): 24–35.

Inskeep, E. (1991) *Tourism Planning: an Integrated and Sustainable Development Approach.* Chapman & Hall, London.

Jaakson, R. (1997) Exploring the epistemology of ecotourism. *Journal of Applied Recreation Research* 22(1), 33–47.

Lane, B. (1994) What is rural tourism? *Journal of Sustainable Tourism* 2 (1 & 2), 7–21.

Lindberg, K. and McKercher, B. (1997) Ecotourism: a critical overview. *Pacific Tourism Review* 1(1), 65–79.

Mowforth, M. and Munt, I. (1998) *Tourism and Sustainability: New Tourism in the Third World.* Routledge, London.

Nepal, S.K. (1997) Sustainable tourism, protected areas and likelihood needs of local communities in developing countries. *International Journal of Sustainable Development and World Ecology* 4(2), 123–135.

Orams, M.B. (1995a) Towards a more desirable form of ecotourism. *Tourism Management* 16(1), 3–8.

Orams, M.B. (1995b) Using interpretation to manage nature-based tourism. *Journal of Sustainable Tourism* 4(2), 81–94.

Wahab, S. (1997) Sustainable tourism in the developing world. In: Wahab, S. and Pigram, J.J. (eds) *Tourism Development and Growth, the Challenge of Sustainability.* Routledge, London, pp. 129–146.

Wall, G. (1994) Ecotourism: old wine in new bottles? *Trends* 3(2), 4–9.

Wall, G. (1997) Sustainable tourism-unsustainable development. In: Wahab, S. and Pigram, J.J. (eds) *Tourism Development and Growth, The Challenge of Sustainability*, Routledge, London, 33–49.

Westlake, J. and Diamantis, D. (1998) The application of environmental auditing to the management of sustainability within tourism. *Tourism Recreation Research* 23(2), 69–71.

World Tourism Organisation (1993) *Sustainable Tourism Development: Guide for Local Planners*. WTO, Madrid.

World Tourism Organisation (1995) *What Tourism Managers Need to Know: a Practical Guide to the Development and Use of Indicators of Sustainable Tourism*. WTO, Madrid.

World Tourism Organisation (1998) Ecotourism now one-fifth of market. *World Tourism Organisation News* 1, 6.

World Travel and Tourism Council/World Tourism Organisation/Earth Council (1995) *Agenda 21 for the Travel and Tourism Industry – Towards Environmentally Sustainable Development*. WTTC/WTO/EC, Oxford.

Ziffer, K.A. (1989) *Ecotourism: the Uneasy Alliance*. Conservation International and Ernst & Young, Washington, DC.

Chapter 4

The Consumer Behaviour Context of Ecolabelling
RICHARD SHARPLEY

Introduction

Resource problems are not 'environmental problems: they are human problems' (Ludwig *et al.*, 1993). In other words, the depletion or degradation of resources, including those upon which the development of tourism depends, results not from scarcity or fragility of those resources but from the excessive or inappropriate ways in which people exploit them. Therefore, any attempt to achieve the sustainable use of resources requires, in general, sustainable lifestyles. More specifically, the successful formulation and implementation of environmentally appropriate policies, including ecolabelling, is dependent upon at least the existence of environmental awareness and, preferably, the positive acceptance or adoption of appropriate behaviour on the part of both industries and consumers.

The development of tourism is no exception. In response to widespread concern about the potentially negative consequences of tourism in destination areas, new, environmentally appropriate or sustainable forms of tourism have been increasingly promoted by the tourism industry since the early 1990s. Moreover, it would appear that such forms of tourism have gained in popularity among tourists; for example, ecotourism now accounts for up to 10% of all international tourism arrivals (Steele, 1995). More recently, increasing attention has also been paid to the ecolabelling of such tourism products, whether to endorse the activities of the organizations concerned, to attract or influence potential customers or to verify their expectations.

There is, then, little doubt about the apparent willingness of the tourism industry to embrace the principles of sustainability and green marketing. Equally, the growth in demand for what may be described collectively as ecotourism suggests that tourists themselves are becoming increasingly amenable to the production and promotion of sustainable forms of tourism. However, the important point here is that, although there exists widespread support for the development of sustainable tourism, its inherent policies, objectives and practices, including ecolabelling, are largely justified on the basis of broad, unsubstantiated assumptions about 'environmental credentials' of tourists. Specifically, it is assumed that, because the demand for and supply of ecotourism-type products is on the increase, tourists are positively seeking out more sustainable forms of tourism, are prepared to adopt modes of behaviour more appropriate to the tourism environments they enter, or are willing to purchase sustainable tourism products as and when the tourism industry supplies them. In short, the existence of the environmentally aware, green tourist is taken for granted.

This assumption is, however, normally based upon the results of general (rather than tourism-specific) surveys which indicate, for example, wider awareness of environmental issues, increasing membership of environmental organizations, greater concern for the natural environment or the existence of the environmentally aware consumer. Thus, it is also implicitly assumed that the consumption of tourism can be equated with other forms of consumption and that, as a result, greater environmental awareness will influence tourists to be more responsive to the development and promotion of sustainable tourism in general and to green messages or ecolabelling in particular.

The purpose of this chapter is to argue that this is not the case. It suggests that a significant degree of ambivalence exists within the context of green consumerism and that, in the specific context of tourism, the alleged emergence of the 'green consumer' certainly does not imply the emergence of the 'green tourist'. Moreover, it also suggests that, within the context of postmodern consumer culture, tourism is consumed in a variety of ways which are in opposition to the notion of the green, environmentally aware tourist. Together, these arguments point to a number of implications for the design, role and potential influence of ecolabelling in tourism.

The Green Consumer as Green Tourist?

Since the late 1960s environmental concern has become, and continues to be, one of the most widespread social and political issues. In the UK, for example, reported 'levels of public concern about environmental issues ran at steadily high levels throughout the 1970s and 1980s' (MacKenzie, 1991: 68), while research in Canada has shown that, in 1990, the environment remained the most important issue for a significant proportion of the population. Furthermore, it would appear that public concern over environmental issues continued to increase in the 1990s, although becoming relatively less important compared with other issues.

It was also during the latter half of the 1980s that, for the first time, environmental concern became translated into the specific activity of green consumerism. Some assert that this has been a passing fad, although surveys suggest that it has become a more permanent shift in consumers' attitudes. For example, Mintel (1994) found that, between 1990 and 1994, the numbers of people who in general considered themselves to be either 'dark green' (i.e. 'always or as far as possible buy environmentally friendly products') or 'pale green' (i.e. 'buy if I see them') consumers both increased slightly, together representing 63% of those questioned.

At face value, these findings appear to be borne out within the specific context of tourism. Reference has already been made to the growth in demand for activities or types of holidays collectively referred to as ecotourism and this would appear to support the argument that greater numbers of tourists are embracing the principles of green consumerism. Indeed, there is little doubt that this is a rapidly expanding sector of the overall tourism market, although there is currently a lack of accurate statistical data to confirm this. At the same time, and again despite a lack of relevant research, it is also safe to suggest that some, but not all, of those who participate in sustainable forms of tourism do so on the basis of deeply held environmental convictions. Therefore, the ecolabelling of tourism products would appear to be an effective means of communicating the green message to an increasingly responsive tourist audience.

Significantly, however, there is no evidence to suggest that the increase in popularity of ecotourism/sustainable tourism as a whole is directly related to the emergence of green consumerism or is a response to the implicit or explicit green credentials of such forms of tourism. In fact, the limited research into the motivations of ecotourists reveals preferences for particular destinational attributes, such as the desire for natural surroundings, but does not suggest that the behaviour of ecotourists is in any way moulded by environmental values (Eagles, 1992). Therefore, it is safe to assume that other, more powerful factors influence holiday or destination choice.

Moreover, there is also little or no evidence to support the fundamental assumption, upon which the concept of sustainable tourism largely rests, that greater environmental awareness in general inevitably leads to what may be described as increasing green tourism consumerism in particular and, hence, that increasing numbers of tourists will respond positively to ecolabelling. Indeed, research into the general relationships between environmental concerns and people's resultant behaviour has revealed a significant lack of consistency between potentially influential factors, such as age, level of education or social grouping, and observed consumer behaviour. In particular, the alleged widespread participation in green consumerism reported by Mintel (1994) has been challenged by Witherspoon (1994) who observes that up to one half of those who claim to embrace green values never transfer these beliefs into their consumer behaviour. She concludes that 'despite the earlier evidence of high levels of environmental concern. . . .the proportion of adults who behave in a consistently environmentally friendly consumerist fashion is very low. *Fewer than one per cent of consumers behave in a consistently environmentally-friendly way'* (Witherspoon, 1994: 125, emphasis added).

These contradictory findings not only point to the inherently complex and frequently ambivalent ways in which consumers respond to environmental concerns, but also highlight weaknesses in research techniques which fail to address the enormous variety of influences on individual consumer behaviour. For example, many surveys into environmental awareness or consumer behaviour are based on assumptions that different social groupings can be identified with 'technocentric' or 'ecocentric' attitudes and behaviour, that such attitudes remain constant over time and determine people's overall involvement in environmental activism or consumption, or that responses to specific questions can reveal an individual's inner beliefs and values. What they fail to explore is the extent to which different environmental issues or problems, or different forms of consumption, elicit different responses in an individual's behaviour. At the same time and more pragmatically, it is likely that most people would claim to be environmentally aware; the extent to which such stated environmental concern becomes translated into green behaviour, however, is dependent upon a whole host of variables related to an individual's needs and values.

It is not surprising, therefore, that surveys which point to high levels of general environmental concern with respect to national or global issues reveal nothing about individual attitudes, values and responses to specific environmental, political or ethical issues. As a result, predicted and actual behaviour is frequently contradictory. In the specific context of rural tourism in the UK, for example, research consistently shows a high level of support for protecting the countryside (Young, 1989) and is frequently cited as evidence of increasing demands for greener, sustainable forms of tourism. Nevertheless, despite about 90% of people believing that the countryside is an important part of British heritage and should be protected at all costs (Countryside Commission, 1996), the great majority of visits to the countryside are still made by car.

Many other examples could be used to demonstrate the divergence between the alleged levels of environmental awareness and actual behaviour, particularly on the part of consumers. Moreover, many other factors, such as perceptions of individual versus government responsibility, deserve consideration. However, the important point here is that, even when people do embrace environmental concerns, they do not always consume or behave according to green values or principles. It is evident, for example, that concerns about air pollution do not prevent people from driving cars or flying to tourist destinations. Thus, it must be concluded that green consumerism must be assessed according to individual products or activities and be based upon a variety of related factors, including a product's cost, availability, substitutability, purpose/use and, in a semiotic sense, its significance. In other words, where a green product costs more, provides inferior performance, involves greater effort on the part of the consumer or simply does not fully satisfy customer needs, environmental values are likely to be of little consequence in the consumer decision-making process.

In the present context, this brief analysis supports the assertion that widespread awareness of general environmental issues cannot be translated into the emergence of the 'green' tourist. This, in turn, suggests that tourism consumer-directed ecolabelling may not elicit widespread responses, even among actual and potential consumers of sustainable forms of tourism. In other words, a significant degree of ambivalence exists in the context of green consumerism; general environmental concern and even a commitment to green consumerism does not mean that its principles will be applied to all forms of consumption. Indeed, in many cases the decision to participate in ecotourism may not be related in any way to environmental concerns. Therefore, effective tourism ecolabelling should be based not on broad, unsubstantiated assumptions about the increasing propensity of tourists to seek out sustainable tourism, but on a more specific understanding of the different ways in which tourism is consumed. This will then provide a more focused foundation for the formulation and targeting of ecolabelling strategies.

The Consumption of Tourism

Tourism researchers have long been concerned with analysing and attempting to develop an understanding of the consumption of tourism. Typically, attention has been focused specifically on the role of tourist motivation within the overall tourism demand process, the main purpose being to enable the prediction of tourist behaviour, with evident practical applications in terms of product design, market segmentation, and so on. Therefore, it is not surprising that attention has primarily been directed towards identifying individuals' needs and wants and how these may be satisfied, in a utilitarian sense, by tourism.

However, much of this work has been weakened by an overly tourism-centric perspective. That is, for many tourists the decision-making process is undoubtedly relatively simple: what sort of holiday do I want (family holiday, beach holiday, skiing holiday, adventure holiday), how much can I afford, and which destination/company best satisfies these needs? Nevertheless, tourism is just one of many forms of consumption and it has become increasingly recognized that, in order to fully understand consumer choices, it is also vital to take into account the broader social and cultural influences that pattern or shape consumer behaviour. As Solomon (1994: 536) argues, overall consumption choices 'simply cannot be understood without considering the cultural context in which they are made'. In other words, in modern societies where consumption has become a defining element of social life, understanding why particular types of tourism are chosen is only half the story. It is also important to understand the meaning of tourism as a form of consumption, particularly if the viability of any element of a sustainable tourism marketing strategy, including ecolabelling, is to be fully assessed.

Underpinning this argument is the claim that a defining feature of postmodern cultures is the emergence of consumerism or consumer culture. In other words, in postmodern societies 'consumption, rather than production, becomes dominant, and the commodity attains the total occupation of social life' (Bocock, 1993). This has come about, in part, from a variety of factors and transformations within the wider social and economic system in post-industrial societies that have enabled the practice of consumption to assume a leading role in people's lives. Such factors include the large, widely available and ever-increasing range of consumer goods and services, the popularity of 'leisure shopping', the emergence of consumer groups and consumer legislation, pervasive advertising, widely available credit facilities and 'the impossibility of avoiding making choices in relation to consumer goods' (Lury, 1996: 36).

However, it is not only the *practice* but also the *significance* of consumption that is of vital importance in the emergence of a dominant consumer culture. It has long been recognized that commodities, whether goods or services, have a meaning beyond their economic exchange or use value. As Lury (1996: 11) explains, 'the utility of goods is always framed by a cultural context, that even the use of the most mundane objects in daily life has cultural meaning . . . material goods are not only used to do things, but they also have a meaning, and act as meaningful markers of social relationships'. In short, social lives are patterned, or indeed created, by the acquisition and use (i.e. consumption) of things.

The primary role of this symbolic process inherent in consumption is considered by many to be its contribution to the creation of a sense of identity and status or in establishing distinctions between different social groups; groups which were identified and demarcated by work roles in the era of modernity now seek identity and status through consumption. As discussed below, tourism has long been a status symbol. Until the mid-20th century it was only the well-to-do who could holiday abroad, and still today certain forms of travel (Concorde, the Orient Express) and certain destinations signify wealth or status.

However, it has been argued that identity-construction or group-distinction is not the only symbolic or social role of consumption. In other words, although some individuals' consumption practices may be identity or status driven, the same consumption objects, including tourism, may be consumed by others in different ways. Nevertheless, the vital point is that the consumption of tourism must be considered at two levels. Firstly, it fulfils a utilitarian purpose – to escape, rest, learn, play sport, and so on – associated with need satisfaction. Secondly, tourism experiences possess a cultural significance or meaning which frames tourists' decision-making process and their behaviour as consumers of tourism products.

It is this second level which is of greatest importance in the present context. For ecolabelling to be effective, it must encourage an individual to place environmental values before the cultural significance of tourism, or to translate cultural significance into environmentally appropriate (tourism) consumer behaviour. The extent to which this may be possible is considered below, but firstly it is important to consider briefly the different ways in which tourism may be consumed.

Holt (1995) identifies a total of four categories of consumption, each of which may be related to the specific sphere of tourism:

(i) Consuming tourism as experience

The consumption-as-experience perspective focuses on the subjective or emotional reactions of consumers to particular consumption objects. It is concerned with the ways in which people experience, or make sense of, different objects or consumption experiences. To a great extent, the ways in which people experience different objects of consumption is by placing them within an interpretative framework. That is, many consumption objects are embedded in a social world which provides the framework for their definition or understanding.

Tourism is no exception to this process. As a form of consumption it is firmly embedded in tourists' social world and the ways in which people experience, or consume, tourism will depend very much on their interpretation of the role or meaning of tourism within that social world. For example, tourism may be interpreted as a form of sacred consumption, a modern spiritual experience (holiday being the modern form of holy day) occurring outside normal (profane) times and places. Tourists' behaviour will, therefore, be framed by this sacralization of tourism and may be manifested in different ways. Some may seek the spiritual refreshment of solitary, romantic tourist places, places which are uncrowded, unspoiled and offer the 'spiritual' benefits of experiencing nature or authentic cultures. In this sense, there is an evident link with ecotourism and the potential for ecolabelling to promote/verify the inherent significance of such destinations, even though the desired experience may not emanate directly or even indirectly from environmental values. Conversely, for others, the sacred nature of tourism may be reflected in their collective experience of tourist sites and destinations, or visiting attractions that have achieved iconic status.

Importantly, the consumption of tourism is also framed by the experiential aspect of modern consumption as a whole, namely, the hedonistic pursuit of pleasure which, it has been argued, results not from physical satisfaction but from romantic daydreaming (Campbell, 1987). Tourism in particular lends itself to this concept of consumption as the pursuit of illusory pleasure, especially as daydreaming suggests desires for the novel, different or the 'other'. Indeed, the anticipation stage of tourism consumption (looking forward to the holiday) is considered by some to be a fundamental ingredient of the tourism experience. Importantly, this suggests that tourism represents the consumption of dreams, an escape to the non-ordinary, sacred, novel 'other'. This may well include the escape from ordinary concerns: work, financial worries and, perhaps, environmental concerns. In this sense, ecolabelling may be counter-productive as it may remind tourists of the 'here-and-now' rather than the dreamworld of the tourism experience.

(ii) Consuming tourism as integration

Consuming-as-integration is the process whereby consumers integrate themselves with the object of consumption; that is, the object becomes part of their identity. This is achieved by either adapting the object to suit their self-concept, or by adapting their self-concept to align it with the socially or institutionally defined identity of the object (more simply, by 'fitting in').

In the case of tourism, integration is, in one sense, automatic as tourists play an integral role in the production of tourism experiences. Nevertheless, much depends on the direction of that integration. A tourist who wishes to be identified with a particular destination's culture or society or with a particular form of tourism may adapt his or her self-concept to 'fit' the identity of the destination or tourism-type. Thus, individuals who see themselves as 'good', environmentally aware tourists will adapt their behaviour by consuming particular types of tourism or by assimilating into the local area. Similarly, tourists in destinations such as Ibiza may adapt their behaviour to integrate into the perceived 'youth-party' culture of the island. In either case, the self is integrated into the object. Conversely, certain types of tourism or tourist experience may be integrated into the individual's self-concept in a process of self-extension. For example, adventure sports, such as white-water rafting, may be used by tourists to convey a message about their own self-image.

In the context of consuming-as-integration, it is evident that ecolabelling may play a powerful role in matching particular tourists to particular destinations or forms of tourism. Certainly, those who consider themselves to be 'good' tourists will be responsive to green messages and may be influenced to buy holidays or use companies that enable them to integrate themselves into, rather than conflict with, the local environment and culture. However, ecolabelling here is essentially 'preaching to the converted'; it will allow certain tourists to consume according to an existing self-image, but it will not influence others to alter their self-image.

(iii) Consuming tourism as play

The consuming-as-play perspective suggests that people utilize objects as a resource or focus for interaction with other consumers, rather than referring specifically to the experiential characteristics of the consumption object. Thus, in the context of tourism, consuming-as-play does not refer, for example, to tourism providing the opportunity to 'play' as in a child-like experience free from responsibility, but to the fact that it is used as a vehicle for socializing with fellow consumers of tourism or sharing particular experiences.

This draws attention to the fact that tourism is, frequently, a social experience, an element of which is 'to be able to consume particular commodities in the company of others. Part of what people buy is in effect a particular social composition of other consumers' (Urry, 1990). In this sense, tourism provides the focus for people to socialize or to fulfil a more reciprocal role in entertaining each other. Indeed, the popularity of many resorts is based on the opportunity for tourists to enjoy their holiday in the company of large numbers of other tourists. Equally, tourism may also be a means of sharing unusual, extraordinary or even unpleasant experiences; the communal interaction with the consumption object allows tourists to commune or experience a sense of togetherness in challenging or difficult situations or environments. Often, this sense of sharing/togetherness may continue long after the tourism experience. In either case, however, the focus is on the communal, social nature of the consumption experience rather than the object of consumption. Therefore, from this perspective on the consumption of tourism, environmental/sustainability considerations will come second to the social or play significance of tourism.

(iv) Consuming tourism as classification

Most commonly, consumption is considered a means of classification. That is, especially within so-called postmodern societies where traditional status markers (job, income, social class, and so on) are of less significance, consumers utilize consumption objects to create self-identity, to classify themselves in relation to others. It has been argued, for example, that traditional social groupings are being replaced by a new and expanding middle or 'service' class, the members of which seek social differentiation and status not through the value or cost, but through different styles, of consumption. That is, different goods and services have different social and cultural values and serve as markers of style; thus, social classification is no longer based on the ability to pay, but on taste.

In the context of tourism, the consuming-as-classification perspective points to the role of tourism consumption in identity and status formation. As mentioned earlier, tourism has long been a marker of social status; initially the ability to travel and, more recently, different means of travel and different destinations have signified social exclusivity. Nowadays, tourism is widely used as an expression of taste, a fact recognized by the travel industry which, in response, is developing more specialized, niche products, such as ecotourism or styles of tourism which, though relatively affordable, have the aura of status or luxury. One example of the latter is the relatively recent introduction of cruise holidays by some of the larger British tour operators, bringing the 'exclusivity' of cruising within the economic reach of the mass tourist.

In terms of sustainable tourism in particular, it can be argued that the increasing consumption of ecotourism and other environmentally appropriate forms of tourism has more to do with the apparent exclusivity of the product rather than its inherent environmental quality. Certainly, many 'ecotours' occur in more exotic destinations, are relatively expensive and by definition are non-mass (i.e. exclusive). This, of course, implies that such forms of tourism will only remain popular while they remain exclusive, a conclusion that holds little promise for the longer-term and more widespread adoption of sustainable tourism consumption practices. Conversely, however, sustainable (tourism) consumption practices may in fact become a social classifier, the 'mass tourist' being, in effect, the lowest common denominator of tourism consumers. In this case, as the following section discusses, consumption-as-classification may represent one of a number of opportunities for the effective use of ecolabelling in tourism.

Tourism Consumption and Ecolabelling

In addressing the issue of ecolabelling in the tourism industry from the point of view of tourist-consumer culture, this chapter has challenged the fundamental assumption that tourists are, in general, becoming increasingly environmentally conscious. More specifically, it has argued that the alleged increase in environmental awareness and the corresponding emergence of green consumerism cannot necessarily be translated into all forms of consumer behaviour. Not only is there evidence of significant ambivalence, with consumers varying their behaviour and applying different values according to different objects and modes of consumption, but also their claimed (environmental) values and actual behaviour are frequently contradictory. In the specific context of tourism, this has arisen partly as a result of the reasons why people consume tourism, but also because of the variety of meanings attached to the consumption of tourism, meanings which potentially supersede environmental concerns.

This has a number of implications for the successful implementation and use of ecolabelling within the tourism industry. At a basic level, if tourists do follow the simplistic process of deciding what kind of holiday they want and, within a variety of (primarily financial) constraints, decide which destination/holiday company will satisfy their needs most closely, then ecolabelling will have little or no effect on the consumption process. For example, a family wanting a 'typical' summer beach holiday in the Mediterranean is likely to be more concerned about food quality, facilities for the children, the standards of accommodation and the price than about the extent to which the tour operator contributes to local environmental projects or to which their chosen hotel recycles waste water.

At the same time, the basic characteristics of tourism should also not be overlooked. Generally, tourism is considered to be motivated by the desire to escape and relax; the consumption of tourism is, therefore, very much focused inwardly on the self. It is also, typically, a relatively expensive form of consumption. Together, these characteristics suggest that tourism is a form of self-reward within which outward looking environmental concern is likely to have a low priority. Hence, the ecolabelling of the product is likely to elicit limited responses on the part of the consumer, even those who may attach environmental principles to other forms of consumption. At the same time, broader 'eco-messages', such as the recent decision by one British tour operator to show a short 'tourist education' film on flights to The Gambia, are also likely to prove relatively ineffective.

The exception to this rather negative conclusion would be, of course, those tourists who positively seek 'green' holidays or, as discussed shortly, those markets which have a tradition of environmental concern. In these cases, there is little doubt that ecolabelling plays a positive role in matching tourists to appropriate destinations or experiences, although the number of tourists who will be influenced by such labelling is likely to be relatively small. It will include those who apply green principles to most, if not all forms of consumption and, in the terminology used here, consume tourism as a means of integrating themselves with the object of their consumption. Conversely, those who consume tourism as experience, particularly the escapist, daydreaming, hedonistic experience referred to above, are unlikely to be positively influenced by ecolabelling. Indeed, it may prove to be a disincentive as it frames the holiday experience within reality, requiring the tourist to 'work' at tourism. Thus, in this rather narrow context, the use of ecolabelling should be carefully targeted at specific markets and attached to particular products which permit consumer–object integration.

However, ecolabelling in tourism undoubtedly has a broader and more positive role to play beyond simply 'preaching to the converted' (or beyond the identification/reward of good practice within the industry), particularly if ecolabelling is manifested as a message as opposed to a symbol or mark. In other words, if the starting point for designing and implementing ecolabelling policies is not the object of consumption (the destination, the tourism experience or the providers of tourism services) but recognition of the different ways in which tourism is consumed, then ecolabelling can exploit these in order to encourage more appropriate tourism-consumer behaviour.

To put it another way, earlier in this chapter it was argued that green consumerism in general is characterized by a significant degree of ambivalence; not only is there little evidence of individual consumers applying green values to all forms of consumption all the time, but there is also a lack of consistency between environmental concern and specific social groups. In short, it is difficult, if not impossible, to segment consumers by their level of environmental concern or their 'shade of green' (Swarbooke and Horner, 1999: 201). This, in turn, implies that it is difficult to target specific ecolabels at specific, traditional market segments; specific income, age, lifestyle, lifecycle, employment and education characteristics cannot be related to environmental awareness.

The model of consumption practices described here, however, does go some way to providing the basis for the more effective targeting of ecolabels at specific segments of the tourism market. Indeed, each of the four consumer typologies outlined above represents a 'segment' for which specific ecolabelling may be designed to encourage, directly or indirectly, environmentally sustainable behaviour.

The 'experiential' tourist

The desired experience focuses upon natural, unspoiled or culturally authentic environments (a dominant destinational-pull among eco-tourists); the focus is very much upon the quality of the environment and the resultant personal experience rather than on the impacts of tourism on such environments. Nevertheless, labelling can explicitly highlight the experiential advantages of such environments while implicitly emphasizing the role of tourists in their protection. Thus, as the demand for such destinations increases, ecolabelling can undoubtedly play a role in raising environmental awareness among tourists, even when such demands are unrelated to environmental concerns. At the same time, where the tourism experience is contextualized by relatively high levels of environmental consciousness in the tourist's home society, ecolabelling of tourism products may encourage tourists to link a 'home' value to an activity that occurs away from their normal society, thereby promoting more responsible tourist behaviour. Conversely, where the sought experience is the consumption of dreams (i.e. the escape from reality), lower-key, indirect ecolabels may be used to sow the subconscious seeds of environmental awareness.

The 'integrating' tourist

As pointed out above, where tourists wish to integrate themselves with the tourism product, particularly in the case of appropriate or sustainable forms of tourism, ecolabelling is an effective means of marketing and verifying desired experiences. Additionally, ecolabelling may encourage integration, even when this is not the primary consumption mode, by highlighting the experiential and destinational benefits of a more proactive stance on the part of tourists. However, careful matching of specific destinations, products and tourists types is essential. That is, sun–sea–sand tourists (as in the example of The Gambia noted above) may be less responsive to eco-messages than other types of tourists, irrespective of the destination.

The 'playing' tourist

Although environmental concern is likely to be secondary to social and inter-personal aspects of the 'play' mode of consumption, in certain circumstances ecolabelling can be used to foster a social or communal sense of responsibility to the environment. For example, small group overland tours, based on the shared experience of 'real' travel, are one of a number of types of tourism where ecolabelling may act as a catalyst in the development of a shared social/group awareness and appropriate mode of behaviour.

The 'classifying' tourist

Ecotourism remains an exclusive form of tourism. Not only does it tend to occur in more distant, fragile or exotic destinations, but it is relatively expensive and is the antithesis of the popularly held perceptions of mass package tourism. It is, therefore, an effective marker of status, hence often referred to as 'ego' tourism (Wheeller, 1992). Equally, some tourists may consider that displays of environmental concern (whether or not founded upon genuine environmental values) are a positive status enhancer. In either case, the environmental aims of ecolabelling may be achieved by appealing to forms of consumer behaviour not primarily shaped by environmental awareness but which nevertheless have a positive impact on tourist destinations. Ecotourism may indeed attract tourists who use the experience primarily as a status symbol but, from the point of view of destination environments and societies, does it matter?

Inevitably, the success of targeted ecolabels based on a consumption-practice segmentation model is dependent on the identification of each segment, a process requiring significant further research. Moreover, the consumption of tourism is multi-dimensional; tourist behaviour is influenced by an enormous variety of factors related to both the individual and the product. Nevertheless, a more in-depth analysis of the socio-cultural context of the consumption of tourism suggests that, in a strict sense, the ecolabelling of tourism products or organizations that satisfy particular indicators of environmental soundness will positively appeal to relatively few tourism-consumers. However, this somewhat negative conclusion may be balanced against a more positive, pragmatic approach to labelling which not only recognizes but exploits the different ways in which tourism is consumed. That is, the model of tourism consumption practices presented here offers the potential to develop a new means of segmenting tourists so that ecolabels may be more effectively designed and targeted at the specific consumer-cultural needs of tourists. In the longer term, this may result in a wider acceptance of and participation in environmentally sustainable forms of tourism which, overall, must be the aim of ecolabelling.

References

Bocock, R. (1993) *Consumption*. Routledge, London.

Campbell, C. (1987) *The Romantic Ethic and the Spirit of Modern Consumerism*. Blackwell, Oxford.

Countryside Commission (1996) *Public Attitudes to the Countryside*, CCP 481. Countryside Commission, Cheltenham.

Eagles, P. (1992) The travel motivations of Canadian ecotourists. *Journal of Travel Research* 31(2), 3–13.

Holt, D. (1995) How consumers consume: a typology of consumption practices. *Journal of Consumer Research* 22 (June), 1–16.

Ludwig, D., Hilborn, R. and Walters, C. (1993) Uncertainty, resource exploitation, and conservation: lessons from history. *Science* 269, (5104), 17 and 36.

Lury, C. (1996) *Consumer Culture*. Polity Press, Cambridge.

Mackenzie, D. (1991) The rise of the green consumer. *Consumer Policy Review* 1(2), 68–75.

Mintel (1994) *The Green Consumer I: the Green Conscience*. Mintel International, London.

Solomon, M. (1994) *Consumer Behaviour: Buying, Having and Being*, 2nd edn. Allyn and Bacon, Needham Heights, Massachusetts.

Steele, P. (1995) Ecotourism: an economic analysis. *Journal of Sustainable Tourism* 3(1), 29–44.

Swarbooke, J. and Horner, S. (1999) *Consumer Behaviour in Tourism*. Butterworth-Heinemann, Oxford.

Urry, J. (1990) The consumption of tourism. *Sociology* 24(1), 23–35.

Wheeller, B. (1992) Eco or ego tourism: new wave tourism. In: *ETB Insights*, vol. 3. English Tourist Board, London: D41–44.

Witherspoon, S. (1994) The greening of Britain: romance and rationality. In: Jowell, R., Curtis, J., Brook, L. and Ahrendt, D. (eds) *British Social Attitudes: the 11th Report*. Dartmouth, Aldershot, pp. 107–139.

Young, K. (1989) Rural prospects. In: Jowell, R., Witherspoon, S. and Brook, L. (eds) *British Social Attitudes: the 5th Report*. Gower, Aldershot.

Chapter 5

Environmental Behaviour Implications for Tourist Destinations and Ecolabels

TANJA MIHALIČ

Introduction

In the flood of tourism ecolabels it is of the utmost importance for destination managers to recognize that, for the environment-conscious tourist, the quality of the environment is of primary and direct concern rather than the environment improving efforts of the destination itself. The question 'What is the air quality at the destination?' is more important for the holiday traveller than the question 'What does the tourism industry do to protect the air quality at the destination?'. Thus, the labels 'good bathing water' or 'authentic place' would attract more visitors than, for example, the label 'waste minimization' even though both aspects are interrelated and ecolabelling activities enables the achievement and maintenance of environmental quality standards as required for environmental quality labels.

If we regard the environmental characteristics of tourist destinations (clear sea water, beautiful and clean beaches, etc.) as tourist product components and a prime attractive force in triggering tourist demand, it becomes obvious that tourist stakeholders on supply and demand sides have a vested interest in environmental protection. This chapter presents how the market mechanism can be routed towards environmental protection, preservation and even towards the upgrading of already degraded environments through various kinds of environmental labelling. The market functioning of ecolabelling is explained by environmental behaviour theories. Environmental awareness, ethics and behaviour in tourism are studied and the gaps between environmentally relevant intentions and actual environmental behaviour are analysed as are their implications for ecolabelling. Further, the chapter attempts to argue that all categories of environmental labelling in tourism are not equally effective in attracting tourist demand and distinguishes between ecolabels and environmental quality labels.

Theoretical Assumptions Underlying the Market Functioning of Environmental Labelling: Environmental Behaviour Theory

It is assumed that consumers prefer and choose products that are ecolabelled. Accordingly, ecolabelling influences demand and supply and thus works through the market mechanism. How and by how much demand and supply are influenced by ecolabelling can be partly explained by environmental behavioural theory. That theory explains the existence of environmental damage through the absence of environmental social ethics and as a product of human ignorance.

According to the first explanation, the absence of environmental social ethics is the main reason for environmental degradation and damage. The term 'environmental ethics' refers to the 'standards and principles regulating the behaviour of individuals or groups of individuals' (Rue and Byars, 1986: 71) in relation to their environment. In general, ethics deals with questions such as 'what is right and what is wrong?', and with moral obligations: 'Is it wrong to buy products from a producer which does not care for the environment? Isn't it right to choose destinations/hotels which have shown they take care of the environment?. Do we as tourists have to help protect the nature and respect the culture of the holiday destination?' The proportion of positive answers here reveals the developed level of environmental ethics.

In theory, it is assumed that humans possess environmental ethics. Further, theory assumes that humans will react in an environmentally friendly way if appropriate environmental information is available. Opponents argue that the environmental wave seen in developed countries should not be mistaken for environmental social ethics (Frey, 1985: 38–39). It is limited to an environmental awareness that can be measured by positive answers to different questions such as those above. The proper questions for measuring environmental awareness would thus be: 'Do we tourists damage the environment? Does the tourism industry destroy the landscape? Do we have to protect the environment from tourism?'. Further, according to some authors, environmental awareness includes the intention to act in an environmentally friendly way (Mueller and Fluegel, 1999: 53). This can be measured by positive answers to questions like: 'Are you willing to use public transport instead of your car? Are you willing to pay a certain amount for environmental protection in your holiday destination?'.

A gap occurs because intentions are not necessarily transferred into actual behaviour. The above-mentioned environmental wave does not necessarily include environmental behaviour. The latter is manifested through environmental activities and can be expressed and measured by positive answers to questions such as: 'When choosing a destination/hotel, do you take environmental criteria into account? Do you follow the guidelines of environmental codes of conduct? Do you use public transport? Have you financially contributed to environmental protection in the destination?'.

The mentioned gap between environmental awareness and behaviour has previously been observed. Mueller and Fluegel (1999: 58) maintain that in one study 89% of Germans declared themselves to be environmentally aware, yet only 45% replied in the affirmative to questions regarding actual environmental behaviour. Lassberg (quoted in Mueller and Fluegel, 1999: 58) showed that 40% of German tourists answered positively to the question: 'Are you willing to pay DEM 2 per holiday day for the protection of the environment?'. We assume that the likely gap between the declarative and actual willingness to pay (between expressed intentions and actual deeds) was not measured and can only speculate how many German 2-week holidaymakers would in practice be willing to forgo a nice dinner on account of environmental protection in a holiday destination.

There is another tourism-specific issue to be discussed in the framework of the first variation of environmental behaviour theory that is based on environmental ethics. The question is whether environmental social ethics also refers to the environmental quality issue. It is obvious that concern about environmental quality could be included in the category of tourism environmental awareness. It could be expressed through questions like: 'What is the quality of bathing water in a destination? How natural or authentic is the landscape?'. We know that tourists turn away from polluted destinations, yet it would be wrong to maintain that such behaviour is guided by ethics. Such behaviour is guided by other motives, such as recreational or health.

Although the first variation of the theory has been criticized, its implementation holds great potential for resolving environmental problems. It defines environmental ethics as an integral part of environmental awareness, a precondition for environmental behaviour. At the same time, we must not forget that not all of the population is environmentally conscious. Environmental social ethics is in its developmental stage and there is no such thing as innate environmental ethics.

The second variation of environmental behaviour theory involves human ignorance due to insufficient environmental research, education and information. The theory here says that environmental disasters occur over a long period. A direct link with specific actions is invisible, therefore a lack of understanding and information are the real reasons why disasters arise. If humans had sufficient information about the consequences of their actions such disasters would not happen. In order to prevent manipulation by the interested parties, research in this area must be intensified and the resulting information must be made public and easily accessible.

Although the said theory is specially treated in the economic literature (Frey, 1985: 39), it is quite justifiably criticized for being inappropriate. There is no doubt that sufficient information on environmental damage, together with knowledge about environmental behaviour, is necessary, yet this is not the only condition needed to prevent damage. Prevention also depends on factors like the above-mentioned environmental ethics. In the case of the tourism industry, we doubt that a seaside hotel owner would invest in an (expensive) sewage purifying plant for ethical reasons only. Thus, environmental information – in this case information on the absence of a purifying plant and information on the poor quality of bathing water – should be available to the public. It would create public disapproval of the inappropriate behaviour of the hotel owner and a push for appropriate environmental behaviour.

The two variations of the behavioural theory discussed complement each other. Environmental ethics can only be developed on the assumption that the reasons for environmental damage and methods (know-how) for improving and preserving the environment are known. Otherwise, knowledge about environmental disasters does not itself guarantee that behaviour regarding the environment will be friendlier. When behavioural theory is applied to tourism we do not distinguish between the two variations mentioned, we refer to both of them. On the one hand, taking into account the human ignorance variation requires discussion of the importance of environmental knowledge (information, research, education and – in the theory often neglected – know-how). On the other hand, the first variation of the environmental theory emphasizes the importance of environmental ethics, the constituent part of environmental responsibility.

Environmental Responsibility

Environmental responsibility refers to the attitudes of individuals, organizations and destinations towards environmental problems as well as their behaviour and is closely connected with the ethical part of their behaviour. It involves environmental awareness and environmental behaviour guided by environmental ethics.

Environmental responsibility in tourism is understood as the awareness of environmental problems caused by tourism, and as the behaviour of tourists and the tourist industry that complies with environmental ethics in tourism, i.e. behaviour with the minimum negative consequences for the natural, cultural and social environments.

The definition refers to environmental responsibility in tourism in a broader sense and takes into account the natural, cultural and social environments (World Bank, 1975: 5; Inskeep, 1991: 339; Mathieson and Wall, 1992: 3). As far as the present understanding of the term ecology is concerned, a narrower definition is also relevant, that is to say a definition that refers to the attitude towards the natural environment only (Mihalič and Kaspar, 1996: 44).

Dividing the terms into environmental awareness, ethics and behaviour is of great importance. In general, and in tourism as already mentioned, there is a difference between the declarative and actual environmental sensitivity of (tourist) demand, which is the difference between environmental awareness and environmental behaviour. In the declarative sense, the environmental awareness of today's tourists is much greater than seen in their (non-environmental) behaviour. So the problem lies in the absence of environmental ethics that should be aimed towards environmental behaviour – on the demand side among tourists, as well as on the supply side among tourism producers and/or suppliers (organizations and/or destinations).

Demand side

From the demand viewpoint, the absence of environmental awareness these days can be seen in the fact that in many cases tourists notice environmental damage when it threatens their own holiday enjoyment (Mueller, 1989: 101) and do not see their contribution to this destruction. They are aware of the fact that tourists do cause environmental damage but 'the tourist is always somebody else' (Krippendorf, 1986: 133). The absence of environmental ethics can also be found in the way of thinking that 'we should enjoy the benefits as long as possible' (Opashowski, 1991: 43), while the absence of environmental responsibility and/or behaviour can be found in the demand for environmentally less friendly forms of tourism and ignorance of environmentally friendlier tourist products.

There has been a strong attempt to create environmental awareness and ethics in terms of environmental agreements and codes. The Tourist Code, as an example, calls for respect for the natural and cultural heritage from the side of tourists (WTO, 1985, Article XI).

Tourists' ecological behaviour manifests itself in the choice of environmentally responsible tourism suppliers, in the choice of environmentally friendlier transport means, in avoiding products and services causing damage to nature (for example, canned drinks). Ecologically responsible behaviour (in the broader sense) also involves learning about the cultural and social characteristics of a host country and in respecting them.

In addition to the strain on the environment caused by travel, the environmental state of the destination is of definite interest to environmentally conscious travellers (Mueller, 1992: 9). Nevertheless, ecologically responsible demand for environmentally friendlier (low impact) tourism products should not be mistaken for demand for environmentally unspoiled destinations.

Supply side

The absence of environmental responsibility is obvious on the supply side, too. In the tourist industry, the absence of environmental responsibility is revealed in ignoring environmental problems, hiding or ignoring environmental information, in the supply of artificial substitutes for natural features (pools instead of the sea) and in an extreme reliance on the quality of the purpose-built part of the tourist supply.

Similar to the environmental codes of conduct on the demand side, there are many codes governing the environmental ethical behaviour of supply stakeholders. The latest example is the Global Code of Ethics for Tourism (WTO, 2000, Article 3), which concerns the question of responsibility of all stakeholders in tourism to 'safeguard the natural environment' and 'protect the natural heritage'.

There are many possibilities for environmentally responsible action in the tourist industry: control over and reduction in emissions harmful to the environment (for example, herbicides on golf courses, raw sewage, etc.), recycling and use of recycled materials, choice of environmentally aware business partners, development and encouragement of environmental forms of tourism, waste reduction, energy and water consumption minimization, preservation of landscapes, or providing environmental information and educating tourists. Tour operators can take ecological criteria into account when arranging programmes, use an ecological checklist when selecting hotels or preparing an energy audit for transport and so on (for examples see Hopfenbeck and Zimmer, 1993; Viegas, 1998; Hamele, 1996).

Many companies are already aware of their responsibility to the environment. They are also cognizant of the fact that through environmentally friendly behaviour they can avoid governmental regulations and also improve their own image, attract visitors and protect the environment for future business. Nevertheless, the absence of environmental responsibility is shown in the lack of easy, acceptable and understandable information on environmental impacts and quality. The European Community adopted the community ecolabel award scheme in order to provide customers with better information on the environmental impact of the products they buy (EEC, 1992). Furthermore, information should also be provided on the environmental quality of the tourism product, such as the cleanliness of the air and water at the destination. The Global Code of Ethics for Tourism (WTO, 2000, Article 6) states that 'tourism professionals have an obligation to provide tourists with objective and honest quality information on their places of destination.' The correct question that would measure the level of present environmental responsibility would be: 'Do we tourism professionals provide information on the environmental quality of the destination?'.

Nevertheless, supply of environmentally unspoiled natural areas is not environmentally responsible if the only environmental feature is the (given) virgin nature, exploited by (an environmentally ignorant) tourism entrepreneur.

Environmental Labelling in Tourism

Environmental or ecolabelling for industrial products is well known and widely used in today's world. Ecolabelled industrial products communicate the message: 'lowered (negative) environmental impacts'. Ecolabels are awarded to products environmentally less harmful in comparison with other products from the same product group (EEC, 1992).

This industrial product ecolabelling scheme cannot easily be applied to ecolabelling in tourism. Tourist products differ from industrial products. They are connected to the destination or, in other words, the destination's attractions are incorporated within an integrated tourist product. From the customer viewpoint, the quality of the natural, social and cultural environments forms part of the tourism product. Thus, for tourist customers, it is not only impact minimization but also the environmental quality of the destination that is the issue. In one study (Lübbert, 1998: 28) German travellers, when asked to evaluate the importance of different labelling criteria, gave 60% to the environmental quality criteria (poor water, clear air) and 26% to the 'lowering negative impacts' criteria (waste minimization and sorting, water and energy saving programmes, purifying plants, etc.).

Categories of environmental labelling

Since environmental quality is the greatest concern of a tourist customer, the ecolabel notion in tourism is often incorrectly restricted to the ecological quality of the tourist destination such as the cleanliness of bathing water, instead of negative impacts. In tourism, we must observe both aspects and so the term 'ecological labelling' is introduced. The term encompasses both ecolabels as traditionally defined for industrial products as well as the labels of environmental quality of tourist places. Therefore, it is necessary to distinguish between:

- the environmental or ecolabels which refer to the impact of tourist products or tourism on the environment (as in the case of the EU's ecolabels for industrial products);
- the environmental quality or eco-quality labels (labels of environmental quality) that refer to the tourist product's environmental attributes, e.g. to the state of the environmental quality of the tourist destination; and
- combined labels that simultaneously refer to the impact of the tourist product on the environment and to the state of the environmental quality of the tourist product/destination.

Accordingly, the ecolabel in tourism identifies the (reduced) negative physical, visual, cultural and social influences of tourism or tourism products, whereas the label of environmental quality refers to the degree of existing environmental (non-)degradation of a tourist destination, irrespective of the cause (Table 5.1, row 1).

Combined labels of tourism products pose a challenge for the future. Although the combined label Blue Flag for beaches and marinas was already developed in 1985, the strengths and weaknesses of combined labels regarding their market potential have not yet been sufficiently researched. Thus, the dilemma of whether future tourism environmental labelling should join environmental quality and impact criteria remains open (Hamele, 1998: 59). In practice, the subject of an ecolabel in tourism is not only the tourism product, but is usually also its producer and/or supplier, for example the tourism enterprise: hotel, tour operator, travel agent, leisure park, carrier, etc. (see Table 5.1, row 3). Ecolabelling can also refer to the environmental management of a tourist resort and reflects the resort's efforts to improve environmental quality.

From the point of view of the tourist destination, the two kinds of environmental labelling are co-dependent. On one hand, lowering the negative impacts of tourism preserves the environmental quality of the destination, yet, on the other hand, preserving environmental quality requires lowering the negative impacts of tourism activities at the destination. At the same time, from the standpoint of the consumer there is an essential difference between the two. The environmentally responsible tourist would find the information on environmental impacts essential to his or her choice of tourism package, hotel or carrier. However, since we already know that destination choice is influenced by environmental attractiveness (e.g. the quality) of the destination in the first place (Tschurtschenthaler, 1986), merely offering low impact tourist products is not sufficient. Customers look for eco quality labels in the first place (Table 5.1, column 3).

We agree that ecolabels in tourism have a noticeable effect on tourism demand, too (see Table 5.1, row 7). The environmentally responsible tourist is clearly willing to buy ecolabelled tourism products in order to contribute to environmental protection. It is possible

Table 5.1. Market functioning of environmental labelling in tourism.

Element No. 1	Ecolabel 2	Eco-quality label 3
1 Measuring	Environmental impacts: at place of residence in transit at destination (on air quality, water quality, etc.)	Environmental quality: at destination (air quality, water quality, visual pollution, etc.)
2 Auditing	Product/service production method/process	Water-quality, air-quality, noise, visual pollution, cultural authenticity, etc.
3 Awarding	Product/service enterprise/organization (hotels, tour operators, travel agents, carriers, etc.)	Destination (place, beach, resort, etc.)
4 Aim	To stimulate the supply and demand of products/services with a reduced environmental impact by informing potential consumer of environmentally sound tourism products and companies	To stimulate protection of the environment and upgrading of environmental quality and to inform potential customers about the environmental quality of the destination
5 Information	Direct message: environmentally sound/ responsible tourism products/ tourism companies Induced message 1: environmentally responsible destination Induced message 2: environmentally sound destination	Direct message: environmental quality of the destination (pure water, unspoiled flora/fauna, etc.) Induced message 1: environmentally sound destination Induced message 2: environmentally responsible destination
6 Assumptions	Customers are aware of environmental problems, possess environmental ethics, act environmentally friendly and buy ecolabelled products (in order to contribute to environmental protection)	Customers are aware of environmental pollution and choose destinations of environmental quality (in order to satisfy their motives for travel, e.g. sports, health, etc.)
7 Market effect	Customers prefer (choose) tourist products/services with reduced environmental impacts	Customers prefer (choose) destinations of environmental quality

to substitute car driving for public transport in the destination, but it is not as easy to substitute destination A for destination B for environmental impact reasons only. There is enough evidence that tourists are turning away from polluted destinations. This is illustrated by the increase in tourism in the less polluted eastern Mediterranean, and elsewhere (Mieczkowski, 1995: 210). In the northern hemisphere, peak tourist demand is influenced by natural conditions: January and February are for winter sports and July and August are for summer vacations (Planina, 1997: 158). Thus, the market mechanism runs in favour of environmental attractions.

Table 5.1 (row 5) also reveals the indirect effects of ecolabels on tourism demand. It is reasonable to believe that the impact minimiz-ion message given by the ecolabel communicates an induced message: if the destination's product and organizations are environmentally responsible, the destination must also be environmentally responsible (induced message 1, row 5). Further, an environmentally responsible destination takes care of the environment and is environmentally sound (induced message 2). Since many potential customers are not sufficiently well informed to distinguish between both aspects, ecolabels in tourism may have a similar market effect as eco-quality labels. Transmission of the wrong messages is also caused by the flood of (not necessarily authorized) environmental logos, the complexity and diversity of criteria and the lack of information on ecolabelling.

There are many signs and labels meeting the standards for eco and eco quality labels. Examples are the German Blue Angel, the European ecolabel and the Blue Flag for beaches and marinas. Unfortunately, the Blue Angel logo, known by 80% of the German population (Hopfenbeck, 1993: 191), or the EU's environmental logo, have not yet been awarded to tourism products So far, the Blue Angel has developed criteria for 76 different product groups and one service (RAL, 1998b). Licensees are transport services, for example environmental tickets for using short-distance public transport instead of private motor vehicles. Part of the logo is the explanation 'because by bus and train' (RAL, 1998a: 64). The transport balance developed by tour operator Hotelplan (see Mezzasalma, 1994) that calculates the energy consumption for tourist packages by car, bus, rail and plane could form the base for awarding another such label for environmentally friendly package tours 'because of lower transport energy consumption'. The European ecolabelling under the Council Regulation on the Community Ecolabel Award Scheme (EEC, 1992), based on life cycle assessments of environmental impacts, refers to 'products' which are interpreted as being equal to 'goods'. For that reason, European ecolabelling of tourism products being equal to services is impossible (see Mihalič, 1998: 35). The Blue Flag for beaches (UNEP, 1996), which is a combined environmental label (indicates environmental efforts and the quality of bathing water), was awarded to 1821 beaches in 22 European countries in 1999 (FEEE, 2000).

Quasi ecolabelling

While there are (too) many environmental labels and logos in the travel industry, there is a need for a more systematic approach in order to offer clear information to the customer and to enable a distinction between objective and 'quasi' ecolabelling. Quasi ecological labelling refers to those forms of environmental labelling that cannot be strictly called ecolabels or environmental quality labels because the criteria or proceedings for ecolabelling are not fulfilled. If independent, neutral organizations and bodies are involved, the environmental management gains considerable credibility (Mihalič, 1997: 280).

Confidence in the objectivity of an ecolabel is a precondition for market functioning. Since there are no objective criteria, it is very difficult for visitors to judge which tourism products are really less damaging to the environment and which destinations truly pay attention to environmental quality. Many eco-logos are awarded only to the stakeholders within a local community, region or only to the awarding association's members. Very often the accreditation body is a tourist association or somebody from the tourism business, which raises the question of credibility. Such eco-logos that are not based on pre-determined expert criteria, where criteria fulfilment is not necessarily controlled and the awarding body is perhaps one-sided, fall into the category of quasi ecolabelling.

Another example of quasi ecolabelling is the descriptive information contained in the brochures of tour operators. They mark their products 'eco' on the basis of the provision of information on the visual pollution of beaches, on visual pollution of the landscape and on the negative impacts on the local culture. The objectivity of such information is questionable since it is shaped by the seller, the tour packager, without any systematic consideration of environmental criteria, procedures or expert involvement.

A further example of quasi labelling found in the tourism market involves eco-denominations for tourism, such as green, ecological, natural, romantic, alternative, human or soft tourism. For example, 'green destination' is normally used to label an environmentally attractive destination (e.g. an environmentally unspoiled destination) and is rarely used for environmentally managed destinations. 'Green tourism' can refer to either of those meanings, while the term 'ecotourism' is most often reserved for both, at the same time meaning 'responsible travel to natural areas' (Western, 1993: 8). Nevertheless, for objective ecolabelling the difference between a self-appointed and an externally awarded eco logo is crucial. Tourist companies often use the above-listed denominations on their own initiative and without any outside validation or control.

Conclusion

Ecological labelling in tourism helps to differentiate tourist offers according to their environmental attractiveness (quality) and the intensity of their (negative) environmental impacts. From the consumers' point of view, environmentally unspoiled destinations are more attractive.

Ecolabels in tourism, similar to ecolabels for industrial products, also influence the competitiveness of the holder in the tourism market. But they are not nearly as important as the information on environmental quality of the destination. This chapter shows that reduction of environmental impacts is an important instrument helping to preserve the environmental quality of a destination, but it is not by itself sufficient. It is often presumed that visitors are environmentally responsible and that they prefer tourist products with lower environmental impacts. Research has shown that, firstly, there is a gap between declarative environmental intentions and actual environmental behaviour and that, secondly, tourists choose their destination according to environmental quality, e.g. according to the quality of bathing water, air, peace and climate and not according to efforts to minimize environmental impacts alone.

Various kinds of ecolabelling can be found in the tourism market. If we ignore the confusion caused by quasi ecolabelling which does not meet all the criteria of independence, transparency and objectivity, 'tourism labels' often combine the criteria of ecolabels and eco-quality labels. Nevertheless, since environmental quality of the destination is a prevailing factor in the selection of a destination, it is reasonable to expect that the number of environmental quality labels (or combined labels) will increase in the near future in order to increase tourist demand and deliver information on environmental quality to potential customers.

References

EEC Council Regulation (1992) No 880/92 of 23 March 1992 on a Community ecolabel award scheme. *Official Journal of the European Communities*, 11 April, 7.

FEEE (Foundation for Environmental Education in Europe) (2000) *The Campaign Today*. URL: http://www.blueflag.org/history/history.htm (22 August 2000).

Frey, B.S. (1985) *Umweltoekonomie*. V&R, Goettingen, Germany.

Hamele H. (1996) *The Book of Environmental Seals of Ecolabels. Environmental Awards in Tourism. An International Overview of Current Development*, 2nd edn. Pera Druck, Lochham/Munich.

Hamele H. (1998) Top Team NaTour – Entwicklung eines Qualitaetszeichens fuer 'Kinder- und Jugendreisen im Sinne einer nachhaltigen Entwicklung' im Kontext der aktuellen Entwicklungen. In: Luebbert, C., Feige M. and Moeller A. (eds) *Fachtagung 'Umweltkennzeichnungen im Tourismus' am 29. Oktober 1998 an der Ludwig-Maximilians-Universitaet Muenchen (LMU)*. Deutsches Wirtschaftswissenschaftliches Institut fuer Fremdenverkehr e.V. (DWIF) an der Universität Muenchen, Munich, pp. 59–61.

Hopfenbeck, W. (1993) *The Green Management Revolution*. Prentice Hall, New York.

Hopfenbeck, W. and Zimmer, P. (1993) *Umweltorientiertes Tourismusmanagement. Strategien, Checklisten, Fallstudien*. Moderne Industrie, Landsberg/Lech, Germany.

Inskeep, E. (1991) *Tourism Planning: an Integrated and Sustainable Development Approach*. Van Nostrand Reinhold, New York.

Krippendoprf, J. (1986) *Alpsegen Alptraum. Fuer eine Tourismus-Entwicklung im Einklang mit Mensch un Natur*. Kuemmerly & Frey, Bern.

Lübbert, C. (1998) Umweltkennzeichnungen fuer touristische Angebote: Einstellungen deutscher Urlauber – Ergebnisse einer Pilotstudie. In: Lübbert, C., Feige M. and Moeller A. (eds) *Fachtagung 'Umweltkennzeichnungen im Tourismus' am 29. Oktober 1998 an der Ludwig-Maximilians-Universitaet Muenchen (LMU)*. Deutsches Wirtschaftswissenschaftliches Institut fuer Fremdenverkehr e.V. (DWIF) an der Universitaet Muenchen, Munich, pp. 22–31.

Mathieson, A. and Wall, G. (1992) *Tourism: Economic, Physical and Social Impacts*. Longman, Harlow, UK.

Mezzasalma, R. (1994) *Oeko Management fuer Reiseveranstalter*. Gerber AG, Schwarzenburg, Germany.

Mieczkowski, Z. (1995) *Environmental Issues of Tourism and Recreation*. University Press of America, Lanham, Maryland.

Mihalič, T. (1997) Umweltorientiertes Tourismusmanagement durch die objektive Oeko-Kennzeichnung (Das Verfahren fuer die objektive Oeko-Kennzeichnung). *Tourism and Hospitality Management* 3, 275-286.

Mihalič, T. (1998) Ecological labelling in tourism. *UK CEED Bulletin. Special Focus: Environmental Valuation* Spring, 33–35.

Mihalič, T. and Kaspar, C. (1996) *Umweltoekonomie im Tourismus*. Paul Haupt, Bern.

Mueller H. and Fluegel M. (1999) *Tourismus und Oekologie*. Forschungsinstitut fuer Freizeit und Tourismus (FIF) an der Universitaet Bern, Bern.

Mueller, H.R. (1989) Ecology management. In: Witt, S.F. and Moutinho, L. (eds) *Tourism Marketing and Management Handbook*. Prentice Hall, London, pp. 99–103.

Mueller, H.R. (1992) Ecological product declaration rather than 'green' symbols schemes. *Revue de Tourisme* 3, 7–10.

Opashowski, H.W. (1991) *Oekologie von Freizeit und Tourismus.* Leske and Budrich, Opladen, Germany.

Planina, J. (1997) *Ekonomika turizma.* Ekonomska fakulteta, Ljubljana, Slovenia.

RAL Deutsches Institut fuer Guetesicherung und Kennzeichnung (1998a) *Environmental Label German »Blue Angel. Product Requirements*, 6th edn. Umweltbundesamt, Berlin.

RAL Deutsches Institut fuer Guetesicherung und Kennzeichnung (1998b) *Information Sheet on the German Environmental Label Scheme »Blue Angel«. Current Facts and Figures, Status: April 1998.* Umweltbundesamt, Berlin.

Rue, L.W. and Byars, L.L. (1986) *Management: Theory and Application*, 4th edn. Irwin, Homewood, Alabama.

Tschurtschenthaler, P. (1986) *Das Landschaftsproblem im Fremdenverkehr dargestellt anhand der Situation des Alpenraums.* Paul Haupt, Bern.

UNEP (United Nations Environmental Programme), WTO (World Tourism Organisation), FEEE (Foundation for Environmental Education in Europe) (1996) *Awards for Improving the Coastal Environment: the Example of the Blue Flag.* WTO, Madrid.

Viegas, A. (1998) *Oekomanagement im Tourismus.* R. Oldenburg Verlag, Munich.

Western, D. (1993) Defining ecotourism. In: Lindberg, K. and Hawkins, D.E. (eds) *Ecotourism: a Guide for Planners and Managers*, vol. 1. The Ecotourism Society, North Bennington, Vermont.

World Bank (1975) *Environment and Development.* World Bank, Washington, DC.

WTO (World Tourism Organisation) (1985) *Tourist Code.* WTO, Madrid.

WTO (World Tourism Organisation) (2000) *Global Code of Ethics for Tourism.* URL: http://www.world-tourism.org/pressrel/CODEOFE.html (viewed 23 February, 2000).

Chapter 6

Tourism Ecolabels Market Research in Germany

CLAUDIA LÜBBERT

Introduction

Ecolabels in tourism focus primarily on the producer. Consumer attitudes and requirements were mainly neglected in the past. In order to avoid following this perspective, the basic hypothesis for this research is that there is an absolute necessity to take consumer attitudes and requirements into account in order to develop a possible concept for an ecolabel in tourism. Unless this label-concept takes into consideration the consumers' demands, a risk prevails that the label will not be recognized and accepted by the tourists. Consequently it would fail as an additional advantage in the sales process.

The German situation is characterized by the existence of a variety of different quality and environmental seals for tourism products as well as destinations (according to Wittmann (1982) and Bieger (1996) the term 'product' is used here for describing goods and services). As German ecolabels in tourism have so far not been very successful, the following question was raised: would a uniform concept applied to the whole of the German tourism industry have been more successful if the view of the consumer was taken into account? Additional elements and characteristics of the label could have been included which would have been neglected by considering only the producers' point of view, thus developing an ecolabel that is accepted by the consumer.

For some time now the German government has supported efforts to introduce a nation-wide ecolabel within the tourism industry. However, one of the most prominent labels, the 'green suitcase', has not been accepted by the tourism industry. Similarly, expanding the possibilities of the 'Blue Angel', which has so far mainly been used for goods, could not be realized up to now. Only the European 'Blue Flag' offers a possibility to mark specific products all over Germany with the same label (i.e. a label for beaches, marinas, gliding fields).

To address the lack of consumer-oriented research in the case of ecolabels in tourism, the author conducted an empirical study as part of a doctoral thesis at the University of Munich (see Lübbert, 1999).

Methodology

The research aims to determine the tourists' requirements for the further development of tourism-related ecolabels. The study is based on an analysis of characteristics of ecolabels in tourism, their functions, possibilities and limits. One result of this research is the analysis of certain 'label-dimensions' which characterize each label. This concluded that a tourism-related ecolabel should include the following: the label-system, the award criteria, field of application (product and spatial area) and label-communication (see Lübbert, 1999).

These label-dimensions are the framework for the following empirical research. To obtain a first impression of these labels' impacts on the consumer, an analysis was undertaken of how widely known the existing product seals of quality are within Germany. In order to obtain information about the tourists' requirements the basic attitudes towards ecolabels and information needs were investigated. Furthermore the study was focused on the interaction between environmental and quality aspects of holidays in general. For a summary of the study see Fig. 6.1.

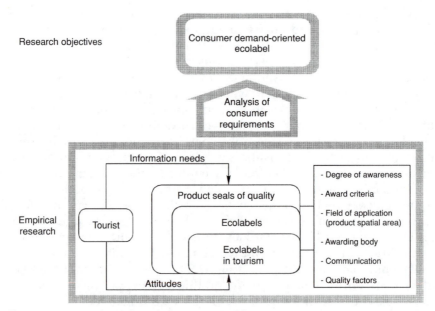

Fig. 6.1.   Research goals and objectives (Lübbert, 1999: 149).

The main research topic was broken down into the following eight hypotheses about consumer attitudes:

1. Product seals of quality are an integral part of consumer decision making (point of reference).
2. Tourism-related seals of quality are significantly less known than product or ecolabels in general.
3. Tourism-related ecolabels are regarded as useful by German tourists.
4. Ecolabels for tourism products should give information about environmental management systems (EMS), measurements for environmental protection and the current status of the environment in the destination.
5. A uniform ecolabel in tourism as opposed to a variety of different solutions will be preferred by German tourists.
6. Award and control of the ecolabel should be based with an independent organization.
7. There is a need for information about the background of an ecolabel in tourism.
8. The ecological quality of the destination's environment is strongly related to the quality of the holiday in general.

Due to a lack of available theories and detailed empirical studies on this subject the initial research focused on the exploration of the topic. Based on the resulting findings, more detailed studies can then follow. A set of three methods was utilized in order to combine qualitative with quantitative research methods. This allowed the analysis of personal wishes, motives and expectations of the consumers. Moreover, the representative validation of several parts of these results could be made.

During the first, explorative phase, focus groups – directed by a moderator and structured by a discussion guideline – were conducted in order to establish the base for subsequent investigations. During the second phase a representative survey was carried out. This ensured that results obtained by explorative methods were validated using quantitative research methods. Furthermore, this initiated a more differentiated analysis of certain questions and attitudes of the target groups. During the third phase, results obtained from the two preceding surveys were further investigated and evaluated using semi-structured interviews (for the design of the empirical research see Fig. 6.2).

Results

The following presentation of empirical results will focus on the representative survey supplemented by additional qualitative data. The

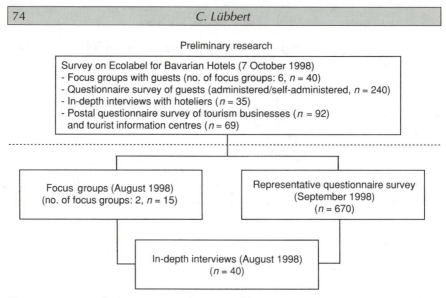

Preliminary research

Survey on Ecolabel for Bavarian Hotels (7 October 1998)
- Focus groups with guests (no. of focus groups: 6, $n = 40$)
- Questionnaire survey of guests (administered/self-administered, $n = 240$)
- In-depth interviews with hoteliers ($n = 35$)
- Postal questionnaire survey of tourism businesses ($n = 92$)
  and tourist information centres ($n = 69$)

Focus groups (August 1998)
(no. of focus groups: 2, $n = 15$)

Representative questionnaire survey
(September 1998)
($n = 670$)

In-depth interviews (August 1998)
($n = 40$)

Fig. 6.2. Research design (triangulation) (Lübbert, 1999: 166).

representative results contain answers by German tourists (German domestic tourists and German tourists abroad; $n = 670$). In order to be able to account for possible differences between these two different target groups, each group has been identified (for detailed results regarding the German domestic tourist segment, see Lübbert, 1998).

The importance of environmental factors in the holiday decision-making process

The first question concerns the general importance given to environmental aspects by German tourists when making the decision on which holiday destination to choose. In the representative survey, the interviewees were asked to name the three aspects which were most important for their holiday choice (see Fig. 6.3). For German tourists holidaying in Germany the most important aspects are 'landscape/scenery' (67.9%), 'value for money' (47.6%) and 'hospitality' (33.6%). For German tourists holidaying abroad it is important to obtain 'value for money' (60.2%) and 'swimming facilities' (56.9%). 'Landscape/scenery' follows in third place with 51.0%. For German tourists holidaying in Germany and abroad, 21.1% and 13.8%, respectively, state that an intact nature is one of the three most important aspects for their decision. The term 'intact nature' in Germany is a popular description for nature which gives the impression of being healthy and

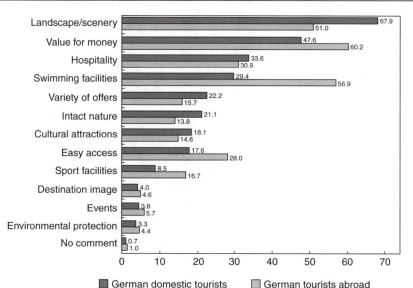

German domestic tourists   German tourists abroad

Fig. 6.3. Question: How important are the following factors when deciding which destination to visit (prompted answers as a percentage) (representative questionnaire survey, *n* = 670) (Lübbert, 1999: 173).

non-disturbed. Based on its popular use, however, the definitions of what exactly constitutes intact nature vary. In the preliminary research (see Fig. 6.2) the Bavarian hotel guests were asked during the focus group discussions to provide the researcher with their interpretations of this term. Intact nature for the interviewees meant a landscape that includes a variety of flora and fauna coupled with a lake or small river. A common image of the Garden of Eden.

'Environmental protection' is the least-mentioned aspect (German domestic tourists 3.3%, German tourists abroad 4.4%). These results were confirmed during the focus group discussions: environmental protection lags far behind in the individual ranking of aspects that determine a successful holiday experience. Only aspects such as 'clean water', 'clean beaches', 'landscape', 'intact nature' or 'environment' were mentioned by participants in the focus groups.

To summarize these results concerning the importance of environmental aspects within the holiday decision-making process, it has to be pointed out that environmental protection plays a relatively minor role for German tourists. However, the importance of environmental factors increases rapidly when looking at aspects which the tourist directly feels (i.e. consumption of the environment), like water, air and nature (especially landscape).

Attitudes and knowledge of product seals

In the representative questionnaire survey general attitudes towards product seals of quality were the main focus. A differentiation between seals of quality for tourism products as opposed to other goods was not undertaken. The survey consisted of a list of different statements regarding seals of quality in general. The interviewee was asked to agree or disagree with these statements. In the following some of the results are presented.

For most of the German tourists, product seals of quality provide useful information when choosing a product (information function) as it enables them to compare similar products (comparison function). Product seals of quality were thought to guarantee a certain quality by 43.5% of German tourists. In the case of dissatisfaction or product failure the manufacturer or service provider could be taken to court (guarantee function). When looking at buying decision making, both the information and comparison function mean that the label gives information about certain characteristics of the products. Product seals of quality are used as orientation guidelines based on test criteria for the label award. In addition, they indicate products which offer value for money as well as branded products (see Fig. 6.4). The interpretation of these results must take into consideration that about half of the German tourists state that they are not specifically concerned about product seals of quality.

Fig. 6.4. Question: Do you agree/disagree with the following statements? (prompted answers as a percentage) (representative questionnaire survey, *n* = 670) (Lübbert, 1999: 177).

These results are confirmed by the qualitative surveys. Here, in addition to the afore-mentioned findings, product seals of quality were regarded as a sign for the quality of the product and factors which concern personal security especially health. Out of 40 interviewees, 37 stated that product seals of quality were beneficial 'overall'.

Another important aspect is credibility. The in-depth interviews showed that trust in a certain product seal of quality is caused by individually positive experiences with this label (22 interviewees). Knowledge about label details (e.g. from specialist journals) is also important for the formation of this opinion (nine interviewees). The media plays an important role in creating positive or negative attitudes (six interviewees, 14 interviewees respectively).

In general, the German tourist develops a negative or suspicious attitude towards product seals of quality when the information offered about the seal is not regarded as being sufficient (see Fig. 6.5). Other negative attitudes derive from the great variety of product seals used, which has caused confusion among consumers ('lost overview'). Also important is that products which are awarded with a seal of quality are often regarded as being more expensive than comparable non-awarded

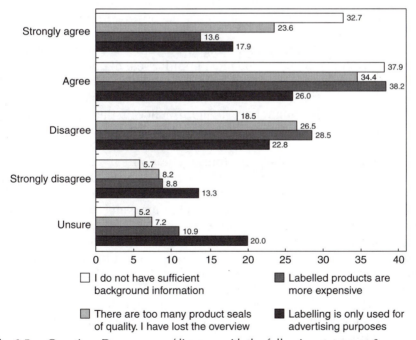

Fig. 6.5. Question: Do you agree/disagree with the following statements? (prompted answers in percentage) (representative questionnaire survey, *n* = 670) (Lübbert, 1999: 179).

products. However, only very few tourists think that product seals of quality are purely being used as promotion tools.

Because of the importance of the consumers' assumption that quality awarded products are more expensive than other products this point was analysed in detail. Of the surveyed German tourists, 59.4% think that labelled products are reasonably priced. About half of the interviewees are ready to pay more for a labelled product (45.4%). The explorative parts of the survey show that tourists fear a price increase for tourism products due to being awarded a seal of quality. This could create a negative attitude when establishing an ecolabel for tourism.

The next question concerned the German tourists' knowledge of existing product seals of quality, especially the range of labels for tourism products. If labels are well known, this represents one indicator for the success of a product seal of quality. The representative survey used a list containing 15 different product seals of quality that are in existence in Germany. This included examples of different kinds of products as well as destinations and tourism institutions.

The results show that seals of quality for goods are significantly better known than seals of quality for tourism products. The most popular seals among German tourists are TÜV (German Technical Supervisory Authority) which indicates safety and security aspects of a product (73.4%) and Stiftung Warentest, a nation-wide seal of quality used for comparing groups of goods according to varying criteria whereby the results are published (68.3%). The third well-known seal of quality is the German Blue Angel, a symbol for environmentally friendly products (62.9%). The most popular seal of quality for tourism products is a label for rural tourism (DLG) (35.8%). However, the DLG sign is also used for several other products, for example to specify the quality of meat. This might have great influence on the high recognition of this seal of quality. Other seals of quality for tourism products are very little known.

Furthermore, ecolabels in tourism are much less well known than the Blue Angel. The 'Squirrel' which is provided for highway restaurants and leisure parks from the ADAC (German Automobile Club) is the most widely known ecolabel in tourism (19.9%). The European Blue Flag is well-known only among 3.6% of the interviewees. The Bavarian ecolabel for hotels, an example of a regional label, is known only by 3.1% of the German tourists. For the interpretation of these specific results, it has to be taken into account that of the total German tourists only 16.1% have holidayed in Bavaria in 1997 (as main holidays; see FUR, 1998). For more details about the interaction between the knowledge of product seals of quality and their usage see Lübbert (1999).

Additionally it is important to consider the different lengths of time since the introduction of a specific product seal of quality into the market and the different target groups. Furthermore, it is evident that differences in label-communication cause different levels of knowledge.

Attitudes towards ecolabels in tourism

The basic attitude towards a seal of quality for tourism products is positive (in the questionnaire the term 'seal of approval' was used). Of the German tourists holidaying in Germany and abroad, 71% and 59.5%, respectively, agree with the statement that an ecolabel for tourism products is 'extremely useful' (prompted answers). However, the agreement about its specific use while making personal holiday decisions is lower: 52.8% of the German tourists holidaying in Germany and 46.0% of the German tourists abroad state that they would take such a label into account while making holiday decisions.

To achieve more specific results, the use of qualitative methods is necessary. During the in-depth interviews, the importance of labelling the quality of the environment (current environmental condition) and nature, traffic and environmental protection was confirmed by 15 interviewees (out of a total of 40). Following this open question the interviewees were asked to evaluate the importance of labelling specific aspects of their holidays (e.g. intact nature, cleanliness). Interviewees also had the opportunity to specify if they regarded certain aspects as being standard requirements and therefore not necessarily needing a seal of quality (see Fig. 6.6). The responses show that a seal of quality

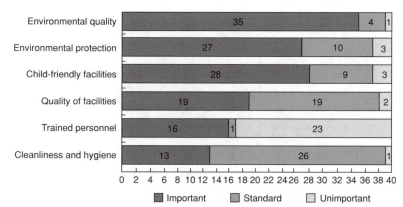

Fig. 6.6. Question: Do you believe it is important/unimportant to award the following elements of a holiday in Germany with a seal of quality? Please state if you believe that one or more elements are standard parts of the tourism products and therefore do not need to be labelled (in-depth interviews, prompted answers; no. of respondents = 40) (Lübbert, 1999: 188).

for intact nature has the highest priority for the interviewed German tourists (35 interviewees). Environmental protection takes third place (28 interviewees) after a seal of quality for child-friendly facilities (29 interviewees). An important finding is that ten interviewees regarded the aspect of environmental protection as standard, not needing an award of quality. Most of the interviewees in the in-depth interviews regard an enterprise or a holiday offer awarded with an ecolabel as helping to minimize pressures on the environment (28 interviewees).

Three main groups of factors regarding the importance of environmental aspects could be detected. Firstly, the factors with highest priority are those that concern the tourists personally, like clean air and water. The second group includes different measures of environmental protection (waste separation, environmentally friendly transport, etc.). One of the least important factors is the environmental management system. The third group concerns information given about the environment (see Fig. 6.7).

In order to translate the survey results into a viable ecolabel for tourism products it is necessary to analyse the reasons for the rather low priority given to environmental management and information provided. This was uncovered using in-depth interviews. The result is that the individual tourist does not feel responsible for the environment in a holiday destination and consequently is not interested in management systems or information (18 interviewees). Clean lakes, for example, are components of the holiday itself (basic conditions). Therefore, tourists are only interested in the current condition of the environment, they are not interested in the process of achieving this. Also, clean lakes and the like are reasons for choosing to spend a

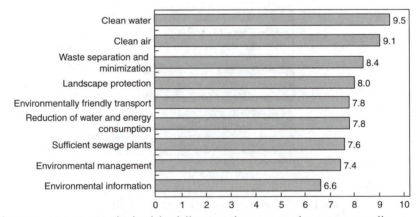

Fig. 6.7. Question: Which of the following elements are for you personally important/unimportant when holidaying in Germany? Please rank them in order of importance: 1 = not important at all to 10 = very important (in-depth interviews, prompted answers; no. of respondents = 40) (Lübbert, 1999: 191).

holiday in a specific destination and are therefore an important element in achieving a quality holiday (eight interviewees). These are elements which the tourist in general is able to comprehend, while understanding the purpose and functioning of management systems might be more difficult (seven interviewees).

Finally the interviewees were asked to contemplate possible criteria for an ecolabel in tourism. The results seem to confirm the importance of environmental aspects in general (see Fig. 6.8). However, it has to be acknowledged that the results might have possibly been influenced by the methodology chosen. The interviewees were already familiar with the topic, although in another context.

Additional results are presented, although in a more summarized form, in the following text and Fig. 6.9 (for detailed requirements of German tourists see Lübbert, 1999: 172 ff.). During the in-depth interviews, the interviewees were asked to evaluate the importance of awarding different tourism products with seals of quality. The labels are most strongly recommended for destinations and holiday parks (8.4 and 8.2 out of 10 possible points). The least important seal of quality from the tourists' point of view is an ecolabel for travel agencies (6.3 out of 10 possible points) (see Fig. 6.9). The different evaluations seem to confirm the results regarding the importance of specific environmental aspects of the holiday.

During focus group discussions and in-depth interviews it was shown that the German tourist prefers an overall ecolabel for tourism products as opposed to several single seals. Furthermore, the interviewees stated that the advantages of a nation-wide label as opposed to

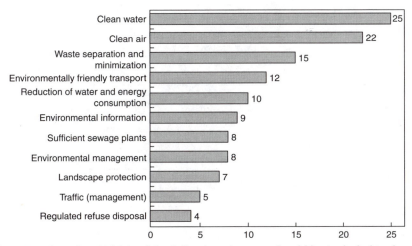

Fig. 6.8. Question: Which of the following elements should be included in the award criteria for an ecolabel in tourism? (in-depth interviews, prompted answers; no. of respondents = 40) (Lübbert, 1999: 193).

a variety of different labels for regions or products are greater than the disadvantages. One big advantage for the tourist would be the clarity of the ecolabel and comparability of the products.

Another important factor is the credibility of an ecolabel which is underlined by its control and award criteria through an economically and politically independent institution. An award given out by an internal institution (companies themselves or tourism organizations) is regarded as being less positive than, for example, a well-known external institution (e.g. Stiftung Warentest) or a nature protection organization. Moreover, there seems to be a correlation between the confidence in a certain award institution and the credibility of the ecolabel. Also, the positive personal experience with the seal is very important.

A further result of the survey is the importance of background information for the ecolabel. The tourist is interested in the institution for award and control, the criteria for award and the methods of validation. But it should also be considered that there is a different level of interest in environmental information regarding the tourism product (e.g. air, lakes, etc., and management systems). Therefore, at this point a general statement about the importance of background information cannot be made. But it is clear that the existence of relevant background information has an impact on the credibility of the ecolabel and therefore should be given attention.

A further result of the qualitative survey is that most of the interviewees think that a relationship between environmental aspects and the quality of their holiday prevails. This is because the environment is

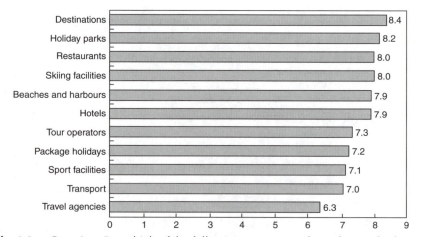

Fig. 6.9. Question: For which of the following tourism products do you think it is important/unimportant that they are awarded with an ecolabel? Please rank them in order of importance: 1 = not important at all to 10 = very important (in-depth interviews, prompted answers; no. of respondents = 40) (Lübbert, 1999: 194).

seen as part of the holiday and therefore part of the product on offer. Consequently, the evaluation of this part of the tourism product influences the evaluation of the holiday as a whole. The specific value of this environmental quality is determined by the form of the trip and the individual preferences and attitudes.

Conclusions

The German tourists' demands on an ecolabel in tourism can be deduced from the results of the empirical research and summarized in six important elements (see Fig. 6.10). For the German tourist the most important elements of a product seal of quality are the information function and the possibility to compare similar products. Therefore, an ecolabel in tourism should aim to function as an orientation guideline (a point of reference) within the process of comparing similar holiday offers. In order to achieve this, it is necessary to have knowledge of the criteria which the tourist uses to compare different offers. Furthermore, product seals of quality provide information on the quality of products (e.g. branded products, or approved award criteria). This requires that traditional quality aspects should be included in the label-concept. In particular, it should be assessed whether environmental aspects are a factor in assessing the quality of holidays.

The ecolabel itself and the label-communication should take into account that tourists expect a positive contribution to the protection of the environment through certain offers which fulfil specific environmental criteria. To strengthen the tourists' confidence in the label it is important that the communicated information about the ecolabel coincides with positive experiences of each individual tourist. The tourists'

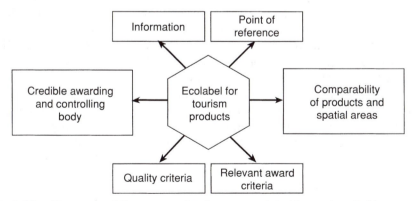

Fig. 6.10. Demands of German tourists from an ecolabel in tourism (Lübbert, 1999: 210).

confidence is influenced by the competence and independence of the institution for award and control, and the credibility of the label. During the process of information and confidence building, the media should be involved by publishing promotional articles. A well-known seal of quality increases confidence among consumers.

German tourists place importance on the award criteria which reflect the current condition of the environment in the destination as far as they are affected directly (e.g. cleanliness of air and lakes, intact nature, etc.). The feeling of quality is especially important to the tourists (e.g. waste disposal). Environmental management systems are not very important in comparison to other aspects. A better knowledge of such management systems for environmental protection could possibly modify this result.

Another important characteristic of an award criterion is its transparency and logic. The criterion should be used for all offers and producers in the same way so that the products can be compared by tourists. Another positive effect of uniform criteria is that the label is more likely to be recognized by the tourists.

To achieve the ideal prerequisites for comparability, transparency and recognition by tourists, the field of application (spatial area and product) in which the ecolabel is awarded should be maximized. Despite this, experience demonstrates it is nearly impossible to find uniform criteria for such a variety of destinations and tourism products. However, it is possible to create a framework of criteria which could be used for all products and, in addition to that, some variable criteria for each product group (Lübbert, 1999).

It seems to be very important that the institution for award and control is economically and politically independent from the entrepreneur who is awarded the label. This institution should have no vested interests in awarding a certain group of entrepreneurs or products with the ecolabel. In addition, this institution should be known as a specialist in all questions of awarding the concerned products. The credibility of the institution for award and control will strongly influence the credibility of the label itself. Moreover, the institution should already be well known in the country concerned, as an unknown institution could be regarded with suspicion.

As a final remark the question remains if it would be possible to carry out the survey in another country in order to achieve comparable results. This would be an important basis for determining if a new European or even worldwide ecolabel could be established.

Acknowledgements

This study was financially supported by the Federal Ministry for the Environment, Nature Conservation and Nuclear Safety and the Federal Environmental Agency.

References

Bieger, T. (1996) *Management von Destinationen und Tourismusorganizationen*. Oldenbourg, Munich.

FUR (Forschungsgemeinschaft Urlaub und Reisen e.V.) (1998) *Die Reiseanalyse RA 97*; Urlaub & Reisen, Kurzfassung, Hamburg.

Lübbert, C. (1998) Umweltkennzeichnungen für touristische Angebote, Einstellungen deutscher Urlauber – Ergebnisse einer Pilotstudie'. In: Lübbert, C., Feige, M. and Möller, A. (eds) *Fachtagung 'Umweltkennzeichnngen im Tourismus'* 29 October 1998, Ludwig-Maximilians-Universität München (LMU), Tagungsdokumentation, Munich, pp. 22–31.

Lübbert, C. (1999) *Qualitätsorientiertes Umweltschutzmanagement im Tourismus*. Empirische Untersuchung und Entwurf eines nachfrageorientierten Modells zur Umweltkennzeichnung touristischer Leistungen, vvf, Munich.

Wittmann, W. (1982) *Betriebswirtschaftslehre*, Ein einführendes Lehrbuch, Band I, Grundlagen, Elemente, Instrumente, Mohr, Tübingen.

Chapter 7

The Process of Developing an Ecolabel

XAVIER FONT AND JOHN TRIBE

Introduction

Despite the increase in tourism ecolabels and awards in the 1990s, it is expected that public authorities, non-profit organizations, industry associations and private companies will continue to show an interest in launching new ecolabelling programmes (UNEP, 1998). This chapter explains the process followed to develop an ecolabel, based on the experience of the authors in a 3-year project preparing the proposals for the Tourfor award. This project was funded by the European Commission, aiming to promote sustainable tourism and recreation in forests in Europe through a new ecolabel (Tribe, 1998; Tribe and Font, 2000a,b,c). The emphasis in this chapter will be on the process followed, and how the experience gained through the Tourfor award can be used to inform the development of other ecolabels in tourism, recreation, hospitality and other related industries. The process outlined here and presented in Fig. 7.1 is an adaptation of the generic new product development process (Rogers, 1996). It is divided into three distinct phases.

The first phase encompasses the positioning and planning of the ecolabel, consideration of the role the ecolabel will have, the organizations already involved in similar initiatives, the target market of potential awardees and the impact on tourism consumption. The second phase will include the development of the criteria for this ecolabel, by evaluating the key environmental impacts in the sector, taking criteria from a broader system and adapting them to the sector, identifying the key criteria for companies to meet, preparing manuals and examples for them to follow. This information should go through a process of consultation and piloting to ensure that a critical mass of the industry can meet the criteria. The final phase will involve the management and marketing of the ecolabel proposal, by budgeting the

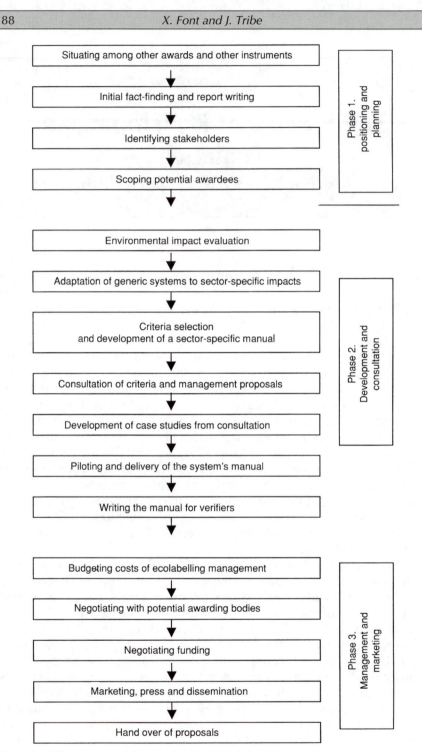

Fig. 7.1. The process of developing an ecolabel.

costs of managing the ecolabel, negotiating with potential awarding bodies likely to take over the idea and negotiating for funding. Once the proposals have been written and there is some idea of the future of the proposal, this can be marketed to potential awardees, non-profit organizations and the industry press in order to assess the degree of interest before handing over the proposals of the ecolabel to the commissioning organization.

Project Management

Perhaps the most important task of developing an ecolabel is the management of the project itself. The project will need to be managed taking into account:

1. The available finance;
2. The available resources;
3. The time period;
4. The fulfilment of the project aims;
5. The satisfying of the project partners.

It is important therefore to designate a manager with overall responsibility for delivering the project. The project manager should in turn be accountable to a steering group who are those senior partners involved in the project for both the technical and financial aspects of the project.

At the commencement of the project the project manager should ensure that there is a detailed specification of the project which establishes the project's aims, anticipated outcomes, and methods and activities for achieving the aims. A budget should be prepared for the project and a critical path analysis which identifies the timing of the component activities of the project. A dissemination strategy for the project should also be prepared. For most projects it is useful to divide the whole period into a number of working phases. The point of this is to break down activities into clear stages of activity, each with specific and measurable outcomes. The steering group should meet at the beginning of each phase (e.g. 6 months) and their agenda should include:

- review of outcomes of last period against objectives;
- planning of objectives for next period;
- review of budget;
- dissemination;
- review of whole project.

At the end of the project, the project manager is responsible for writing the final technical and financial reports of the project. The project management framework outlined above and shown in Fig. 7.2. is

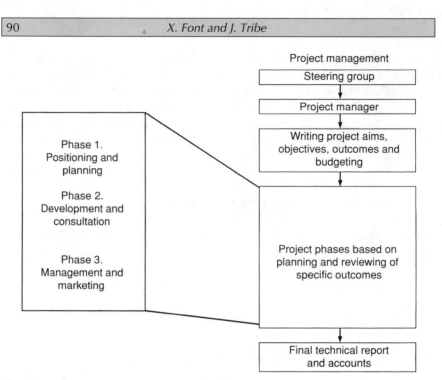

Fig. 7.2. The management of an ecolabel project.

the generic shell within which most ecolabels will be developed. This gives way to the first of the three phases, the positioning and planning of the ecolabel.

Phase 1. Positioning and Planning

The first phase will be characterized by the positioning of the ecolabel proposal and the careful planning of the ecolabel. Several tasks will be carried out. These include considering who else is doing similar work; potential overlaps and collaborations; identifying which stakeholders may want to participate or endorse the proposal; scoping the market and collecting data in a usable format; and understanding how the ecolabel may impact on the consumption of tourist products and services.

Situating among other awards and other instruments

Currently there is a wide variety of small, regional, alternative and overlapping ecolabels in tourism, without one that is recognized by the industry and tourists alike as the leading one (see Chapter 13). It has been stated elsewhere in this book that 'the future belongs to international ecolabels' (see Chapter 15), yet in the short term new ecolabels are being proposed to solve problems specific to parts of the tourism industry. The development of international ecolabels will have to go through a process of merging several ecolabels to create an overall umbrella generic enough for the whole tourism industry with overarching criteria for the management of the broader ecolabel. Yet this international tourism ecolabel will need criteria specific to the different sectors of the tourism industry, and therefore the input of specialist teams.

One of the initial tasks when developing an ecolabel should be to understand the role it is supposed to play. In order to do so the developers should situate it among other awards already in place or being developed, and against other instruments to promote good environmental practice (Font and Tribe, 2001; Tribe *et al.*, 2000). Organizations developing tourism ecolabels ought to ensure they understand how their new ecolabel can relate to others, how it can complement them, and the possibilities for cooperation with them. Unless this is understood and planned from the beginning, the ecolabel will always be in competition and possibly fail to succeed.

Besides situating the new ecolabels against others, the team should also assess the alternative instruments available to promote environmental performance within the specific sector in tourism in which they are going to operate. Table 7.1 presents some of the categories of environmental instruments available, and the relative positioning of awards and ecolabels. Usually ecolabels will cover environmental performance issues that are not already covered by 'harder' tools such as regulations and economic approaches, but ecolabels can be used as marketing and recognition tools for other 'soft' approaches.

Table 7.1. Categories of environmental instruments (Tribe *et al.*, 2000).

Regulations	Economic approaches	Soft tools
Laws and regulation	Taxes, subsidies and grants	Community programmes national and local networks
Special status designation	Tradable rights and permits	Tourism ecolabelling
	Deposit-refund schemes	Environmental management systems
	Product and service charges	Certification/award schemes
		Guidelines, treaties and agreements
		Citizenship and education

Initial fact-finding and report writing

The ecolabelling team should instigate initial information gathering and literature searching processes in order to find out the state-of-the-art in the sector targeted, including the markets, consumer behaviour, products, suppliers and current issues affecting the sector. This will be particularly important if the team developing the ecolabel is multidisciplinary – and in general it will be – including at least environmental management and tourism experts. If several people in different offices (or even countries) are involved, it may be necessary to turn the initial fact-finding into internal reports, stating conclusions and recommendations for the development of the ecolabel (Font, 1997; Hulmi, 1999; Castro-Rego, 1999).

Identifying stakeholders

Identifying key stakeholders at this stage will be crucial. Stakeholders already involved in the subject will have on the ground knowledge of good practice, and they can provide support to the initiative through time and expertise, and through public endorsement of the ecolabel. A list of stakeholders should be compiled and information sent to them regarding the development of the ecolabel, inviting them for their initial comments and contributions, and suggestions for other contacts. The responses of this initial contact will divide the list of stakeholders into those that want to be involved and those that will be kept informed of progress.

Scoping potential awardees

From the initial fact-finding process it will be necessary to focus on the target market for this ecolabel. The type of company the ecolabel is aiming to target will determine the difficulty of the scoping task. There are usually directories of tourism companies available, although these may not have the information necessary. If the award is trying to improve the environmental performance of the management of golf courses or natural parks, for example, it is quite likely that the tourist boards will have directories for them, or at least, addresses. The same can be said for other listed tourism companies such as hotels. It gets harder when targeting tour operators and travel agencies, since in some countries directories are kept but in others not, and also in others they are both in the same list. The smaller the size of the company, the harder it is to find a directory that includes it. Also it gets much harder when the award is trying to encourage the links between two industries (farming and tourism; management of parks and recreation; hunting and tourism; or in the case of Tourfor, tourism and forest management). The listings available may not be representative of the sector, and may include only those organizations that are proactive towards it.

The scoping exercise is unlikely to give a comprehensive list of the target market population, and instead the ecolabel organizer may opt for a sample to test the market and an indication of the market size (Aaker *et al.*, 1995). The team might deploy a mixture of secondary sources plus judgemental and snowball sampling when collecting the market sample data, with the difficulty of having to justify the method used and the possibility to extrapolate the findings to the overall population.

Data regarding the potential awardees should be saved in a database for ease of use, as it will become the basis for the consultation and future targeting of potential awardees. This database should include information such as company name, address, contact name, as well as some parameters to help in the classification of companies, depending on the type of company targeted and the data available. Examples could be number of employees, hectares of land, annual turnover, number of beds, camping plots or members, list of facilities and amenities. The list needs to be assessed on a case-by-case basis. Depending on the country and the size of the database, it may be necessary to register it to comply with national data protection legislation.

Identifying expected impact on tourist behaviour

One last task of the initial planning phase is to identify how the ecolabel expects to impact on the tourist's behaviour. Few ecolabels carry out this task, mainly for two reasons. First, for many awards, the appeal of receiving the award is peer recognition, not increased consumer awareness or purchases. This is indeed the case in many awards given to zero-price tourism service providers, where the increased awareness of the tourist site may only increase the environmental pressure, but not bring any added income. Second, the ecolabel organizer may not be able to reach the tourist markets, let alone influence them, since this is a costly exercise. The consequence is that many tourism ecolabels are developed with little understanding of how they will actually impact on tourist behaviour. There are some exceptions (see Chapters 4, 5 and 6).

Phase 2. Development and Consultation

The initial framework-setting phase will give way to the development of the ecolabel, including the evaluation of environmental impacts, the outlining of the criteria for the ecolabel on the basis of broader and established systems, and the development of support systems for applicants such as a manual of implementation. Consultation about the criteria will be necessary for potential sites and stakeholders, and the manual will be piloted. A manual for verifiers should be written to ensure consistency and fairness in the process.

Environmental impact evaluation

First, an initial identification of key environmental impacts can be carried out through reviewing the literature (i.e. Forestry Commission, 1990; Liddle, 1997; Hammitt and Cole, 1998). Listings of potential impacts will be developed, and whenever possible, linked to specific activities or practices. Second, it is necessary to understand the current environmental performance of the target market. This can be done by surveying the scoping list in the previously created database, subsequently approaching a selection of best practice organizations, and creating a forum for the presentation of cases (Tourfor, 1999). This will be a useful way to gather data regarding what the industry considers they should be doing and the issues they currently tackle, ensuring the relevance of the ecolabel and early commitment of key players.

Expert panels can be used to compare the literature with the industry performance. The thoroughness of the process will depend on the resources available, but the expected output at this stage is to develop a working list of priorities for the ecolabel's criteria (Tourfor, 1998; WWF, 2000).

Adaptation of generic systems to sector-specific impacts

Efforts should be placed again at this point to relate the previous findings to the overall progress in environmental management in other sectors. There are already widely researched and tested guidelines for the assessment of environmental impacts, carrying out environmental reviews and evaluating environmental effects, with published guidance notes (for example, LGMB, 1995a, 1996a; TQM, 1996). There are also environmental management systems applied internationally such as ISO 14001 and EMAS, with general manuals for their implementation (BSI, 1996) as well as guidelines for writing the elements of an environmental management system (LGMB 1995b,c; 1996b,c).

These systems are broad enough to embrace tourism impacts, and though not specific to tourism or hospitality, there are good tried and tested reasons for the industry to move towards them. The organizers of a new ecolabel will benefit from adapting these generic systems to the specific impacts prioritized in the previous step and the industry's ability to implement the systems suggested here. The generic systems adapted here will also provide a basic framework for the management of the ecolabel.

Criteria selection and development of a sector-specific manual

The working list of prioritized environmental impacts in the sector will be the baseline from which to select the criteria to apply for the ecolabel. Each ecolabel will use different criteria according to its purpose (UNEP, 1998). Those with broad, loose criteria will tend to attract companies that want to be awarded for their current achievements, and there may be considerable differences between the companies awarded. Broad criteria will be a good idea when the ecolabel is trying to raise awareness of best practice within the industry, but it will have little significance to the potential tourist (Font and Tribe, 2001). Consumers will be more likely to be receptive to ecolabels with clear criteria that standardize the awardees' provision of services, since this way they will know what to expect.

Companies wanting to apply for the ecolabel will benefit from criteria that are clearly stated, explaining what it is meant by each of them, what the tourism company has to do to achieve those criteria, and what the evidence in terms of outcomes will be once each criterion has been met. Table 7.2 gives an example of writing an environmental policy as one ecolabelling criterion, with an explanation to potential awardees of the requirements that need to be met. Yet for most ecolabels it will be useful to go beyond this by writing a manual for potential awardees that shows how to meet the criteria (Tribe *et al.*, 2000). The length and depth of this manual will depend on the industry requirements and the availability of alternative sources of information.

Consultation of criteria and management proposals

Consultation will be crucial in order to ensure the relevance of the proposals to the industry's needs and abilities. This will take place in two stages. First, the criteria previously selected need to be tested (Font *et al.*, 2001b). This will involve finding out the current industry's ability to understand what is expected of them, whether those systems are currently in practice and whether companies feel they could

Table 7.2. Environmental policy as a criterion for an environmental management system ecolabel (Tourfor, 2000).

What it is	Statement of environmental commitments for the organization and the management of the site, which will act as a guide to help the organization develop its aims and objectives for the site and should describe the principles and intentions and provide the direction for action. The policy should be seen as an integral part of the organization's overall strategy. The key aim of an environmental management system (EMS) policy is the minimizing of environmental impacts
What you have to do	1. Develop an environmental policy for the site 2. Policy development should be undertaken at the highest management level 3. Demonstrate a commitment for including stakeholder opinions 4. Demonstrate a commitment to complying with environmental legislation
The expected outcomes	The expected outcomes from writing a policy will be the commitment to environmental management demonstrated through a policy statement, integrated into the organization's culture and provides direction to the EMS The documented results will be a written policy statement framing the environmental commitments for the management of the site, although this does not have to conform to a specific length or format

implement them. The consultation will also help in adapting the criteria and simplifying the wording, and up to a certain extent deciding on the strictness of the criteria. Second, it will be necessary to consult the relevance of the ecolabel and the proposals to manage it (Font *et al.*, 2001a). This will include the industry's willingness to apply for this award, perceived benefits from it, the application method and cost, the verification methods, the period of verification. The ecolabel organizers may find ways to work collaboratively with the applicants to ensure longer-term links to improve the information available to applicants, such as training courses, leaflets and newsletters and updates on the manual of implementation, among others, to increase the perceived benefits of applying (i.e. Green Globe).

Development of case studies from consultation

Best-practice case studies found at earlier stages can now be put into the context of the elements of the environmental management system they relate to (i.e. examples of a policy, how to conduct a site review, how to write a programme of actions, methods to operationalize an environmental programme, methods to keep records of actions, examples of environmental improvements and how these were monitored, how to carry out an internal audit). This will be a time-consuming exercise since it may involve site visits to collect data and some difficulty in collecting examples, yet it is crucial to the successful introduction of new practices through the application for the ecolabel. These case studies can be inserted into the manual for applicants (Tribe *et al.*, 2000) or published as a separate volume (Font and Tribe, 2000).

Piloting and delivery of the system's manual

Piloting will be an essential element of the development of the ecolabel, to ensure potential users understand what is suggested and expected of them. The piloting of the manual can be twofold. First, the team developing the ecolabel can engage a small sample of tourism companies in testing the manual, by providing them with the material and support. Second, the team can assess the environmental performance and management of a tourism company against the proposed criteria and manual (Flynn *et al.*, 2001), to see the differences in performance and management when the manual is not available, as well as checking whether they will have the information necessary for verification without the manual's help.

Findings from the piloting process need to be evaluated, and if necessary addressed in the manual. Once the final draft of the manual has been accepted, it needs to go to print ready for the launch of the ecolabel. Desktop publishing and printing are expensive and time consuming, and if not carefully planned can delay the launch. Professional publishing can take up to 6 months, and the cost of publishing the manual will depend on the numbers, length of the manual, quality of paper, binding and colours.

Writing the manual for verifiers

The manual for verifiers will be a combination of the manuals for applicants, the criteria for verifying and the process of verification. Verifiers will need to be aware of the contents of the manual for applicants in order to understand the suggested actions to meet the requirements of the criteria. Also if applicants were not given the detail suggested earlier on in Table 7.2, this will still be needed by potential verifiers as part of the forms of assessment. The process of verification, including the method and cycle of verification should be one of the ecolabel's management criteria consulted in an earlier stage of the process, but will basically consist of looking for evidence of the site's performance against the criteria.

The process of verification can be on site, desk or a combination of both (Font and Tribe, 2001). Site visits will allow the verifier to check the current state of the tourism organization and will be useful in checking tourist attractions, hotels, parks, airlines and any other organizations whose operations take place within premises they can control. Desk reviews will allow the verifier to check the management and control of any potential environmental impacts, such as the development of environmental policies, results from environmental site reviews, environmental programmes and evidence of operationalizing those programmes, and any auditing carried out.

Phase 3. Management and Marketing

During phase 2, the key instruments and structure of the ecolabel were developed, yet it is still necessary to consider the mechanisms to get the proposal off the ground. The final stages of preparing the ecolabel will involve the practical issues in relation to budgeting the costs of running the ecolabel, negotiating funds and terms and conditions with potential awarding bodies. Marketing the ecolabel proposal will involve dissemination to the general public, interested stakeholders and potential awardees, in order to ensure that the ecolabel has the backing of the industry at the hand over of the proposals.

Budgeting costs of ecolabelling management

The costs of running an ecolabel can be summarized as office administration costs, verification costs, regional or worldwide coordination costs (if applicable), verification costs, marketing costs and PR event costs.

For the Tourfor award it is estimated that if the Foundation for Environmental Education in Europe (FEEE) was to run this award, the expected coordination cost for the first year would be £50,000, and thereafter the cost of managing the award and verification would be around £500 per application, with a minimum threshold of 50 sites. Focusing an ecolabel too narrowly may limit the potential market. For example to promote Tourfor only on forest tourism and recreation sites may make the cost–benefit analysis unfeasible. It may therefore be sensible to broaden the scope of the award to all countryside tourism and recreation sites to ensure a wider appeal of the award.

If sites are expected to pay most of the £500 it will cost for an application, the awarding body will have to provide a package of benefits. Achieving the award for sites with an operational EMS should be the culmination of the benefits. Yet applying for the award will be much more beneficial for sites if as part of the application they can gain expert advice in implementing an EMS, take part in training opportunities and develop in-house expertise.

External funding will be necessary to create the infrastructure within the awarding body and to initially establish the award within the participating countries. For Tourfor to be developed as an award, EU funding opportunities and commercial sponsorship need to be explored to meet these costs. However in establishing a business plan for the running of an ecolabel it is important to establish a break even point within the first 2 years. Ecolabels which depend on subsidies and grants are unlikely to be sustainable in the long term. Hence the need for a realistic business plan which can generate a self-financing scheme in the medium term.

Negotiating with potential awarding bodies

For an award to be run consistently and within several countries in Europe one or more organizations are required to administer and manage the award and to provide the verification service for qualification to the scheme. There are several options available for managing the award. The organization will need expertise to administer and verify the award. Alternatively it should have links with other companies who can provide this expertise. Two options are considered here:

In option 1 the award would seek a well-known co-partner. An example here is the Blue Flag award for beaches. Management of this award is the responsibility of the Foundation for Environmental Education in Europe (FEEE). FEEE operates in EU member states through a recognized NGO (non-governmental organization) such as the Tidy Britain Group in the UK and Keep the Archipelago Tidy Association in Finland. The NGO carries out the administration, surveying and registering of all beaches applying for the award within the country.

The Foundation for Environmental Education in Europe already runs the Blue Flag for Beaches award. It has high recognition and has experience in coordinating administering organizations in each member state. FEEE is an independent organization which gives the outcomes of its award schemes a high level of credibility. FEEE also has a strong European network of organizations and staff expertise already available, so the process of operationalizing the award would be quick, between 6 months to a year from when funding was available.

Option 2 is for the award developer to act as a certification body itself. This option would be the simplest and quickest to develop, as it cuts out lengthy negotiations with third parties. This option would also be the most cost effective initially. It would not, however, have the authority or credibility as a fully and independently verified award.

Neither would it be likely to have a network of organizations in other countries already developed so development would be limited initially to the country of the award developer.

An award also needs a strong emblem for it to quickly gain recognition. Association with organizations of good reputation and authority would give an award credibility and integrity. Again two options are considered.

In option 1 the way of achieving this is for it to adopt the emblem of an award or organization which already has a good reputation in this area and which is already successful in running and managing award schemes, for example the Blue Flag. Using an emblem already in the market would prevent emblem-proliferation with another award being added to the many already in existence. This would reduce any confusion to the public of another ecolabel appearing on the market. The Blue Flag for Beaches award is known in many countries and its aims are understood, so by seeking to work under the umbrella of this title, part of the education and marketing process would have already been achieved.

In option 2 the award could use its specific prototype name and logo. The benefits of this are that the prototype name and logo may already have gained a level of recognition. Through dissemination and consultation carried out during the ecolabel development, stakeholders may already be familiar with the prototype logo and the aims of the award. By continuing to use this logo, there would be an automatic link for stakeholders with the project, so they will not be faced with an entirely new scheme that would require new introductions.

Marketing, press and dissemination

A dissemination strategy needs to be devised, and this should be developed and adapted according to opportunities. One of the initial tasks should be to prepare a press release to outline the ecolabel development process. A website should also be constructed and launched at an early stage in the project. It should be regularly updated as the project develops. A key factor in the success of a web page is to use a short web address and to position the site in the major search engines. The success of a web page can be gauged by use of a webcounter which registers the number of hits to a page.

When research is conducted to collect data for the project it should be used as a marketing exercise so that information about the project is disseminated at the same time as data is collected. A publication strategy should include a number of different media. Academic and professional journals should be used to disseminate the technical aspects of the development of an ecolabel. Newspapers and magazines can be targeted with items of more general interest. Where possible a publisher which has a leading presence in the field should be used to publish the manual for an ecolabel. In this way costs can be kept to a minimum and the publisher will take on the responsibility for marketing.

Conferences should also be used as a key part of the dissemination strategy. The development team should target conferences which are related to the theme of their ecolabel, and where this is not possible an opportunity arises to organise a unique conference for this particular purpose.

Finally it is important to have a high profile event which will attract interest in terms of participants and press for the final proposals for an ecolabel. The emphasis here should be on people, place and purpose. The right people means people who are significant in endorsing an ecolabel, people who are of a high enough profile to attract interest in the ecolabel and people who represent organizations which will be important in the successful introduction of the ecolabel. The right place means selecting a venue which will excite interest in the project. The purpose of the event should be to generate press and stakeholder interest. To do this it may be a good idea to make some initial awards to demonstrate how the ecolabel will work in practice.

Conclusions

This chapter has outlined the phases and tasks involved in developing an ecolabel, as a basic guideline for any organization embarking on such a project. This has been done by reflection on the experience of the authors in preparing a proposal for a new ecolabel for the EU LIFE programme. This chapter suggests that the development of new ecolabels needs to be understood within the framework of the current proposals, and increased competition in this area will require a closer engagement of stakeholders and understanding of the ecolabel's impact on applicants, the industry as a whole and the tourist. The ecolabel should be developed within the frame of existing tried and tested criteria and verification processes yet adapted to the industry through consultation, to ensure comparability and complementarity with other initiatives and the ability of a critical mass to achieve the requirements. If the ecolabel is to improve environmental performance, rather than award current practices, applicants will need guidelines and manuals for the implementation of environmental management systems as well as environmental information and training sources. Once the key tools for the ecolabel are developed, it will be necessary to find the means to run it, by assessing the costs of verification, and manage it, negotiate with potential awarding bodies willing to support it and negotiate funding methods. The last stages will involve the dissemination of the proposals to gain industry and stakeholder awareness and commitment, before handing over the proposals to the commissioning organization.

References

Aaker, D., Kumar, V. and Day, G. (1995) *Marketing Research*, 5th edn. John Wiley & Sons, New York.

British Standards Institute (1996) *Implementation of ISO 14001: 1996*. BSI, London.

Castro-Rego, F. (1999) The Portuguese perspective to forest tourism. In: *Tourfor (1999) Environmental Management of Forest Tourism and Recreation*, Conference proceedings, 21 November 1998. Buckinghamshire Chilterns University College, High Wycombe, UK www.tourfor.com

Flynn, P., Font, X., Tribe, J. and Yale, K. (2001) Environmental management systems in outdoor recreation: the case study of a Forest Enterprise (UK) site. *Journal of Sustainable Tourism* (in press).

Font, X. (1997) Forest-based tourism in Great Britain: markets, products and suppliers. *Cahiers du Tourisme* N. 204. Centre des Hautes Etudes Touristiques, Aix-en Provence, France.

Font, X. and Tribe, J. (eds) (2000) *Forest Tourism and Recreation: Case Studies in Environmental Management*. CAB International, Wallingford, UK.

Font, X. and Tribe, J. (2001) Promoting green tourism: the future of environmental awards. *International Journal of Tourism Research* 3 (1), 1–13.

Font, X., Tribe, J. and Yale, K. (2001a) The Tourfor (tourism in forests) project progress report: results from its consultation exercise, Submitted to *Tourism Geographics*.

Font, X., Yale, K. and Tribe, J. (2001b) Introducing environmental management systems in forest recreation: results from a consultation exercise, submitted to *Managing Leisure*.

Forestry Commission (1990) *Forest Nature Conservation Guidelines*. Forestry Commission, Edinburgh.

Hammitt, W. and Cole, D. (1998) *Wildland Recreation: Ecology and Management*. John Wiley & Sons, New York.

Hulmi, R. (1999) Forest tourism in Finland. In: Font, X. (ed.) *Tourfor (1999) Environmental management of forest tourism and recreation*, Conference proceedings, 21 November 1998. Buckinghamshire Chilterns University College, High Wycombe, UK www.tourfor.com

LGMB (1995a) *EMAS Help-desk Guidance Notes: Undertaking an Environmental Review*. Local Government Management Board, London.

LGMB (1995b) *EMAS Help-desk Guidance Notes: Writing and Environmental Policy*. Local Government Management Board, London.

LGMB (1995c) *EMAS Help-desk Guidance Notes: Writing an Environmental Programme*. Local Government Management Board, London.

LGMB (1996a) *EMAS Help-desk Guidance Notes: Environmental Effects Evaluation (EEE)*. Local Government Management Board, London..

LGMB (1996b) *EMAS Help-desk Guidance Notes: Writing an Environmental Policy: Update.* Local Government Management Board, London.

LGMB (1996c) *EMAS Help-desk Guidance Notes: a Guide to the Management System and Audit Stages of EMAS for UK Local Government.* Local Government Management Board, London.

Liddle, M. (1997) *Recreation Ecology.* Chapman & Hall, London.

Rogers, B. (1996) *Creating Product Strategies.* International Thomson Business Press, London.

Tourfor (1998) Fourth international partners meeting: Tourfor Environmental Management System and Criteria, minutes of meetings 22–25 November 1998. Buckinghamshire Chilterns University College, High Wycombe, UK www.tourfor.com

Tourfor (1999) *Environmental Management of Forest Tourism and Recreation,* Conference proceedings, 21 November 1998; Buckinghamshire Chilterns University College, High Wycombe, UK www.tourfor.com

Tourfor (2000) *The Tourfor Award Pack.* Buckinghamshire Chilterns University College, High Wycombe, UK.

TQM (1996) *Environmental Management Systems: Your Handbook.* TQM International, Cheshire.

Tribe, J. (1998) Tourfor: an environmental management systems approach to tourism and recreation in forest areas. In: Hall, D. and O'Hanlon, L. (eds) *Rural Tourism Management: Sustainable Options.* International Conference Proceedings Scottish Agricultural College, Ayr, UK, pp. 561–577.

Tribe, J. and Font, X. (2000a) The Tourfor project and lessons for the UK woods and forest. *Access to Woodlands: Threats and Opportunities* Conference proceedings, 9 March 2000, Royal Agricultural Society of England and Royal Forestry Society, Warwickshire.

Tribe, J. and Font, X. (2000b) Tourfor: Managing the environmental impacts of access and tourism in Europe's forests. *Quarterly Journal of Forestry* 94(3).

Tribe, J. and Font, X. (2000c) *Tourfor: Tourism, Forestry and the Environment,* Finnish Forest Institute (METLA) research papers. METLA, Helsinki

Tribe, J., Font, X., Griffiths, N., Vickery, R. and Yale, K. (2000) *Environmental Management of Rural Tourism and Recreation.* Cassell, London.

UNEP (1998) *Ecolabels in the Tourism Industry.* United Nations Environmental Programme, Paris.

WWF (2000) *Pan-Parks Principles and Criteria Workshop,* 10–12 April 2000. World Wide Fund for Nature, Zeist, The Netherlands.

Chapter 8
Pitfalls of Ecolabelling
VINOD SASIDHARAN AND XAVIER FONT

Introduction

The potential of tourism ecolabels as a method to improve the industry's environmental performance is acknowledged and celebrated (UNEP, 1998). Ecolabels are meant to 'awaken' tourists with respect to the impacts of their tourism-related actions and decisions (Weissman, 1997); enable them to make informed choices while selecting tour operators, travel agencies, resorts/hotels and/or other tourism service providers for their vacations (Rhodes and Brown, 1997); and act in favour of environmentally sensitive tourism enterprises through their purchasing decisions (Grodsky, 1993; Hemmelskamp and Brockmann, 1997). Simultaneously, tourism enterprises would be pressured to improve their industrial practices thereby reducing tourism-related environmental impacts (West, 1995). Utilization of tourism ecolabels would be highly compatible with sustainable tourism initiatives (Jensen *et al.*, 1998). The potential of ecolabels to maintain and even enhance the physical environment by educating potential tourists regarding the environmental attributes of tourism enterprises and fostering environmentally sensitive business operations among such enterprises would make the concept particularly appealing to developing countries currently promoted as ecotourism destinations.

Despite the potential benefits from ecolabels, to date no conclusive evidence exists to support their assertive claims that ecolabels improve the environment (Weissman, 1997). Social science research suggests that environmental education of consumers and increasing environmental awareness does not stimulate environmentally responsible purchasing behaviour (Hemmelskamp and Brockmann, 1997; see Chapter 5). Similarly, despite the environment-oriented educative potential of tourism ecolabels, potential tourists may not respond favourably to ecolabels and the enterprises that market their eco-sensitive tourism services and products (see Chapter 4). It is for the above reasons that this chapter will review the potential pitfalls that ecolabelling programmes may encounter, based on the four phases outlined in Chapter 7 when reviewing the process of developing an ecolabel: (i) project management; (ii) positioning and planning; (iii) development and consultation; and (iv) management and marketing.

Project Management

Many of the pitfalls that an ecolabel may encounter come from the nature of the funding sources, the relationship between the funding body and the organization developing the ecolabel and the management of the ecolabel.

Getting the green light: matching projects to funds

If the funding body has already decided that they want to develop a tourism ecolabel under their umbrella of projects, they may approach directly a recognized organization, or publish a call for tenders for proposals fulfilling the specific outcomes outlined by the funding body's brief. Alternatively, the funding body may put an open call for proposals for actions to improve environmental performance, and a research team may propose the development of an ecolabel as a way to meet the funding body's aims and objectives.

The funding body will have a portfolio of several projects funded, with a specific structure to manage them. They will be the ones outlining how the proposal has to be written, its length, level of detail and contents. They will also decide when the call for proposals comes out, how it is advertised, how long bidding teams have to prepare the call, the maximum of funds available per project, what percentage of the cost will the funding body contribute, the encouraged origin and composition of bidding teams, the expected duration of projects and so on. For example a call for proposals could be published by the European Commission (EC), giving a 3-month period to prepare proposals for tools to encourage environmental performance of small and medium companies, specifically within the context of rural Europe. Projects should be of practical nature and not research projects, with particular preference for demonstration projects, they are expected to last between 2 and 3 years, and the European Commission will fund a maximum of 50% of the project. There is no information of whether future funds will be available to take forward any recommendations, and initially it should be expected that projects will be self-funding after the initial period. Finally, in this call the EC particularly welcomes proposals including women, and at least one East European country.

The bidding team will have to read into these criteria to ensure they can meet the requirements as closely as possible. Some proposals will fit more naturally under the available calls than others and the bidding team may have to rethink their project around the available resources, but one thing is clear: proposals can be matched to available funds more often than funds to proposals.

Once a call for proposals has been identified, the next step is to write a proposal that fulfils the criteria outlined. Writing a project proposal will involve several tasks. First, explain in detail the contents of the project itself: what will be done when and by whom. Second, relate the project proposed to the aims of the funding body, outlining how the funding body's requirements are met, and the deliverables the funding body will receive at the completion of the project. Third, outline the project team and project management, to demonstrate the proposal can actually be delivered and the team has the expertise to do it. Fourth, prepare the budget of the project by collecting data about the costs, usually following the cost forms, categories and margins given by the funding body. This is a lengthy process that will require the team to juggle all the above requirements in order to ensure that the funding body prioritizes this project proposal above others. The proposal will be written emphasizing the positive aspects and usually overselling the expected outcomes and targets in order to get the funds. Too many proposals are problem based, not solution oriented, focusing on why tourism damages the environment, rather than how an ecolabel can realistically have an impact and how it can be made operational.

There will be a time gap between the submission of proposals and hearing the outcomes, usually of some months, to allow for proposals to be assessed and prioritized. Assuming the bid is successful, the proposal submitted will form the baseline document against which the bidding team's work will be assessed. If the funding body requires modifications to the project proposal or the budget, the team in charge of developing the ecolabel should have the opportunity to modify the proposal. This will be done by preparing an inception report, which will become the basis of the contract between the funding body and the team commissioned to carry out the work. Modifications in the budget may mean cutting down the amount or length of time for research, or by funding only the preliminary stages of the overall proposal. Between writing the proposal and hearing the results the state of the art in the industry may well have changed, since developments by competing ecolabels may change the industry's needs. Also this time gap may mean that the bidding team has changed by the time the results are made public. All this can be negative if the new team does not have the expertise required or the ecolabel is already redundant before developing it, although it can also be seen in a positive light if the inception report allows renegotiation of objectives and proposed actions. All in all, the goal posts may have moved a long way since the ecolabel proposal was first thought out, potentially making the ecolabel redundant.

Reporting on progress

Regular progress reports will be required by the funding body from the contractors to demonstrate their progress to date. Funds are usually released in stages, and part way through the project there may be one or more extensive interim reports that, if successful, will trigger the mechanism to release an instalment of funds. Progress reporting cycles can make project development awkward, since dates and tasks may not coincide, and reporting on results in the middle of a task is never easy and becomes artificial. Contractors will try to match the project development and the project management deadlines by aiming to plan the phases of the project around reporting dates. In this instance one may need more or less time to undertake all the tasks for a specific phase, but due to the reporting dates, tasks have to be rushed to meet a reporting deadline, or there is extra time to start the next phase and therefore less to report about.

At the end of the project, the contractors will have to prepare a final technical report detailing how the objectives outlined in the project proposal or inception report have been met. The contractors will be requested to provide evidence of the work done and to present the project deliverables, which will include any reports, documents, leaflets, databases, videos, newspaper cuttings, recordings and so on that can be used to prove performance. The contractors will also have to provide their accounts, usually audited by an external accountancy firm, to justify all expenses necessary to undertake the project. This could well be a requirement to release the payment of the last instalment of funds from the project. There is a gap between completing the project, carrying out the audit of accounts, having them accepted by the funding body and receiving the final payment. This means the contractors will require considerable cash flows to pay salaries and others in advance until the final payment is received. This limits the type of organization that can apply to undertake a project of this nature. Furthermore, unless part way through the project new funds were secured to continue, the development of the ecolabel will have to be put on hold, which will mean losing valuable staff and expertise.

Positioning and Planning

Three key pitfalls will be highlighted from the positioning and planning stages. First, the fact that too often funding bodies prefer to retain ownership of the ecolabel over the objective of encouraging sustainable tourism. Second, the process of ecolabelling is dominated by developing countries, yet the majority of ecotourism destinations are in developing countries where the local companies will have greater difficulties in meeting strict and expensive measurement and monitoring requirements, and it will be harder to involve them in the process. Third, stakeholders approached for involvement in the development of the ecolabel may not be representative of all the interests at stake, and only those seeing a direct benefit for themselves may be able to dedicate the resources to influence the outcomes.

Situating the ecolabel: retaining ownership

The development of a new tourism ecolabel would start with the identification of existing ecolabelling programmes and environmental certification schemes focusing on a sector of the tourism industry. An inventory analysis and initial fact-finding relating to the objectives, geographical scope and coverage (international, regional, national, subnational), and focus areas (such as facilities, services and location) of available ecolabelling schemes (UNEP, 1998) would assist the prospective ecolabelling programme in delineating the overlooked needs of various groups involved in tourism. Ideally, the ecolabelling programme would (market) position its new ecolabel towards meeting those requirements and needs of the tourism industry stakeholders which existing ecolabels have largely ignored.

It has already been suggested elsewhere in this book that there are too many ecolabels, quite often overlapping geographically and across sectors of the industry. The reason for this is that too many funding bodies run ecolabels with limited resources, considering their member-ship (if industry associations) or local companies (if publicly run) as the target market for the award. The economies of scale necessary to make a public awareness project work mean that most ecolabels are provincial: unless a large number of sites can be awarded, the message will not be meaningful to the potential tourist. A large number of ecolabels appear because funding bodies want to be seen to promote green tourism and they have a me-too aproach. These tend to reinvent the wheel by developing a new set of criteria, usually quite similar to other ecolabels, but not so similar that this new ecolabel can be questioned. Also most ecolabels have no market focus, since they are run on a can-do approach, rather than considering what the market is willing to pay for. These ecolabels are an attempt by tourist destinations or industry associations to compete among themselves, rather than a genuine effort to promote sustainable tourism. Also too many ecolabels appear as demonstration projects (see Chapter 1) yet these are not taken further on their own, or taken over by an umbrella ecolabel. Few examples can be seen where two ecolabels decide to standardize criteria or merge for the benefit of clarity. Also funding bodies may be willing to put funds aside to run their own ecolabel, but will not be willing to lose ownership of the idea and its management by joining efforts with stronger schemes run elsewhere. A possible solution would be to streamline the number of ecolabels, while still allowing for locally run organizations to retain some ownership.

Eco-protectionism and domination by developed countries

Evidently, nearly all existing ecolabelling programmes and schemes for manufactured goods have their origins in developed countries, for example the United States, Canada, Germany, Austria, Sweden, France, Japan and Australia (Hemmelskamp and Brockmann, 1997; Kusz, 1997; Eiderströem, 1997; Parris, 1998; Lal, 1996) with negligible developing-country representation. This pattern of predomination by developed countries in ecolabelling schemes would extend to such programmes for the service-oriented tourism industry. The criteria set forth by tourism ecolabelling schemes would be based on local interests of developed countries and would seldom take developing countries and their local industry perspectives into account (West, 1995; Lal, 1996). Owing to their limited capability to meet these standards, the tourism enterprises of developing countries would have little control over the politicized criteria of ecolabelling schemes (West, 1995) set forth by developed countries. Attempts to establish harmonized, mutually recognized tourism ecolabelling standards that accommodate the perspectives of tourism enterprises of developing countries would be largely unsuccessful due to the conflicting public agendas and environmental priorities of developed and developing countries. Since most of the large-scale tourism enterprises operating in the areas of developing countries as well as the tourists brought in by them originate in Western, developed countries, ecolabelling programmes could be influenced by these enterprises for protectionist purposes (Lal, 1996; Wildavsky, 1996), i.e. eco-protectionism. Under such conditions, local tourism enterprises, most of which are incapable of meeting the environmental standards and criteria prescribed by ecolabelling schemes, would be portrayed as being eco-insensitive in the eyes of Western tourists. Even if the small, local companies had a good environmental record, they may be excluded from the consultation process or even from applying due to language and information barriers.

Consequential loss of the 'environmentally conscious tourist' market share for local tourism enterprises (of developed countries) that fail to receive ecolabels would lead to the market exclusion and decline of most of these enterprises due to their dependency on these tourists for business profitability. Efforts by local tourism enterprises and local governments to avert these circumstances would lead to their boycott of foreign ecolabelling schemes, and the subsequent establishment of local ecolabelling agencies that nullify the influence of their Western counterparts. Most importantly, tourists visiting these areas would be faced with the dilemma of choosing between tourism enterprises that have been ecolabelled by different ecolabelling bodies. Many of their decisions would be based on the amount of information provided to them by ecolabelling agencies regarding the environmental impacts of the tourism enterprises that carry their environmental seals of approval.

Stakeholder involvement: a lopsided affair

The credibility of ecolabelling programmes for the tourism industry will depend on the guarantee of independence and neutrality pertaining to the composition of its board members and representation of stakeholders from the tourism industry involved in the ecolabelling process (West, 1995). Although the stakeholders may comprise representatives from both public and private sector of the tourism industry, discrepancies in the composition (e.g. more large-scale enterprise representatives than others), and the consequent involvement of diverse stakeholders in ecolabelling decisions may not necessarily produce justifiable consensus on issues pertaining to tourism sector category selection and criteria finalization. In the case of 'externally verified' ecolabelling schemes that disallow involvement from stakeholders of the tourism industry, ecolabelling decisions would reflect the judgements of the group with adequate time and resources (personnel and financial) to participate in the ecolabelling process (West, 1995). Most tourism ecolabelling schemes are prone to be plagued by greater involvement from large-scale enterprises of the private sector (Grodsky, 1993) working towards the development of environmental standards that best suit their business interests. On the other hand, the fear of failing to meet the set standards would discourage most small-scale enterprises from participating in the initiation phase of ecolabelling programmes (Kusz, 1997). Moreover, the lack of time and resources (monetary and personnel) would deter other groups, such as government personnel, citizens groups and tourists, from attending intensive working sessions during crucial phases of ecolabelling programmes (West, 1995).

Development and Consultation

The process of development will be crucial to the future of an ecolabel. Two pitfalls will be hightlighted here, in relation to measuring and monitoring environmental impacts, and prioritizing impacts as part of the criteria for certification. The outcomes from this phase decide how difficult it will be to achieve the ecolabel and will have a key impact on the cost of applying for certification.

Environmental impact evaluation: lack of scientific credibility

Ideally, the environmental impacts associated with the selected tourism sector would be evaluated by environmental scientists using the life cycle assessment (LCA) or 'cradle-to-grave' environmental accounting methodology (Grodsky, 1993; Wildavsky, 1996; Hemmelskamp and Brockmann, 1997; Rhodes and Brown, 1997; Jensen *et al.*, 1998). This would include the environmental impacts generated from raw materials, energy consumption, air and water emissions, and solid waste (Rhodes and Brown, 1997; Weissman, 1997). By definition, the life cycle analysis technique used to assess the environmental impacts of the tourism enterprise would include:

1. Life cycle inventory: the identification and quantification of energy consumption, raw materials used and the wastes discharged into the environment by the enterprise during the course of providing tourism-related services;
2. Environmental impact analysis: the computation of the cumulative environmental impacts produced by the inputs and outputs over the life of the enterprise (Salzhauer, 1991; Grodsky, 1993); and
3. Improvement analysis: the utilization of information gathered through the previous steps to reduce the environmental impacts of enterprises during their respective lifecycles (Salzhauer, 1991).

Despite the availability of clear outlines for performing life cycle inventories, the impact analysis and improvement analysis phases of life cycle assessment for tourism enterprises would be onerous and complicated due to the multi-resource dependence of tourism and the plethora of related environmental impacts. Although the scale and magnitude of environmental impacts may vary, all tourism enterprises and sectors produce environmental impacts. Life cycle assessments are also harder in tourism companies where production is not standardized and there are more raw materials used, and most of these impacts are far-reaching and costly to measure.

For this reason most ecolabels use simpler evaluation standards, based on arbitrary and unscientific indicators and criteria (Salzhauer, 1991; Dudley *et al.*, 1997). Ecolabelling is seen by opponents as an inherently flawed, value laden concept (West, 1995) essentially nothing but a marketing tool that could be used by large-scale tourism enterprises to gain a competitive edge (Eiderströem, 1997; Weissman, 1997). The lack of a universally accepted methodology for assessing environmental impacts (West, 1995; Wildavsky, 1996) during the various stages of the life cycle of tourism enterprises, the inadequacy of detail and sophistication of the databases utilized for conducting life cycle inventories and the reluctance of tourism enterprises to disclose operations-specific information (Grodsky, 1993; Davis, 1997) cumulatively give rise to a serious set of problems. Assessments of these impacts and the subsequent development of evaluation criteria and manuals for potential awardees would depend on the priorities of parties with vested interests (Hemmelskamp and Brockmann, 1997) in the tourism industry. Owing to the unavailability of set scientific methods and information required for the identification of impacts that have the greatest potential to adversely affect resources, the tourism impacts considered would be those which tourism enterprises find least difficult to address (West, 1995).

Criteria selection: a product of compromises

Stakeholder involvement would be minimal during the environmental impact identification phase of ecolabelling programmes. Environmental scientists, researchers and specialists (often recommended and funded by large-scale enterprises from the private sector) with expertise would be responsible for analysing environmental impacts associated with tourism sectors, owing to the lack of resources among the majority of stakeholders to do the same. As a result, environmental impact analyses would be conducted and interpreted by a selected few within the limits of monetary and personnel resources provided to them by the affluent, large-scale enterprises from the private sector thereby incapacitating other stakeholders from participating in the analyses. Besides small-scale tourism enterprises, most stakeholders would have little involvement when it comes to making decisions regarding allowable thresholds of environmental damages/impacts for tourism sectors, in terms of scale and magnitude.

The development of impact assessment criteria would be based on compromises between environmental protection and the demands of tourism enterprises (West, 1995; Dudley *et al.*, 1997; Kusz, 1997). Thus, impact assessment criteria would emerge as a compromised product, and not necessarily as a means for evaluating a tourism enterprise's environmental sensitivity (Kusz, 1997) due to the 'overinvolvement' of private-sector tourism enterprises in ecolabelling programmes. As a result, impacts that could have a negative effect on enterprise profitability would be prioritized whereas complex issues such as impacts on biodiversity, ecosystems and indigenous populations are likely to receive lesser attention. Concomitantly, ecolabelling schemes would address environmental impacts prioritized by private-sector tourism enterprises, rather than focusing on scientifically important, far-reaching environmental impacts (Salzhauer, 1991). Furthermore, macro-scale (regional and global level) environmental impacts are likely to be overlooked by tourism ecolabelling schemes due to the 'site specific' focus and interests of private-sector tourism enterprises. Consequently, the foibles of inventory and impact analyses generated through life cycle assessments of the tourism industry would lead to inaccurate, unscientific improvement analyses (Salzhauer, 1991) for tourism enterprises. The lack of a systematic, scientific technique for assessing inventories and impacts of diverse enterprises within the tourism industry, as well as the overall uncertainties and inaccuracy of the analyses would mandate the need for improvements in the overall structure of life cycle assessment.

Management and Marketing

Pitfalls related to the management and marketing of the ecolabel will usually be the direct outcome of the value placed by both applicants and the market on the ecolabel. Ecolabelling programmes suffer from small marketing budgets compared to the amounts spent by private companies, and the label's low exposure, coupled with design and market mistakes made at earlier stages, put the ecolabelling agency under pressure to make ends meet. Low industry applications, financing difficulties, relaxation of standards and low educational value are potential pitfalls with an impact on the image of the ecolabel.

Applications and environmental performance

Tourism enterprises falling within one of the predetermined tourism sectors would apply to the ecolabelling agency. The tourism enterprise would be awarded the ecolabel if it meets the final criteria. For example, a tour operator applying for an ecolabel would be awarded it only if the tour operator surpasses or at least meets the threshold levels established for the final criteria of environmental impacts (Grodsky,

1993) associated with the tour operator sector of the tourism industry. The tour operator is then allowed by the ecolabelling agency to use the ecolabel certification, symbol or logo in its marketing efforts in return for a licensing fee (Kusz, 1997; Shimp and Rattray, 1997).

The pitfall in the process basically comes from the nature of the applicants. In the first instance, the companies applying will be those that already have a high record of environmental performance, and therefore the label will only recognize past performance, rather than help in environmental improvement. The difficulty for the ecolabelling agency is to convince other organizations of the value of making improvements to apply for the award, otherwise the value of the label is limited.

Companies will be certified for a limited period, after which they will have to reapply. Some ecolabels base their criteria on the need for continuous environmental improvement, such as those based on environmental management systems, yet others have a fixed set of criteria that are re-evaluated against technological and innovative advancements. The ecolabelling agency will be faced with the problem of choosing between aiming for improvement on a cyclical basis, which means that companies will have to make efforts to meet the targets and new applicants will find it harder to apply, or not updating the standards, in an effort to establish a minimum threshold that companies lagging behind can aim for, yet the ecolabel runs the risk of not responding to changing situations.

Financial viability: the inevitability of criteria relaxation

In the long term, lack of involvement in tourism ecolabelling schemes could become prevalent even among industry stakeholders (Kusz, 1997). The high costs of operating environmentally sensitive tourism projects are often affordable only to large-scale, multinational enterprises. The tourism industry mainly comprises smaller agencies such as privately owned, small-scale tour operators, travel agents, lodges, hotels, etc., usually lacking the financial capability to provide eco-friendly tourism services and to support the high start-up and compliance monitoring costs associated with the application for ecolabels (Grodsky, 1993). Very few small-scale tourism enterprises would be capable of meeting the strong criteria and standards developed by ecolabelling schemes. The resource (both personnel and financial) inadequacy and incapability of most tourism enterprises in developing countries to meet the stringent standards and criteria set by ecolabelling schemes would discourage them from participating in tourism ecolabelling programmes. The budgeting costs of ecolabelling management are often steep. Additionally, high licensing fees are charged by the ecolabelling agency for permitting tourism enterprises to use the awarded ecolabels in their marketing efforts, the future tightening of criteria, the possibility of non-recertification due to unsatisfactory standards, and the costs associated with recertification after 1–3 years (Salzhauer, 1991; Shimp and Rattray, 1997). Although some of the tourism enterprises may manage to meet the set criteria, the high costs and expenses associated with ecolabelling management would potentially deter such enterprises from continuing with ecolabelling schemes. The cumulative effect of non-involvement from small enterprise stakeholders in tourism ecolabelling schemes and the consequent insufficiency of sponsors for funding ecolabelling programmes may result in the lowering of certification standards (West, 1995) in order to increase industry participation and increase the mileage of such programmes.

Negotiation of environmental performance standards and loss of innovation

Non-involvement from the tourism industry may also arise due to profit-oriented private sectors' uninterest in synergizing with stakeholders belonging to environmental groups that have anti-business agendas (Salzhauer, 1991). The inhibitory effect of stringent criteria and standards on tourism industry stakeholder involvement would pressurize environmental interest groups and stakeholders to re-evaluate and ease their set standards for acceptable levels of environmental impacts, in response to the fear of environmental interests being marginalized from the ecolabelling process. Besides the lowering of eco-certification standards, ecolabelling programmes run the inherent risk of negating the potential of the tourism industry to make innovative improvements in ameliorating negative environmental impacts. Tourism enterprises that meet the highest standards of environmental sensitivity would be awarded the same ecolabel as those that meet the minimal standards identified in the evaluation criteria (Shimp and Rattray, 1997). Upon receiving an ecolabel for attaining the standards determined by the ecolabelling programme, most enterprises would have little incentive to devote resources towards furthering their quest for innovative ways to reduce detrimental resource impacts (Wildavsky, 1996). The inadequacy of resources and incentives to meet the prohibitive costs of investing in innovative technology for complying with stricter standards in the future, while maintaining profit margins (Salzhauer, 1991) would preclude most small-scale tourism enterprises from future recertification by ecolabelling programmes.

Education of tourists: dissemination of information or distortion of facts?

Ideally, tourism ecolabels would provide tourists with a detailed description of the ecolabelled tourism enterprises' environmental impacts with the objective of influencing their behaviour in favour of enterprises offering environmentally sensitive tourism services and products (Lynch, 1997). The information provided to tourists would evolve from ecolabelling agencies' evaluation criteria developed as a compromise of tourism industry and environmental interests. Therefore, this information would not provide a true, holistic account of all environmental impacts produced by a particular tourism enterprise. As a result, tourism ecolabelling schemes may provide potential tourists with only a subjective, filtered and distorted narrative (Wildavsky, 1996; Davis, 1997), thereby misinforming and depriving them of a validated, in-depth environmental impact analysis that would stimulate informed decisions on locally, regionally and globally relevant issues (Shimp and Rattray, 1997). Further, the plethora of value-laden, diverse and, often, contradictory information provided by various tourism ecolabelling schemes would impede tourists from making objective judgements regarding the environmental impacts of tourism enterprises (Wildavsky, 1996). Additionally, the absence of a 'neutral', well-recognized agency for overseeing, monitoring and regulating all tourism ecolabelling schemes in developing countries would potentially raise the levels of suspicion and distrust among tourists towards the credibility of the environmental claims raised by tourism enterprises and their ecolabelling agencies.

Tourism ecolabels would provide tourists with information pertaining only to the environmental impacts of a tourism enterprise. Socio-cultural impacts having dire consequences on the quality of life of host destinations and indigenous populations are likely to be downplayed by ecolabels. Tourism enterprises would use the ecolabel as a tool for concealing the socio-cultural impacts caused by their operations and services. Tourists would have to be educated with respect to the utility, purpose and scope of tourism ecolabels as most tourists remain unaware of the existence of ecolabels, and much less understand their meaning (Morris *et al.*, 1995; Eisen, 1997).

Conclusion

This review aimed to flag potential pitfalls and to show warning signs for any organization considering the development of a new ecolabel, or making changes to their current programme. This was done by classifying the pitfalls into four groups, depending on the stages of the development of the ecolabel, following the structure proposed in the previous chapter. First it reviewed pitfalls from the 'Project management' of the ecolabel, with specific reference to the nature of ecolabels are projects and issues relating to funding and reporting. Second, it outlined pitfalls from the 'Positioning and planning' of the ecolabel. Since funding bodies are usually the first to use ecolabels as a method to make themselves look environmentally friendly, they retain ownership of their ecolabel before other priorities. Furthermore, this section highlights the fact that most ecolabels are Western responses to worldwide problems, particularly noticeable in developing ecotourism destinations, pinpoints the difficulties of stakeholder involvement which are not unique to ecolabels.

Third, the section on 'Development and consultation' focused on the difficulties of assessing environmental impacts, and the relation between these and the choice of certification criteria, considering issues such as the economies of scale in environmental management and the difficulties for small companies to compete. Finally this chapter focused on pitfalls around the 'Management and marketing' of the ecolabel once running, looking at the type of applicants certified against the ecolabel's objectives, the financial pressures on ecolabelling programmes and implications for standards, the relaxation of standards to gain applications and exposure, the difficulties for small companies at the destination to comply with requirements, and finally the questionable educational value of some ecolabels. Those ecolabels avoiding these mistakes will have a greater chance to succeed in promoting good environmental practice in tourism, which ultimately should be their aim.

References

Davis, G. (1997) How green the label? *Forum for Applied Research and Public Policy* 12, 137–140.

Dudley, N., Elliott, C. and Stolton, S. (1997) A framework for environmental labeling. *Environment* 39, 16–20, 42–45.

Eiderströem, E. (1997) Ecolabelling: Swedish style. *Forum for Applied Research and Public Policy* 12, 141–144.

Eisen, M. (1997) Ecolabeled products find home at depot. *Forum for Applied Research and Public Policy* 12, 124–127.

Grodsky, J. (1993). Certified green: the law and future of environmental labeling. *The Yale Journal on Regulation* 10, 147–227.

Hemmelskamp, J. and Brockmann, K. (1997) Environmental labels – the German 'Blue Angel'. *Futures* 29, 67–76.

Jensen, A., Christiansen, K. and Elkington, J. (1998) *Life Cycle Assessment: a Guide to Approaches, Experiences and Information Sources*, Environmental Issues Series no. 6. European Environment Agency, Copenhagen.

Kusz, J. (1997) Ecolabel investments: what's behind label? *Forum for Applied Research and Public Policy* 12, 133–136.

Lal, R. (1996) Eco-labels – an instrument to hasslefree marketing. *Colourage* 43, 15–18, 32.

Lynch, J. (1997) Environmental labels: a new policy strategy. *Forum for Applied Research and Public Policy* 12, 121–123.

Morris, L.A., Hastak, M. and Mazis, M.B. (1995) Consumer comprehension of environmental advertising and labeling claims. *Journal of Consumer Affairs* 29, 328–350.

Parris, T. (1998) Seals of approval: environmental labeling on the net. *Environment* 40, 3–4.

Rhodes, S. and Brown, L. (1997) Consumers look for the ecolabel. *Forum for Applied Research and Public Policy* 12, 109–115.

Salzhauer, A. (1991) Obstacles and opportunities for a consumer ecolabel. *Environment* 33, 10–15, 33–37.

Shimp, R. and Rattray, T. (1997) Ecoseals: little more than a pretty package. *Forum for Applied Research and Public Policy* 12, 128–132.

United Nations Environment Programme (UNEP) (1998) *Ecolabels in the Tourism Industry*. United Nations Publication, UNEP, Paris.

Weismann, A. (1997) Greener marketplace means cleaner world. *Forum for Applied Research and Public Policy* 12, 116–120.

West, K. (1995) Ecolabels: the industrialization of environmental standards. *The Ecologist* 25, 16–20.

Wildavsky, B. (1996) Sticker shocker. *National Journal* 28, 532–535.

Chapter 9

Ecotourism Certification and Evaluation: Progress and Prospects

MEGAN EPLER WOOD AND ELIZABETH A. HALPENNY

Introduction

Ecotourism is a label that has the distinction of being attached to both an industry and a sustainable development strategy. Its definition, 'responsible travel to natural areas that conserves the environment and sustains the well-being of local people' (The International Ecotourism Society (TIES), 1991) is difficult to grapple with in the real world of actual business operations. False labelling has made it difficult, if not impossible, for the consumer to distinguish the genuine product. The lack of regulation has left responsible businesses scrambling to prove their legitimacy. As early as 1992, responsible tour operators and lodges started refusing to be labelled as ecotourism businesses because of the lack of credibility of the term in the market place.

The success of the ecotourism industry may be fuelling some of the suspicion that has arisen. Ecotourism businesses now number in the thousands, and can be found lining the major arteries of destination cities including Nairobi, Quito, Kathmandu and Belize City. Despite this boom, there is no international system to monitor the ecotourism label and only two national certification programmes in the world; in Costa Rica (described later in this chapter) and Australia (detailed in Chapter 11).

Ecotourism certification could play a valuable role in boosting the market for legitimate ecotourism, however, there are substantial difficulties with creating a valid system. These difficulties are, in part, due to the distinctiveness of ecotourism from other forms of tourism. Below, ecotourism as a concept and business is explored briefly. Later in the chapter, suggestions are made on how certification for ecotourism could differ from that of mainstream tourism.

Ecotourism as a Sustainable Development Tool

Ecotourism is rooted in its role and history as a sustainable development strategy. Its components can be identified as travel to a natural area, that: (i) benefits local communities; (ii) supports conservation efforts both locally and nationally; and (iii) includes interpretation of natural and cultural environments. These elements give ecotourism a high standard to achieve from the outset. For an ecotourism 'product' or 'experience' to be true ecotourism, its benchmarks for excellence include many of mainstream tourism's, but usually put more stress on the protection of natural resources, support of protected areas, in-depth interpretation of natural and cultural resources, and more requirements for achieving genuine local involvement.

The Ecotourism Market

Ecotourism has been differentiated from nature tourism for over 10 years, because of its unique mission (as described earlier in the TIES definition). Because ecotourism is defined by its sustainable development results, not solely by consumer activities, the ecotourism market is difficult to quantify. Experts have long insisted upon the need to create an operational definition that would allow for quantification. Some have argued it is unquantifiable, while others have insisted that its positive contributions in destinations must be quantified. There has been little progress on this issue in part due to the small and medium-sized nature of ecotourism companies and their inability to coordinate large-scale market research. Rough estimates have been published during the last decade, including a World Tourism Organization (WTO) estimate stating that nature tourism generates 7% of the world travel receipts (Ceballos-Lascurain, cited in Lindberg *et al.*, 1998). Drawing largely on a recently completed paper by Wight (2001) which provides an overview of all ecotourism market-related data published in the last decade, a profile of the average ecotourist is outlined in Table 9.1. This profile is based on a variety of results from studies of ecotourism markets in North America, Asia and Australia.

The motivations that distinguish ecotourists from other mainstream tourists are clearly identified by several studies as an interest in 'uncrowded destinations in remote wilderness areas' (Eagles, 1992; Crossley and Lee 1994), while 'learning about nature' appears to be particularly important among certain age groups and types (TIAA, 1994; Bureau of Tourism Research, 1998).

Certifying the Ecotourism Sector of the Tourism Industry

The ecotourism sector is a collection of industries that are inter-connected to both mainstream tourism and other global economic activities. They are affected by the same global and regional events as all other businesses are: climate change, warfare and terrorism, economic boom and bust, and so on. Table 9.2 details some of these industries and highlights other factors associated with ecotourism. It is the ancillary groups in Table 9.2 that have expressed strong interest

Table 9.1.   Estimated ecotourist profile (Wight, 2001).

Age: 35–54, although minimum age appears to be lowering to 30. The maximum average age is also increasing as baby boomers continue to age.
Gender: generally slightly more females than males, especially in younger age groups.
Income: generally ecotourists, especially as international travellers display higher income levels than mainstream travellers.
Education: highly educated, most are college graduates
Party composition: most (60%) travel as a couple, 15% with families, and 13% prefer to travel alone. There is some evidence to indicate that family travel rose significantly in the 1990s and may not be reflected in this statistic.
Trip duration: varies significantly, especially with activity. In a study of North American 'experienced ecotravellers' many (50%) preferred trips lasting 8–14 days.
Expenditure: ecotourists generally spend more than mainstream tourists, however they also expect value for their additional expenditure, i.e. a quality experience.
Activity preferences: varies with destination, however visiting national parks, hiking, water-based activities, admiring nature, camping and touring all appeared often in survey results. Additionally cultural/aboriginal experiences may also be a significant attraction.
Primary reason for travel: (i) experiencing various elements of nature and scenery was cited most often in surveys; however (ii) new experiences, wildlife, learning, and local cultures, also figured prominently.

Table 9.2.   Ecotourism stakeholders.

Ecotourism industries (direct stakeholders)	Ancillary groups (other stakeholders)
Information services/travel agents/retail	Non-government organizations
Airlines	(including conservation and
Outbound tour operators	community groups)
Inbound/ground operators	Local communities
Ecolodging/accommodations and meals	Regional and national governments
Local entrepreneurs/vendors/outfitters	(including marketing boards, tourism
	ministries, etc.)
	Development agencies
	Universities and researchers

in providing certification systems for ecotourism. The private sector has become involved, but only because of the initiation of projects by non-government organizations (NGOs), regional and national governments, development agencies, and universities. As a result, a fragmented set of initiatives has been launched throughout the world, which lack any coordination at present. The International Ecotourism Society (TIES), which is the largest international ecotourism organization in the world, has been very cautious about taking responsibility for a global system of ecotourism certification. The reasons for this will be explained in this chapter. Many new certification initiatives were launched in 1999, including those in the Galapagos and Saskatchewan. The longest established ecotourism programme, Australia's Nature and Ecotourism Accreditation Programme (NEAP) has recently completed a second round of criteria evaluation and category expansion. A selection of these can be seen in the directory of ecolabels.

Comments on the varying criteria and programmes are beginning to proliferate in the ecotourism literature. A number of cogent points have been made. Gnoth (1998) illuminates some of these:

> It may be hard to create an ecolabel that has appeal to the different facilitators in different countries. Indeed economic, cultural and other sociodemographic variables may well generate ethical dilemmas and unfair situations. In other words, destinations in Europe can possibly afford more stringent requirements for an ecolabel than Tanzania or Thailand.

This problem is particularly acute when considering ecotourism, which stresses local involvement and benefits – particularly in developing countries – and downplays any role for international business. Creating indicators that are highly sensitive to local development and socioeconomic factors must be the objective when it comes to creating a set of standards that reflect ecotourism principles. None the less, without any international standards for ecotourism certification there is a greater possibility of opportunism, graft and corruption, and profit-making approaches at the local level. Two highly respected guidebook authors, Blake and Becher who worked hard to create an objective system in Costa Rica, have commented that:

> We are concerned about the proliferation of tourism certification processes – especially those based on paid membership in the certifying organization and self-evaluations. We worry that if the public sees that different certifying organizations recognize different lodgings, the general perception will be that all evaluation methods are subjective and any lodging can buy its way into a certification. Ideally we believe that a sustainable tourism umbrella organization should certify the certifiers, to prevent misuse of the process.
>
> (Blake and Becher, 1998)

This problem was recognized as being a fundamental issue at the UN Commission for Sustainable Development (UNCSD) Dialogue Session on Sustainable Tourism in April 1999 in New York City. Over 500 NGOs were represented in this process, as were industry, trade unions and municipalities. In the NGO dialogue speech on 19 April 1999 (which author Epler Wood helped to draft, record and distribute), the NGOs suggested that the UNCSD, 'invite public, private, and NGO certification initiatives to join in an evaluation process to determine what are the best procedures for tourism certification and monitoring and widely distribute the results of this process'. According to the UNEP document, *Ecolabels in the Tourism Industry* (UNEP, 1998), 'there is a need to develop a means of measuring the effectiveness of tourism ecolabels, and a need for internationally recognized standards for environmental labels.'

The questions remains, how much do tourists actually want this information? Recent research demonstrates a serious lack of empirical evidence to support the notion that consumers are 'ready to change their behaviour, e.g. to desist from previous non-sustainable activities, or willing to pay a higher price for tourism products with green attributes' (Hjalager, 1999). It is fascinating that a global movement to certify ecotourism has been launched and even become fragmented without any measurable data on the demand for this service. While ecotourists receive most of their information about ecotourism trips via word-of-mouth or directly from tour operators, they also gather information from travel agents, and information services such as guide books, trade shows and the Internet. A report by the Travel Industry Association of America (TIAA) shows that travel planning is surging on the Internet, with 52.2 million online travellers using the net for this purpose in 1999, a 54% increase over 1998 (TIAA, 1999).

Ecotourism reporting on the Internet will reach many consumers, and NGOs such as The International Ecotourism Society and Conservation International (J. Sweeting, personal communication) are seriously exploring this option. An example of certification reporting can be found at the Costa Rican Sustainable Tourism Certification website (www.turismo-sostenible.co.cr/EN/index-en.shtml). However, while reporting to consumers is vital, the underlying issue is what sector of the industry can be legitimately certified. In preliminary research done by The International Ecotourism Society in 1994 with its industry members, it was quickly determined that international tour operators would be difficult, if not impossible to certify, because their services are largely subcontracted to inbound operators.

Ecotour trips are frequently organized through an inbound tour operator, which may work in conjunction with an outbound tour operator to provide a specialized tour in another country. Inbound operators arrange accommodations and guides, they take the lion's share of responsibility for fostering biodiversity conservation and well-being of local people, and they brief travellers on situations such as begging, tipping and appropriate clothes, making them excellent targets for certification. However, these small businesses are generally dwarfed by their outbound colleagues, and often lack personnel or resources to devote to the process.

The outbound tour operator is essentially a marketing and sales organization. It takes responsibility for selecting and packaging the tour product, overseeing the creation of itineraries that will meet its market's needs. It handles all insurance and liability for tours, and provides the passengers with the information they need before departure. Outbound ecotourism operators also handle most retail air arrangements for their clients, using travel agents that work in-house and work directly with airlines to secure wholesale rates and related deals. Outbound operators also create the brand name that sells ecotourism products; however, they do not take direct responsibility for the way ecotours are delivered at the destination. They generally contract local operators around the world to carry out the tours and therefore resist involvement in certification, because they do not directly control product delivery on the ground, nor would it be economically feasible for them to pay for certifying partner businesses worldwide.

International trips are usually purchased at home, and travellers fly to the trip destination. Airlines play an integral role in tourism. Some are working towards more environmentally responsible practices that support a variety of environmental programmes, such as the UNESCO benefit programme 'Coins for Conservation'. In this programme, travellers flying home on cooperating airlines are asked to donate their leftover foreign currency to conservation projects. However, overall, airlines have played little or no role in the debate regarding certification of the ecotourism industry.

The primary accommodation facilities used in the ecotourism sector are ecolodges. Ecolodges are small businesses (as opposed to large chains of hotels) usually found in remote natural areas. They vary from simple low-impact tents, which can be easily relocated to minimize environmental degradation, to state-of-the-art ecolodges with all the comforts found in traditional hotels but with fewer environmental impacts. Ideally ecolodges should offer educational experiences, be developed and managed in an environmentally sensitive manner, afford protection of the environment in which it is located, provide employment with the chance for advancement to local people and promote the patronage of local suppliers and vendors (Hawkins *et al.*, 1995). Criteria for ecolodges are still being developed as these facilities evolve. Both Australia and Costa Rica's certification programmes list criteria. Additional supporting standards can be found in Hawkins *et al.* (1995) and Mehta and Baez (2001). Certification of ecolodges may ultimately be the best way to achieve a legitimate ecotourism programme with international standards that is locally implemented. While ecotours offer a set of fluctuating services that vary each time they are offered, ecolodges are fixed facilities that can be monitored at appropriate intervals.

Local vendors are another major component of the ecotourism equation. They are the chief suppliers of goods and services used at the destination. Examples of local vendors include boat outfitters, tour guides, handicraft sellers, and local eateries and restaurants. Local people are frequently the vendors and their ability to deliver quality services determines if they can take part in the ecotourism project. This ultimately determines how well ecotourism is delivering local benefits. A lack of appropriate training for local communities often hinders their ability to take part (Epler Wood, 1998). In ecotourism evaluation of community involvement identifying and measuring 'socioeconomic indicators' is difficult and is rarely undertaken by sustainable tourism programmes.

Quantifying Sustainability

Finding methods to create fair green labels based on quantifiable indicators was the challenge of the 1990s. In the case of products such as light bulbs, it was quickly determined that product testing overseen by independent experts in environmental and technical fields would be the primary source of data. Tourism business professionals call tours and lodges 'products', but the products they sell cannot be tested like light bulbs.

Tourism's sustainability within the environment has been investigated. Consulting and Audit Canada summarized the risks from unsustainable tourism practices for the World Tourism Organization (Consulting and Audit Canada, 1996). This excellent paper produced the first working set of 'core indicators' for sustainable tourism. While providing a very useful set of principles, the authors also commented that tourism monitoring would be dependent on 'qualitative measures, because environmental and social indicators are not always quantifiable'.

In the UNEP publication, *Environmental Codes of Conduct for Tourism* (UNEP, 1995), the problem of quantifying sustainability in the field of tourism is evident from the results. The authors of this valuable compilation of tourism codes of conduct attempted to summarize the primary components of sustainable tourism guidelines and are left with a list of immeasurable items, such as 'environmental commitment, recognizing responsibility, taking the environment into account, and cooperation with other sectors' (UNEP, 1995). The more recent UNEP publication, *Ecolabels in the Tourism Industry* (UNEP, 1998), offers much more guidance to organizations seeking to establish ecolabel programmes. The author points out that the number and stringency of the criteria clearly gives the signal for which types of businesses should participate. While all 28 programmes surveyed reviewed water, waste water, solid waste, energy and purchasing criteria, the core principles of ecotourism articulated in The International Ecotourism Society's *Ecotourism Guidelines for Nature Tour Operators* (The International Ecotourism Society, 1993) and in the upcoming *Ecolodge Guidelines* (Mehta and Baez, 2001) often far exceed these basic standards.

Until very recently, environmental commitment was the message for sustainability within the mainstream tourism industry. This led to initiatives such as the original Green Globe programme, which was established in 1994 by the World Travel and Tourism Council. This programme initially accepted a pledge of commitment, but made no attempt to quantify or undertake independent assessments of their participants before offering a green seal. The original Green Globe is now called a membership programme, and it has 500 members in 90 countries (Green Seal, 1998) making it the largest ecolabelling programme for tourism in the world. The Green Globe programme became an independent profit corporation in 1999. It is now implementing its new industry certification process, which is being carried out with Sociète General Surveillance (SGS), the world's leading verification/auditing agency. This programme helps tourism companies to set standards that are possible to measure and verify through the implementation of internal environmental management systems, using the ISO 14000 model as its terms of reference. As of November 1998, Green Globe industry certification had only been tested in Negril, Jamaica, with support from the US Agency for International Development. Four hotels were certified, 13 statements of intent were issued, and over 30 hotels registered for certification (Hagler Bailly, 1999). In spite of its short implementation history and low participation numbers, the Green Globe corporation sought endorsement as the global scheme for tourism certification at the UN Commission on Sustainable Development (UNCSD) Conference in New York City in April 1999. While this proposal was not accepted, many participants agreed that a worldwide standard on tourism labelling was needed to address mounting consumer confusion. (Note that as of April 2000, Green Globe had certified 18 hotels worldwide (M. Cain, personal communication, 2000).)

Special local criteria for certifying ecotourism

At the 1999 UNCSD, author Epler Wood participated in crafting the NGO dialogue speech for Industry Initiatives in Sustainable Tourism.

The statement, read on the floor of the UN suggested that the Commission on Sustainable Development (CSD) should promote an international process to agree and finalize sets of indicators for sustainable tourism, taking into account regional considerations, the needs of local stakeholders, the scale of tourism development, and environmental and socio-cultural considerations.

The ecotourism world would have much to gain from this procedure. The International Ecotourism Society works with its 1700 members in 70 countries to make ecotourism a sustainable development tool. Many member businesses are small and locally based with many regional concerns to consider. In part, this is because they have relied on local participation and local stakeholder involvement in the development of their businesses. It is difficult to imagine how an international certification programme could appropriately set standards for the ecotourism world, given the number of local concerns. For example, TIES members routinely work with local communities who often retain indigenous lifestyles and want to conserve their traditional land management practices. The Maasai in Kenya, the Aborigines in Australia, and the Amazonian peoples of the rain forest are all stakeholders in the development of ecotourism. Are international certification systems really capable of incorporating these sensitive socio-cultural concerns? To study this point, a comparison chart (Table 9.3) was formulated to look at the standards set by the Costa Rica Tourism Institute Certification Programme for Socioeconomic Impacts (1997) versus the work done by Green Globe (1998) on Social and Cultural Development.

The emphasis in the Costa Rican programme on the support of local business, training, cultural development, health, and local infrastructure are all distinct from the more general points reviewed in the Green Globe standards. This is not surprising because Costa Rica, as a nation, has many concerns about supporting and developing local business. These standards were evolved via a local stakeholder programme that clearly reflects the concerns of Costa Ricans. It is much more likely that a national certification system will include local concerns of this nature, and will be more sensitive to the issues of local people. The survey done by UNEP (1998) also shows that national schemes have a higher number of demands and criteria than international schemes.

In general, it is likely that ecotourism certification programmes will include more criteria regarding socio-cultural impacts than mainstream tourism. Ecotourism companies often make far-reaching efforts to develop programmes that are of genuine benefit to local people because of their commitment to the principles of ecotourism and sustainable development (Christ, 1998; Drumm, 1998; Sproule, 1998). However, minimizing socio-cultural impacts often does not result in cost-savings for tourism companies. Experts (W. Meade, personal communication, 2000) working on industry certification programmes confirm that if

Table 9.3. Comparing tourism ecolabel criteria (Costa Rica Tourism Institute, 1997; Green Globe, 1998).

Costa Rica certification: socioeconomic impacts, 1997	Green Globe/Green Seal standard: social and cultural development, 1998
Employment	1. The organization shall have a policy in relation to the advantageous employment of persons living in nearby communities in both construction and operation activities
1. The business should use personnel from the region for more than 60% of its employees	
2. The business shall have the training necessary to enable local people to occupy positions in the hotel	2. The organization shall advise and direct persons living in nearby communities seeking employment of opportunities for training, career planning and job placement opportunities
3. The business shall use persons from the community and from the home country for positions at the level of administration and management	
Local products	3. Whenever practicable and ethical the organization shall buy products and services through local businesses and artisans
4. The business contributes to the support of human resources for work that is complementary to tourism	
5. The business uses promotion material to inform clients of recreational activities available in the community	
6. The business promotes the use of locally produced goods	
7. The business sells local handicrafts and other goods made locally	
8. The hotel uses locally produced handicrafts in the rooms	
9. The materials and equipment used in the hotel are produced locally or with important components made nationally	

Local issues

10. The hotel has special rates to promote domestic tourism
11. The business has policies and relationships, either commercial or of support, that help local business
12. The business helps with local transportation for the community
13. The business contributes to cultural development (seven criteria)
14. The business contributes to health programmes (three criteria)
15. The business contributes to local infrastructure and security programmes (seven criteria)

Visitor information

4. The organization shall participate in local and regional activities to clean up the environment and/or support regional or local organizations that are working on environmental and social problems
5. The organization shall be familiar with the management policy of protected natural areas in its region of operation, comply with this policy and explain it to its customers
6. The organization shall take action to ensure that prostitution and drug dealing does not take place on its premises
7. The organization shall endeavour to inform its customers of sensitive local customs and ways of life, important environmental issues, and how best to contribute to the regional economy

certification does not result in greater profitability for mainstream travel corporations, they are unlikely to subscribe.

> After being in the middle of environmental labelling research for years, I have come to the conclusion that for destination managers, environmental brands, logos, and awards are only useful if they directly contribute to cost reduction, have marketing value and increase sales, or improve competitiveness.
>
> (Mihalič, 1998).

In an independent assessment on corporate accountability for UNCSD by the NGO Taskforce on Business and Industry (Barber, 1997), it was pointed out 'clean production is a concept sometimes reduced to mean only eco-efficiency. However, efficiency is just one aspect of clean production.' In the world of ecotourism, eco-efficiency standards play only a limited role in the guidelines and standards outlined in ecotourism documents published by The International Ecotourism Society and organizations such as the Ecotourism Association of Australia.

Ecotourism also stresses the importance of supporting the conservation of natural resources, particularly the industry's role in building consumer and corporate support for the protection of natural areas. Green Globe businesses are asked to be familiar with the management policy of protected areas, comply with the policy, and explain it to its customers (Table 9.3). In the Costa Rican system, a whole chapter is devoted to how ecotourism can support natural areas. Ecotourism businesses are asked to encourage their clients to visit protected areas, maintain detailed information on natural areas of interest to clients, follow the stipulated management requirements of protected areas and inform their clients about these requirements, maintain and manage their own natural reserves, and support the maintenance of local protected areas.

The support for parks and natural resources is vital to all industry, but it is strictly an indirect benefit for most tourism businesses, which cannot be easily tied to the bottom line. It is easy to take photos of beautiful natural environments for marketing purposes without paying for the privilege. In the case of ecotourism, the connection is more direct. Market research shows that ecotourists are expecting to visit wild and scenic areas as their primary objective. The protection of natural areas is therefore directly beneficial to the ecotourism industry. This is not to argue that all tourism businesses are not ultimately dependent on a clean and healthy environment. The point is that ecotourism must deliver protected environments including forests, birds, whales and all manner of wild resources, or they are not delivering what they have promised to their customers.

Again, for the nation of Costa Rica, it makes sense to ask small-scale hotels to support parks. Setting an ecotourism standard for Costa Rica or other developing countries is likely to be quite different from standards in developed countries like the United States. The likely contrast in objectives for a developing country versus a developed country underlines the importance of creating standards and certification programmes for ecotourism that suit the destination and its stakeholders.

Monitoring Sustainability

Recent work on the part of Colorado State University and The International Ecotourism Society shows that quantifying the sustainability of ecotourism at the destination level is difficult but may be achievable. These two significant tests of methodology and technique provide important lessons that should be applied in the future.

Evaluating Ecotourism in Amazonas, Brazil

Dr George N. Wallace and Susan M. Pierce of Colorado State University set out to study the sustainability of ecotourism projects in the rainforests of Brazil based on a set of principles they created for sustainability associated with measurable indicators (Wallace and Pierce, 1996). Surveys were used to determine how well the tourism project met each indicator. Three researchers trained in interview techniques went into the field and surveys were read to each subject.

This project features a very thorough sampling strategy to determine sustainability. The aim was to survey all the tourists at each site (80 surveyed), all the employees at each site (89 surveyed), and approximately 10% of the local inhabitants (75 surveyed), including known opinion leaders, those living in a village and those living in a more dispersed pattern. A four-point scaling system was used and a simple matrix system summarized the aggregate performance of the Amazon lodges and tour boats sampled. A workshop was held after the project was completed and the aggregate results were presented. The individual results of the surveyed businesses were also given to each business. Sampling took place in one season which, according to the authors of this chapter, led to some problems with the number of surveys completed.

A research institution undertook this project and therefore the researchers had complete freedom to establish their own principles and their own indicators for quantification. Wallace and Pierce comment that indicators should be selected using the Delphi approach, a research technique that allows a consensus to be reached between local stakeholders before selecting the significant indicators. A consensus process might best be applied to the selection of core principles as well. These principles function as the gateway to achieving sustainability in the monitoring programme and would need to be carefully honed, with stakeholders, before being applied on a broader scale.

The International Ecotourism Society's Green Evaluations

In 1993 The International Ecotourism Society published a set of international guidelines, *Ecotourism Guidelines for Nature Tour Operators* (The International Ecotourism Society, 1993). Stakeholders were surveyed to develop these guidelines. To accomplish this, three focus group meetings (which included industry, academia and conservation NGOs) helped to draft and review the final guidelines. The resulting 20-page booklet is distributed by TIES in Spanish and English worldwide, with over 5000 now in circulation.

The *Green Evaluations* programme was launched in 1995 to investigate how well tour operators were meeting the guidelines published in the 1993 booklet. TIES teamed up with the Ecuadorean Ecotourism Association to do a pilot evaluation of tour operators in Ecuador. The Ecuadorean-based NGO programme, CARE-SUBIR, gave partial funding. Clemson University was hired to formulate the surveys, and act as an independent monitoring body to collect and analyse the survey data. Only consumers were surveyed. One in five consumers on each trip was randomly selected by the participating tour operators (30), given surveys to fill out during their tours, instructed to seal their completed questionnaires in return envelopes, and encouraged to deliver their envelopes to their guide in Ecuador or directly in the mail to Clemson University. Problems with sampling arose with this project also, as tour operators did not follow these procedures uniformly, and an inadequate number of surveys were returned. The project was extended to run for a full 15 months to improve the response rate. This did help to collect enough data for an aggregate study (608 completed questionnaires), but still left many individual companies without an adequate number of responses for statistically valid results (Norman *et al.*, 1996).

At a conference in Quito, Ecuador, in March 1997, the aggregate results of Green Evaluations were presented and private reports were given to each participating tour operator with a certificate of participation. The Ecuadorean Ecotourism Association, the Ecuadorean Ministry of Tourism, and several Ecuadorean universities expressed interest in another round of evaluations. Researchers and industry members participating in the event agreed that more surveying would need to be done by individuals trained in survey techniques to ensure quality control. Using consumers as the only evaluators was also judged to be inadequate. Quito conference participants agreed that surveys of the industry, consumer surveys, and exit surveys of consumers by trained students would all be needed. By triangulating the results from three sources more accurate, reliable results would be achieved.

Conclusion

The nature tourism industry has a good reason to support a valid ecotourism label. First and foremost they need to protect themselves from false ecolabelling, and distinguish themselves as businesses that protect the environment. Governments of nations where ecotourism is a significant source of revenue, both foreign and domestic, also need a credible ecotourism label, as Australia and Costa Rica have amply demonstrated. International NGOs and development agencies also need a viable ecotourism label. Without proper certification programmes, they are inhibited from funding and implementing ecotourism as a sustainable development strategy.

A more systematic international system for ecotourism certification has not been reached because:

- Ecotourism relies on the protection of local natural resources and delivering benefits to local people. Local certification systems are more likely to be sensitive to local issues and genuinely involve local stakeholders in the development and implementation process thereby creating a more meaningful product.
- Only recently have there been international forums such as the UNCSD Dialogue Session on Sustainable Tourism (April 1999) on setting sustainability standards for the tourism industry at large. It will take time to show that ecotourism merits a separate certification approach from mainstream tourism, with different indicators. The reasons for a separate approach are amply demonstrated in this chapter, but are far from having worldwide approval.
- Ancillary players and not the tourism industry largely drive demand for ecotourism certification programmes. This has led to fragmentation. No unified leadership from industry has emerged.
- There is little research that credibly demonstrates that there is a market demand for certified ecotourism companies. This further undermines industry support for certification programmes.
- The ecotour industry brands and markets its services in developed regions that are generally not where the product is actually delivered. Product delivery, which is often in developing countries, is not usually under the direct supervision of the marketing enterprises. The marketing enterprises work with a wide variety of contractees who deliver their services around the world. The marketing entities see little to gain from being involved in certification,

due to the number of contractees they would have to involve in the process, not to mention the likely cost of checking on these programmes. They therefore suggest that their inbound colleagues should take all responsibility.

- Local companies in developing countries are much smaller than the marketing enterprises that represent them. Ecolodges and inbound ecotour companies rarely have the resources to pay for ecotourism certification, nor the human resources to undertake environmental management planning of any kind, especially if they are in developing countries.

- Local vendors deserve attention as full stakeholders in an eco-tourism certification process. These vendors are often from rural and indigenous communities and would need to be fully supported if they are to take part in the design process. And they would need on-going training to help them to maintain the quality control standards that would be required by any certification programme. At present such training for local communities is scarce and often inappropriately designed.

- Certification that is strictly market-based would only favour the largest companies and leave out legitimate stakeholders. Designing any other type of system will require significant subsidies that have generally been unavailable worldwide.

Many of these impediments are overlooked as new entities seek to enter the certification business. It can be frustrating to discuss the difficulties, because a number of private companies – such as Green Globe – are seeking to sell certification as part of a consulting service. They will argue that ecotourism certification can be market based (G. Lippman, personal communication, 1999). Given the above analysis, we believe it is fair to conclude that any ecotourism certification programme will need significant subsidies to fairly distribute the benefits of the programme to local players.

With these parameters fully in mind, it will be up to the international community to begin to support, and actively seek, ways to unify local ecotourism certification programmes via international agreements. It is recommended that:

- Ecotourism certification programmes should be developed locally via stakeholder processes that fully involve local communities. Guidelines need to be developed that are internationally recognized on the required steps for successful certification in order to prevent the possibility of graft and corruption, or the profit motive from overtaking the mission of the programme at a local level (Table 9.4 provides a draft set of criteria).

- International efforts to certify local ecotourism certification programmes need to be developed via an international stakeholder

Table 9.4.   Guidelines for successful ecotourism certification (Epler Wood, 1998).

1. Indicators for sustainability must be arrived at by research into appropriate parameters, based on current best practice
2. Indicators for sustainability must be reviewed and approved via a stakeholder process
3. Indicators for sustainability must be arrived at for each segment of the industry, e.g. hotels, tour operators, transportation systems, etc.
4. Indicators for sustainability will vary according to the region and must be arrived at via local stakeholder participation and research
5. Certification programmes require independent verification procedures that are not directly associated with the entity that is being paid to certify. University involvement is ideal for this process
6. Certification programmes, particularly for the small ecotourism business sector, are unlikely to pay for themselves through fees, and will need national, regional or international subsidization
7. Certification programmes can be given to the operating entity, but should specify the products or locations that fulfil relevant criteria as certified
8. Certification should be ground tested before full-fledged implementation to ensure all systems are properly in line, due to the difficulty of verifying appropriate performance standards without advance testing

process that is led by a consortium of international NGOs, industry, and UN representatives. UNCSD or WTO sponsored events could be international forums for this process.
- International funding to study and support the progress on this issue, hold international meetings, develop indicators, and provide support to local initiatives is urgently needed to prevent further fragmentation and more consumer confusion.

Based on active participation in stakeholder meetings worldwide, and the extensive research presented in this paper, the authors recommend the guidelines shown in Table 9.4 for ecotourism certification. The need to develop an evaluatory framework for future ecotourism certification programmes is fully in line with the UNCSD Task Force on Business and Industry goals that seek to 'identify the elements and conditions necessary for voluntary initiatives to make effective contributions to sustainable development, and report progress towards greater responsibility and accountability of industry and business' (TOBI, 1999). The special factors facing the tourism industry are only beginning to be understood in this process. Ecotourism is an even more specialized case. As the ecotourism industry grows and evolves, an international agreement on certification will prevent consumer confusion and allow for effective monitoring of local efforts.

Acknowledgements

Special thanks for the review of this document by The International Ecotourism Society board of directors and advisers, especially Pam Wight and Hitesh Mehta for their insightful comments.

References

Barber, J. (1997) *Minding Our Business: the Role of Corporate Accountability in Sustainable Development*. Integrative Strategies Forum NGO Taskforce on Business and Industry, Washington, DC.

Beacher, A. and Blake, B. (1998) *Reflections on 'Green Ratings'* (El Planeta Platica August, online at Planeta.com)

Bureau of Tourism Research – Australia (1998) *Profiles and Motivations of Nature-based Tourists visiting Australia*, Occasional Paper No. 25. Bureau of Tourism Research, Canberra.

Christ, C. (1998) Taking ecotourism to the new step. In: *Ecotourism: a Guide for Planners and Managers*, Vol. 2. The International Ecotourism Society, North Bennington, Vermont, pp. 183–195.

Consulting and Audit Canada (1996) *What Tourism Managers Need to Know*, Project 570–0872. World Tourism Organization, Madrid.

Costa Rica Tourism Institute (Instituto Costarricense de Turismo) (1997) *Certification for Sustainable Tourism*. Costa Rica Tourism Institute, Costa Rica.

Crossley, J. and Lee, B. (1994) *Ecotourists and Mass Tourists: a Difference in 'Benefits Sought'*. Proceedings of the Travel and Tourism Research Association Conference, Bal Harbour, Florida.

Drumm, A. (1998) New Approaches to Community-based Ecotourism Management. In: *Ecotourism: a Guide for Planners and Managers*, vol. 2, in press. The Ecotourism Society, North Bennington, Vermont, pp. 197–213.

Eagles, P.F.J. (1992) The travel motivations of Canadian ecotourists. *Journal of Travel Research* 31(2), 3–7.

Epler Wood, M. (1998) *Meeting the Global Challenge of Community Participation in Ecotourism: Case Studies and Lessons from Ecuador*, América Verde Working Paper No. 2. Latin America and Caribbean Division, USAID and The Nature Conservancy, Arlington, Virginia.

Gnoth, J. (1998) [Communication via the TRINET internet mail listserve service]

Green Globe (1998) *Green Globe Standard*. Green Globe, London.

Green Seal (1998) *Green Seal Environmental Standard for Lodging Properties: Draft for Public Comment*. Green Seal, Washington, DC.

Hagler Bailly (1999) *Assessment of Voluntary Environmental Rating and Certification Programs: Environmental Audits for Sustainable Tourism*. Hagler Bailly (consultants), Arlington, Virginia.

Hawkins, D., Epler Wood, M. and Bittman, S. (1995) *The Ecolodge Sourcebook for Planners and Developers*. The International Ecotourism Society, North Bennington, Vermont, USA.

Hjalager, A. (1999) Consumerism and Sustainable Tourism. *Journal of Travel and Tourism Marketing* 8 (3), pp. 1–20.

The International Ecotourism Society (TES) (1991) *TIES Board of Directors Meeting Minutes*, Miami, Florida.

The International Ecotourism Society (TES) (1993) *Ecotourism Guidelines for Nature Tour Operators.* The International Ecotourism Society, North Bennington, Vermont.

Lindberg, K., Furze, B., Staff, M. and Black, R. (1998) *Ecotourism in the Asia-Pacific Region: Issues and Outlook.* Forestry Policy and Planning Division, Rome Regional Office for Asia and the Pacific, Bangkok and United States Department of Agriculture, Forest Service, with The International Ecotourism Society, North Bennington, Vermont.

Mehta, H. and Baez, A. (2001) *Ecolodge Guidelines.* The International Ecotourism Society, North Bennington, Vermont.

Mihalič, T. (1998) [Communication via the TRINET internet mail listserve service] 20 November 1998.

Norman, W.C., Frauman, E., Toepper, L. and Sirakaya, E. (1996) *Green Evaluation Program and Compliance of Nature Tour Operators.* The International Ecotourism Society, North Bennington, Vermont.

Sproule, K. (1998) Guidelines for community-based ecotourism programs: lessons from Indonesia? In: *Ecotourism: a Guide for Planners and Managers*, vol. 2, The International Ecotourism Society, North Bennington, Vermont, pp. 215–236.

TOBI (1999) *The Multistakeholder Review of Voluntary Initiatives* (brochure). NGO Taskforce on Business and Industry, Washington, DC.

Travel Industry Association of America (TIAA) (1994) *Adventure Travel: Profile of a Growing Market*, conducted by US Travel Data Center, Washington, DC.

Travel Industry Association of America (TIAA) (1999) *Internet Usage By Travellers Continues Rapid Growth* (online at WebTravelNews.com).

United Nations Environment Programme (UNEP) (1995) *Environmental Codes of Conduct for Tourism*, Industry and Environment Technical Report No. 29. UNEP, Paris.

United Nations Environment Programme (UNEP) (1998) *Ecolabels in the Tourism Industry*, Industry and Environment Technical Report No. 29. UNEP, Paris.

Wallace, G.N. and Pierce, S. (1996) An evaluation of ecotourism in Amazonas, Brazil. *Annals of Tourism Research* 23, 843–874.

Wight, P. (2001) Ecotourists: not a homogeneous market segment. In: Weaver, D.B. (ed.) *Encyclopedia of Ecotourism*. CAB International, Wallingford, UK.

Chapter 10

Environmental Management Tools in Canada: Ecolabelling and Best Practice Benchmarking
PAMELA A. WIGHT

Tourism Lags in Applying Environmental Management Tools

The search for innovation and for cost-effective ways to improve industry's environmental performance has led to the development of a wide array of environmental management (EM) tools. These tools can be used internally by companies to better design and manage their operations, as well as to monitor their results, or they can be used by governments and others to lead industry towards environmental improvement. Although environmental impact assessment (EIA) was one of the first specific environmental management tools, it has limitations, and there is now a large 'environmental management system' tool box available. This allows companies to:

- evaluate and improve their processes and operations (e.g. environmental audits, safety audits);
- design environmentally sound products (e.g. life cycle assessments, risk assessments);
- communicate with all their stakeholders (e.g. mission statements, environmental reporting, environmental purchasing/procurement, ecolabelling);
- monitor their progress and compare it with that of other companies (e.g. benchmarking, full-cost accounting, performance indicators).

EM tools are structured or systematic instruments for improving decision-making or information management, or for effecting changes in the behaviour of others, with the overall aim of improving the environmental performance of industry. They can be used by companies or by government (UNEP, 1995a). Table 10.1 shows examples of various types of EM tools. It should be noted that these EM tools cannot be rigidly classified, since there are overlaps between many of them, most are still evolving, and some terms are used differently in different parts of the world. However, the table does serve to demonstrate analytical differences, and the fact that ecolabels and benchmarking are but two of a range of EM tools.

Ecolabelling in Canada

Tourism lags behind other industries in using these EM tools. However, there has been a strong move to ecolabelling in tourism. Despite this move, there is no consistent approach to ecolabelling in Canada, nor, in fact, for the whole of North America. This is somewhat ironic, since one of the first tourism organizations, globally, to examine environmental practices and to inculcate environmental improvements in their organizational culture, was Canadian Pacific Hotels and Resorts (CPH&R) in the late 1980s. This high-quality hotel chain developed its own *Green Partnership Guide*, a systematic manual to guide

Table 10.1. Environmental management tools (including ecolabelling and benchmarking).

Function of environmental management tools	Examples of environmental management tools
Analysis and evaluation	Corporate environmental benchmarking
	Cost–benefit analysis
	Environmental auditing, for liabilities, management, activities (review, surveillance, survey, appraisal or evaluation)
	Environmental impact assessment
	Full cost accounting
	Initial environmental assessment
	Life cycle assessment
	Risk assessment
	Technology assessment
	Sustainable development indicators
Action	Ecolabelling (and communication)
	Environmental management system
	Environmental policy
	Total quality environmental management
	Economic instruments
	Voluntary agreements
	Multi-stakeholder partnerships
Communications	Corporate environmental reporting
	Environmental procurement (and action)
	Mission statement

environmental and social action at the level of each hotel, and for each department (Troyer, 1992). This guide was used by the well-known International Hotels Environmental Initiative in developing their first hotels environmental manual. CPH&R has a corporate environmental department, and has environmental committees at each property. CPH&R also went on, in Phase 2 of its environmental programme in the 1990s, to develop relationships at the local level with ecotourism operators who must meet a set of seven 'ecofriendly criteria'. It was one of the earliest hotel chains to recognize the fact that customers are actually not primarily motivated by the accommodation, but by the surrounding environment (whether urban, natural or cultural).

Canada's Code of Ethics and Guidelines for Sustainable Tourism

In 1990, the Tourism Industry Association of Canada (TIAC) joined with the National Round Table on the Environment and the Economy to initiate a dialogue on 'Sustainable Tourism'. This resulted in a Code of Ethics and Guidelines for Sustainable Tourism (TIAC, 1992) which were directed at travellers, but more particularly at industry and segments of the industry, ministries and tourism associations. They were intended for voluntary adoption. Unlike many codes that developed in the 1990s, a unique feature of the document is that it includes all of the aspects outlined in Table 10.2.

These guidelines are still very relevant today, but have not been as widely disseminated by industry sectors as had been hoped. What has

Table 10.2. Unique characteristics of Canada's Code of Ethics and Guidelines for Sustainable Tourism.

Codes for both tourists and for industry

Specific guidelines to expand the codes, both at an overall industry level, and in detail for five industry subsectors: accommodation, foodservices, tour operators, ministries and tourism industry associations

Publication in both English and French

Guidelines related to the natural environment, and also to social and cultural perspectives

A range for scales, from local to global

Guidelines on a comprehensive range of topics for each tourism subsector, including:

1. Policy, planning and decision-making	7. Environmental protection
2. Guests/the tourism experience	8. Marketing
3. The host community	9. Research and education
4. Development	10. Public awareness
5. Natural, cultural and historic resources	11. Industry cooperation
6. Conservation of natural resources	12. The global village

happened instead, is a number of fragmented efforts at the subsector or destination level, focusing on developing codes or labels or environmental awareness. Examples are the code of conduct for whale-watching which developed among operators in British Columbia; a similar code among East Coast operators and those in the Gulf of St Lawrence. Similarly, Société Duvetnor instigated a project in conjunction with other ecotourism organizations in Québec: Le Québec Maritime and the Bas-Saint-Laurent Tourism Association. The project is a quality label, for tourism business in the region, with categories which relate to: the environment, the guest, the business, the community and protected areas. At the city level, Toronto has a Green Tourism Association, a non-profit organization committed to establishing an economically sustainable green tourism industry in Toronto. Also, Vancouver has its Oceans Blue Foundation, which promotes environmentally responsible tourism practices through cooperation among communities, governments, environmentalists and the tourism industry in port cities. Some other specific initiatives are described below.

Saskatchewan ecolabelling: Horizons Quality Seal

One early Canadian initiative with an ecolabelling component was in the Province of Saskatchewan. By 1994, Saskatchewan had guidelines for ecotourism operators in the Manitou Sand Hills area. These guidelines formed part of a Land Use Plan for an area of about 110,000 acres of crown land, to combine resource, visitor, and impact management, through operator guidelines. The guidelines were developed by a mixed group representing government, farmers, and local agencies, who consulted with affected parties during the process. The operators were required to be accredited by the Ecotourism Society of Saskatchewan (ESS), which reviews ecotourism operations to ensure responsible practices and conduct. The guidelines covered: code of ethics, educational responsibility, environmental impact, measures to protect flora and fauna, cultural sensitivity and other considerations.

One of the principles of ecotourism in Saskatchewan is that 'the purchase of an ecotourism package will include a contribution to the conservation of habitats and species in the areas to be visited'. Operators were required to turn a portion of revenues over to the environment. Ecotourism customers visiting the Sand Hills have been contributing Can$10 each to a local environmental impact assessment and restoration fund. These funds are collected by operators and deposited in a financial institution. The fund is administered by a Standing Committee of area residents and advisers.

After the success of the programme in the Manitou area, the ESS began working on a province-wide accreditation programme to assist operators in developing superior experiences and a high standard of excellence for nature tourists. The ESS has now developed 'Horizons', an initiative of nature-based attractions, tourism businesses, conservation organizations and agencies involved in economic development and tourism. It has been developed in response to the need to promote genuine ecotourism operations throughout Saskatchewan, and it represents a seal of quality, or ecolabel. Accreditation relates to standards (Table 10.3), but criteria have been designed differently for: attractions, accommodation and guided tours.

There is a five-step application process. It includes completion of an application document, followed by a visit from a team of ESS members who will help complete a more thorough and detailed confidential report. The process takes several weeks. Saskatchewan feels that ecotourism accreditation provides an assurance that products and services will be delivered with a commitment to the environment and ecological processes, and a commitment to providing quality experiences. The system seeks to expand the business opportunities available to members, and to help conserve the natural resources upon which they depend. ESS accreditation goes beyond ecolabelling, and provides benefits to ecotourism businesses, their customers, the natural environment, and land managers charged with its protection and conservation. It also provides benefits to local communities, in terms of opportunities to monitor, regulate and participate in economic diversification and cultural enrichment.

Canadian Tourism Commission Product Clubs

The Canadian Tourism Commission (CTC) is the federal body responsible for tourism. They initiated the tourism Product Club programme

Table 10.3.   Ecotourism Society of Saskatchewan Accreditation.

Accreditation standards topics

1. Interpretation and education
2. Infrastructure, general management and programme activities
3. Aesthetic client environment
4. Environmentally friendly food and accommodation services
5. Local traditions and cultures
6. Client safety
7. Local economic participation
8. Monitoring and client feedback
9. Adherence to laws and policies
10. Peer review
11. Fees for cost recovery and conservation

in 1996. Product clubs are designed to foster partnering opportunities for small and medium-sized enterprises (SMEs). They may focus on a range of activities, from human resource development and training, to product packaging, to establishing accreditation for the industry. The main objectives are to:

- bring tourism SMEs together to enhance existing products or to create new products;
- encourage communication among small and medium-sized tourism businesses;
- work with them on industry development issues;
- encourage SMEs to coordinate their efforts to sustain a vibrant and profitable Canadian tourism industry.

Canadian Biosphere Reserves Association

Some of the current 24 product clubs have developed codes or standards, as a form of quality control. One is the Canadian Biosphere Reserves Association (BRA). The Canadian Biosphere Reserves have principles for developing tour packages in and adjacent to biosphere reserves. Principles relate to benefiting visitors, conservation, the economy and adjacent communities. All suppliers of nature-based tourism products are expected to adhere to these principles by following certain criteria (Table 10.4). Clients are asked to comment about adherence to both operators *and* the BRA.

The Conservation Lands of Ontario

Another product club, the Conservation Lands of Ontario (CLO), has strong environmental ethics in its operations. The CLO is a grouping of five Conservation Authorities. Conservation Authorities are charged with water management and environmental responsibilities. The CLO had a history of excellent cooperation, and in 1996, when the province cut their funding by 70%, they decided to work with the local private sector and communities to develop new tourism products and programmes to increase revenues for all. The activities focus on:

- developing near-urban outdoor conservation experiences;
- developing packages that focus on existing winners in the areas;
- making sites more accessible to visitors;
- sharing information on best practices by organizing ecotourism partnership forums.

CLO members range from outfitters, country inns and restaurants, to herb gardens, aboriginals, or a llama trek operation. Members exceed all applicable government environmental laws and regulations. In fact, a number of membership requests have been turned down where businesses were felt to be insufficiently environmentally friendly. CLO

Table 10.4. Biosphere Reserves Association tourism criteria.

Does the operation practise the 5-Rs (Respect, Re-use, Recover, Recycle, Reduce) in all aspects of the package?

Is promotional material free of guarantees of seeing specific species of wildlife?

Are promotional materials culturally sensitive and accurate?

Are visitors provided with pre-trip materials detailing the trip itinerary and providing background information about habitats, species and local cultures?

Do wildlife viewing activities avoid repeated or sustained disturbance?

Does your operation avoid altering the behaviour patterns of wildlife species?

Does the activity minimize impact on sensitive natural areas?

Does the operator ensure that culturally sensitive sites are protected from visitor impact or inappropriate activity?

Has concurrence been obtained from affected communities about the nature and scope of the operation?

Does the programme inform the visitor about habitats, species and local human communities?

Does the programme include a recognition of the significance of the area visited for conservation?

Does the programme address relevant natural area management issues and possible solutions?

Are supplies purchased from within the local community whenever available and reasonable to do so?

Does the operator hire guides and other labour from the local community where available?

Does the operator give financial or measurable in-kind support to the local community?

Does the activity involve visitors in volunteer conservation activities?

Does the activity contribute financially to local conservation?

Does the operator keep a record of observations of visitor impacts and share it with resource managers?

Is the operator prepared to deal effectively with environmental emergencies caused by the tour operation?

Is there an understanding of the Limits of Acceptable Change for the area visited?

Are all necessary operating licences in place?

Are staff members readily available who are trained in First Aid?

Has the operator purchased liability insurance?

Does the operator apply the correct use of waiver forms?

---

interpreters impart important environmental messages to participants on all their tours, and these include an attitude of social responsibility towards the sustainable use of natural resources. Members of CLO agree to adopt an ecotourism code of practice (Table 10.5) when they become members, and sign a Tour Operators Agreement committing to sustainable tourism practices. Currently, 10% of membership fees are directed to worthy environmental projects; also, a percentage of sales

Table 10.5. Ecotourism Code for Conservation Lands of Ontario members.

Strengthen conservation efforts	Support CLO partners who have a
Respect other cultures' sensitivities	conservation ethic
Efficient in use of natural resources (water and energy conservation)	Network with others, particularly locally, about the code
Recycle	Use media to raise environmental
Employ tour guides who follow code	awareness
Use locally produced goods	Support ecotourism education/training
Never intentionally disturb wildlife or habitats	for guides and managers
Keep vehicles to designated roads and trails	Give clients appropriate educational materials and guidance
Keep rules and regulations on natural areas	Commit to best practice
	Maximize quality experiences for hosts and guests
	Ensure truth in advertising

goes to regional environmental projects. The CLO brand is now well recognized in Ontario, and represents a regional ecolabel.

Wilderness Spirit: a private sector brand, or ecolabel

Branding is a concept which consumer product marketers have used for some time, but is relatively new in tourism. A strong brand can clarify destination characteristics for tourists who might have little knowledge of it. Branding verbalizes and operationalizes core values and signals attributes and benefits to tourists. These core values may have strong symbolic value for the visitor. Tourism branding can also be developed among discrete operations sharing similar characteristics, where they offer themselves jointly and separately, through a distinctive brand name and shared values (e.g. Holiday Inn). The values may be exhibited by standards related to quality, activity or other similar elements, which indicate to the visitor that they might have confidence that the experience will be what is expected.

The first example of such branding (or ecolabelling) in a private sector partnership of tourism SMEs has just emerged in Canada. *Wilderness Spirit©* is a group of nature lodges that have agreed to cooperate to share in the benefits of group marketing, information sharing and problem solving. The lodge operators realized that success in the business comes not from a sales approach, but a marketing approach, where products are delivered that satisfy the clients' needs, wants and desires. The advantages of a 'brand' are that the client may be encouraged to try other brand operations, knowing that they match their expectations, since they fall within the ecolabel. Members agreed that quality standards will be the fundamental characteristic of the brand, and that environmental components will be important to their standards. However, this brand has quality standards that encompass many more aspects than environmental components (or ecolabels), including most aspects that will affect a guest and their experiences. This makes the ecolabel more representative of sustainability indicators. Major categories for *Wilderness Spirit* standards are summarized in Table 10.6. Travellers are invited to provide their comments about lodge adherence to the standards both to individual operators and to *Wilderness Spirit*, to strengthen and improve the brand.

Benchmarking in Canada

As mentioned earlier, ecolabelling is only one of many EM tools. There is a need for independent or credible bodies to back or monitor the ecolabels. Canada is a vast land, with many different situations, from ecosystem diversity to cultural diversity, from dense to sparse local populations, from tourism regions with a history of cooperation, to areas which are only recently being developed. To this point there has been no move to develop a national set of standards or labels in tourism. UNEP (1998) suggests that internationally recognized standards are required for ecolabels, but that ecolabels need to be adapted to the local situation. Some question whether Canada can be viewed as a 'local situation', due to its extreme size and diversity (indeed, for a programme as subsector specific as whale-watching, there are differences in the BC, the St Lawrence River, and the Maritimes guidelines, due to the differences in the types of whales and their environmental context [P. Corbeil, personal communications, 2000). Instead, Canada has focused on another EM tool, that of benchmarking best practices for tourism SMEs (see Table 10.1).

Although the *demand side* for nature, culture and adventure has been fairly well established, the *supply side* of the industry has been less well known. Canada's tourism SMEs are characterized by challenges of remoteness, geography, lack of economies of scale and frequently by extreme seasonality. Most operators are struggling to provide the type of overall product demanded by internationally

Table 10.6. Categories for Wilderness Spirit brand standards.

Nature-based and other experiences	Service standards
Accommodation	Safety
Facilities	Environmental sensitivity
Services	Community sensitivity
Equipment	Codes and guidelines
Communal facilities and services	Product quality cycle

experienced and knowledgeable travellers. They need to be conversant with a number of requirements, including: environmentally and culturally sensitive operations, quality customer service, effective marketing, provision of an appropriate menu of activities, quality interpretation, value for money, experience orientation and product quality consistency, all conveniently packaged, and effected within the context of effective business management.

SMEs have exceptional problems in keeping abreast of numerous issues: from trends to factors for success; from marketing to operational efficiencies; from sustainability issues to business practices. Their constraints are numerous, not the least of which is *time* to research and investigate all those aspects. In addition, they constitute a very fragmented sector, which is not well developed in terms of linkages and internal communication, nor in terms of outside partnerships, such as with the travel trade. Over the last few years the Canadian Tourism Commission (CTC) has worked with *industry-led* research priorities. One of the major strategies recommended for implementation, was the preparation of a Best Business Practices Catalogue, a leading edge concept in tourism.

Pam Wight & Associates (1999) was commissioned to provide a results-oriented tool, to effectively deliver key strategies and actions which demonstrably contribute to successful practice, and which are practical, innovative and relevant to ecotourism and adventure travel. The document is a *Catalogue of Exemplary Practices in Adventure Travel and Ecotourism*. This is essentially a best practices benchmarking (BPB) study. As such, it incorporates environmental components, but goes beyond environment to incorporate a range of practices required for sustainability.

Ecolabelling and Benchmarking

Dooley and Kirkpatrick (1993) state that

> Ecolabel is a term used to describe an officially sanctioned scheme in which a product may be awarded an ecological label on the basis of its 'acceptable' level of environmental impact. The acceptable level of environmental impact may be determined by consideration of a single environmental hurdle which is deemed to be particularly important, or after undertaking an assessment of its overall environmental impacts.

Thus the focus of ecolabels is topically, the environment. Benchmarking via the Canadian Catalogue, by contrast, covers a range of aspects of an operation, including environmental, social and economic areas. It is possible to be selective about the benchmarking process (some benchmarking studies have *not* included environmental matters.

By the same token, corporate environmental benchmarking covers *only* the environmental arena). The relationship between environmental benchmarking and benchmarking, may resemble the relationship between ecolabelling and overall accreditation (which should encompass environmental, social and economic topics). In Fig. 10.1 the shaded areas conceptualize the topic areas covered by benchmarking and by ecolabelling.

The idea of benchmarking in tourism is a relatively new one. There have been a number of global examples of regional, provincial/state or national tourism bodies evaluating tourism operations, or collating materials related to success stories, which describe select successful practices. However, these studies have been limited in their range of topics, or in the rigour of their approach, or both. Some of the weaknesses of such tourism case studies are that:

- self-assessment manuals provide direction, but are static, and do not go 'outside the box' to incorporate creative best practices
- case studies tend to describe the performance of one operation (which may have weak performance in some operational areas, as well as strengths, but case studies rarely examine the weaknesses).

What sets the Canadian benchmarking study apart from other such initiatives, is that it:

- evaluated all core competency areas in the tourism operation, not only environmental;
- included more than the 'business' aspects of an operation, and went beyond a specialized topic (such as energy);
- used a rigorous national process for generating potential best practice operators;
- obtained a range of expert input for framing effective criteria for evaluation;

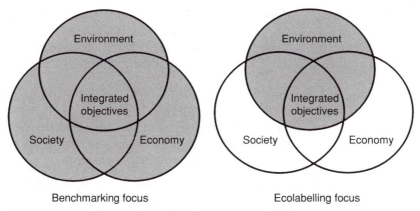

Benchmarking focus   Ecolabelling focus

Fig. 10.1. Areas of focus of benchmarking and ecolabelling.

- developed an objective process for evaluating all submissions related to performance;
- provided a document with a focus on the practices (not operators/ companies) which are treated systematically rather than selectively.

Essentially, the Catalogue is the first comprehensive best practice benchmarking study in the tourism sector. It is understood that the CTC intends to repeat this benchmarking process, at which time, monitoring activities may be able to take place. A follow-up document would be useful for identifying progress in this sector, and tracking increased effectiveness.

What are benchmarks and benchmarking?

There is some confusion around the terminology of benchmarks and benchmarking. The American Productivity and Quality Center (APQC, 1999) says benchmarking is 'the process of identifying, learning, and adapting outstanding practices and processes from any organization, anywhere in the world, to help an organization improve its performance'. Similarly,

> benchmarking is an important component of total quality environmental management . . . Benchmarking is a process of comparing and measuring an organization's business processes against best-in-class operations to inspire improvement in the organization's performance. The insights gained from benchmarking provide organizations with a foundation for building operational plans to meet and surpass industry best practices and promote an overall awareness of environmental improvement opportunities.
>
> (Global Environmental Management Initiative, 1994)

- *Benchmarking gathers the knowledge* about the know-how, the judgements, enabling factors, and such tacit knowledge that facts and explicit knowledge often miss (APQC, 1999). Benchmarking is always carried out with the goal of putting improvements into action.
- *Benchmarks measure performance* in terms of numbers, speed, distance, and so on. Benchmarking is action, through which one discovers the specific practices responsible for high quality performance, together with understanding how these practices work, and subsequent actions in applying these to one's operation.

It should be quite explicit that benchmarks are not the same as benchmarking. The essential difference is that benchmarks are facts, while benchmarking enables improvement to operational performance.

What is best practice?

There is no single set of best practices that works everywhere, every time. One single 'best practice' does not exist, because best is not best for everyone. Each tourism operation is somewhat different in geography, political situation, vision, culture, environment or technologies. The practices that are best for a company are those that are appropriate for the particular stage of development in which the firm finds itself. They will change as the company itself changes. 'Best practice' in this case is not meant to represent 'the one' practice to consider; it means those practices that have been shown to produce superior results.

Best practice benchmarking: what it can contribute to an operation

Best practice benchmarking (BPB) is a technique used by many companies in all sectors, globally, to assist them to become as good as, or better than successful operators, in the most important aspects of their operations. The size of the company does not matter, although often those implementing BPB are multinationals in non-tourism sectors. The main characteristic is that they recognize that profitability and development comes from a clear understanding of how their operation is doing, not just against its performance in the previous year, but against the best they can measure. A 1990 study into industrial productivity by the Massachusetts Institute of Technology concluded: 'a characteristic of all the best-practice American firms we observed, large or small, is an emphasis on competitive benchmarking: comparing the performance of their products and processes with those of world leaders in order to achieve improvement and to measure progress' (Department of Trade and Industry, 1999). Such firms do not view outstanding companies as competition, but as motivators.

Benchmarking goes beyond the current global moves to ecolabelling, certification and accreditation in the tourism industry. Some benefits of BPB in tourism are that it enables operations to:

- benefit from the discoveries and practices of others, so that they do not have to struggle to reinvent the wheel (and there is little need to invest time, research effort, cost, and so on, particularly when it may have already been done better or more cheaply or effectively);
- re-examine their current processes and operations, which often leads to improvement by that fact alone;
- accelerate change for the better, by using proven practices, demonstrating use, overcoming inertia and possible complacency and revealing gaps in operations;

- view totally different ideas 'outside the conventional mould' of the current operation. Some ideas may come from non-similar operations, as well as similar operations, and thus may present innovative perspectives or gaps in practice;
- make implementation more easy, and speedy, due to the involvement of the 'owners' of the process;
- better understand their markets and their competitors;
- develop a stronger reputation;
- gain faster awareness of important trends or innovations, and how they can be applied advantageously;
- avoid the cost of making their own mistakes.

Benchmarking can act as a catalyst for change. By examining one's operation in the light of other successful operations, it may be that weaknesses are revealed, which can create the impetus for change. Strategic benchmarking systematically evaluates alternatives and improves performance by understanding and modifying other successful strategies. This type of approach is not about trying to replicate other company practices, nor to obtain confidential information; it is about building on the success of others to improve future performance. By frequent benchmarking iterations, an organization is always researching *current* best practice, not outdated practices.

Steps in benchmarking

Companies who decide to do their own benchmarking have to answer some basic questions, which may vary by such aspects as the size of their firm. In any case, operators need to have a clear idea of *why* they are benchmarking and a strategy for implementing it. Questions to address are:

- what will we benchmark?
- who will we benchmark against?
- how will we obtain the information?
- how will we analyse the findings?
- how will we use the findings?

In the Canadian benchmarking study, these questions were answered somewhat differently from the way any individual tourism operator might answer them, since the study was on behalf of all operators in the sector, rather than focused on one size or type of operation. While a large tourism company might want to gather a considerable amount of information, particularly as it relates to competition, a small tourism company might want to focus on issues which are critical to it, or where it knows it has a weakness. The more precisely an operator defines what it wants to measure, the more useful the information obtained will be. The Catalogue benchmarking process aimed to:

- obtain information for all types of ecotourism and adventure travel operations;
- look at all seasons;
- examine all sizes of operation;
- look at all geographic areas and ecosystems;
- examine all areas of company practice (core competencies), from environmental protection, to community relationships, to the development of new product, and many more; not simply 'business' practices.

On the one hand, this was exceptionally challenging, but on the other, its comprehensive nature makes the final product usable by all operators in ecotourism and adventure travel, as well as in many more areas of tourism. It also is helpful for tourism stakeholders beyond operators, including: government, consultants, industry associations, non-governmental organizations, resource managers, and many others.

The Canadian benchmarking process

Objectives of the catalogue
The principal purpose of the assignment was to develop a Catalogue of Best (Exemplary) Practices in Adventure Travel and Ecotourism, to enable the sharing of a range of successful practices among various players in the industry: operators, and key stakeholders and the tourism industry. It was to be a practical tool to transmit a range of lessons to other operators, so as to enable them to improve their own tourism offerings.

Who to benchmark against?
There are a range of ways to benchmark, and organizations to benchmark against. A tourism operator may gather information from trade sources, such as magazines and brochures and associations. However, some of the most valuable information may come from direct exchange with others, who recognize the benefits of sharing. Benchmarking may be:

1. Against other parts of one's own company; but as one of the characteristics of ecotourism and adventure travel operations is that they are fairly small, internal benchmarking tends not to be a useful option.
2. Between parallel industries; companies in parallel industries may have very different (and useful) approaches to similar problems.

3. Against direct competitors; this works well when there are some similarities between competitors.
4. Against totally different industries; the best idea is to compare against very specific activities.

In the Catalogue, the third option was selected: benchmarking the best of the industry. They might be considered competitors, but more importantly should be considered to be those with similar situations, and even to be potential partners. Many of the best practice companies were those most willing to share information with each other. They are in a constant learning mode, and recognize the value in this approach.

Steps in developing the catalogue
1. SOLICITING EXPERT INPUT. Two initial information needs were: a qualified list of operators, considered by industry experts to have good practices to survey; and expert opinion on possible criteria which would assist in evaluating 'best practices'. Both types of information were obtained from approximately 100 agencies or individuals, some of whom were out-of-country experts, including academics, and board/committee members of The Ecotourism Society. These contacts generated almost 350 operators across the country, all of whom were considered to be essentially pre-qualified for survey purposes.

2. DEVELOPING BEST PRACTICE CRITERIA. The operator evaluation criteria were finalized after a range of types of input from:

- the client;
- agencies and experts;
- other operator evaluation criteria;
- tourism standards, guidelines and ecolabels;
- non-tourism sectors standards;
- certification criteria (such as Australia's National Ecotourism Accreditation Programme);
- management systems designed to measure performance (such as the balanced scorecard);
- professional expertise.

This helped to refine the various areas of practice in which operations were required to be proficient. The nine areas of practice are described as core competency areas (see Table 10.7). Evaluation criteria for all areas of practice were developed.

3. DESIGNING THE SURVEY INSTRUMENT. Once the criteria were developed, the challenge was then to develop a survey which performed two functions: evaluated practices; and elicited substantive and useful responses. Evaluation criteria were often hidden in and throughout the survey. Table 10.7 shows, for each core competency, one example of

Table 10.7.   The nine core competencies and sample evaluation criteria.

Core competency	Example evaluation criteria
Business management	Has a formal business plan to guide operations
Product and delivery	Has a safety/risk minimization and/or emergency response plan
Customer service and relations	Size of groups
Training and human resources development	% staff accredited
Resource rotection and sustainability	Has minimum impact policies regarding wildlife
Social and community contribution	% staff employed from the area/region in which operations take place
Packaging	Packages with other types of operators
Marketing and promotion	Has a written marketing plan
Product development	Uses customer/market research in product development

the evaluation criteria used. Note that the range of competencies cover a range of environmental, social and economic topic areas. The design of the operator survey was of fundamental importance to the Catalogue. It had to be sufficiently straightforward so as not to deter respondents, and to balance evaluation with questions which could reveal useful practices. Thus the survey was, of necessity, substantive. Each competency grouping had 5 to 14 questions, for a total of 84 questions. However, some 'questions' had multiple sections, or required a significant description of practice. So respondents had to invest considerable time to answer the survey.

4. ADMINISTERING THE SURVEY.   The survey was administered to operators by e-mail, fax and mail. In addition, the survey was translated and administered concurrently in French, particularly to Quebec operators.

The sharing of best business practice tools and strategies has been well known as an improvement method in Japan, through the application of a principle called Shukko (or the loaning of employees to other firms). This may happen within or between companies, to assist all organizations to move forward. However, sharing is sometimes seen elsewhere as the 'revealing of company secrets', and it was not assumed that all operators contacted would immediately see the benefits in participating in this project. The consultants intrigued and attracted their interest and 'buy-in' through a covering letter which described a range of *benefits* to operator participation.

5. EVALUATING AND RANKING RESPONSES.   Some survey questions were for evaluation only; others were for obtaining information; others were for

both evaluation and information. Points were allocated for each evaluation question; in addition, further points were allocated for particularly
innovative practices. Once evaluated, operations were ranked. Three
major groupings emerged: excellent, fair and poor. All the excellent
operations had their practices included. In addition, those with a
fair 'overall' rating were examined with respect to specific core
competencies. If they had high individual competency ratings, or
described particularly innovative or useful practices, they, too, were
included, since the Catalogue was practice-focused.

The quality of responses from operators varied hugely, for a variety
of reasons. The operation with the highest number of points was 1057,
and the lowest number of points allocated was 241. Some operators
indicated that they could not fill in the survey due to time or season
constraints of the project; others did not answer some questions/
sections; others provided poor quality answers to some questions (for
example, saying yes, or no, instead of providing the requested description of practice). This helps to explain the large spread of points. What
was notable was the extraordinary effort by some operators to comply
with survey responses and also to requests for other information
(references, customer comments). Some supplied photographs, videos,
a range of brochures, commendations, different types of promotional
materials, and their guidelines, codes of practice or other relevant
information.

The evaluations, in essence, should be viewed as evaluations of the
survey responses, rather than of the actual operation. Some operators
may run a quality business, but unless this information is described,
the evaluators cannot know. This outlines a weakness in the project. It
is probable that for certain operators, the degree of comfort with a written survey may vary; and possibly such comfort levels for SMEs may be
lower than for the industry overall. This may be even more pronounced
for aboriginal respondents. However, there were a number of aboriginal
operators who responded ably, and were included in the Catalogue.

6. STRUCTURING AND COMPILING THE CATALOGUE.   During evaluation, those
practices worthy of description were recorded. The selected practices
were then grouped under the relevant core competencies. The bulk of
the Catalogue is devoted to practices. These were discussed in separate
chapters devoted to each core competency topic (Table 10.7), present-
ing useful practices against which operators can compare their own
performance. It was important to maximize the use of the operators'
own words to resonate with potential readers, and to be convincing and
practical, yet in a style which added sparkle and was easy to read.

Developing the presentation framework of the Catalogue involved
considerable research and professional knowledge, drawing from the
consultants' applied and practical experience, as well as principles and

Table 10.8. Core competencies and subsections, related to ecolabelling.

Resource protection and sustainability	Social and community contribution
1. Being sensitive to the environment	1. Taking ownership of your region of operations
2. Conserving and managing energy, water, waste and transportation	2. Consulting with and involving local people and groups
3. Developing policies for purchases and suppliers	3. Employing local people
4. Minimizing impacts on wildlife	4. Purchasing local goods and services
5. Minimizing impacts on natural environments, and guiding visitor behaviour	5. Sharing with, or contributing other benefits to local communities
6. Supporting regional conservation efforts	6. Adapting to unique local conditions over time
7. Contributing in other ways	7. Minimizing impact on, and being sensitive to communities
	8. Enabling guests to experience local communities and culture

theory. In essence, subheadings had to be developed for each core competency, which enabled the range of practices to be described and linked (some of these are shown in Table 10.8). In addition, the practices could not merely be listed. A concise written framework within which to insert and integrate the practices was required. Thus the body of the Catalogue is composed of a written framework, plus numerous operator quotes and practices. In addition to the examples and the written framework, good business tips and practices were sprinkled throughout the text, with the objective of being visually stimulating and interesting for the target audience: operators. For example:

Good Business Practice: *Contribute dollars or in-kind toward the environment that supports your operation.*

Good Business Tip: *Guests usually find opportunities for real local contact to be a tremendously enriching experience.*

The appendix of the Catalogue provided, as a tourism showcase, those operations with practices selected for inclusion. This took the form of an alphabetical listing of all selected operations, with information presented in the form of a template for travel trade buyers.

Sample catalogue contents particularly related to ecolabelling topics
Although the Canadian Catalogue covers the spectrum of operator core competencies, since it aimed to provide a balance of practices for economically, socially and environmentally sustainable operations, it is noteworthy that environmentally and socio-culturally sustainable practices were given considerable weight in the document. The types of sections dealt with in these two chapters of the Catalogue are shown

in Table 10.8, and naturally each of the sections had a range of sub-sections, approaches, practices and supplementary information. For each of these core competency subheadings, a range of practices was described, both systematically in the text and using boxed examples (practices) from specific operators. For instance, in the section on 'Minimizing Impacts on Natural Environments and Guiding Visitor Behaviour' (Section 5), one example of the way that operators act to influence visitors is described in Box 10.1.

In the section 'Minimize Impacts on Wildlife', the environmental practices of another operator are boxed and described in Box 10.2.

In the 'Social and Community Contribution' chapter, in the section dealing with 'Employing Local People', a range of practices are described (relating to recruitment, developing pride through 'owner-ship', etc.). Employment practices were highlighted by example, such as in Box 10.3.

Box 10.1.   Guide visitor behaviour by education and example

Niagara Nature Tours interpreters carry domestic ginger in their pockets with a pocket knife. When they are on the trail and see wild ginger, guests can see the plant, smell the rhizomes, and guides cut a little piece of the ginger from their pocket, so each person gets to taste it. 'Guests see by example that we do not dig up the plants to let them taste it, and then we can explain about the ethics of edible wild harvesting.'

Box 10.2.   Be aware of various types of habitat sensitivities

Sawyer Lake Adventures is unusually sensitive to the specific needs of the many types of habitats and wildlife. Their guidelines, therefore, are not 'firm', but vary with the species, the age of animal, the season, and so on (e.g. mother with young, breeding season). In addition, they are sensitive not simply to the animals themselves, but to animal travel corridors and use areas. Thus they consider feeding, bedding, antler rubs, scrapes or roosting spots, and the need to visit at a time of day when the wildlife are not using them.

Box 10.3.   Employ local/regional staff and experts

Bathurst Inlet Lodge: Our owners (Inuit and Kablunak) are experts in their own right, and are involved in the interpretation. In addition, we supply a staff natu-ralist (a professional biologist) who lives in Rankin Inlet in the winter (when the lodge is closed), and who has been involved with the Lodge since 1972. We are also joined by the retired Anglican Bishop of the Arctic, who is an arctic histo-rian, linguist and expert on the Copper Inuit. Bishop Sperry shares stories of the North based on his extensive experience (since 1951), and his years of service to the people of the arctic, both in the NWT/Nunavut and in Arctic Quebec.

Box 10.4.   Partner with aboriginal communities and businesses

---

Wilderness Spirit: When our trips start or end on a First Nation's land we make people aware of it and encourage them to look around. When we operate in Nunavut, clients will be given opportunities to spend time in local communities before and after trips. The costs of accommodation also make it most practical to participate in community homestay programmes when visiting remote communities. These programmes have the added benefit of giving clients a chance to experience the aboriginal people's living conditions.

Boreal Wilderness Guides: We are bringing 20 German ecotourists and billeting them on the reserve for 3 days. Each native family will receive $100.00 per tourist day during the tour. This helps provide employment in regions of 90% unemployment

---

In the section 'Enable Guests to Share or Contribute Benefits to Local Communities and Culture', one boxed example was as in Box 10.4.

Feedback on the catalogue
From the outset, there have been positive responses from operators, about how practical and user-friendly the Catalogue proved to be. Some operators indicated that the very act of responding to the survey highlighted areas of their operation which they felt they could re-examine for improvement purposes. For example, Voyageur/ Klondike Ventures wrote: 'I have just completed the survey. I found it to be a helpful tool to test where we are, in having a complete operations plan and strategy. I would request your honest feedback on our current operation, what might be missing, etc.' This was echoed by others, who indicated that they found the range of questions insightful, and they also wanted to hear specific feedback about their operations, regardless of whether they were selected for inclusion in the Catalogue. These represent real learning and improvement-oriented organizations.

The CTC has received positive feedback on the Catalogue, and consequently has commissioned a further work on best practice partnerships in tourism SMEs. Similarly, the consultants received many unsolicited comments from operators who had received the Catalogue to indicate that the document provided an excellent resource for improvement, and a source of innovative ideas for them. Companies that use best practice benchmarking report that the time and effort are repaid many times; best practice operations are learning operations.

Conclusions

As environmental protection comes to play a more central role in companies' operations, it is also being recognized that better environmental management and better management are the same thing. Environmental management tools are providing the framework needed for continuous improvement, proactive initiatives by industry, and creative partnerships to yield real and sustainable improvements in environmental performance. Much work needs to be done in developing EM tools, particularly in the development of both concepts and terminology. However, this growth in EM tools is a hopeful sign, and enables companies and governments to take practical steps to improve industry's environmental performance, improve management of performance, and help industry and government replace confrontation with mutual understanding and partnership (UNEP, 1995b). Ecolabelling is one EM tool, and its use in select destinations in Canada has been described. However, at the national level, Canada has moved from a Code of Ethics and Guidelines for Sustainable Tourism, to benchmarking best practices.

An environmental journal has pointed out: 'we need an ongoing catalog of "what works". What innovations at the local level are working? We need a place where we can all go to find out. We need a much more ambitious, cumulative database of "what works" for sustainable development' (Environmental Research Foundation, 1997). The *Catalogue of Exemplary Practices in Adventure Travel and Ecotourism* responds to this call, and acts as a best practice benchmarking milestone; it is the first rigorous study of its kind in the tourism industry, oriented to transmitting a full spectrum of practices for sustainability including those relevant to ecolabelling.

This Catalogue may thus help to stimulate a grassroots effort throughout Canada in adventure travel and ecotourism to improve a range of sustainability practices, including environmental. The Catalogue provides a large menu of activities, practices and tips, which have been proven successful in the industry. It not only provides information on practices among similar operations (whether by activity or season), but also among dissimilar tourism operations; this can lead to 'outside the box' creative thinking. Benefits of the Catalogue include:

- providing a practical tool for use by the industry, which provides not only tips and key pointers, but also 'how to' activities;
- enabling industry to emulate the best by implementing change and measuring performance;
- acting as a measurement of business performance against the best of the industry (i.e. provide a reference value against which to compare performance);

- acting as an enabler for achieving and maintaining high levels of competitiveness;
- demonstrating the benefits of partnerships within and outside the sector;
- showcasing quality Canadian ecotourism and adventure travel operations representing a range of activity/product types, and all regions of the country;
- allowing operators to select those practices best suited to their particular climate, culture and ecosystem, instead of being bound to uniform standards.

Strategic benchmarking is a systematic business process for evaluating alternatives, implementing strategies, and improving performance, by understanding and adapting successful strategies. The CTC is working to realize the benefits of strategic best practice benchmarking by disseminating the Catalogue on its website and encouraging best practices to be applied. It will increase these benefits if it systematically implements the benchmarking exercise in the future as a form of monitoring.

One of the elements required in both ecolabelling and benchmarking, is monitoring. The Catalogue allows individual operators to monitor their own performance against those of peers and best practice operators. What is required for continued monitoring is a follow-up document to track progress in the sector. Also helpful would be a study which tracked increased effectiveness in the industry, and where use of the Catalogue had contributed to this improvement.

Should an ecolabelling programme be pursued, the groundwork of having benchmarked best practices would be useful in setting up practical quality criteria, and the Catalogue could operate as a base manual providing guidelines. These could be used by the tourism industry overall in developing a quality label, or by operators in applying for the label. What would be further required is credible verification of operator standards. From this point of view, the Canadian experience in benchmarking could be used or applied by other organizations or destinations, with a view to encouraging improved standards throughout their industry, or as a base for a certification programme.

References

Department of Trade and Industry (1999) *Best Practice Benchmarking.* Web site: http://www.dti.gov.uk/mbp/bpgt/m9jc00001/m9jc000011.html

Dooley, D. and Kirkpatrick, N. (1993) *Environmental Glossary.* Pira International, Leatherhead, UK.

Environmental Research Foundation (1997) Catalog what works. *Rachel's Environment & Health Weekly* 570, 30 October. http://www.rachel.org/bulletin/index.cfm?St=2 (2 September 2000).

Global Environmental Management Initiative (1994) *Benchmarking: the Primer – Benchmarking for Continuous Environmental Improvement.* Global Environmental Management Initiative, Washington, DC.

Troyer, W. (1992) *The Green Partnership Guide: 12 Steps to help Create an Environmentally-Friendly Setting for our Guests, Ourselves and our Future.* Canadian Pacific Hotels and Resorts.

UNEP (1995a) Environmental Management Tools: Facts and Figures. *UNEP Industry and Environment* 18(2–3), April–September, 4–10.

UNEP (1995b) Tools for Sustainable Industry. *UNEP Industry and Environment* 18(2–3), April–September, 3.

UNEP (1998) *Ecolabels in the Tourism Industry.* United Nations Environment Program, Industry and Environment, Paris.

Pam Wight & Associates (1999) *Catalogue of Exemplary Practices in Adventure Travel and Ecotourism.* Canadian Tourism Commission, Ottawa. http://travelcanada.ca/en/ctc/partner_centre/index.html

Chapter 11

Ecotourism Accreditation in Australia

RALF C. BUCKLEY

Introduction

Promotional materials for a number of tours and lodges in Australia bear a prominent ecolabel, a green tick with the words ECO TOURISM in a rectangular format. This signifies accreditation under the Nature and Ecotourism Accreditation Programme. Some bear two ticks, indicating Advanced Ecotourism Accreditation. From 2000 onwards, there will be two different single-tick labels, one for nature tourism and another for ecotourism. There may also be a label for individual guides under the National Nature and Ecotour Guide Certification Programme, NNEGCP. NEAP provides accreditation for individual tourism products rather than entire companies. As of January 2000, 237 products from over 100 companies have either basic or advanced ecotourism accreditation under NEAP.

Nation-wide listings in classified telephone directories (Buckley, 1999) suggest that there are at least 1500 operators in the Australian nature, eco- and adventure tourism (NEAT) sector. Many of these, however, are very small and probably do not currently constitute viable businesses; and many have no pretension to be ecotours. Of the tourism products which are advertised or generally recognized as falling within broad definitions of ecotourism (Buckley, 1994; Tourism Queensland, 1997) a high proportion have obtained the NEAP ecolabel. Accreditation has also, however, been granted to several products which would probably not be considered as ecotourism by environmental groups.

Context

Australia does not have the proliferation of localized tourism ecolabels characteristic of European nations such as Germany and Austria. For the mainstream tourism industry, Australia has neither destination-quality nor environmental-performance ecolabel schemes of its own. It has a detailed accreditation-based environmental performance ecolabel which was designed specifically for ecotourism operations, and has been expanded recently to include all forms of nature tourism. This scheme, the Nature and Ecotourism Accreditation Programme (NEAP) is described in detail below.

One of the peak national tourism industry associations, Tourism Council Australia, has a very broad quality-certification label, encompassing various aspects of business practices. For its environmental components, however, it has adopted NEAP. Green Globe 21 has recently been established in Australia and is currently carrying out a membership marketing campaign. Green Globe in its original format was not supported by Tourism Council Australia, which instead elected to develop its own scheme and support the Nature and Ecotourism Accreditation Programme as above.

Australian companies have been keen entrants in international award schemes such as British Airways' Tourism for Tomorrow Awards; but as noted elsewhere, these are not strictly ecolabels, nor are they specific to Australia. Australia also has its own environmental award scheme, the Banksia Awards for the Environment (www.banksia-foundation.asn.au). This includes 14 different categories, all of them cross-sectoral. Tour operators can apply for any appropriate category, but there is no category specific to tourism, or any other industry sector.

Voluntary ecolabel schemes, public or private, are relatively uncommon in Australia in any industry sector. In 1991, a national ecolabel scheme called Environmental Choice Australia was introduced for the wholesale and retail trade. It was operated by ANZECC, which is a ministerial-level coordinating council of national and state Environment Ministers in Australia and New Zealand. The Environmental Choice logo was intended to indicate only that environmental claims made by manufacturers and retailers had been subject to external verification. Consumers interpreted it, however, as some kind of governmental environmental endorsement, and were disillusioned when they found this was not the case. The entire scheme was abandoned 3 years later.

Various ecolabel schemes, local or international, have been proposed and/or trialled in a range of other industry sectors including agriculture, wool production, marine fisheries, aquaculture, forestry, packaging and paper, and whitegoods. In general, Australian consumers are now used to recycling logos on plastic manufactured items, though they may not be able to differentiate between the various symbols. They are used to seeing 'made from recycled paper' on paper products, and 'biodegradable' on detergents. And they are used to seeing energy-efficiency labels on domestic appliances. Most of these claims, however, are only treated as meaningful by consumers where they are backed by Australian Standards established under legislation.

Evolution of NEAP

The first practical step towards the establishment of NEAP was taken by the tourism portfolio in the Australian federal government, who hired consultants to draft a national ecotourism accreditation scheme. The consultants produced a document that included detailed procedures but very little in the way of substantive accreditation criteria. Fortunately, the then fledging Ecotourism Association of Australia (EAA) undertook to compile a second and far more substantive draft. The first version of NEAP implemented in practice (NEAP I) was published in 1996 by the Australian government. It was developed by a team from the Ecotourism Association of Australia, the Office for National Tourism, and Victoria Tour Operators Association, with assistance from over 30 individual tour operators.

NEAP's principal difficulty, in its early stages, was relatively low industry sign-up. There are several likely reasons for this.

- The EAA was not as well known as it is now, and operators may not have been convinced that NEAP would be an effective marketing tool.
- Perhaps relatively few individual products in the nature and adventure tourism sectors were able to qualify for ecotourism accreditation, even though the criteria were pitched at a level quite easy to achieve.
- At least for a period, there was a perception that the term ecotourism was being abused as a meaningless marketing tool by some operators, so other operators which had already established a reputation for good environment management performance may have wished to dissociate themselves from this perception.
- In particular, it seems there were some residual concerns from an earlier attempt at a national directory of Australian ecotour operators, where it was widely perceived that the relative environmental claims made by different tourism operators did not correspond well to their relative environmental performances in practice.

Concerted effort by the EAA during NEAP's early years, with support from a number of state government agencies such as the Environment Branch of Tourism Queensland, increased industry sign-up to the point where by early 1999, a major proportion of Australian tourism operators conforming to the general perception of ecotourism had one or more products with basic or advanced accreditation under NEAP.

While valuable in distinguishing those particular products to potential purchasers, however, NEAP in its initial form still had relatively limited reach within the Australian nature and adventure tourism sector as a whole, and hence relatively little ability to improve its aggregate environmental management, because the vast majority of products in this sector are simply not within the ambit of the scheme at all. During 1999, therefore, NEAP was revised to include a third level of accreditation, broader and more basic than existing levels. Hence there are now three levels of accreditation: nature tourism, ecotourism and advanced ecotourism.

This second version of NEAP (NEAP II) was developed by the accreditation panel for NEAP I, and distributed for public comment at the Ecotourism Association of Australia annual conference in October 1999.

Structure of NEAP II

NEAP II incorporates eight sets of criteria, as follows:

- natural area focus
- interpretation
- ecological sustainability
- contributions to conservation
- working with local communities
- cultural component
- client satisfaction
- responsible marketing.

Different levels of detail are provided, as appropriate, under each of these headings. For example, criteria for ecological sustainability take up more space than all other criteria combined. For each specific technical issue, a number of specific, testable and, in many cases, quantified criteria are listed. Some of these are specified as essential core criteria, others as bonus criteria. Each individual criterion may apply to accommodation, tours, and/or other activities. To gain ecotourism accreditation, a tourism product must meet all the core criteria in relevant categories. To gain advanced ecotourism accreditation, it must also meet 80% of relevant bonus criteria. Additional bonus points may be awarded by the NEAP accreditation panel if the applicant can provide evidence of innovative best practice. The panel also has the task of interpreting some of the vaguer criteria.

Accreditation Criteria

The most critical criterion for a natural area focus is that the product must be 'based around activities that help clients to personally experience the natural environment, such as by using at least three senses'. Presumably, a half-day whitewater raft trip, downhill mountain-bike race or resort ski pass could fulfil this criterion, though of course these might fail other criteria for accreditation. A four-wheel drive tour, helicopter tour or gondola ride would not satisfy this criterion, since clients could see and possibly hear their environment, but could not smell, taste or touch it. If any of those tours included a stop where clients could disembark, however, the criterion would be met.

Interpretation seems to be a key component of NEAP II. Different levels of interpretation are specified for the three different levels of accreditation, namely nature tourism, ecotourism and advanced ecotourism. Note that too strong an emphasis on interpretation may weaken the value of NEAP II as a consumer ecolabel, since interpretation is much easier to provide than ecological sustainability. It remains to be seen whether this will be an issue in practice. Specific criteria cover:

- access to interpretation,
- accuracy of information,
- interpretive planning,
- staff awareness and training.

The section on ecological sustainability is the most detailed part of NEAP II. Most of it would apply internationally. A number of specific criteria which might be considered standard in other countries, however, are listed only as bonus criteria under NEAP II. Some of the terminology is also rather idiosyncratic. For example, 'stag watching' refers not to male deer, but to standing dead trees. Specific criteria cover:

- environmental knowledge of staff,
- planning and preparedness for environmental emergencies,
- location in an area where tourism is an appropriate land use,
- environmental planning and impact assessment,
- site disturbance, landscaping and rehabilitation,
- drainage, soil and water management,
- construction methods and material,
- visual impacts,
- light,
- water supply and conservation,
- waste water,
- noise,
- air quality,
- waste minimization and litter,
- energy minimization for both buildings and transport,
- minimal disturbance to wildlife,
- minimal-impact practices for specific activities, as below.

NEAP II specifies core and bonus accreditation criteria for minimal-impact practices in a range of specific activities:

- spotlighting,
- marine mammal and megafauna viewing,
- walking,
- camping,
- vehicle use, including four-wheel drive and bicycles,
- boating, powered and non-powered,
- aircraft use,
- rock climbing and abseiling,
- caving,
- snorkelling and scuba diving,
- horse, camel and alpaca tours.

As an example, the core criteria for minimal-impact powered boat tours include the following:

- design and operate boats for maximum fuel efficiency,
- no erosion from wash,
- go slow enough not to affect other users,
- do not anchor or ground on seagrass or live coral,
- install moorings at frequently used sites,
- do not discharge contaminated bilge water or untreated ballast water,
- discharge sewage and sullage only into on-shore treatment facilities, or in large, well-flushed waterbodies,
- use no antifouling in lakes and rivers, and only tin-free antifouls in marine environments,
- carry out maintenance in 'appropriately' designed and managed facilities,
- do not scrub down hulls in sensitive environments if they are coated with antifouling containing heavy metals or biocides.

Bonus criteria include:

- no discharge of sewage, sullage, bilge or untreated ballast water into open water,
- installation and operation of mooring in cooperation with other tour operators,
- use tar epoxy antifouls only,
- use only diesel, four-stroke or electric engines, preferably with noise suppression equipment.

NEAP II includes a proactive contribution to the conservation of natural areas as a criterion for all levels of accreditation. Such contributions may include direct conservation initiatives in natural areas visited, such as provision of visitor data, physical assistance in litter removal, weed control, etc., or assistance with research, training or monitoring. They may also include broader contributions such as membership of a conservation group, or support for student projects.

Under the heading of working with local communities, NEAP II considers issues such as:

- local employment and local purchase of goods and services,
- client briefings to minimize cultural impacts,
- consultation with community representatives,
- support or discounts for local non-profits, schools or resident groups,
- consultation and involvement of traditional custodians of indigenous cultures,
- interpretation relating to indigenous cultures.

NEAP II includes a set of criteria related to client satisfaction. The core criteria for four of six bonus criteria are not specific to ecotourism or even tourism in general, and it is not clear why they should be included in an ecotourism accreditation scheme. The other two bonus criteria, however, are of particular interest. The first of these is that clients should be told how the product has been changed to meet NEAP criteria. The second is that the product should be subject to peer review, for example, by other ecotour operators. It would be interesting to investigate, once NEAP II has been in operation for a couple of years, how many operators have taken advantage of this particular bonus criterion.

The final set of criteria under NEAP II relate to responsible marketing. Clearly, this is of particular interest in the ecolabel context. Core criteria relate principally to accurate representation of the product, and presentation of information on NEAP and ecotourism more generally. Bonus criteria include the provision of information such as the tenure of protected areas presented in images, and means of accessing additional information about the specific destination and ecotourism in general. Interestingly, one of the critical criteria in other responsible-travel marketing guidelines, namely that advertisements should only illustrate views, activities or situations which a normal client might reasonably expect to experience themselves, is not specifically included.

A final section in NEAP II, referring to innovative best practice, mentions issues such as the following:

- interpretation promotes tangible environmental actions;
- operator has established an EMS accredited to ISO 14000, determined limits of acceptable change at the site, and set up an impact monitoring programme;
- the product uses a rehabilitated site, or a site with low conservation but high scenic value;

- the operator provides funding for research or management in public lands, above compulsory licence fees;
- a privately managed area for nature conservation is created;
- the operator has been involved in a social impact study;
- the operator uses only NEAP-accredited accommodation and transport.

Strictly speaking, none of these is new in the sense of recently invented. They are, however, innovative in the sense that they are currently rare within the Australian tourism industry.

Other Tourism Ecolabels in Australia

NEAP II is by far the best-known tourism ecolabel in Australia, but by no means the only one. A number of Australian tourism companies are also members of other ecolabel schemes such as Green Globe, PATA Green Leaf, and the International Hotels Environment Initiative. The national tourism industry association Tourism Council Australia also operates a quality label scheme. The Asia-Pacific node for the new Green Globe 21 is based in Australia, in association with the Cooperative Research Centre for Sustainable Tourism. The precise structure and operation of Green Globe 21 are still under development. Currently, it appears that the Green Globe ecolabel will be available on the basis of an auditable commitment to continuous improvement in various areas of environmental management. This contrasts with NEAP and NEAP II, which incorporate detailed substantive criteria and thresholds for various levels of accreditation. The PATA Green Leaf scheme has been amalgamated with Green Globe 21, but this was straightforward since it apparently never developed detailed criteria. NEAP is very different, and it seems unlikely that it would be amalgamated with Green Globe 21, at least until the latter has progressed considerably in technical detail.

Conclusion

In Australia, there has been extensive debate over ecolabels, and indeed other quality labels, in the tourism industry. Australia has an active industry-based ecotourism association which operates an accreditation programme co-founded by the national government. Although only a small number of tourist products have received accreditation to date, the scheme is currently being expanded through the addition of a less stringent nature tourism category. At the same time Australia now hosts the Asia-Pacific node of the revised Green

Globe 21, which is intended to cover the entire tourism industry worldwide. Other international programmes, such as those established by the International Hotels Environment Initiative and the Pacific Asia Travel Association, are also represented in Australia. This has led to concern over consumer confusion. Attempts are currently under way to integrate these schemes.

References

Buckley, R.C. (1994) A framework for ecotourism. *Annals of Tourism Research* 21, 661–669.

Buckley, R.C. (1999) NEAT trends: current issues in nature, eco and adventure tourism. Ecotourism Association of Australia Annual Conference, Fraser Island.

Queensland Department of Tourism, Small Business and Industry (1997) *Queensland Ecotourism Plan.* QDTSBI, Brisbane.

Chapter 12

Ecolabels for Tourism in Europe: the European Ecolabel for Tourism?

HERBERT HAMELE

Tourism and Environment in Europe within the context of Sustainable Development

In 1999, at dozens of international conferences and workshops in Europe, tour operators and travel agencies, destinations and companies in tourism, politicians, consumers and environmental organizations and a long list of experts and consultants again stressed the need for more sustainable development in tourism, more than they did in the years before. This chapter addresses such issues as what 'sustainable' tourism means, how tourism and the environment in Europe may develop, how organizations should be reacting and what benefits may arise from ecolabels.

Sustainable tourism: defined by many interests

Tourism within the framework of sustainable development has to be defined by a wide range of players and interests: by tourists (satisfaction, behaviour, etc.), the host population (jobs, identities, wealth, etc.), the local tourism companies and economy (occupancies, added value, local multiplier, etc.), culture (heritage preservation, etc.) and the environment and nature (consumption of energy and materials, biodiversity, environmental quality, etc.). The needs of future generations and the environmental, social and cultural carrying capacities are setting the quality and limits for growth.

© CAB *International* 2001. *Tourism Ecolabelling*
(eds X. Font and R.C. Buckley)

Tourism and environment: double problems in 2010?

One might say that to stay at home or to stay in a holiday destination for some weeks makes no difference to environmental impacts. However, the higher level of services offered in accommodation, sport and leisure facilities, the construction of accommodation (especially holiday villages) and other facilities and – above all – transport from, to and within the destination requires much more energy, water and land, and produces more waste and emissions than staying at home. It is also obvious that due to the carrying capacities, more and more of the quality of nature and the environment is being put under threat; for example in southern Mediterranean countries the consumption of fresh water is less and less sustainable. This also, therefore, has an effect on the quality of the overall tourism product.

At the end of the 20th century 50% of international tourism was going to and taking place within Europe. Tourism has been estimated to be a continuously growing market worldwide:

- Until 2010, international arrivals in Europe will probably double from about 400 million to about 800 million, with high growth rates in Central/Eastern Europe and in Eastern Mediterranean Europe. Including the residential tourists (e.g. French holidaymakers in France), in 2010 approximately 500,000 mostly micro, small- and medium-sized companies in accommodation, will probably welcome more than 1 billion tourists (1,000,000,000).
- The tourists will probably: (i) drive or fly more than 1000 billion km across and to Europe (mostly by car and aeroplane), which will significantly contribute to global warming; (ii) spend more than 5 billion nights in hotels, guesthouses or campsites; (iii) consume more than 1 billion m^3 of drinking water and more than 1 billion megawatts of energy; and (iv) produce approximately 5 million tonnes of unsorted waste.

How to react?

The common challenge for all organizations within tourism is to save and strengthen competitiveness through variety and attractiveness of Europe's tourism in the future years, and to combine environmental and other quality aspects within the framework of sustainable development. The ever-growing environmental problems in Europe, also caused by tourism (as stated by the European Environmental Agency), are challenging politicians and managers on local, regional and international levels to concentrate finances and activities on instruments and practices which promise synergies: saving costs by consuming less energy and water and by producing less waste, creating jobs and unique selling propositions by use of local products and rising quality, saving successful destinations by changing 'throw away' into 'keep and restore' mentalities.

In practice a wide range of instruments can be used to put the tourism industry on the path to sustainability. Regulations, of course, are essential for defining the legal framework within which the private sector should operate and for establishing minimum standards and processes. Economic instruments are also being increasingly used to address environmental issues. However, voluntary approaches like ecolabelling are certainly the best way of ensuring long-term commitments and improvements. This applies particularly to an industry such as tourism, which is composed of many small and medium-sized firms (SMEs), and which has a vested interest in not degrading the environment (UNEP, 1998).

What benefits may arise from ecolabels?

In general, an ecolabel for a service product group in tourism as a voluntary environmental product-policy instrument may have following benefits (CREM, 2000):

- They can help tourism suppliers to identify critical issues, speed up the implementation of eco-efficient solutions, and lead to effective ways of monitoring and reporting on environmental performance.
- While ecolabels can help to sell tourism products, they also decrease the use of resources such as energy and water, reducing costs for the operator. Ecolabels are thus both a marketing and on environmental management tool.
- Ecolabels provide consumers with easily accessible and recognizable information on best environmental practice within a product group (facilitate the use of environmental performance as one of the possible decision criteria).
- Guarantee an external source of monitoring and public reporting (to consumers and business-to-business market).
- Provide SMEs with an instrument which is less costly than working with EMAS.
- Raise environmental awareness among all stakeholders.
- Advance good environmental practice in the tourist sector.

More and More Ecolabels for Accommodation Services in Europe

In the 1990s an increasing number of tourism associations began to pay attention to ecologically sound tourism. In 2000 they offered more than 40 environmental certificates and awards for nearly all kind of tourism suppliers on regional, national and international levels in order to stimulate the market towards better environmental performance; about 30 of them were for accommodation services. For hotels and restaurants, campsites and youth hostels, farm holiday and alpine huts there are now approximately 20 regional and national environmental certificates and awards exist in Austria, Germany, Denmark, Luxembourg, the UK, The Netherlands, Italy, France, Spain and Switzerland. International ecolabels have been developed and implemented in the Nordic Countries or by private organizations on a European level. What is the present situation for European countries then?

Austria

The valley of Kleinwalsertal was the pioneer for ecolabels in tourism: since 1989 the 'Silberdistel' has been a model for many other destinations and regions in Austria and in Germany. Other local ecolabels (Saalbach-Hinterglemm) and regional labels (Lungau, Kärnten) still exist with their specific criteria. The regional 'Umweltsiegel Tirol' (Environmental Seal of Quality, Tyrol) in 1995 was adopted by the neighbouring Italian region of Südtirol (South Tyrol) and about 230 accommodation companies in 1998 were labelled with this well-known certificate. Since 1996 the regional labels in Austria have been in competition with the official 'Österreichisches Umweltzeichen für Tourismusbetriebe' (Austrian Ecolabels for Tourism Organizations), the first official nation-wide ecolabel for tourism services in Europe. Since 1999 this national Austrian label has been more and more accepted (nearly 100 companies) and seems to be best positioned to beat the competition there. The large number of criteria (about 100) as well as the independent testing and awarding procedure to which hotels, inns, guesthouse and mountain huts have to submit, are among the most sophisticated in Europe.

Germany

In Bavaria about 50 hotels and restaurants in 1999 were awarded as 'Umweltbewusster Hotel- und Gaststättenbetrieb' (Environmentally Conscious Hotel and Restaurant Businesses) (since 1991). Most of the other Länder (federal regions) in Germany have been joining the Deutsche Hotel- und Gaststättenverband (the German Hotel and Restaurant Association, DEHOGA) initiative 'Wir führen einen umweltorientierten Betrieb' (We run an environmentally orientated organization) (since 1993) and run regional awards with slightly different criteria. Some hundreds of companies from Mecklenburg-Vorpommern to Baden-Württemberg have been awarded. Since 1999 the regional partners of DEHOGA agreed to national harmonization. Local ecolabels exist, for example on the island of Borkum or the small region of Uckermark/Brandenburg.

In 2000 a dozen of the leading national tourism associations (including DEHOGA) are on the way to develop a common national brand for environmentally friendly tourism: an umbrella label for, if possible, all tourism services complete with a unified logo and, for each case, an appropriate catalogue of criteria. Thus it is planned that restaurants, leisure facilities, public transport providers, health spas, local governments and tourism providers will all determine the contents of such a brand together. The advantages of such an umbrella label are clear: by means of a unified, recurring logo the participants expect not only a higher level of acceptance among their customers but also, as a result of synergy, a marked reduction in marketing costs.

Denmark

The 'Gronne Nogle' (Green Key, since 1994) in Denmark in 1999 has been awarded to more than 100 hotels, youth hostels and restaurants. A private label for the environmental quality of holiday houses is run on the Island of Moen. Since the end of last year the Green Key has been in competition with the 'Nordic Ecolabel'.

Switzerland

In the region of Graubünden since 1994 the 'Öko-Grischun' has been awarded to 14 companies. It is likely that in 2000 the procedure and criteria will be updated.

Luxembourg

The Ecolabel für Luxemburger Tourismusbetriebe (for Luxembourg Tourism organizations) in 1999 certified the first 16 hotels, campsites and farm houses. In this smallest of the European member states the interest of accommodation companies to participate in this national scheme is still growing.

United Kingdom

Since 1996 in the UK, caravan and campsites, holiday parks and park home estates have been able to apply for the David Bellamy Conservation Award. In 1999 more than 200 applicants were awarded. In the same year in Scotland approximately 200 hotels and youth hostels participated in the Green Tourism Business Scheme and reached the bronze, silver or gold level. As a whole group all the Scottish British Trust Hotels have received the bronze level.

France

At the end of last year the French office of the Foundation of Environmental Education in Europe (FEEE) awarded the first 'Clefs Verts' (Green Keys) to 42 campsites. It is planned to develop the scheme also for hostels and holiday centres in France.

Spain

Local and smaller regional ecolabelling schemes exist on the Balearic (Alcudia) and Canary (Lanzarote) islands. 'El Distintivo de Garantía de Calidad Ambiental' (The Emblem of Guarantee of Environmental Quality) is the official ecolabel of the region of Catalonia. In 1999 the first campsite was awarded. More campsites followed in 2000 and the scheme will probably be developed for hotels and other accommodation services.

The Netherlands

Campsites in The Netherlands can participate in the private 'Milieu-barometer' scheme. Based on their participation in 1999 the first 63 sites got the 'Milieukeer' label (golden level of 'Milieubarometer'). This national labelling system will now be developed for hotels and swimming pools.

Belgium

In the region of Brussels-Capital from 2000 all types of companies, including accommodation, may apply for the 'Entreprise éco-dynamique' label (eco-dynamic enterprise). At present ten hotels are looking forward to reaching the 1, 2 or 3 star level.

Italy

Next to the joint Austrian/Italian 'Umweltzeichen Tirol-Südtirol' there are a few private run local certificates and ecolabels in Italy (e.g. at the Adriatic Sea). In 2000 the National Department for Environmental Protection (ANPA) stimulated and coordinated the discussion among the Italian stakeholder associations in order to prepare for the (possible) European Ecolabel for accommodation services.

Multinational schemes

Since 1990 the private company Verträglich Reisen, München, has been awarding accommodation services in Sweden, Finland, Germany, Austria, Switzerland and Italy with its 'Blaue Schwalbe' (Blue Swallow) label. In 1999 more than 100 companies fulfilled the criteria and have been published in the consumers' magazine *Verträglich Reisen* (120,000 copies). Since 1997 the ADAC Verlag, München, has been labelling campsites with the 'Öko-Pikto' (a green leaf) in its *Europäischer Camping und Caravaning Führer* (European Camping and Caravaning Traveller) (more than 300,000 copies). The 'green leaf' has been awarded to 231 campsites for their environmental initiatives and measures, especially for the use of solar energy.

Since 1997 in the eastern alpine area, the Deutscher Alpenverein, München, together with its partners in Austria and Italy are awarding alpine huts with the 'Umweltgütesiegel auf Alpenvereinshütten' (Environmental Seal of Quality for Mountain Huts) (four companies in 1999). The European Centre of Eco-Agro Tourism ECEAT, Amsterdam, is awarding 'Ecological Holiday Farms in the Countryside', for example in Germany as 'Urlaub auf Biohöfen in Deutschland'. This year the criteria and procedures have been developed for further countries in Eastern and Western Europe.

The Nordic Ecolabel is the common ecolabel of Sweden, Finland, Norway, Iceland and Denmark. It is the first and only official multi-national ecolabel for tourism services and could be seen as a model for the European level. Its criteria demand concrete limits in the consumption of water, energy, cleaning and washing substances and in the production of unsorted waste. The limits depend on the size, services and climatic situation of the companies. At the time of writing (May 2000) three companies have been awarded.

Are these Ecolabels Successful?

Bearing in mind the common goal of more sustainable tourism and the necessity to combine governmental and private, legal, financial and voluntary instruments, all of these above-mentioned ecolabels should represent a 'soft' approach to regulating the market. Authoritarian action, whether at national or European level, should be avoided as long as there is a spontaneous reduction in damage to the environment as a result of self-regulatory practices and commitment to the environment of establishments or resorts, factors which should be high on their list of choice criteria.

Many tourism service providers engage wholeheartedly in these environmental award schemes. In order to encourage them to take part, there has to be large-scale outreach to the public in order to publicize the awards or tourist products that qualify for ecolabels. The criteria for awarding these labels in most cases are laid down so that they offer just reward for the genuine efforts taken in the most important fields of action. The schemes, especially the official ones, are accompanied by appropriate measures, in particular guidelines, checklists and advice (e.g. on how hotels could be re-organized) for applicants. In these cases they have considerable effects, leading to numerous initiatives to reduce water and energy consumption, waste production and various traffic-related problems, and to preserve biodiversity and the beauty of the landscape. For this investment to be worthwhile and to enable the long-term objectives to be achieved, the label or award must not be just a marketing ploy, but must have a lasting effect.

Ecolabelling is a marketing tool to move the demand. So the most important thing, apart from the intrinsic quality of the services thus acknowledged, is to reach the public and the consumers. Here, the results obtained have been somewhat disappointing. The vast majority of holidaymakers are unaware of the existence of the environmental schemes in the tourism sector. And it is unlikely that any tangible results will be obtained while the major tour operators, tourist clubs, tourist information and reservation networks, the press and TV fail to publicize more actively the 2000 and more hotels, campsites, hostels and restaurants which were given such awards in 1999.

The European Ecolabel for a Common Tourism Market?

If ecolabels should serve to lay down minimum environmental standards below which it would be inaccurate to speak of 'quality tourism' and which, in conjunction with social, cultural and economic criteria, would make it easier to identify European areas which are contributing to more sustainable tourism in Europe, could the official European Ecolabel better support these objectives? The common European market calls for unified competition rules, not least in the international tourism sector. For this it is essential that prices and services are comparable and that consumers can access reliable and distinguishing information with ease. Developing a Europe-wide ecolabel could be an important step to make environmental soundness a more important issue in international tourism and to encourage existing ecolabelling schemes to harmonize, to join their efforts and to become more successful.

General objectives and principles

The general objective of European environmental policies is to contribute to sustainable development. The European Ecolabel scheme is established in Council Regulation no. 880/92, following the objective goals and priorities of the Fifth Environmental Action Programme and its revision, and it is in consonance with Agenda 21. The European Union's institutions are currently working on the revision of this EU Ecolabel Regulation, which will allow the implementation of ecolabels for services. This revision should be completed before the end of 2000.

The scheme is part of a broader strategy aimed at promoting sustainable production and consumption. This aim can be achieved in the context of a 'framework for an integrated life-cycle oriented product policy' (The EU Ecolabel Homepage: http//europa.eu.int/ecolabel). The objective is to promote products (meaning goods or services) which have the potential to reduce negative environmental impacts, as compared with the other products in the same product group, thus contributing to the efficient use of resources and a high level of environment protection (Common Position (EC) No. 6/2000). Tourism and particularly tourist accommodation have been identified as initial priorities for the development of ecolabels applied to services.

Information, as it is used by the scheme, is the main character of a market-based environmental policy. It is essential to diffuse information about the environmental effects of a service during its whole life cycle for supporting sustainable consumption (EU Ecolabel homepage).

Characteristics of the scheme

- The label is *selective*. The label is only given to those accommodations which fulfil the criteria.
- It is *transparent* (a clear indicator of the level of environmental performance of the specific accommodation), but also protective with regard to *confidential* information provided by individuals, public companies, interest groups, interested parties or other sources.
- It works with a *multi-criteria* approach, it is not based on a single parameter.
- It is *voluntary*, it is for the establishment to decide whether or not to apply.
- It has a *European dimension*. This avoids having to make an application in every country, including time-consuming and costly procedures and eliminates consumer confusion.

Methodological requirements for setting ecolabel criteria

The process of identifying and selecting the key environmental aspects as well as setting the ecolabel criteria will include the following steps:

1. *Feasibility and market study*: it will consider the various types of the product group in question on the Community market, the quantities provided, imported and sold, and the structure of the market in the Member States. Consumer perception, functional differences between types of services and the need for identifying subgroups will be assessed.

2. *Life cycle considerations*: key environmental aspects for which criteria will need to be developed will be defined through the use of life cycle considerations, and will be performed in accordance with internationally recognized methods and standards. The principles laid down in EN ISO 14040 and ISO 14024 will be duly taken into account, where appropriate.

3. *Improvement analysis*: the improvement considerations will take into account in particular the following aspects: the theoretical potential for environment improvement in conjunction with possible changes induced in the market structures; technical, industrial and economic feasibility and market modifications; and consumer attitudes, perceptions and preferences, which may influence the effectiveness of the ecolabel.

4. *Proposal of the criteria*: the final ecological criteria proposal will take into account the relevant environmental aspects related to the product group (Common Position (EC) No. 6/2000).

The potential value of a European ecolabel for tourist accommodations

A European ecolabel may provide *harmonization* on a European level: one official ecolabel and one ecolabelling system for different tourist destinations. The tourist sector is an internationally operating sector and many providers of tourist services operate in different European countries. At the EU workshop of July 1999, the ECTAA (the group of national travel agents' and tour operators' associations within the EU) highlighted the increasing European integration of tourism markets and stressed the importance of a harmonized language providing a clear message to consumers when it comes to identifying ecological forms of tourism. Providing one ecolabel for accommodation in different European destinations may:

- improve the recognition of best environmental practice for the consumer (one official label for accommodation in different destinations compared with many different labels, mostly private ones currently);
- stimulate the use of an ecolabel by tour operators (one label on accommodation in different destinations in tourist brochures, on the Internet, etc.);
- serve as a valuable tool for internationally operating providers of tourist services (the use of one system/set of criteria will limit the costs of applying for the ecolabel in different countries);
- encourage more direct and indirect cooperation and coordination among different national and regional ecolabels (a European ecolabel could serve as a guideline for national and regional initiatives); and
- provide a valuable example of European best practices in tourist accommodation for other areas in the world.

First steps of the European Commission for 'the European ecolabel for tourism services'

Based on these official requirements and aims for the potential benefits, in March 1999 the Commission, together with Competent Bodies, relaunched the 'Ecolabelling initiative in tourism' started by the Greek and the French Competent Body as early as 1994, when legislative restraints hindered a follow-up. At a 'European Hearing on Instruments favouring Sustainable Tourism and Green Purchasing' in Athens, the Ecolabel Unit at the European Commission outlined the significance of sustainable tourism and the necessity of credible benchmarking instruments. In two following meetings, participants of DG Environment, Competent Bodies and experts from Austria, Finland, Greece, Sweden and Spain prepared the ground for the initial workshop in July 1999. Here 70 participants including international stakeholders, representatives of the tourism industry, SMEs, tour operators, NGOs, Competent Bodies and Commission services had the opportunity to discuss a European labelling approach among a wider circle. The workshop ended by summarizing preliminary conclusions and the commitment for further networking for the next steps. Based on these conclusions most Member States were in favour of the next step: launching a new feasibility study (autumn 1999–autumn 2000) and an 'Ad Hoc Working Group on Tourism'. The feasibility study started in January 2000 and involves several tasks such as:

- analysing the nature of the European tourism market;
- characterizing the main different types of services;
- grouping them and analysing options for product groups;
- assessing best environmental practices and environmental impacts;
- identifying barriers and success factors;
- commenting on options for flexibility;
- investigating synergies and links to EMAS; and
- setting up an indicative priority list for feasibility and action at the European level.

In case of positive signals from the feasibility study, a third phase on criteria setting could start in 2000/2001, including a closer look at the entire life cycle (see: http://www.europa.eu.int/comm/environment/ecolabel.htm).

Little enthusiasm at the ECOTRANS panel discussion at ITB 2000

At the Internationale Tourismusbörse (ITB) in March 2000 in Berlin, the European network for Sustainable Tourism Development, ECOTRANS, invited Susanne Chlan of the Austrian Environmental Label, Wolf Michael Iwand of the TUI Group, Walter Leu of the European Travel Commission and Horst Nitschke of the ADAC to discuss the 'European Ecolabel for Tourism: yes or no?'. The following summary of the discussion may give a concrete idea of the issues, which necessarily have to be considered for the second and third phase on criteria setting for the European Ecolabel:

The TUI itself does not award an environmental label, however it does emphasize the environmentally conscious way of running the business of 215 of the hotels listed in its catalogues. 'We can check this ourselves and we guarantee this', said Mr Iwand, and asked: 'Who checks the current Ecolabels and the proposed European environmental label for tourism?'. The TUI knows its customers well and has noted that detailed information about environmental quality is rarely sought.

Much more important are the qualities which a customer associates with a brand: safety, health and a 100% money-back guarantee.

Thus, the ecolabels are not only competing with one another but also with the brands which are being promoted with big advertising budgets. This also became apparent when the Austrian environmental label was introduced: an environmental label cannot survive without marketing and an advertising budget. The Commission plans to call upon the member states for funding; so far they do not even provide for their own environmental labels very generously.

It is the European Travel Commission's view that the international market needs an authority, which will be responsible for a unified core message of all ecolabels. This is something which the European Commission might be able to provide. An alternative would be a 'Tourism Standard Agency' which could use licensing deals and fines to enforce compliance with agreed environmental qualities.

The ADAC, through Europe's largest caravan and camping guide, has long-standing experience with checking standards of quality of campsites. It awarded the 'grünes Blatt' (green leaf) to 200 of over 5000 campsites which switched to environmentally friendly solar technology. Horst Nitschke is not as pessimistic when it comes to customers' interest in environmental information: he refers to the success of the ADAC's summer service, which provides information on water quality in various holiday regions. Marketing advantages cannot be the only relevant factor, the tourism industry's responsibility for the future is at least as important a criterion. The current abundance of environmental labels is a reflection of the (industry's) will to act. With a view to the different underlying conditions of camping grounds across Europe, Nitschke is sceptical as to whether this multitude of criteria could be contained in a unified environmental label.

According to Wolf Michael Iwand, 'If you are taking the Eastern expansion of the EU into account, this becomes even more difficult . . . as the EU has to ensure a level competition and therefore cannot exclude the Eastern European countries'. 'Smallest common denominator for the EU-Ecolabel?', asks ECOTRANS. This is out of the question for Susanne Chlan. The Austrian environmental label has stricter guidelines than the EU and would only agree to be integrated into an EU-label if these are not compromised. What are the alternatives to an EU-ecolabel? Apart from a Tourism Standards Agency, an EU-supported concerted effort among the national environmental labels and an 'EU-label for ecolabels' were also discussed at the ITB. A title like 'EU acknowledged label for tourism' could serve to tell labels apart. In summary, there was little enthusiasm for a unified European environmental label, and a more sceptical view dominated (ECOTRANS, 2000).

Conclusions: The Nordic Ecolabel – a Model for Europe?

Despite all the scepticism and difficulties there are many experiences, voluntary initiatives and readiness among all of the interested groups to join efforts and to take common steps towards a European ecolabel. It is also not necessary to re-invent the wheel. For example, the Nordic Ecolabel, with its ambitious set of criteria, its reliable procedure and its flexible limits per country, might be a model for Europe. The more detailed explanation on the Nordic Ecolabel website (SIS Miljömärkning AB, 2000) is likely to be a good source of ideas for the further development of the 'first official European Ecolabel for Tourism', perhaps in 2002, the global 'Year of Ecotourism'.

Acknowledgement

This chapter is based on the research carried out by the European Network ECOTRANS, which hosts the most comprehensive database of ecolabels and environmental awards for tourism at www.eco-tip.org. The database contains among other things a 'spotlight' on the topic of ecolabels with current information, brief descriptions of all European environmental awards in the tourism sector, a list of award recipients and hundreds of positive examples of environmentally friendly tourism.

References

CREM and ET&P/CH2M-HILL (2000) FEMATOUR study, draft report to European Commission, D6 Environment,

ECOTRANS (2000), panel discussion at ITB 2000, 13 March 2000, Berlin (press release).

SIS Miljömärkning AB (2000) The Nordic Swan and Nordic Ecolabel for Tourism, www.svanen.nu. last updated 25 May 2000, viewed June 2000.

UNEP (1998) *Ecolabels in the Tourism Industry*. United Nations Environmental Programme, Paris.

Chapter 13

Turnover and Trends in Tourism Ecolabels

RALF C. BUCKLEY

Introduction

Ecolabels in tourism industry are relatively new and far from static. To gauge the likely future of ecolabels in the tourism sector, it is useful to examine what has happened to the various tourism ecolabels established or proposed in the past. Have they grown, survived unchanged, been merged with other schemes or disappeared? Have they lived up to their initial promises as regards technical content and operational processes such as audit and transparency? Have they become recognized by tourism companies, by individual consumers or by regulatory agencies? Are new schemes similar to old ones or are they significantly different and, if so, how?

This chapter examines turnover and trends in the number, content and scope of labels since they were first established. Their quality and effectiveness are addressed in Chapter 14.

Tourism ecolabels are little over a decade old. They commenced operation in 1987, when the Foundation for Environmental Education in Europe (FEEE) awarded its first 'Blue Flag' for beaches clean enough to swim from, and the Federation of German Travel Agencies (Deutsche Reisebüro Verband) awarded its first 'International Ecolabel' for environmentally oriented individuals, organizations and destinations. One year later in 1988, the 'Kleinwalser Valley Environmental Award' (formerly the 'Silver Thistle'), was first awarded, to accommodation operators in the German municipality of Mittelberg-Kleinwalser Valley.

Since then the number of labels has grown rapidly, and there are currently so many localized labels that they may mean little except to local consumers. Substantive criteria, focus, performance, industry uptake and customer awareness are far less mature for ecolabels in tourism and recreation than in manufacturing and forestry (Font and Tribe, 2001).

Methods

We used a variety of sources to compile a comprehensive directory of ecolabels in the tourism industry. In particular, we relied heavily on two reports (UNEP, 1998; AubE, 1998), and two websites (Ecotrans, 2000; Naturfreunde Internationale, 2000). The two written compendia incorporate most of the tourism ecolabels in operation up to 1997, including smaller single-nation schemes in languages other than English. The websites are more up-to-date but provide less detailed information. The EcoTour site (Naturfreunde Internationale, 2000) includes more labels, but in summary form only, and without links to web pages for the individual labels listed. The Eco-Tip site (Ecotrans, 2000) is less comprehensive, but does include weblinks for some labels, and some of its contents have been updated to February 2000.

To determine trends and turnover in these tourism ecolabels, we used three main approaches. First, we extracted relevant information from the reports and websites listed above. Second, we contacted the sponsoring organization for each ecolabel scheme, by mail or e-mail, and invited them to contribute information for the directory of ecolabels in this book. And third, we searched the World Wide Web for references either to the name of the ecolabel, or to the organization which sponsors or operates the ecolabel scheme.

Searches were conducted in January–June 2000, using a variety of search engines, but principally the powerful Google engine (www. google.com) and the Systran machine translation software (Altavista, 2000). Indirect references (e.g. in newspaper or magazine articles, or publicity materials for tourism operators which had been awarded the label) were followed up in an attempt to track down a current primary website for each the ecolabel schemes, either in English or in the primary language of the country concerned. The rationale behind this approach is that any tourism ecolabel except the most small-scale and localized, needs to be accessible to companies, consumers and travel agents worldwide or at least nationally if it is to be successful; and in the modern global tourism marketplace, this is unlikely to be achieved without a website. Certainly, the well-known ecolabel schemes in the tourism sector, as well as environmental awards and accreditation programmes, do indeed have their own websites.

The report by UNEP (1998) was a representative rather than exhaustive review of tourism ecolabels existing at that time. Hence, even though the other sources list many more ecolabel schemes than the UNEP report, the additional labels are not necessarily new in origin. Indeed, it is clear from the summaries in the EcoTour website that many of them were already in existence at the time of UNEP Report. Therefore it is not possible, from these web-based materials alone, to determine a complete history and life-cycle for every tourism ecolabel which has ever been established. To achieve that level of detail would require interviews, in the relevant local language, with staff from the various organizations currently operating each of the ecolabel schemes or which were operating them when they were last in existence. That would be an expensive and difficult undertaking well beyond the resources of this investigation, particularly since many of these labels no longer exist, or have been taken over by different operating organizations.

By combining the approaches outlined above, however, it has proved possible to identify changes both to the labels listed by UNEP (1998), and major labels listed only in other sources. Further information is provided in the directory of labels later in this book.

Results

The UNEP report on tourism ecolabels (UNEP, 1998) tabulated schemes in four categories, namely international, regional, national and subnational. The same structure will be followed here, also including other labels under these four headings. The current status of these schemes may be summarized as follows.

International schemes

Green Globe 21 (Green Globe, 2000) is the only large-scale global ecolabel covering the entire tourism industry, operating as an environmental management and awareness programme for the travel and tourism industry. The strengths of Green Globe 21 are its recognition within the tourism sector, due largely to a massive marketing campaign by the former Green Globe; and its strategic alliances with organizations such as UNEP, the World Travel and Tourism Council (WTTC), the World Tourism Organization (WTO), the International Air Transport Association (IATA), the International Hotel and Restaurant Association (IH&RA) and the Pacific-Asia Travel Association, and with regional tourism ecolabels such as PATA's Green Leaf and Denmark's Green Key. Green Globe 21 has also entered into agreements with international environmental audit companies in relation to certification. Further detail is provided in the Directory of Ecolabels and the Discussions below.

There are two labels run by private consultancies as part of their environmental management services. Whilst international in scope, they are lacking in critical mass, particularly since they now compete directly with Green Globe 21. Ecotel, a private label assigned to hotels certified by a private consulting company, still exists but has been applied to only 40 hotels in all, and appears to be largely a promotional device by the consulting company HVS international, based in the US. The hotels certified are mostly based in Central America, with some in the US, Japan and India. Another consulting company, RUES Hotel Management and Consulting, runs the label Ecofriendly Hotels Worldwide, which started in Bolivia with 22 hotels affiliated in 1994. Initially, the scheme focused on North and Latin America, although since 1998 it has also approached independent hotels in Europe, and it has recently signed a co-operation contract with a Bavarian tour operator (Kahlenborn, personal communication).

The distinction between ecolabels, awards and accreditation programmes is not always clear (Chapter 2). UNEP (1998) listed two programmes run by the conservation organization Audubon International, the Audubon Cooperative Sanctuary Programme and the Audubon Signature Cooperative Sanctuary Programme, under the heading of international tourism ecolabels. Strictly, these are environmental conservation awards given to sites used incidentally for tourism and recreation, rather than ecolabels intended specifically to promote sustainably managed tourism. Whilst the objective of these awards is to recognize good conservation practices, the recipients may use them to promote their tourism activities. At least one US mountain resort is currently negotiating for Audubon accreditation (Proteau, personal communication). Hence, even if the distinction is clear to the sponsoring organization, it may not always be apparent to the consumer. Indeed, even if these awards are not intended as ecolabels, they are being used that way, in the broad sense of a label using the environment to promote a product.

The perspective of Audubon International itself is expressed as follows by Howard Jack, Vice President and Chief Operating Officer (Jack, personal communication):

> These programmes are designed to educate and assist property owners and managers in how they can voluntarily develop or manage their properties in ways that are better for the environment, particularly wildlife and water. Our certifications in those programmes give the participating businesses' properties recognition for what the businesses have learned and accomplished, as reflected in the steps taken to develop or manage the properties. We understand that certification in the ACSP or the ASCSP can have important 'good will' marketing or community relations benefits for many of the participating businesses, which often might well be a motivating factor for participation. One of those types of benefits is the incidental value some of the participating businesses find certification provides in attracting tourists to their facilities . . . [But] ecolabelling for tourism is not the focus of our programmes . . . [and] many, if not most, of our members do not cater to tourists. We do not wish to create a misimpression or skew the focus of the programmes by suggesting in any

way that these are labelling or certification programmes for ecotourism purposes.

Similarly, there are voluntary environmental codes in many industry sectors which individual companies may sign up to or otherwise endorse publicly. These may well have been set up simply to promote improved management of environmental or social impacts. If they are used by individual companies as a marketing device, however, then from a consumer perspective they become ecolabels, albeit weak ecolabels without certification. Both Green Globe and the PATA Green Leaf (see below) allow individual tour companies to use their labels, at least for an initial period, simply by signing on to a code or commitment. The recently launched 'Tour Operators Initiative for Sustainable Tourism Development' (Orizzonti, 2000), a voluntary environmental code supported by the United Nations Environment Programme, the United Nations Educational, Scientific and Cultural Organization and the World Tourism Organization, is not intended as an ecolabel; but it is not clear that consumers, travel agents or tourism marketing programmes will make this distinction. Similar consideration apply to a number of the awards, programmes and labels reviewed in Chapter 14.

In addition to codes produced by tourism organizations and industry associations, a number of tourism accommodation, transport and tour providers have their own corporate environmental management programmes in place. For example, British Airways has an environmental code attached to its internal partnership policy, e.g. for suppliers to BA Holidays. Government agencies and voluntary groups have also produced environmental guidelines, manuals and codes of conduct for tourism. These are not intended as ecolabels in the sense of a distinguishing device for consumer choice, but they may easily be misunderstood as such.

The best international example of a single-company system is the environmental certification programme run by the German company Turistik Union International (TUI, 2000). Under this programme, TUI: (i) encourages improved environmental management by hotels listed in their brochures; (ii) includes environmental information on these hotels in TUI holiday brochures; (iii) requires contract partners to complete a TUI environmental checklist; and (iv) collects environmental information on these partners through guests as well as employees on site. Currently, TUI advertises 200 of its 10,000 contractual partners worldwide as having sound management. Although TUI does not intend or promote this programme as an ecolabel (Latussek, personal communication), it has all the characteristics of a global environmental accreditation scheme for both German and English-speaking tourists. Tourists booking holidays through TUI can see clearly that: (i) the TUI programme covers a very large number of tourism providers; (ii) some operators are listed with environmental credentials whereas others are not; and (iii) that there is an independent audit system which they themselves can contribute to. This is more than most self-described ecolabel schemes can claim. It therefore seems likely that the TUI programme may well have more practical impact on consumer choice than any ecolabel scheme, perhaps even Green Globe 21.

TUI also runs two award schemes: the 'TUI Environmental Champion', which recognizes five hotels each year for their environmental performance as judged from guest questionnaires; and an 'International Environment Award', which recognizes the work of NGOs in tourism destinations.

One of the best known environmental awards, often treated as a tourism ecolabel, is the British Airways Tourism for Tomorrow Awards. These are well known, highly coveted, and heavily used in international marketing by the recipients. The current format of the awards gives them a wide international coverage and publicises some examples of good practice (Neale, 1998; Buckley and Sommer, 2000; Somerville, personal communication; Foxlee, personal communication). The selection process and criteria, however, are not set up as a label scheme.

A number of other international organizations are also showing interest in operating tourism ecolabel schemes. These include the Brazil branch of the World Wide Fund for Nature (Woolford, personal communication); and the World Bank, which commissioned a study in 1998 to investigate the options for an international label with particular emphasis on developing countries (Kahlenborn, personal communication).

Regional schemes

The majority of regional labels relate to European initiatives, generally part-funded by the European Union. The strongest of the regional schemes is the European Blue Flag label (FEEE, 2000) operated by the Foundation for Environmental Education in Europe (FEEE) and funded by the European Commission DG XI (Environment) as a tool in the Campaign on the Implementation of the Bathing Water Quality Directive. This is the best example of a thriving regional label, with over 1800 beaches and over 600 marinas accredited in 2000. Accreditation must be re-earned every year, and accreditation criteria are publicly available on the Blue Flag website (FEEE, 2000). In recent years the Blue Flag programme has expanded towards Eastern Europe, covering 21 countries to date. FEEE has also encouraged similar initiatives elsewhere, both through publications (UNEP/WTO/FEEE, 1997), and by establishing contacts with relevant organizations in the

USA, South Africa, Egypt and Southeast Asian nations (Kahlenborn, personal communication). It appears that forthcoming changes in the programme's funding structure, however, may force the organizers to rethink its pricing, criteria, operations and geographical targets in the near future.

The European Charter for Sustainable Tourism in Protected Areas is a pan-European project aiming to improve the environmental management of tourism and recreation in national parks. Funding was provided by the European Union (LIFE94 ENV/F/000878) until 1999, and the project is currently pending further funding. It was co-ordinated by the Parcs Naturels Régionaux de France and the Federation Europarc. Outcomes to date include the guidelines, application procedures, a steering committee and case studies from pilot parks. It cannot yet be considered a functional tourism ecolabel.

A regional tourism ecolabel of particular note is the new Nordic Ecolabel for Hotels, a Scandinavian scheme covering Iceland, Norway, Sweden, Finland and Denmark. This ecolabel is especially interesting for two reasons. Firstly, it has been established under the umbrella of the Swan label, a broad ecolabel which already has good penetration in manufacturing products, from paper to machinery, in Scandinavia. Hence it can take advantage of the greater maturity of ecolabels in forestry and manufacturing than in tourism. Secondly, it is one of the few tourism ecolabels based on quantitative environmental performance criteria, e.g. for energy consumption *per capita*, wastewater quality, etc., which apply uniformly across the entire scheme. To receive accreditation, a hotel must meet these criteria irrespective of its initial circumstances; so consumers can be assured that certified hotels meet basic minimum standards of environmental performance. This contrasts with labels such a Green Globe 21, which currently require only a commitment to improvement against internal company-by-company benchmarks. The current criteria for the Nordic Ecolabel for Hotels apply from October 1999 to September 2002, when they are to be reconsidered and perhaps revised. The label has only recently started operation, and fewer than ten hotels have been accredited to date. Hamele (Chapter 12) considers it to be the best example of international co-operation in tourism ecolabelling. Recommendations made to the European Commission under a new 'Feasibility and market study for developing a product group in tourism accommodations for the European Union Eco-label scheme' (FEMATOUR) may well reflect this (CREM, 2000).

The European Golf Association Ecology Unit, part of a golf industry association, advertises the 'Committed to Green' label, commenced in 1997 in a launch by the European Commission president, Jacques Santer. To date, 80 of an estimated 5200 European golf courses are involved in a pilot programme, but none of them have been certified.

Accreditation criteria have not been formalized, and the scheme appears somewhat embryonic.

The Blue Swallow scheme (Blaue Schwalbe) for tourist hotels is a regional label, though it is restricted by the requirement that hotels must be accessible from Germany by public transport, without air travel. In practice it is heavily weighted towards Central Europe, though it does also have members in Scandinavia. It began in 1990 with seven hotels, and currently has about 80 members. It is organized by Verträglich Reisen, a non-profit organization from Germany, which publishes a magazine including details of the hotels. Other regional awards include Europa Nostra and Top Team Natour, a national youth competition run by Deutsche Bundesstiftung Umwelt.

The Tourfor award (see Chapter 7) is the working title for a proposed ecolabel aimed at tourism and recreation in European forests and woodlands (Buckinghamshire Chilterns University College, 2000). Funded by the EU (LIFE96 ENV/UK/000413) the project has been developed and piloted in the UK, Finland and Portugal. Detailed proposals were submitted to the LIFE office in January 2000, with a recommendation for the Foundation for Environmental Education (FEEE) to take over the award. The principles for this label can be extended to any rural tourism and outdoor recreation provider, not merely forest sites, so it could easily be merged with other tourism ecolabels.

A new initiative by the World Wide Fund for Nature International, the PAN Parks Initiative (WWF, 2000a) aims to certify good management of environmental and social impacts of tourism in a selection of large national parks in Europe. It has been developed by WWF International with funding from Molecaten, a Dutch leisure and tourism group. Its long-term vision is the consolidation of parks with importance beyond their national boundaries, likely to sustain key wildlife in Europe. The project has engaged a variety of parks, mostly in Eastern Europe, and is currently developing criteria (WWF, 2000b). WWF's access to sponsorship underpins the continuation of this programme, at least in the short to medium term.

At a more localized but still crossborder scale, there are several small tourism ecolabels in and around Austria. Kleinwalser Valley, a tourist destination area on the border between Germany and Austria operated its 'Silver Thistle' ecolabel until 1993/94, according to the Eco-Tour website. According to the Eco-Tip website, this has now been superseded by the 'Q-Plus-Kleinwalsertal' ecolabel (TIS Corporation, 2000) which covers all forms of tourism enterprise, including ski and snowboard schools. As of 1999, 148 businesses had earned the Q-Plus label. As of 1998, the Tyrolean Environmental Seal of Quality (Austria and Italy) had been granted to 229 enterprises in the Tyrol and South Tyrol, according to the Eco-Tip website. According to the Eco-Tour website, new criteria for this label were being developed in 1998, for application in 1999. Whilst being regional in the sense of crossing national boundaries, these labels effectively have only local relevance and scope.

The only non-European regional scheme reported here is the Green Leaf ecolabel from the Pacific Asia Travel Association, PATA. This was first awarded in 1995, as part of the PATA 'Code for Responsible Tourism' launched in 1992. This programme is apparently still in existence, although there is limited information available: the organization's web page www.pata.org does not list either criteria or accredited products. Membership of Green Leaf is apparently based simply on signing the code and paying fees. This label has entered into a strategic alliance with Green Globe 21 and there are plans to integrate it into this broader programme.

National schemes

There are a variety of national schemes, most of which cover only specific types or components of tourism operations, such as ecotours, golf courses, destinations, campsites or hotels. Most of these schemes are organized by national industry associations or non-profit organizations with an interest in the particular type of tourism concerned. They are generally intended to improve environmental performance within that sector, although individual companies may use them for a variety of other purposes. National schemes can generally only grow by increasing their market share within their own particular sector (see Chapter 16), or by expanding to related sectors. Principal amongst these is the Nature and Ecotourism Accreditation Programme in Australia, described in detail in Chapter 11.

The Seaside Award from the UK's Tidy Britain Group (Tidy Britain Group, 2000) has accredited 260 beaches to date. This compares with the 41 British beaches and 26 marinas accredited under the Blue Flag programme, reflecting a difference in focus for the two schemes, however, rather than difference in stringency. The Seaside Award is based mainly on the provision of tourist facilities, principally in resorts, and places less importance on water quality. This award has a good coverage of resort beaches in the UK, and is currently increasing its scope to include rural beaches with fewer facilities. Possibilities for further expansion, however, are clearly limited.

A Worldwide Fund for Nature ecolabel for rural tourist accommodation in France, Gîtes Panda, also seems to have been adopted extensively, to judge from tourist accommodation listings (Fédération des Parcs naturels Régionaux de France, 2000). It is Gîtes de France that undertakes most of the certification work, endorsed by WWF

France. The relevant WWF website (WWF, 2000c) does not provide information on criteria. This label has potential for growth within the Eurogites system of marketing booking rural accommodation in Europe.

The David Bellamy Award for environmental management by holiday parks in the UK's British Holiday and Home Parks Association (BH&HP, 1999) is also fully operational, with three levels of accreditation. Although named as an award, this is effectively operated as a label scheme. Parks are assessed by the UK Conservation Foundation, co-funded by Bellamy. There are currently 120 parks with gold, 108 with silver and 26 with bronze awards.

Austria currently has a variety of tourism ecolabels, but only one seems to be national: the Bundesumweltzeichen, referred to in English-language materials as the 'Austrian Ecolabel for Tourism', or in the Eco-Tour website as the 'Austrian Environmental Mark for Tourism Enterprise.' This was operated in 1999–2000 by the Austrian Consumer Association, and in 1998 by Umweltberatung GmbH. It took over the successful 'Öko Tourismuspreis in Oberoesterreich', which was developed by the Upper Austrian Tourist Board in 1991, but ceased operations in 1997/98. To date, the Bundesumweltzeichen label has been awarded to around 100 companies. According to the Eco-Tip website, there are several other tourism ecolabel schemes in Austria, but they are all smaller either in scope or geographical coverage. They include 'Dörfurlaub in Österreich,' which listed 37 businesses in 1998; 'Grüne Baum' (Green Tree) with two awards in 1998 and one in 1999; 'Grüne Hand' (Green Hand), with no information available since 1995; and another local scheme in Lungau. These may well be subsumed in time into the Bundesumweltzeichen label.

The German automobile association Allgemeiner Deutscher Automobil-Club eV (ADAC) is known internationally, but its websites (ADAC, 2000) apparently do not refer to its 'Environmental Squirrel' label in either German (Umwelteichhörnchen) or English. The Eco-Tour website suggests that in 1998 it has two sets of operational criteria, one for holiday parks and the other for motorway service stations. The Eco-Tip website says that ADAC made only one Environmental Squirrel award in 1997, none in 1998, and one in 1999, and that the scheme may soon be discontinued. The Eco-Trans website mentions, however, that ADAC now runs another tourism ecolabel, 'Grüne Baumchen' (Green Sapling) with 11 accredited businesses in Germany and ten in Switzerland, as of 1999. This appears to be quite distinct from the 'Grüne Baum' (Green Tree) label run by Collegium Touristicum Carinthiae in Austria.

The 'Grüne Koffer' (Green Suitcase) label proposed by the German NGO Ökologischer Tourismus in Europe has been under development intermittently since 1991, but is not operational. Criteria have been planned for destinations, companies and travel agents respectively, but none have yet been implemented. The future of the 'Grune Koffer' will depend on whether Germany adopts a unified national tourism ecolabel.

One German label with some weight at present is the 'We are an environmentally oriented establishment' tag, run by the Deutscher Hotel- und Gaststättenverband (DeHoGa, 2000). Around 900 businesses had qualified for the label by the end of 1997, most of them under regional schemes which have mutual-recognition agreements with the central DeHoGa label. These regional labels may also use the DeHoGa name, as for example in the Schleswig-Holstein label mentioned on the Eco-Tip website. Outside Germany, the Deutscher Hotel- und Gaststättenverband is known best for its 40-item environmental code of conduct, which has been publicized on green-travel listservers. This code covers a range of basic issues such as water and energy conservation, and sewage and waste management.

The small nation of Luxembourg has its own tourism ecolabel (Stiftung Öko-Fonds, 2000), which exemplifies the evolution of ecolabels in tourism. The Luxembourg Ecolabel started with the creation of a steering committee in 1996. In the following year it was organized as a competition and award scheme. This then led to benchmarking and definition of criteria for the current ecolabel, which has started full operation in the 1998/99 season. According to the Eco-Tip website, the label incorporates 100 criteria. By May 2000, 19 companies had received accreditation, out of a total of 700 accommodation providers in the Grand Duchy of Luxembourg. It will be interesting to follow its future growth and progress.

In Ireland, the EU LIFE programme (LIFE94 ENV/IRL/000399) funded a project to develop a destination ecolabel under the acronym NASC. The project was undertaken by the West Coast of Ireland County Councils and the University College of Galloway. Its aim was to define an area-based 'environmental quality mark' designed to promote sustainability by involving environmental managers in land-use planning. The concept was one of assured quality and environmental integrity within a given geographical area, initially for use in develop-ment and marketing of sustainable tourism, but with ultimate potential to be extended to the marketing of all goods and services originating within that area. The project cost 800,000 Euros and was completed in 1997. Official sources claim that a strategy is being prepared to implement the results in the country on a broader basis, especially in the context of fulfilling county council duties under Agenda 21. To date, however, there seems to be little concrete evidence of outcomes.

Most Danish hotels belong to the national hotel industry association HORESTA (www.danishhotels.dk), which operates an ecolabel called The Green Key (Grøne Nøgle, Grüner Schlussel) (www.thegreenkey.com). The Green Key scheme is variously reported to include either 56 criteria, according to the EcoTour website; or 74, according to the Eco-Tip site. Criteria include energy and water conservation, waste management, and provision of environmental information. Over 100 businesses have currently met these criteria. The scheme is currently under revision, to be taken over in 2001 by HORESTA and the new Danish 'Destination 21.' This label has also reported plans to introduce itself to the broader Scandinavian market in the near future, and has apparently signed a partnership agreement with Green Globe 21 (Kaas, personal communication).

The Green Key name is also used for a French tourism ecolabel (Ifrance, 2000) run by the Foundation for Education and Environment in Europe (FEEE), the same organization running the Blue Flag. According to Eco-Trans, 42 campsites and caravan parks had been granted the Clefs Vertes label in 1999.

Apart from the Australian NEAP scheme, only one national tourism ecolabel ever appears to have been established outside Europe, and it now seems to be defunct. This was the Green Leaf label in Thailand, which was mentioned in UNEP promotional material from a few years ago. Its last-known secretariat address was at the Tourism Authority of Thailand, however, and the current TAT website (Tourism Authority of Thailand 2000) makes no mention of it. It seems likely that it may have been subsumed into the PATA Green Leaf programme, now joining Green Globe 21.

Subnational schemes

Both UNEP (1998) and the Eco-Tour and Eco-Tip websites list a number of small-scale subnational labels and awards, all of them in Europe. They are examined in more detail in Chapters 12 and 14. Subnational tourism ecolabels seem to be most prevalent in countries which have strong local or regional subnational governments: over 15 in Germany, several in Austria, and three in Spain. Most of these are for hotels, campsites and other tourist accommodation, and a few seem to be destination labels encompassing entire local communities.

The local label Eco-Grishun or Öko Grischun (Eco Ibex) in Graubunden, Switzerland, apparently does not have its own listing on the Worldwide Web. It is mentioned in the Eco-Tour website, but with no detail to determine if it is still operational. The Eco-Tip website says that 14 businesses have been awarded between 1 and 56 'ibexes', and that the scheme is currently being revised to incorporate substantive performance criteria as well as process criteria.

The Spanish labels are all run independently, apparently with no plans for integration. The local government authority for Alcudia in

Majorca (Ajuntament d'Alcudia 2000) still operates its 'Distintivo Ecotouristico' award for hotels and restaurants, but its scope is limited. The main focus is on energy, water and paper conservation. The label in the Canary Islands has not had the take-up expected, and the Catalan label is still embryonic. A broader tourism ecolabel for the entire Balearic Isles, referred to by UNEP (1998), is not yet operational.

The Green Tourism Business Scheme in Scotland was established in 1998 by the Tourism and Environment Forum and is operated by the Quality Assurance section of the Scottish Tourism Board (Scottish Tourist Board, 2000). As of April 2000, 27 businesses had received gold awards, 77 silver and 98 bronze, with several more pending awards. According to the Eco-Tip website, it has 100 criteria. The Scottish Golf Course Wildlife Initiative, also mentioned by UNEP (1998) is apparently not an ecolabel. Neither of the Scottish schemes is mentioned in the EcoTour website.

Discussion: Green Globe 21

Perhaps the most important developments in the field of tourism certification are the global schemes. The most significant appear to be Green Globe 21 and the programme run by the German Touristik Union International (TUI); the former for its international recognition within the tourism industry, and the latter for its effectiveness in influencing holiday decisions by individual tourists (see Chapter 16). Given that the TUI scheme claims not to be an ecolabel, this leaves Green Globe 21 heading the global stakes in tourism ecolabelling. It will therefore be considered in some detail.

As described in the directory of labels, Green Globe 21 is a re-branding of the Green Globe ecolabel established by the World Travel and Tourism Council. Green Globe 21 is now established as a self-supporting corporation, independent of WTTC. It has appointed global auditors and three regional operators, for the Americas, Asia-Pacific and Africa-Europe regions respectively. The Green Globe name is relatively well known in the tourism industry, and Green Globe 21 has the potential to become an effective international environmental performance label for the entire tourism sector. To date, however, though it has made some useful steps in that direction, it has also made some stumbles.

The critical issue is the balance between marketing, to increase its penetration in the industry; and substance, to persuade consumers to treat it seriously. Whilst Green Globe 21 has promised to incorporate meaningful technical criteria and audit, that claim is in itself part of the Green Globe 21 marketing campaign, and it is too soon to judge whether the scheme can live up to its promises. Even if its coordinators and most of its client companies have the best intentions, customer acceptance can easily be lost if any of its accredited companies demonstrate poor environmental performance.

Green Globe 21 has recently received significant criticism in a report for WWF-UK on tourism certification (Synergy 2000; Windebank and Woolford, 2000). Some of the concerns raised are similar to those summarized in Chapter 2, but there are also issues relating to credibility and consumer behaviour, as below. Green Globe 21 Asia-Pacific has responded to the WWF report via an open e-mail to an international green-travel listserver (Koch, 2000).

The first major criticism raised by WWF-UK (2000) is that Green Globe 21 claims to be advised by both WWF and the World Tourism Organization, but to date has not asked for or taken any such advice, at least from WWF. The response from Green Globe 21 (Koch, 2000) is that its International Advisory Council met in November 2000. This is all very well, but if Green Globe 21 really wants advice from WWF and WTO, it would seem more effective to provide them with draft materials, confidentially if necessary, as soon as these are produced.

The second major criticism by WWF-UK is that Green Globe 21 will allow companies to use its logo as soon as they sign up for the scheme, typically 2 years before they actually become accredited. Fully accredited companies can use a subtly different logo, essentially the basic logo plus a tick, but most consumers will probably not recognize this distinction. Koch's response is that companies which sign up for the scheme have 'made a public commitment to improve their environmental performance and to achieve tangible environmental improvements'.

Unfortunately, however, this means that either intentionally or otherwise, individual companies may be able to display the Green Globe 21 logo for up to 2 years even if they have extremely poor environmental management at the time of sign-up. Even if only a small proportion of enrolling companies follow this path, consumer acceptance of Green Globe 21 is likely to be damaged very seriously. As Koch (2000) notes 'there is a good deal of trust in the integrity of companies in this step'. From a consumer viewpoint, however, the whole point of certification schemes is so that consumers do not have to take the integrity of companies on trust. Green Globe 21 has taken some precautions against this risk, in that companies must go through a 1-year registration period initially, without using the logo (Koch, 2000). Presumably, Green Globe 21 intends to use this step to screen out applicants which it thinks will not do credit to the programme. How this may work in practice remains to be seen.

The third major concern raised by WWF-UK is that Green Globe 21 is based on process rather than substance, and specifically, that it is modelled on the ISO 14000 series of standards for environmental management systems. The Green Globe 21 response (Koch, 2000) is that ISO 14000 'is the most widespread quality environmental standard used by industry generally'. This is true, but that doesn't mean it works, just that it has been widely adopted. There have been calls for many years (e.g. Buckley, 1989, 1996) for the tourism industry to adopt routine environmental management tools from other industry sectors; and certainly, environmental management systems are one such tool. ISO 14000, however, is by no means state-of-the-art, and has been heavily criticized precisely because it is process-based and provides no guarantee of substantive performance (Gunningham and Grabowsky, 1998). Effective processes are necessary, but not sufficient.

The fourth criticism is that even after the 2-year pre-audit commit-ment phase, Green Globe 21 is based solely on continuous improve-ment by each individual company against its own pre-accreditation baseline, not on meeting industry-wide performance thresholds. Experience from quality labels in other industry sectors (Chapter 2), and tourism ecolabels in Europe (Chapter 6), suggests that consumers tend to give little credence to industry-run schemes which are based on processes rather than substantive criteria. It is true that quantitative performance standards need to be customized closely both to the type and size of tourism activity, and the environments where they operate. Performance criteria for a small boat tour, for example, will be completely different than those for a large resort. Similarly, standards for *per capita* energy and water consumption for hotels in equatorial regions, for example, will be quite inapplicable in polar regions. It is, however, quite possible to develop quantitative performance standards for specific types of tourism activity in specific environments, as shown by the new Nordic Ecolabel for Hotels summarized above.

According to Koch (2000), 'Green Globe 21 will be releasing its new generation of [eight] Company Sector Guides in early 2001, which include benchmarking . . . as [a] key component'. Again, it remains to be seen how much substantive information these guides contain, and to what degree Green Globe 21 requires acccredited companies to meet or better the benchmarks. For example, if they are incorporated only as targets or company-by-company indicators rather than industry-wide threshold standards, they will provide consumers with little grounds for confidence. This applies particularly for tourists from Europe and North America, who are already familiar with this issue from other industry sectors, such as the chemical, manufacturing and automobile industries. If companies only have to show improvement against their own internal benchmarks, they may specify artificially lax benchmarks so they can appear to show improvement without actually making any change. Note that the on-site audits proposed by Green Globe 21 would not take place until the end of the initial 2-year commitment phase (Koch, 2000). At best this is naïve, and at worst, as suggested by

Windebank and Woolford, it could be greenwash. It is all too easy for well-intentioned environmental practitioners to become inadvertent marketing tools for companies where environmental performance is not a high priority (Beder, 1997).

Perhaps equally important, the environmental parameters used to assess corporate improvements relate only to so-called 'brown' environmental issues such as energy efficiency and waste management, including greenhouse gas production. These are important indicators of environmental performance, certainly; but they are not sufficient. Equally important are so-called 'green' issues relating to land use and biodiversity. If these parameters are not included, then a tourism operator or developer which had, say, caused the local or even global extinction of plant or animal species by clearing their last remaining habitat for a resort or golf course, could still obtain certification from Green Globe 21 simply by installing energy efficient light globes. This would make a nonsense of the entire scheme.

Another possible way to address these concerns is to ask, if WWF-UK or anyone else were to design a tourism ecolabel and certification scheme with the maximum chance of actually improving environmental performance in the tourism sector worldwide, how might it differ from Green Globe 21 as it currently stands?

The philosophy of Green Globe 21 seems to be that global improvement requires a global certification scheme. This does indeed seem to have advantages for brand recognition, but there are at least two alternatives. One option is a proliferation of national schemes, as occurs for ecolabels in other industry sectors. The advantages and disadvantages of these approaches were reviewed earlier in this book (Chapter 2). Another option would be for Green Globe 21 to act solely as a global umbrella, accrediting national tourism accreditation schemes rather than individual tourism operators, products or destinations. This approach has much to commend it in developed nations, but may not be practicable in some developing nations.

Similarly, the philosophy of Green Globe 21 seems to be that realistically, the scheme can only hope to achieve significant market penetration if initial certification is based only on commitment rather than performance. Schemes such as the Nordic Ecolabel for Hotels or the Australian Nature and Ecotourism Accreditation Programme demand demonstrated performance before any accreditation is granted, and they seem to be thriving; but they have relatively low market penetration to date.

Again, Green Globe 21 seems to have adopted the philosophy that improvement within each individual company is enough to justify accreditation; or perhaps, that setting external standards, though desirable, would take too long for a global ecolabel scheme covering all types of tourism activity. The former seems questionable, but the latter may well be correct. There will always be a balance between proceeding immediately with what is available at the time, or improving the scheme but starting later.

And finally, Green Globe 21 seems to have focused its attention initially on parameters such as energy consumption and greenhouse gas generation, which can be improved by individual companies in small quantifiable increments and can therefore provide positive feedback to those companies and encourage further improvement. This is a reasonable philosophy, but it needs a set of backup criteria for equally important if less easily quantifiable issues such as biodiversity impacts. What would happen, for example, if a company certified by Green Globe 21 caused a threat to a rare species? It would only take one or two well-publicized incidents for the entire scheme to be thrown into disrepute.

In summary, therefore, it seems that there are several critical features of Green Globe 21 which could be read either as greenwash, naivety or judgement calls which may well prove correct. We shall have to wait several years to determine which proves to be the case. Meanwhile, as a surrogate measure of the scheme's intentions, we can watch to see how much notice is taken of advice by organizations such as WWF-UK.

Discussion: General Trends

Currently at least, there seems to be an enormous proliferation of small-scale and specialist tourism ecolabels in Europe, particularly in Germany and neighbouring countries but also in the UK. Most are aimed principally at hotels, guesthouses and campgrounds, but there are also 'destination' labels run by local municipalities. There is a corresponding proliferation of environmental prizes and awards in the European tourism industry. Consumer reaction to this plethora is not known. Some of the smaller seals and awards mentioned in the report by UNEP (1998) no longer appear to be active, although it is difficult to know if they have formally ceased operations. Others appear to have been incorporated into national schemes. Some, however, seem to be still operating at their original small scale, and a number of new schemes have been established recently. It would therefore be premature to conclude that there is no longer a place in the tourism sector for localized ecolabels.

A number of countries have national tourism ecolabel schemes. Some of these are run by private industry associations, some by non-government organizations. And for some at least, national governments seem to have a more or less active role either in endorsing the label or operating the ecolabel programme. All of these national schemes are operated principally in the language of the country concerned, suggesting that they are aimed principally at domestic tourists, inbound agents and/or domestic tour regulators. Some of them, however, are also publicized in English, presumably so as to be accessible to international visitors and outbound agents from other countries. Most of these national schemes are in European nations. Most are aimed at the accommodation sector and focus on energy, water and waste management. There is also an effective national ecolabel in Australia, but it is restricted to the specialist nature and ecotourism sector. A national tourism ecolabel in Thailand appears to be no longer operational.

Of the regional ecolabels, the most successful seems to have been the Blue Flag label for beaches and marinas. Blue Flag is particularly interesting for several reasons. When first established, it was a destination-quality label, and one for which there was strong public demand: it showed clearly which beaches were safe to swim from, in a region where many are not. It was taken up widely by both destinations and consumers, and established a public reputation which made it easy to expand to marinas. The addition of marinas, however, appears to have created some confusion amongst consumers, who have come to treat the Blue Flag logo as a sign of water safe to swim in. Apparently, this has led to people swimming in marinas; whereas the Blue Flag label for marinas is in fact an environmental performance label, aimed at environmentally concerned boat owners. A third interesting feature of the Blue Flag Programme is that in the UK, it is operated by a pre-existing organization, Tidy Britain. This franchising arrangement for Blue Flag operates in parallel with the original Seaside Award established by Tidy Britain, which is also still operational. In contrast with Blue Flag, the Green Leaf ecolabel established by the Pacific-Asia Travel Association seems to have had rather low uptake, and is now to be subsumed into Green Globe 21. There is also a new regional ecolabel for hotels in Scandinavia, which ranks highly both on technical criteria and international cooperation, but to date it has barely started operations.

As noted in the previous section, it is perhaps at the international level that the most interesting developments are occurring. Foremost amongst these is Green Globe 21, considered above, but there are several other significant initiatives. The Tour Operators Initiative for Sustainable Tourism Development has been established recently by the World Tourism Organization (WTO) and the United Nations Environment Programme (UNEP). Green Globe 21 has announced its support for the WTO/UNEP initiative. It remains to be seen how they may link up in practice.

The TUI programme, which is effectively though not avowedly an ecolabel, operates quite independently of either of the above. It is primarily a German initiative, although its materials are also available in other languages including English. It uses a web-based feedback form to obtain comments directly from tourists, both on the environmental quality of destinations and the environmental performance of operators. This approach seems likely to have considerable appeal to tourists from business and professional backgrounds, and younger age brackets, who use computer communications routinely. International schemes run by environmental organizations, such as The Audubon Society and the World Wildlife Fund, are also likely to remain independent.

It would be feasible for national or regional schemes such as NEAP in Australia and Blue Flag in Europe, which have well-developed criteria and procedures and good consumer recognition in their target markets, to be integrated into a global scheme such as Green Globe 21. This currently seems unlikely, however, until the latter has established equally good consumer recognition and reliability in their specific target markets. Accreditation under either of these schemes, however, might perhaps be taken as automatic evidence for equivalent accreditation under Green Globe 21. Particular industry sectors, notably golf, have originated a number of specialist schemes which could well be integrated, initially with each other and ultimately with Green Globe 21. Since the golf industry may not view its destiny as lying entirely within the tourism sector, however, this is uncertain. And finally, until Green Globe 21 can demonstrate its credentials, independent company schemes such as that of TUI are likely to remain operational.

Discernible patterns and trends in the above are rather weak. The main features seem to be as follows:

- there are many more tourism ecolabels in Europe than elsewhere, especially small-scale schemes, and especially in and around Germany;
- some of the small tourism ecolabels established over the past decade seem to have become inactive, but more have arisen;
- by far the majority of tourism ecolabels are for the accommodation sector and are based principally on energy, water and resource conservation, and waste management;
- new national tourism ecolabels are incorporating more and more quantitative and substantive performance criteria and older ones are being revised to include such criteria;
- global tourism ecolabels have not yet subsumed regional, national and local ones;
- in practice there are now effectively at least two global tourism ecolabels, whereas a few years ago there was only one; but they operate in rather different ways.

It is extremely difficult to make any reliable projections from the above. The author would hazard the following guesses:

- global tourism ecolabels will expand, but this does not necessarily imply that tourists will pay any attention to them;
- the two main current global tourism ecolabels, as well as the international ecolabels run by environmental organizations, will continue to exist in parallel for a while, and probably for at least the next half-decade;
- if regional, national and local ecolabels are subsumed into any of the global schemes it is most likely to be Green Globe 21, since that is one of the latter's explicit aims;
- the proliferation of small local ecolabels is likely to continue even if they also become linked into global schemes;
- specialist national and regional ecolabels are likely to survive, because they contain far more technical environmental information than the global schemes, are hence more meaningful to environmentally concerned tourists.

In additional to interactions between the various tourism ecolabel schemes as above, the future of tourism ecolabels is likely to be influenced by a range of external factors, as follows:

- the overall level of environmental concern amongst tourists from various countries, which affects demand for environmental performance labels;
- increasing pollution and environmental deterioration worldwide, which affects tourist demand for environmental quality labels;
- national and multilateral government frameworks for corporate environmental reporting and community right-to-know (CRTK), which may allow individual consumers, or environmental and community groups, to establish their own independent environmental assessments of different tourism companies directly, bypassing generalized ecolabel schemes;
- developments in trade practices law and litigation in individual countries, with particular reference to environmental claims in corporate advertising;
- developments in international trade law relating to ecolabels;
- changes in the structure of the global tourism industry such as a possible trend to franchising or purchase of small independent tour and accommodation providers by large international chains;
- changes in the global structure of tourism marketing, e.g. possible increased use of the internet, e-commerce, and any associated quality assurance programmes.

Tourism ecolabels, as with any form of quality label, are only likely to remain in demand as long as there are significant environmental differences between operators and or destinations; and people who want to act on these differences, but do not have time or resources to establish the details themselves. The demand for environmental information need not necessarily be from individual tourists; it may be from travel agents, government land management or regulatory agencies, or from investors. For the past two decades, these circumstances have indeed applied in the tourism industry, although to very different degrees in different countries, and a wide range of ecolabels have therefore evolved in tourism as in many other industry sectors.

Any form of quality label scheme, however, especially if run by a private organization, can generally remain viable only as long as people rely on it to make real decisions. And to be effective as a decision-making tool, an ecolabel in tourism needs two critical characteristics. The first is broad coverage and high penetration so that the label is well-known and easily recognized, and users know that all of the tourism operations or destinations they are comparing have been considered by the ecolabel scheme, so that the absence of a label means as much as its presence. The second critical component is technical content and audit processes, so that users know there is a real and reliable difference, in relation to parameters which they care about, between operations or destinations which have been awarded the label, and those which have not. Currently, the global schemes have broad coverage, though not necessarily high penetration; the local schemes have the technical criteria. The challenge for tourism ecolabels is whether any single scheme can deliver both.

Overall Conclusions

Tourism ecolabel schemes undergo turnover, where old schemes are abandoned or modified and new ones established. Turnover in the recent past can help to gauge likely trends in the near future. To gauge turnover, one can examine the current status of major tourism ecolabels, using a variety of sources. Current patterns are not clear. There is still a proliferation of localized tourism ecolabels in Europe, especially Germany and neighbouring nations, but many of these seem to be inactive. There are several functional national schemes, but generally only for particular subsectors of the tourism industry, such as the David Bellamy Award for holiday parks in the UK, and the Nature and Ecotourism Accreditation Programme in Australia. Only one regional label, the European Blue Flag for beaches and marinas, seems to be enjoying continuing strong growth. There is a proliferation of award schemes rather than ecolabels as such. There is only one self-described global tourism ecolabel, Green Globe 21, but there are other initiatives such as the TUI scheme which are international tourism ecolabels in all but name, and which may appeal more effectively to consumers. The future still seems cloudy!

Acknowledgements

I thank Xavier Font for providing updated information on many of these ecolabel schemes and for editorial assistance in compiling the text of this chapter. Except for Somerville and Foxlee, all personal communications cited in the text were to Xavier Font.

References

ADAC (2000) *The ADAC Home Page*, www.adac.de, last updated June 2000, viewed June 2000.

Ajuntament d'Alcudia (2000), *Alcudia Government Home Page* (in Spanish), www.alcudia.net, last updated August 2000, viewed September 2000.

Altavista (2000) *Systrans Powered Translation Software*, http://babelfish. altavista.com/translate.dyn, viewed June 2000.

AUbE (1998) *Beschreibung und Bewertung der Umweltauszeichnungen im Tourismus*, Bielefeld (Germany) Akademie für Umweltforschung und -bildung in Europa (AubE).

Beder, S (1997) *Global Spin*. Scribe, Melbourne. 288 pp.

BH&HP (1999) *David Bellamy Conservation Awards*, www.ukparks.com/ bellamy.htm, last updated November 1999, viewed June 2000.

Buckinghamshire Chilterns University College (2000) *The Tourfor Home Page*, www.tourfor.com, last updated January 2000, viewed June 2000.

Buckley, R.C. (1989) Environmental planning and policy for the Australian tourism industry. *Proceedings of the National Environmental Law Association 8th Annual Conference*, 11–22. NELA, Adelaide.

Buckley, R.C. (1996) Sustainable tourism: technical issues and research needs. *Annals of Tourism Research* 23, 925–928.

Buckley, R.C. (2000) Review of Gunningham and Grabowsky, Smart Regulation. *Environmental and Planning Law Journal* (in press).

Buckley, R.C. and Sommer, M. (2000) *Principle and Practices for Partnerships Between Tourism and Protected Areas*. CRC Tourism, Gold Coast and Tourism Council Australia, Sydney.

CREM (2000) *Feasibility and market study for a European Eco-label for tourist accommodations (FEMATOUR)*, Commissioned by the European Commission, DG ENV, Amsterdam: Consultancy and Research for Environmental Management (CREM), August 2000.

DeHoGa (2000) *The German Hospitality Industry Web Page*, www.dehoga.de/ index-englisch.htm, last updated June 2000, viewed June 2000.

Ecotrans (2000) *Ecolabels and Awards in Tourism in Europe*, http://www.eco-tip.org/Eco-labels/ecolabels.htm, last updated 27 January, 2000, viewed June 2000.

European Golf Association Ecology Unit (2000) www.golfecology.com, viewed June 2000.

Fédération des Parcs naturels Régionaux de France (2000) *The Federation of French Regional Nature Parks Home Page*, www.parcs-naturels-regionaux. tm.fr, last updated June 2000, viewed June 2000.

FEEE (2000) *The Blue Flag Campaign*, www.blueflag.org, last updated May 2000, viewed June 2000.

Font, X. and Tribe, J. (2001) Promoting green tourism: the future of environmental awards, *International Journal of Tourism Research* 3(1), 1–13.

Green Globe (2000) *Green Globe Home Page*, www.greenglobe21.com, last updated April 2000, viewed June 2000.

Gunningham, N. and Grabowsky, P. (1998) *Smart Regulation*. Clarendon Press, Oxford. 494 pp.

Ifrance (2000) *The Clefs Vertes Home Page*, www.ifrance.com/clefsvertes/, last updated June 2000, viewed June 2000.

Koch, H. (2000) *Green Globe Comments on WWF-UK Tourism Certification Report 29/8/2000*. Email posted to green-travel@peach.ease.lsoft.com, 14 September 2000.

Naturfreunde Internationale (2000) *Eco-Tours Page: Environmental Seals and Awards*, http://www.eco-tour.org/information_en.html, last updated June 2000, viewed June 2000.

Neale, G. (1998) *The Green Travel Guide*. EarthScan, London.

Orizzonti (2000) *The Tour Operators Initiative for Sustainable Tourism Development*, www.toinitiative.org, last updated March 2000, viewed June 2000.

Scottish Tourism Board (2000) Green Tourism Businesses in Scotland, www. greentourism.org.uk, last updated April 2000, viewed September 2000.

SIS Eco-Labelling AB (2000) *The Nordic Swan Home Page*, www.svanen.nu/ nordic/Swanindex.htm, last updated May 2000, viewed June 2000.

Stiftung Öko-Fonds (2000) *The Luxembourg Ecolabel Home Page*, www.emweltzenter.lu/emweltzenter/oekofonds/ecolabel/virstellung.htm, last updated March 2000, viewed June 2000.

Synergy Ltd (2000) *Tourism Certification: an Analysis of Green Globe 21 and Other Certification Programs*. www.wwf-uk.org/news/news148.htm, last updated August 2000, viewed September 2000.

Tidy Britain Group (2000) *The Seaside Award and Blue Flag campaigns*, www.tidybritain.org.uk/psea, last updated May 2000, viewed June 2000.

TIS Corporation (2000) The Kleinwalsertal tourism page, www.tiscover.com/ kleinwalsertal, last updated June 2000, viewed June 2000.

Tourism Authority of Thailand (2000) *Sawasdee Thailand 2000*, www.tat.or.th, last updated August 2000, viewed September 2000.

TUI (2000) *The TUI group environmental management Home Page*, www.tui-umwelt.com/, last updated June 2000, viewed June 2000.

UNEP (1998) *Ecolabels in the Tourism Industry*. United Nations Environmental Programme, Paris.

UNEP/WTO/FEEE (1997) *Awards for Improving the Coastal Environment: the Example of the Blue Flag*. UNEP Industry and Environment, the World Tourism Organisation and the Foundation for Environmental Education in Europe, Paris.

Windebank, S. and Woolford, J. (2000) *Green Globe Greenwash? Tourism Certification Struggling for Credibility.* Email posted to green-travel@ peach.ease.lsoft.com, 29 August 2000.

WWF (2000a) *The Pan Parks Home Page*, www.panparks.com, last updated May 2000, viewed June 2000.

WWF (2000b) *Pan-Parks Principles and Criteria Workshop.* World Wide Fund for Nature (WWF), 10–12 April 2000, Zeist, The Netherlands.

WWF (2000c) *WWF France Home Page*, www.panda.org/resources/inthefield/ country/france/page3, viewed June 2000.

Chapter 14

Quality Analysis of Tourism Ecolabels
ROLF SPITTLER AND UTE HAAK

Introduction

Ecolabelling within the tourism industry is a recent phenomenon. The number of labels has increased in the last 10 years, and it is difficult to answer accurately how many ecolabels are in existence at present. Some ecolabels have been abolished and new ones have come into being (see Chapter 13). As represented in Fig. 14.1, only three ecolabels existed in tourism in 1989, while in 1998, 44 labels, which until the present day have been awarded at least once and have not been abolished, could be distinguished.

The development of this 'jungle of labels' would have been prevented by the timely introduction of a uniform environmental quality seal (the word seal is preferred to label in the German language). Legislation regulating environmentally friendly tourist resorts (the Bundeswettbewerb umweltfreundliches Fremdeverkehrsorte), which was put into effect in 1996, served according to the Federal Government as a practical test for the possible introduction of an environmental quality

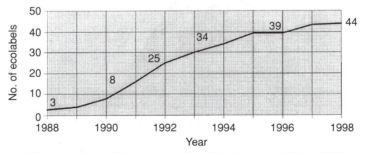

Fig. 14.1. Development of the number of ecolabels from 1988 to 1998.

© CAB *International* 2001. *Tourism Ecolabelling*
(eds X. Font and R.C. Buckley)

seal for German tourist resorts. The Federal Government is striving to push the dialogue regarding the introduction of an environmental quality seal further. In order to develop and to counteract the current 'chaos of seals', a uniform and consumer-friendly environmental quality seal is needed in Germany. The results of this research aim to provide recommendable concepts and suggestions for the seal's development and realization. In order to do so, the traveller will be given a guide through this 'jungle of labelling in tourism'. Additionally, the representation of the strengths and weaknesses of the individual ecolabels will motivate their promoters to check and optimize the contents and basic conditions of their labels.

The promoter awards an ecolabel to a certain applicant, if they fulfil the label's requirements of environmental and/or social compatibility. Ecolabel is the collective term for the following types: environmental quality signs, environmental quality seals, symbols for environmental protection, environmental seals, environmental competitions, environmental prizes and similar terms used synonymously ('campaigns', 'environmental plaques', 'certificates', 'eco-seals', 'ecolabels', 'eco quality seals', 'tourism quality seals'). These types of ecolabels differ qualitatively by means of their contents and basic conditions (see Fig. 14.2).

This chapter presents research carried out in 1998, uncovering 46 ecolabels in tourism, evaluated against the framework presented in Fig. 14.6. The chapter compares the quality of management and criteria of different ecolabels, based on literature review and expert input. The rationale and methodology developed to evaluate labels has a value in itself and can be used to compare the performance of labels in this chapter against future improvements and newer labels that have entered the market after 1998.

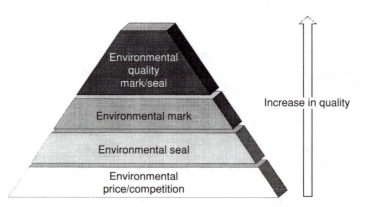

Fig. 14.2. The increase of quality in relation to different types of ecolabels.

Ecolabels in Tourism: a Snapshot

At the time of carrying out this research (1998), 46 ecolabels were identified. The 'Green Suitcase' and 'Top Team Natour' were still in the planning or preparatory phase, but are, nevertheless, still considered in the following statistics. Most promoters of ecolabels originate from Germany and Austria. In Fig. 14.3, the ecolabels are alphabetically listed according to their area of application, both by nationality and multiple nationalities (international to worldwide). The area of application is the geographical area within which the target groups can apply for the label, ranging from municipalities to worldwide schemes.

The promoters awarding these ecolabels include environmental federations, trade associations and governmental organizations. A further important factor of ecolabelling is the focus area or areas. The consumers are, with regard to an ecolabel, primarily seen as the target group. The focus area relates to the potential group of users that can apply to the promoters for an ecolabel. The nature of focus areas can vary widely (see Fig. 14.4, listing all the focus areas which can be a target for five or more labels). A complete overview of the focus areas per ecolabel is given in Table 14.1. The table shows that 26 ecolabels (57%) have hotels and restaurants as their focus area. A quarter of all ecolabels are awarded to private landlords, and 22% of all ecolabels can be applied for by municipalities. In order to receive an ecolabel, the applicant must meet the criteria of the awarding body of the label. The

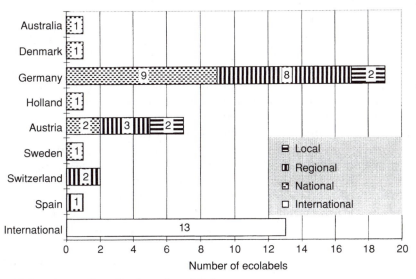

Fig. 14.3. Areas of application of ecolabels.

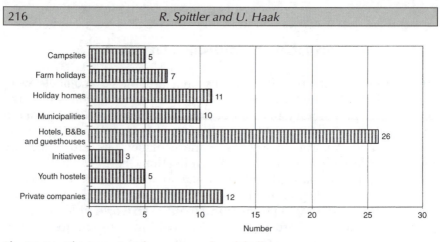

Fig. 14.4. The important focus areas of ecolabelling.

set of criteria for each ecolabel is very different and has distinctive qualities. The supervision of the 'outstanding (successful) applicant' is handled differently in the case of each ecolabel, because each ecolabel demands specific control mechanisms.

Table 14.1 gives an overview of the ecolabels reviewed in this chapter, with some overlaps with the labels listed in this book's directory. The ecolabels have been divided into three categories: 'ecolabels for accommodation', 'ecolabels for resorts' and 'ecolabels for other focus areas'. The ecolabels for projects are indicated by a (P) in the column 'remarks'.

In general, ecolabels are primarily addressed to consumers or tourists as a target group. The requirements, features and characteristics of German tourists are represented in Fig. 14.5. Most German tourists are environmentally conscious and demand an 'intact nature and environment' in the resort. However, on the whole, environmental 'behaviour' is only minimally shown by tourists. A small proportion of tourists align their travelling behaviour with environmental-oriented conduct, while a large proportion display a readiness to behave in an environmentally conscious manner when participating in certain activities. Much confidence is expressed in the 'problem solving authority' of the environmental protection organizations within the area of environmental protection; some confidence in relation to governmental organizations does exist, but confidence in the industry or trade associations is minimal. For the greater part of the travellers, environmental information about their resort is important (see Neitzel *et al.*, 1994: 3; Preisendörfer, 1996: 76; Laßberg, 1997: 35).

Review Rationale and Methodology

In the following section, the ecolabels specified in Table 14.1 are examined and evaluated in terms of their quality. The following were the focal points in the investigation:

- The aims of this investigation are to give recommendable concepts and suggestions for the conception and implementation of a uniform and consumer-friendly environmental quality seal in Germany.
- The aim is to provide more clarity for the tourists on the strongly 'sealed' travel-market.
- To encourage promoters to optimize their ecolabels.

The quality of an ecolabel is predominantly determined by 'contents' and 'basic conditions' (see Fig. 14.6). The emphasis lies on the contents, which determine to a large extent the standard of an ecolabel or its quality. Only if the awarding procedure and the set of criteria are arranged according to certain guidelines (for suggestions see Chapter 3), can an ecolabel also be a quality seal.

For quality seals, there are no legal regulations, their meaning is not determined and the conditions of their awarding procedure are not legally defined. Whether anyone can use the words 'quality seal' with an arbitrary definition and contents is a matter for further investigation. In linguistic usage and also in law, the terms quality marks and quality seals are synonymous. However, specific rules exist for the term quality mark. Thus, the question arises whether these rules should be adopted in the case of the term quality seal or whether the use of the term quality seal should be forbidden, if the requirements for the use of a quality mark are not fulfilled at the same time (see Gorny, 1992: 3).

During the evaluation, two types of ecolabels must be differentiated:

1. Ecolabel for a certain standard of environmental and social compatibility for applicants, who can receive this commendation if acting with concern for its environmental and social compatibility. An important characteristic of this type of ecolabel is a detailed and adequately arranged catalogue of criteria, which allows an accurate evaluation. All criteria pertaining to contents and basic conditions as specified in Fig. 14.6, influence the quality of this type of label and must therefore be monitored.

2. Ecolabels for projects are those where the specific individuals, organizations or initiatives are involved in a project with environmental and social objectives. Project ecolabels have very specific and focused criteria, and these allow only the evaluation of certain aspects. Criteria are formulated by a jury, and the set of criteria is limited to the

Table 14.1. A selection of ecolabels for certain environmental and social compatibility standards in tourism in 1998.

Name	First year awarded	Reach	Focus area(s)		Remarks
Ecolabels for accommodation organizations					
ADAC-Squirrel Environmentally friendly holiday resorts (HR), holiday parks (HP) and holiday centres (HC)	1996	NW	1 (HR,HP, HC)	Allgemeiner Deutscher Automobil Club e.V. (ADAC)	Inspection methods are being implemented, action
Blue Swallow	1990	IEW	3,4,5	Verträglich Reisen	Environmental seal (in A, CH, D, F, FIN, I)
Environmentally friendly hotels and restaurants	1994	R	3	Hotel- und Gaststättenverband Hessen e.V.	Criteria: 40-point catalogue of the DEHOGA, further development of the criteria, competition and environmental plaque
Environment oriented hotels and restaurants	1993	R	3	Dehoga Lippe e.V.	Criteria: 40-point catalogue of the DEHOGA, competition and environmental plaque, awarded once
Environment oriented hotels and restaurants	1994	R	3	Hotel- und Gaststättenverband Schleswig Holstein e.V.	40-point catalogue of the DEHOGA, competition, environmental plaque at the fulfilment of 80% or more of the points
The best choice for the environment	1992	R	3	Collegium Touristicum Carinthae (CTC)	Area of application: Kärnten, 100% fulfilment of the lowest criteria, environmental; quality seal
Green Globe award	??	IEW	3 (only hotels)	Green Globe	Initiative of the WTTC*
Green Hand – We are doing something for the environment	1991	L	3,4	Gemeinde Saalbach	Initiative of accommodation operators
Green Key	1994	NW	3 (only hotels)	HORESTA Dänemark	Geographical coverage: Denmark, 56 criteria, environmental certificate

Name	Year	Type	Criteria	Organization	Description
IH&RA Environmental award	1990	IEW	3	IH&RA International Hotel and Restaurant Association	Environmental prize: first prize = $5000, worldwide advertising, for the further participants there exist certificates (P)
Eco-Grischun	1994	R	3,10	Verein Ökomarkt Graubünden	
Austrian Ecolabel for Tourism	1997	NW	3,4,5,6, 8,9,12	Umweltberatung Gesellschaft für ökologische Projektabwicklung, Bildung und Forschung mbH	First development of a country wide environmental seal in the travel industry in the EU
Q for you	1992	R	2,3,4,5, 6,7,8,9, 14	Verkehrsvein Saas-Fee	Aim: general improvement in the area of services and environment of a tourist region, certificate
Biosphere Hotels	1997	R	3 (only hotels),5	Biosphere Hotels Association	Initiative of Spanish hotel owners*
TUI International Environment Award	1991	IEW	3 (only hotels),5	Touristik Union International	Money prize as high as DM 20,000 (P)
TUI Environment Champion	1997	IEW	3 (only hotels),5	Touristik Union International	Only voted for by TUI guests
TUI environmentally aware hotel management	1997	IEW	3 (only hotels),5	Touristik Union International	Only for TUI associates
Environmentally aware hotels and restaurants	1991	R	3	Bayrische Staatsregierung	Detailed, extensive set of criteria, environmental seal
Environmentally friendly hospitality companies	1995	R	3,4,5,6	Landesfremdenverkehrsverband Mecklenburg-Vorpommern e.V.	40-point catalogue of the DEHOGA, competition, environmental plaque at the fulfilment of 80% or more of the points
Environmentally oriented companies in Niedersachsen	1997	R	3,4,5,6	DEHOGA Landesverband Niedersachsen	40-point catalogue of the DEHOGA, competition, environmental plaque at the fulfilment of 80% or more of the points
Environment plaque 'For Environment's sake'	1992	L	3,4,5	Inselgemeinde Juist	DEHOGA carries out analysis and evaluation of the questionnaires

Table 14.1. *Continued.*

Name	First year awarded	Reach	Focus area(s)		Remarks
Environmental seal Kleinwassertal (Silver Thistle)	1988	L	3,4,5	Gemeinde Mittelberg	International pioneer in environmental seals for tourism
Environmental seal Lungau	1992	R	3,4,5,6, 8,9	Ökoausschuß des Gebietsverbandes Lungau	Diploma as label for companies*
Environmental seal Tirol-Sudtirol	1994	R	3,4,5,6, 8,9	Tirol Werbung und Südtirol Tourismus Werbung	In 1995 Sudtirol joined, inspection by trained independent environmental seal examiners
Environmental seal Waste Avoidance	1990	L	3,4,5,7, 8,9	Borkum	Action catalogue with 47 criteria
We are an environmentally friendly organization	1993	NW	3	DEHOGA Deutscher Hotel- und Gaststättenverband e.V.	40-point catalogue of the DEHOGA-Leitfadens is set of criteria, competition and environmental plaques
We are an environmentally friendly organization	1993	R	3,4,5,6	Hotel- und Gaststättenverband Baden-Württemberg e.V.	Criteria: 40-point catalogue of the DEHOGA and own questionnaires, competition and environmental plaques
Ecolabels for resorts or parts of resorts					
Blue Flag Europe	1987	IEW	2 (beaches and marinas)	Foundation for Environmental Education in Europe (FEEE)	Nationally distinctive campaign, BUND-evaluation is just for the BRD
Federal competition for environmentally friendly tourist resorts	1996	NW	2 (FVO)	Deutscher Fremdenverkehrsverband (DFV) e.V.	27 federal prizes, pilot-projects for the introduction of green suitcases
National Capital for the protection of nature and the environment	1990	NW	2 (cities/ resorts)	Deutsche Umwelthilfe e.V.	Not just limited to tourism, competition

Village holidays in Austria	1991	NW	2 (villages)	Verein Dorfurlaub in Österreich	Strongly restricted set of criteria, initiatives
European Prize for Tourism and Environment	1995	IEW	2 (FVO > 500 beds)	European Commission	Its continuation is not yet decided upon (P)
Green Suitcase	In planning stages	NW	2 (FVO)	Ökologischer Tourismus in Europa (ÖTE) e.V.	In planning since 1991, environmental quality seal
International Ecolabel of the DRV	1987	IEW	2,13	Deutscher Reisebüro Verband	Environmental tourism prize of commerce and industry
Swedish Environment and Tourism Prize	1995	NW	2,13	Schwedenwerbung	Geographical coverage: Sweden, 1 prize of 10000 SKR (P)*
TAT-resorts 'Municipalities in ecological competition'	1995	R	2,11 (resorts < 10.000 inhabitants)	Deutsches Institut für Urbanistik/ Deutsche Bundesstiftung Umwelt	Especially for the new federal states, additionally initiatives can also participate in the competition (P)

Ecolabels for other focus areas

ADAC-Squirrel for environmentally friendly motorway restaurants	1993	NW	1 (motorway restaurant)	Allgemeiner Deutscher Automobil Club e.V. (ADAC)	Certificates for environmentally friendly measures in various areas are awarded
British Airways Tourism for Tomorrow Awards	1992	IEW	11	British Airways	Environmental prize: prizes in various categories (P)
EIBTM'97	??	IEW	??	EIBTM-Holding Ltd	*
Recommendable tour operators	1998	NW	1 (tour operators)	BUND – Arbeitkreis 'Freizeit, Sport, Tourismus'	Competition was held for the first time in 1998
Europe Nostra Awards	1997	IEW	13	Europa Nostra Awards, Niederlande	Protection and expansion of European cultural heritage (P)
Landscape of the year	1989	IEW	1 (landscape)	NFI Naturfreunde Internationale	It cannot be applied for by regions or landscapes, but is awarded by the NFI (P)

Table 14.1. *Continued.*

Name	First year awarded	Reach	Focus area(s)		Remarks
National Ecotourism Accreditation Programme	1991	NW	13	Ecotourism Association of Australia	Environment management and criteria for tourism (P)
Top-Team-Natour	1999	NW	1 (youth holidays)	AG Jugendreisen mit Einsicht	Quality mark for youth travel
Tourism Prize	1995	NW	11	Toerisme and Recreatie/AVN	Geographical coverage: The Netherlands (P)*
Environment Prize of the German Golf Federation	1991	NW	1 (golf-related)	Deutscher Golfverband	Continuation is still unsure

Target group categories: 1, special focus areas (motorway restaurants, holiday parks, holiday resorts, holiday centres, golf courses, cross-border landscapes, youth travel, tour operators); 2, cities, resorts, parts of resorts; 3, hotels and restaurants; 4, private landlords; 5, apartments, holiday houses; 6, farm holidays; 7, government organizations; 8, youth hostels; 9, campsites; 10, agricultural producers; 11, tourism and environmental initiatives; 12, repeat homes and bungalow parks; 13, individuals, groups, organizations and companies; 14, cafes, bars, skiing schools, traffic societies and organizations, retail businesses, post companies, public transport, museums.
Geographical coverage: area of application, IEW, International – Europe wide – world-wide; CW, National; R, Regional; L, Local. (P) Ecolabels for projects.
*These ecolabels could not be included in the evaluation and analysis, since despite several requests, no documents were made available by the promoters.

	Marginally available	Available	Fully available
Environmental consciousness	○	○	✓
Demand for intact nature and environment In the holiday resort	○	○	✓
Environmental behaviour			
• In general with tourists	✓	○	○
• In certain activities	○	✓	○
• In the so-called core of the tourists	○	○	✓
Faith in the ability to solve problems of certain organizations in the area of environmental protection			
• Government organizations	○	✓	○
• Environmental organizations	○	○	✓
• Trade associations	✓	○	○
Demand for environmental information on the holiday resort	○	○	✓

Fig. 14.5. The demands, features and characteristics of the German tourist.

quality requirement, which includes social aspects, environmental aspects and transparency. In relation to the basic conditions of financing such projects, only those directly responsible for the project are examined, and with respect to marketing, whether its approach is in accord with its target group(s). All criteria for the design and the legal framework also apply here.

Criteria which apply to both types are highlighted in Fig. 14.6 by a black outline. In the column 'remarks' in Table 14.1, the ecolabels for projects are marked with a (P). Of the 46 ecolabels, approximately one-quarter are for projects and the remaining 35 focus on environmental and social standards.

Procedures

The appraisal procedure is schematically represented in Fig. 14.7. The contents are the 'heart' of an ecolabel, and therefore that is where the emphasis is placed during this evaluation. There are many prerequisites that must be fulfilled for a quality seal, with different importance and therefore weightings. The differences in significance are represented by the weighting factor (WF), which shows the value of the criteria of ecolabels. In the case of the type 'ecolabel for a certain standard of environmental and social compatibility', the total of the ten criteria have a weighting factor of 100%. This means that if all criteria carried the same value, each would have a weighting factor of

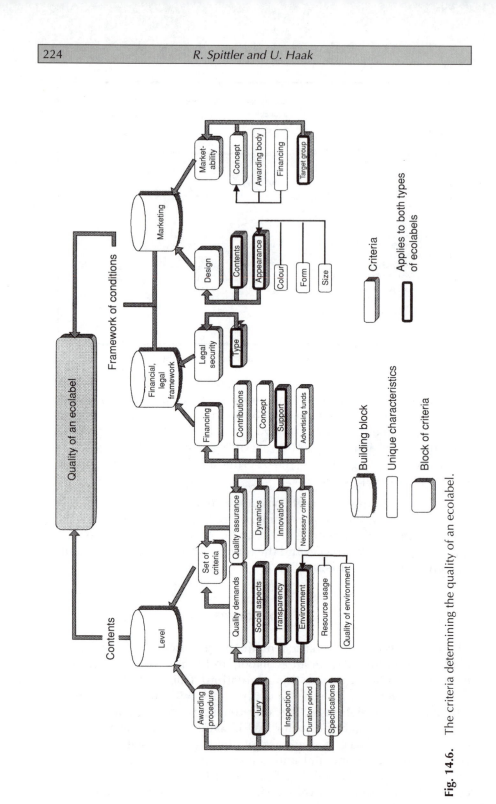

Fig. 14.6. The criteria determining the quality of an ecolabel.

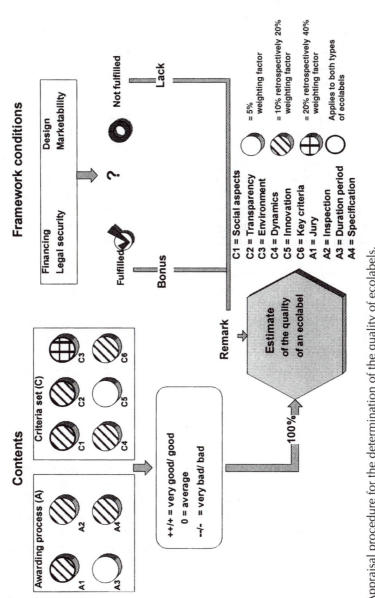

Fig. 14.7. Appraisal procedure for the determination of the quality of ecolabels.

10%. Under normal conditions, a criterion is classified as having a weighting factor of 10%. The WF of a criterion is doubled (20%) when it is of great importance, and reduced to 5% if it is a less important criterion. In the case of the type 'ecolabels for projects', four criteria determine the quality. The environmental aspects make up 40% of the total and the remaining three criteria account in each case for 20%. For each ecolabel, the individual criteria are judged in each case in terms of very positive to positive (++/+), average (0), or bad to very bad (–/––). A representation of the evaluation model for the criteria or areas of criteria are pointed out in Figs 14.6 and 14.7.

The basic conditions should also not be ignored. Ecolabels with a short life span or so-called 'one-offs' are in the consumer's perception more confusing than informative. In comparison, a secured financial framework and legal security ensure a long life span for the ecolabel. Additionally, the consumer must possess knowledge of the ecolabel for this to be effective, and therefore professional marketing should provide the necessary information for the consumer. The four areas of criteria 'financing', 'design', 'legal security' and 'marketing' are classified in each case as fulfilled or not fulfilled.

All criteria are examined in terms of the type of 'ecolabel for a certain standard of environmental and social compatibility'. In the case of 'ecolabels for projects' only the criteria emphasized by black outlines in Fig. 14.7 are judged. For each ecolabel a checklist will be created, in which all important data, criteria and if necessary single features will be included and judged. The results of the individual checklists are summarized in tabular form for all ecolabels.

Criteria

Contents

A quality seal for a high standard of environmental and social compatibility presupposes a high-quality set of criteria, of which the quality is always protected and can be regarded as a reliable and dynamic testing method used by an objective jury. Projects with a high-quality environmental and social compatibility presuppose appropriate procedures. These quality requirements are described below for both types of ecolabels.

Awarding procedures
Ecolabel for a certain standard of environmental and social compatibility: the quality of this procedure is substantially determined by the composition of the jury, method of inspection, the duration period of the label's validity, and the specifications which should be fulfilled, in

order to be able to award an ecolabel (see Fig. 14.7). The awarding procedure is weighted as approximately a third (35%) in the evaluation of the quality requirements. Of that 35%, 10% is assigned to the criteria 'jury', 'inspection method' and 'specifications' and 5% of the total quality can be derived from the 'duration period' (see Table 14.2).

Ecolabels for projects: the criteria 'inspection', 'specifications' and 'duration period' are omitted, due to the project-specific peculiarities. With generally only a few projects awarded with an ecolabel, an in-depth 'inspection' is assumed. Since the 'specifications' are kept predominantly general and cover a broad spectrum, they cannot be classified. The 'duration period' is omitted, since labels awarded to projects are generally a one-off. The criterion 'jury' is weighted as 20% of the evaluation of the quality requirements.

Table 14.2. Evaluation criteria for the testing method (WF = weighting factor).

Criteria	WF (5)	+/++	0	–/––
Jury	10 (20)	High to very high participation by environmental organizations and governmental bodies	Participation by environmental organizations and governmental bodies or awarded only by governmental bodies	Little or no participation by environmental organizations and governmental bodies
Inspection	10	Trained independent investigators, personal and unannounced at all applicants during initial inspection, at least every 2 years	Environmental advisers, personal inspections carried out randomly, at least every 3 years	Only written inspections, only very irregular inspections to no inspections
Duration period	5	≤ 2 years	> 2–3 years	> 3 years
Specifications	10	At least 90% of the individual criteria must be fulfilled (ecolabels with a grading system can only be awarded once to categories lower than 90% and have to be at least 50%)	At least 80% of the individual criteria must be fulfilled (ecolabels with a grading system can only be awarded once to categories lower than 80% and have to be at least 50%)	Less than 80% of the individual criteria must be fulfilled

The composition of the awarding organization must predominantly consist of members of environmental and governmental organizations, as otherwise the reliability of the ecolabel is questioned by the consumer (see Fig. 14.5). Some participation of trade associations in the jury is acceptable, yet a dominance of representatives from trade associations does not generally guarantee the neutrality of the jury. This leads to a loss of confidence by the consumer, endangering the reliability of the testing method. The 'inspection' must always take place when an application for a label is first received and should be carried out personally by independent investigators. The authors suggest that further inspection should take place every 2 years. This inspection method ensures that only applicants who really fulfil the criteria receive an ecolabel. An unreliable inspection method encourages the abuse of ecolabels and endangers its reliability.

The 'duration period' must be determined by the time interval in which the awarding criteria are reviewed and updated, i.e. every 2 years. In the case of long duration periods, there is an increased danger that the organization to which the ecolabel is awarded will rest on its laurels and cease to be ecologically proactive. Moreover, future legislation may have caught up long ago with the criteria of today, and an ecolabel which includes criteria that are required by legislation loses its credibility. The 'duration period' weighs less than the criteria 'inspection' and 'jury' and, therefore, carries the weighting factor of 5% in the evaluation.

The set of criteria does not only have to set high quality standards in theory, but these must also be put into practice. The quality of the ecolabel, and the perception of quality by the potential tourist, depends on how many of the criteria need to be fulfilled, and the 'marks' for each criteria that are needed to achieve accreditation. A grading system dividing ecolabels into several categories (e.g. gold, silver, bronze) is in certain cases acceptable, but that requires high numbers of applicants to be fully developed. The prerequisites are: transparency towards the consumer; an applicant which only fulfils the requirements to a certain extent may only be awarded an ecolabel once; and the lowest fulfilment of a criterion may not fall below 50%. The main aim must be to motivate the applicants in such a way that they regularly improve their standard of environmental and social compatibility.

Set of criteria

Ecolabel for a certain standard of environmental and social compatibility: environmental and social aspects and its transparency towards the consumer determine the quality of the set of criteria. This quality is ensured on a long-term basis by dynamics, innovations and essential criteria (see Fig. 14.7). The set of criteria is weighted as 65% of the total evaluation. The criteria 'dynamics', 'essential criteria', 'social aspects' and 'transparency' each carry 10% of the weighting, the 'environmental aspects' 20% and 'innovative projects' 5% in the evaluation of the ecolabel's quality (see Table 14.3).

Ecolabels for projects: the criteria for quality assurance are omitted due to project-specific characteristics. Projects are supposed to meet the criteria of 'innovation'. 'Essential criteria' and 'dynamics' are omitted, since only certain basic conditions are addressed. The set of criteria has a weighting of 80% in the evaluation. The criteria 'social aspects' and 'transparency' each account for 20%, and the 'environmental aspects' for 40% (see Table 14.3).

An ecolabel will have certain quality requirements to ensure the sustainability of the tourism operations. 'Social aspects' such as culture preservation, economic prosperity, community development and the subjective well-being of the 'hosts' must be taken into account. The 'environmental aspects' take a special position in ecolabelling and, therefore, carry the weighting factor of 20%. Consumption of resources must be reduced and the quality of the environment in all relevant areas must be increased. An ecolabel for a high environmental standard must consider the following areas: waste, effluents, energy, climate, noise, landscape and nature, air, traffic and water. The quality of the label is limited if the organizers do not require supporting evidence of these targets, or they merely award on the basis of compliance with legal criteria. The criteria must be presented to the consumer by the label organizer so that tourists can understand exactly the conditions of the ecolabel which must be met by the applicants. Lack of 'transparency', will cause confusion among consumers and the ecolabel will lose its credibility.

For the quality assurance point, the standards of environmental and social compatibility must be improved constantly and must be superimposed on the legal specifications so that a high inherent quality is always and continuously guaranteed. This requires a regular evaluation and updating of the criteria. If this aspect of the 'dynamics' is neglected, the ecolabel will lose its value over the years. Additionally, 'innovative projects' transferable to a large proportion of the applicants must be stimulated. Only then will the ecological demands be increased and will today's innovations of individual applicants become common practice for the majority of the industry. Compared with the importance of the criteria 'dynamics' and 'essential criteria', the importance of the criterion 'innovative projects' is considered lower and, therefore, carries the weighting factor of 5% in the total evaluation. A certain standard of environmental and social compatibility ('necessary criteria'), which go beyond the legal requirements, must be reached by the ultimate and successful applicant. These applicants

Table 14.3. Evaluation criteria for the set of criteria (WF = weighting factor).

Criteria	WF	+/++	0	-/--
Quality requirements				
Social aspects	10(20)	All important aspects are considered in an appropriate framework	Some are considered	None or very little are considered
Transparency	10(20)	All criteria are directly communicated openly and described in detail to the consumer by the promoter	Some criteria are communicated in detail to the consumer	No disclosure of the criteria takes place
Environmental aspects	20(40)	In (almost) all relevant areas there exist prerequisites for measures to decrease the consumption of resources and to protect the quality of the environment which go (far) beyond the legal requirements	In important areas there exist prerequisites for measures to decrease the consumption of resources and to protect the quality of the environment which go beyond the legal requirements	Only in some areas there exist prerequisites for measures to decrease resource consumption and/or to protect the quality of the environment
Quality assurance				
Dynamics	10	At least every 2 years the criteria are reassessed and updated	At least every 4 years the criteria are reassessed and updated.	The criteria are reassessed and updated > 4 years or not at all
Innovation	5	Innovative projects in the area of environmental and social compatibility, which possess a pioneer character, are considered	Innovative projects in the area of environmental and social compatibility are considered	No innovative projects are considered
Essential criteria	10	High to very high requirements in terms of a minimum standard of environmental and social compatibility	Average requirements in terms of a minimum standard of environmental and social compatibility	Little or no requirements in terms of a minimum standard of environmental and social compatibility

must have distinguished themselves within their industry in environmental and social respects, otherwise the ecolabel loses its credibility.

Basic conditions

The financial and legal framework and marketing are basic conditions
for the quality of an ecolabel (see Fig. 14.6). The authors suggest that
these basic conditions are relatively less important than the contents,
and therefore the evaluation takes place in terms of 'criteria blocks',
determining whether or not these 'criteria blocks' are fulfilled as
a whole. In ecolabels for a certain standard of environmental and
social compatibility all 'criteria blocks' with their specifications, as
mentioned in Table 14.4, apply. In the case of ecolabels for projects,
all criteria for 'design' and 'legal security' also apply, yet due to the
project-specific characteristics, only the agencies responsible for

Table 14.4. Criteria blocks for the evaluation of the basic conditions.

Criteria	(Predominantly) fulfilled	Hardly or not at all fulfilled
Financial framework		
Financing	The ecolabel depends (after an introduction period) predominantly upon member contributions and advertising funds. Further financial support from governmental bodies, organizations and associations is ensured. A dependency upon industry associations does not exist. A financing concept is in place	The ecolabel is also dependent upon support after the introduction period. There exists a dependency upon industry associations. A financial concept does not exist or only exists in vague terms
Legal security	The ecolabel is formally legally secured with the RAL (Deutsches Institut für Gütesicherung und Kennzeichnung, German institute for quality assurance and labelling)	The ecolabel is not formally legally secured
Marketing		
Design	The actual contents are simply and clearly represented and inform the consumer. The appearance or the selection of the colour, form, size and symbol supports the information to the consumer	The actual contents are hardly or not recognizable to the consumer. The appearance is unsatisfactory
Marketability	Marketing takes place professionally and according to the target group. It is financially covered, a marketing concept exists	Marketing hardly takes place or is not according to their target group

the project will be examined in relation to financing and with respect to marketing, to assess whether this takes place according to the appropriate target group. Ecolabels for projects can only be used by associations/federations and/or governmental organizations, and contributors and advertising funds are, therefore, omitted. Financing and marketing concepts are presupposed in the case of ecolabels for projects.

Financial and legal security are key issues, since ecolabels must be financially and legally safeguarded. Financially, this must be achieved after a certain introduction period predominantly through member contributions and sponsoring. Further financial support is to be sought from associations and organizations. A strong financial dependency upon a trade association should be avoided. 'Legal safeguarding' can be achieved by ensuring the label complies to national quality assurance standards (in the German case, the association with the German institute for quality assurance and labelling, RAL). This would give an ecolabel the highest level of seriousness and wide acceptance and increase its credibility towards consumers.

Marketing issues are also crucial, since the consumer must be aware of the existence of an ecolabel. A prerequisite for such consumer awareness is a professional marketing approach, focusing on the right target groups and executed by experts. Additionally, the design or 'logo' of the ecolabel must provide the consumer with clarity on the nature and meaning of an ecolabel. A logo should communicate the following information to the consumer: who the awarding body is, to whom the ecolabel is awarded, the reason why it was awarded, an indication of its criteria, the duration period of the ecolabel and, where appropriate, a classification. Additionally, the appearance of the logos must be selected in such a way that they attract the utmost attention, are easy to recognize and represent the labels' characteristics in the best possible manner.

Ecolabels

Forty-six ecolabels were distinguished, as shown in Table 14.1. Ten of these are ecolabels for projects and 36 are ecolabels for a certain standard of environmental and social compatibility. Based on available documents, both types of ecolabels are judged in each case, adopting the above-mentioned evaluation methods and criteria.

An evaluation of individual criteria and an overall estimate of the quality for ecolabels can be inferred from Table 14.5. More emphasis has been placed on the ecolabels for projects as, due to their project-specific characteristics, only four criteria were checked. A direct comparison in terms of quality between the two types of ecolabels is only partially possible, and this was not the aim of this research.

The ecolabels for a certain standard of environmental and social compatibility are divided into three categories: 'ecolabels for the area of accommodation', 'ecolabels for locations' and 'ecolabels for other focus areas'. Ecolabels with a very high quality are marked by an asterisk (✠). The following four categories of quality are used:

1. Low quality ☹
2. Average quality 😐
3. High quality ☺
4. Very high quality ☺☺

Additionally, other characteristics of an ecolabel are included in Table 14.5 in the column 'remarks'. Additional characteristics taken into consideration were: how long the ecolabel has been in existence, how often it was awarded and, if necessary, noteworthy, special features of an ecolabel. If necessary, it is noted whether this characteristic is an advantage or a disadvantage for the respective ecolabel.

Analysis of the Test Results

Of 46 ecolabels, 39 were evaluated. (During the evaluation, a distinction was made for 'Blue Flag Europe' between beaches and marinas. In the analysis of the statistics, therefore, two ecolabels are considered.) Six ecolabels could not be included in the evaluation because, despite repeated requests, no documents were made available by the promoters of the labels ('EIBTM'97', 'Distinctions Award', 'Swedish Environment and Tourism Price', 'Biosphere Hotels', 'Tourism Pride of the Netherlands' and the 'Environmental Seal Lungau'). The 'environment champion' of the TUI was not included, since the evaluation criteria do not apply to the structure of this ecolabel. Of the ten criteria, only the 'duration period' (1 year = very good) and the 'social aspect' (no consideration = very bad) can be evaluated. With relation to the other eight criteria, no evaluation was possible, since the environmental compatibility of the hotel can only be determined by the perception of the guests. Only the opinions of the guests who answered the questionnaire, are considered. Additionally, the environmental compatibility of the hotel is only broadly examined with just one question; a further differentiation is not made and therefore objective results cannot be guaranteed. However, based on a particular question on the questionnaire, the TUI-guests evaluate the environmental activities of the TUI-hotels as very good to unsatisfactory. The five best hotels are distinguished annually.

The so-called 'recommendable tour operator'-label of the BUND (Bund für Umwelt und Naturschutz Deutschland, Federation for the protection of the environment and nature) was excluded from this

Table 14.5. Evaluation criteria and estimates on the quality of ecolabels.

Criteria	Duration period				Quality requirements			Quality protection			G	Financial, legal		Marketing		Characteristics (advantage or disadvantage)	Estimates/remarks
	V1	V2	V3	V4	C1	C2	C3	C4	C5	C6		F1	F2	M1	M2		
Weighting factor in %	10	10	5	10	10	10	20	10	5	10	100						
Ecolabels for certain environmental and social compatibilty standards																	
Ecolabels for accommodation organizations																	
Blue Swallow	—	—	++	++	0	++	+	++	—	++	+	🖐	🖐	✓	✓	Disadvantage ☺	Has moved to the background
ADAC-Squirrel: environmentally friendly holiday facilities, holiday parks and centres	0	—	—	—	0	++	0	—	0	—	–	🖐	🖐	(✓)	✓	⊗	Since 1996, one holiday park has been awarded a label
The environmentally friendly hotel and guest towns organization (Hessen)	—	+	++	0	—	++	+	0	0	0	0	(✓)	🖐	✓		☺	
The environmentally friendly hotel and guest towns organization (Kreis Lippe)	—	0	—	0	—	++	0	—	—	0	–	(✓)	🖐	✓		Disadvantage ⊗	Until now only awarded once in 1993
The environmentally orientated hotel and guest towns organization (Schleswig-Holstein)	—	+	++	0	—	++	0	0	—	0	0	🖐	🖐	✓		Disadvantage ☺	Awarded once 1994/1995

Label																	Rating	Comment
The best choice for the environment (Kärnten)	—	++	0	+	+	++	++	0	0	++	+	(✓)	📖	✓	✓	Advantage	☺	280 criteria (76 essential criteria)
The Green Hand – we do something for the environment	0	++	++	–	—	++	+	+	0	+	+	✓	📖	✓	✓	Advantage	☺	Awarded annually since 1991
Green Key	—	++	++	+	–	++	0	—	0	++	0	📖	📖	✓	✓		☹	
Eco-Ibex (Öko-Grischun)	0	0	++	—	–	+	++	++	++	+	+	✓	📖	✓	(✓)		☺	
Austrian symbol for environmental protection for tourism operations	0	++	++	++	0	++	++	+	++	++	++	✓	📖	✓	✓	Disadvantage	☺☺	Awarded once since 1997
Q for you	0	++	++	0	+	0	++	++	0	++	+	✓	📖	✓	✓		☺	
TUI-environmentally friendly hotel management	—	+	++	—	—	++	++	++	0	0	+	✓	📖	✓	✓	Disadvantage	☺	Only hotels associated with TUI
Environmentally conscious hotel and restaurant business (Bavaria)	0	+	0	–	0	++	++	0	++	+	0	(✓)	📖	✓	✓		☹	
Environmentally conscious hotel and restaurant business (Mecklenburg-Vorpommern)	—	+	++	—	++	++	+	++	+	0	0	📖	📖	✓	✓			
Environmentally orientated organizations in The Netherlands	—	+	++	0	—	+	kE	++	0	0	0	📖	📖	✓	✓	Disadvantage		First awarded in 1997
Eco-Label for the benefit of the environment (Juist)	—	–	++	++	—	+	++	–	—	++	0	(✓)	📖	✓	✓	Advantage	☹	Awarded since 1992
Environmental Seal of Quality (Kleinwalsertal)	—	0	++	++	—	++	++	+	+	+	+	✓	📖	✓	✓	Advantage	☺	Awarded since 1988, pioneer
Environmental Seal of Quality (Tirol–Südtirol)✵	0	++	++	++	–	++	++	++	–	++	++	✓	📖	✓	✓		☺☺	

Table 14.5. *Continued.*

Criteria	Level — Set of criteria											Framework of conditions				Characteristics (advantage or disadvantage)	Estimates/remarks
	Duration period				Quality requirements			Quality protection				Financial, legal		Marketing			
	V1	V2	V3	V4	C1	C2	C3	C4	C5	C6	G	F1	F2	M1	M2		
Weighting factor in %	10	10	5	10	10	10	20	10	5	10	100						
We are an environmentally orientated organization (DEHOGA Deutschland)	—	+	++	0	—	++	0	0	—	—	—	☞	☞	✓	(✓)	☹	Basis for ecolabels for federal states
We are an environmentally orientated organization (DEHOGA Baden-Württemberg)	—	+	++	0	—	++	0	++	0	+	0	(✓)	☞	✓	✓	☺	
Ecolabels for resorts or parts of resorts																	
Blue Flag beaches/bathing areas (specific areas in Germany)	+	++	++	0	—	++	++	0	0	++	+	✓	☞	(✓)	✓	☺ Disadvantage	Controversial/pilot phase
Regional Capital for Nature and Environmental Protection✠	E	++	++	++	—	++	++	++	++	E	++	✓	☞	✓	☞	☺☺ Advantage	Awarded annually since 1990
Environmentally friendly Federal Competition (FVO)	0	+	++	—	—	0	++	kE	++	0	0	☞	☞	✓	(✓)	☺ Disadvantage	First awarded in 1997
Holiday villages in Austria	0	++	—	—	++	++	++	0	++	++	+	✓	☞	✓	✓	☺	
Green Suitcase✠	++	++	++	++	—	++	++	++	—	++	++	✓	☞	✓	kE Disadvantage	☺☺	In planning since 1991

Ecolabels for other focus areas

Criteria	V1	C1	C2	C3	G	F1	F2	M1	M2		
ADAC Squirrels: the environmentally friendly motorway service stations	0	—	—	—	0	📖	📖	(✓)	(✓)		☹ Ten motorway restaurants have been awarded since 1993
Blue Flag for Sports Boat Harbours (BRD)	0	++	++	++	0	📖	✓	✓	✓	Advantage	☹ Awarded since 1987
Top-Team-Natour	+	0	++	++	+	📖	✓	✓	✓	Disadvantage	☺ First awarded in 1999
The Environmental Award of the German Golf Association	—	++	++	kE	0	📖	📖	✓	✓	Disadvantage	☹ Awarded once in 1993

Ecolabels for projects

Criteria	V1	C1	C2	C3	G	F1	F2	M1	M2		
Weighting factor in %	20	20	20	40	100						
British Airways Tourism for Tomorrow Awards	0	+	++	++	+	📖	📖	✓	✓	Advantage	☺ Awarded annually since 1992
Europa Nostra Awards	kE	——	++	—	—	(✓)	📖	✓	✓	Disadvantage	☹ First awarded in 1997
European Prize for Tourism and the Environment✣	++	+	++	++	++	✓	✓	✓	✓	Disadvantage	☺☺ First awarded in 1995
IH&RA Environmental Awards✣	++	——	++	++	++	📖	📖	✓	✓	Advantage	☺☺ Awarded annually since 1990
The International Environmental Award (Association of German Travel Agents)	—	+	++	++	+	📖	📖	✓	✓	Advantage	☺ Awarded annually since 1989

Table 14.5. *Continued.*

Criteria	Level Duration period	Set of criteria Quality requirements		Quality protection	G	Framework of conditions Financial, legal		Marketing		Characteristics (advantage or disadvantage)	Estimates/remarks
	V1	C1	C2	C3	G	F1	F2	M1	M2		
Weighting factor in %	20	20	20	40	100						
Landscape of the year✱	++	++	++	++	++	✔	☞	✔	✔	Advantage / Disadvantage	☺☺ Awarded since 1989 – No application by regions, awarded by NFI
National Ecotourism Accreditation Programme	kE	+	++	+	+	(✔)	☞	✔			☺ Eco tourism association
Municipalities in Ecological Competition✱	++	+	++	++	++	✔	☞	✔			☺☺ Ends in 2000
TUI International Environment Award	——	—	++	++	+	☞	☞	✔			☺

Assessment criteria: F1 = Financing, F2 = Legal Security, M1 = Design, M2 = Marketability, C1 = Social aspects, C2 = Transparency, C3 = Environmental aspects, C4 = Dynamics, C5 = Innovation, C6 = Essential criteria, V1 = Jury, V2 = Inspection, V3 = Duration period, V4 = Specifications, kE = Immeasurable.
() = conditional, E = Criteria is excluded
Evaluation G: ++ = very good, + = good, 0 = average, – = bad, — — = very bad, ✔ = Criteria fulfilled, ☞ = Criteria not fulfilled.
Quality is: ☹ = low, 😐 = average, ☺ = high, ☺☺ = very high.
✱ = Exemplary ecolabels.

publication, for which BUND is partially responsible, since an objective evaluation could be questioned and thus the rigour of the entire investigation would suffer.

In the case of the 'Blue Flag (Europe)', the label was differentiated into beaches and marinas. Only its German branch, i.e. that of the German Society for Environmental Education (Deutschen Gesellschaft für Umwelterziehung) was investigated. According to experience, the quality of this label in other countries is seen as equivalent at best, but is generally worse. The 'Landscape of the Year' of the Naturfreunde Internationale (NFI) cannot be applied for directly by regions or landscapes, but certain regions are appointed the 'landscape of the year' by the NFI. Because in the case of this ecolabel only a very special focus area is addressed, it is nevertheless included in the evaluation in the category 'ecolabels for projects' with an appropriate annotation.

While in the case of ecolabels for a certain environmental and social compatibility, ten criteria could be evaluated, in the case of ecolabels for projects, only four criteria were judged, due to their project-specific characteristics. Therefore, a direct comparison in terms of quality between the two types of ecolabels is only possible to a certain extent, and the representation of the quality of the ecolabel occurs separately for both types (see Fig. 14.8a and b). The two types of ecolabels are very different in terms of their quality. While four ecolabels for a certain standard of environmental and social compatibility (the 'Environmental Squirrel' of the Allgemeiner Deutscher Automobil-Club for environmentally friendly motorway restaurants and environmentally friendly holiday resorts/parks/ centres, the DEHOGA-label 'We Are an Environmentally friendly Operation' and the ecolabel of DEHOGA Lippe e.V.) and the ecolabel for projects, the 'Europa Nostra Awards', are of low quality, the following ecolabels with a very high quality are to be seen as positive examples of their respective types of ecolabel:

Type 'ecolabel for a certain standard of environmental and social compatibility'

- National capital for nature and environmental protection of the Deutschen Umwelthilfe (German Assistance for the Environment).
- Green Suitcase of the Ö.T.E. (Ökologischer Tourismus in Europa, Association for ecological tourism in Europe).
- Austrian Ecolabel for Tourism.
- Tyrolean Environmental Seal of Quality of the Tirolwerbung and Südtirol Tourismus Werbung.

Type 'ecolabel for projects'

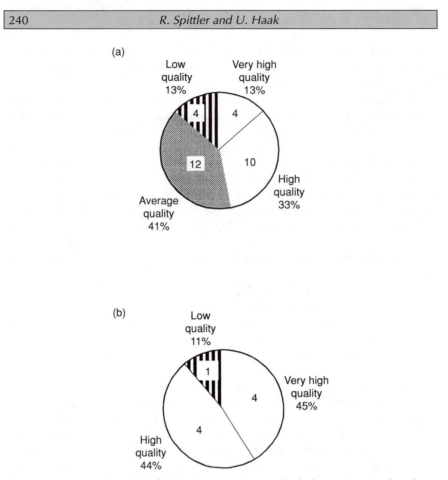

Fig. 14.8. (a) Quality of ecolabels for a certain standard of environmental and social compatibility. (b) Quality of ecolabels for projects.

- European Prize for Tourism and Environment of the EU Commission.
- IH&RA Environmental Awards.
- Landscape of the Year of Friends of Nature International (Naturfreunde Internationale, NFI).
- TAT-resorts: 'municipalities in ecological competition' (Gemeinden in ökologischen Wettbewerb) of the German Institute for Urban Matters (Deutschen Instituts für Urbanistik).

Of the 30 investigated ecolabels for a certain standard of environmental and social compatibility almost half (46%) possess a high to very high quality. Thirteen per cent have a very high quality, i.e. they have few, if any, shortcomings. A third of all ecolabels possess a high quality, i.e. some shortcomings with respect to their sets of criteria or awarding procedure can be indicated. The remaining 54%, or more than half of the ecolabels for a certain standard of environmental and social compatibility have many to substantial shortcomings in their contents (see Fig. 14.8a). Of the ecolabels for projects, eight (89%) possess a high to very high quality, and one has a low quality (see Fig. 14.8b).

During the more in-depth evaluation of the individual criteria – in the case of the ecolabels for projects, only the criteria 'jury', 'social aspects', 'transparency' and 'environmental aspects' were evaluated (see Fig. 14.9) – the most frequently occurring shortcomings become clear. The requirements are met to a high extent (good to very good) in the case of the criteria 'transparency', 'environmental aspects' and 'duration period' with the majority of ecolabels. Yet results are poorer for the criteria 'dynamics', 'inspection' and 'essential criteria', and there are many shortcomings in the criteria 'innovation', 'jury', 'social aspects' and 'specifications' for many ecolabels. Social aspects are considered hardly or not at all by 60% of the ecolabels and half of the ecolabels do not have environmental associations participating in the jury. With a third of all ecolabels, no innovative measures are promoted and the specifications are much too low, i.e. fewer than 80% of the criteria must be fulfilled.

During the evaluation of the basic conditions (see Fig. 14.10), the following trends for ecolabels can be determined. The design is acceptable throughout in the case of each ecolabel; formal legal security, on

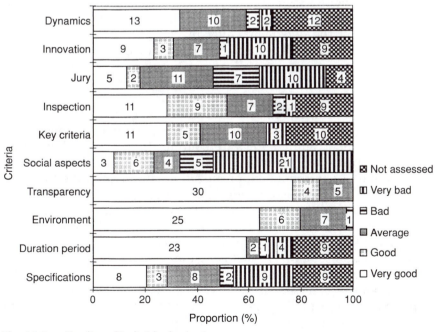

Fig. 14.9. Quality of individual criteria.

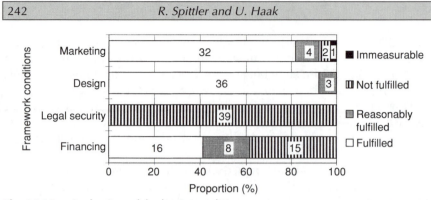

Fig. 14.10. Evaluation of the basic conditions.

the other hand, is not included in any of the labels. Marketing occurs, with some exceptions, according to the appropriate target group for all ecolabels. With regard to financing, many labels are dependent on trade associations and therefore more than two-thirds of ecolabels do not or only marginally meet the requirement for financing.

Conclusions

The awarding bodies were predominantly very cooperative in the supply of the necessary information and documents. Some, on the other hand, only sent the documents after repeated requests. Few did not respond despite repeated requests and their ecolabels could, therefore, not be considered during the evaluation. Questions can be raised on the quality of these labels, and can be judged with regard to 'transparency' towards the consumer as being rather precarious.

   One in five ecolabels in tourism withstands a critical analysis and indicates a high quality standard, with few potential improvements. The most frequent shortcomings were an insufficient consideration of the social aspects and innovative measures, the lack of or insufficient participation of environmental organizations in the jury, the financial dependency on trade associations and missing formal legal frameworks. Particularly in the area of social aspects, a set of criteria must be developed for many of the ecolabels, to serve as a measuring instrument. With the help of this instrument, it should be possible to determine the qualitative status of the social performance by the applicant (e.g. accommodation operators). Table 14.5 points out the strengths and weaknesses of each ecolabel. The evaluated criteria for each ecolabel were added depending upon the evaluation group (++ to −−) and the percentile proportions are represented in Figs 14.11 and 14.12. The quality profiles of the two types of ecolabels are presented

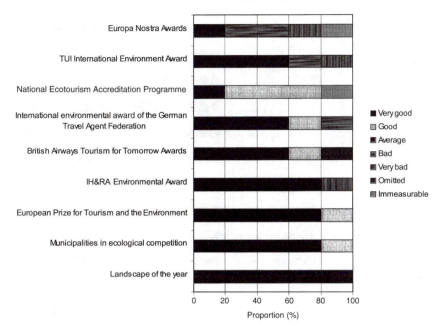

Fig. 14.11. Quality assessment of tourism ecolabels for projects.

separately per quality category, since a direct comparison between the quality of these two types should be avoided.

There are too many ecolabels. The tourism ecolabelling euphoria must be counteracted. In the short term, the existing labels must be identified, systemized and improved qualitatively. On a long-term basis, a uniform, clear system must be created for the consumers. The fact that this is no longer a utopia, is demonstrated by Austria with its 'Austrian Ecolabel for Tourism', where regional seals subordinate themselves or are superseded. In Germany, the 'Green Suitcase' of the Association for Ecological Tourism in Europe (Ökologischen Tourismus in Europa, ÖTE) was originally meant to be awarded to environmentally compatible accommodation operators, tour operators and tourist resorts. For that purpose, a general framework of criteria was created in 1991. In 1994, particular criteria for tourist resorts were developed. But even at present, trade associations reject the 'Green Suitcase' and prevent its introduction into the market, by implementing their own labels. So far, ecolabels were only developed by the trade associations for certain areas. An ecolabel for several industries, as was already generally conceived with the idea of the 'Green Suitcase', has so far not been implemented by trade associations. The political environment is favourable for the introduction of a nation-wide, uniform and consumer-friendly environmental label in Germany. If the criteria for the 'Green Suitcase' are revised, this label can be a good

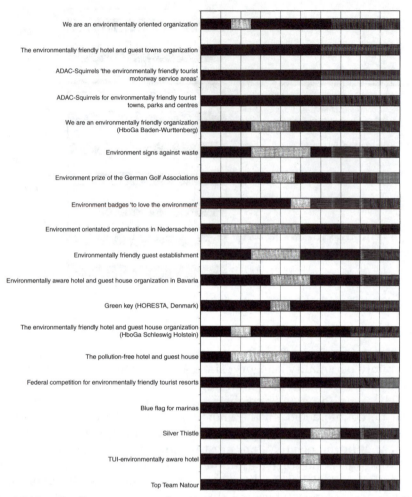

Fig. 14.12. Quality assessment of tourism ecolabels for environmental and social compatibility (legend as Fig. 14.11).

starting point for an environmental quality seal for German tourist resorts, with possibilities for expansion across countries and sectors.

Acknowledgements

This chapter is based on a report prepared by the Academy for Environmental Research and Education in Europe (Akademie für Umweltforschung und -bildung in Europa, AUbE) with the support of the Federation for the Protection of the Environment and Nature (Bund für Umwelt und Naturschutz Deutschland, BUND) in 1998.

References

Gorny, D. (1992) Gutachten zu Rechtsfragen betreffend die Vergabe des Gütessiegels 'Grüner Koffer'. Im Auftrag des Ö.T.E, Frankfurt.

Laßberg, D. v. (1997) Urlaubreisen und Umwelt – Eine Untersuchung über die Ansprechbarkeit der Bundesbürger auf Natur- und Umweltaspekte in Zusammenhang mit Urlaubreisen. *Schriftenreihe für Tourismus und Entwicklung.*

Neitzel, H., Landaman, U. and Pohl, M. (1994) Das Umweltverhalten der Verbraucher – Daten und Tendenzen; Empirische Grundlagen zur Konzipierung von 'Sustainable Consumption Patterns', Elementen einer 'Ökobilanz Haushalte'. Texte Umweltbundesamt 75/94.

Preisendörfer, P. (1996) *Umweltbewußtsein in Deutschland, Ergebnisse einer repräsentativen Bevölkerungsumfrage 1996.* Bundesministeriums für Umwelt, Naturschutz und Reaktorsicherheit, BMU (Hrsg.), Bonn.

Chapter 15

The Future Belongs to International Ecolabelling Schemes

WALTER KAHLENBORN AND ATTINA DOMINÉ

Introduction

The number of tourism ecolabels probably exceeds 100 and new labels are created every few months. The labelling schemes for the hotel sector are especially numerous. But additional schemes do exist (or are envisaged) for other subsectors of the tourism industry, for example tour operators, restaurants, golf courses, marinas, destinations and tourist attractions like beaches or nature reserves. In spite of the large spectrum of existing schemes, there are still manifold opportunities for new schemes. In many regions and for many tourism-related activities there is still a need for new labels. However, who would favour even more labelling schemes?

The tourists who are the targets of ecolabels are often more put off than attracted by the vast number of schemes available to them. Not knowing which scheme to trust, a large number of them probably ignore these schemes altogether. Those who do not ignore them risk becoming victims of schemes set up to deceive tourists by labelling harmful practices as environmentally friendly. The gap between the need for further labelling in all those areas of tourism where no such schemes exist and the disadvantages of a jungle of labels can only be overcome by an extension of existing schemes or by the introduction of new larger schemes. The latter solution would then be followed by the abolition of smaller, older schemes. The enlargement of the schemes can take shape in two ways: including more branches within one scheme or extending the 'labelling area', that is, the region within which the scheme is applied.

Obviously, extending a labelling scheme of, for example, golf courses on to marinas would be relatively difficult. The set of actors involved is completely different as are the criteria which would have to be applied. The extension of the 'labelling area' would be easier.

© CAB International 2001. Tourism Ecolabelling
(eds X. Font and R.C. Buckley)

Certainly, labelling schemes which operate not only within a regional or national context, but within an international context face specific problems. They have some disadvantages compared with smaller-scale labels, but they also have particular benefits and offer specific opportunities for an active environmental policy.

In the past national and regional labelling schemes have spread much faster than international ones (Hamele 1996; DWIF, 1998; Kahlenborn *et al.*, 1999). In part, for this reason, international ecolabelling schemes for the tourism industry have attracted little attention by the academic community. This chapter aims to shift attention somewhat on to the international schemes. The objective of the chapter is to underline the growing importance of international schemes and to analyse the implications of these schemes for environmental policy.

All tourism ecolabels which are used in more than one country can be grouped under the term international tourism ecolabels. Yet the differences between ecolabels belonging to this group are great. Some ecolabels are applied only in small border regions between two countries, while others are applied regionally or even globally. Bilateral tourism ecolabels belong to the former group. These schemes, restricted to and characterized by a particular tourism region, are of little importance to the issues being discussed in this chapter.

First, the chapter deals with likely future development and examines the potential for an increase in international labelling schemes. Next, the challenges of international schemes are investigated. In the third section the positive contributions to environmental policy are studied. Finally, a short résumé is drawn from the findings of the chapter.

The Future of International Schemes

Several obstacles can be named which have hindered the development of international schemes in the last years. The inertia of small and medium-sized firms within the tourism industry has made life difficult for national and regional schemes. Only in a few cases has it been possible to establish larger schemes. Additionally, countries with a high proportion of domestic tourism have little incentive to support international schemes. Furthermore, one of the biggest tourism countries, the USA, has traditionally shown little support for labelling schemes in general. In fact, few national or regional labelling schemes have been developed within the USA so far. International schemes are likely to face resistance from certain sections of the US industry.

For instance, the US Council for International Business (USCIB) does not support ecolabels. Rather it advocates alternatives such as guidelines for environmental advertising claims, environmental reports by industry and eco-auditing standards. The EU Committee of the American Chamber of Commerce has even called on the EU to turn its ecolabel programme into a 'self-declaration' scheme (EWWE, 1996a,b; ENDS, 1996). The critical stand of the USA towards ecolabelling in tourism was also evident during the 1999 session of the Commission on Sustainable Development (CSD-7) which focused on tourism (Earth Negotiations Bulletin, 1999). In spite of all these obstacles, the future probably belongs to international labelling schemes in the tourism industry. That is not to say that national and regional schemes will disappear totally, but international schemes will take over substantial parts of the 'labelling-market'. There are a number of reasons which support this hypothesis.

One important argument for a rapid extension of international schemes is 'globalization'. Due to a growing number of foreign customers, the tourism industry is more international than most other branches of industry. Nevertheless, in the past it has been one of the industries least influenced by globalization. Large segments of the industry were and still are dominated by small companies which are national or regional in their organizational and legal structure and activities. The tourism industry, however, is now undergoing a process of far-reaching transformation.

The airlines, the part of the industry in which concentration has occurred to the greatest extent, are rapidly setting-up global alliances. The hospitality industry is teaming-up in international chains; a move not always connected with a shift in ownership, but resulting in standardization of management, marketing, etc. At the same time, the first noteworthy international holdings of tour operators are emerging. The quickening pace of worldwide competition is forcing more and more companies in the travel and tourism industry to adjust their business strategies and to adapt to the requirements of a global market.

Part of the comparative advantage of the new transnational companies and international chains in the tourism industry is their ability to realize economies of scale in the global promotion of their services. International ecolabel schemes fit well into this strategy. Not only is it easier for international companies to adapt their local service providers to the standards of one international label, but an international ecolabel scheme is also much easier to use in a global marketing strategy. Furthermore, the phenomenon of globalization strengthens the case for international schemes, not least because of its impacts on the demand side. An ever more entangled world economy is producing an increasing number of international travellers as is the growing desire of tourists to spend their vacations abroad. International tourists are obviously served better by international schemes than by national ones. For tourists who are travelling abroad, it is difficult and often impossible to know about the specific national schemes in the destination country or region. As a consequence, they will either not take the existing schemes into account in their decision-making process or they might risk relying on ecolabelling schemes which do not deliver what they promise: the most environmentally friendly services. Therefore, the more tourists become accustomed to using ecolabels in tourism, the more they will ask for standardized international schemes.

A further argument in favour of a stronger role for international schemes is the costs connected with ecolabelling. The management and operation of effective ecolabelling schemes is not cheap. Usually, the companies which apply for labels have to pay for the costs of the scheme through labelling fees. The fees are sometimes a clear obstacle for the participation of companies. International schemes – once up and running – are likely to cover more service providers than national or regional schemes. By realizing economies of scale, they can operate with lower costs. As a consequence, international schemes should be able to offer lower fees than national/regional competitors and therefore attract even more companies in the long run.

International schemes will also profit from the selection process inherent in the 'labelling market'. Labels which do not receive enough attention from tourists will usually find it difficult to keep participating companies in the labelling scheme in the long run. With fewer companies bearing the label, fewer tourists will become aware of and pay attention to the particular scheme and, as a result, even fewer companies will be interested in that particular label. In the end, the label scheme will have to be removed. In Germany, for instance, five regional and local ecolabel schemes for tourism have been abolished in recent years (see Chapter 13). In contrast, successful schemes which achieve widespread attention are likely to grow even more. International schemes which can profit from the large potential market they serve are likely to be on the winning side of that race.

Finally, yet another reason for a bright future for international labelling schemes is the growing attention being paid by several international bodies to tourist-sector eco-schemes. The World Bank and the EU are considering either introducing or actively supporting the development of new international labelling schemes. Also, UNEP is increasing its activities in the tourism sector and strongly supports tourism ecolabels (UNEP, 1999). Such support certainly will not guarantee the success of international schemes in the future, but it is an important precondition.

Environmental Policy Challenges of International Schemes

From the point of view of environmental policy, the likely rise of international schemes is difficult to evaluate. The effectiveness of labelling schemes depends on a number of factors (e.g. ownership, criteria), the geographical scope of the scheme being one example. Furthermore, the geographical range of a scheme, i.e. national or international, has many different implications, some advantageous and others disadvantageous to environmental policy. Some of the implications will be considered briefly below.

Regional conditions

One problem connected with international ecolabels is that different economic regions/countries face different environmental problems. For example, waste reduction is of utmost importance for tourism facilities on the Seychelles whereas the reduction of heating energy is of comparably low importance. In contrast, in France, the reduction of heating energy has far more importance due to the colder climate and greater use of energy for heating purposes. Although important, waste reduction is not as important in France as it is for small islands. In order for international tourism ecolabels to be effective, the eco-labelling criteria have to take regional variations in environmental conditions into consideration (Piotrowski and Kratz, 1999). If they do not, such schemes will almost certainly run counter to the differing priorities of national environmental policies.

Potential misuse

Another problem of international schemes is that they are more prone to misuse. Package operators, for example, might use international tourism ecolabels to green-wash aeroplane travel to distant destinations. By including a hotel with a well-known green label in a package holiday, tourists might be induced to believe the whole package is environmentally friendly. Obviously, national schemes can be misused as well, but international schemes open more possibilities for marketing bad practices over greater areas of time and space.

While marketing with ecolabels is in the interest of environmental policy, the misuse of ecolabels is not. The chances of successfully intervening in cases of misuse are slim. However, it is up to national environmental policy makers to make sure that international ecolabels reflect a high environmental standard, even though they cannot prevent all forms of misuse. First initiatives by NGOs in this direction during the previously mentioned CSD-7 session were unfortunately blocked by industry.

Institutional context

A further aspect which distinguishes international from national schemes and which is of importance to the implementation of environmental policy objectives is the institutional context within which the schemes are allocated. Of course, international schemes can be run (like some national/regional schemes) by just one institution. In this case, the schemes are easy to set up and will face few internal problems. They may, however, find it difficult to receive the initial public recognition which they need to survive.

For that reason a group of organizations rather than one single one is normally responsible for, or at least actively involved in, the establishment of a labelling scheme. In the past, however, it has proven very difficult even for national schemes to achieve agreement between the relevant actors on the structure, range and criteria of the scheme. For an international scheme, this problem is even larger. To involve the relevant actors, more organizations have to participate in the constituting process. However, the background and interests of these actors are likely to diverge even more than is the case for a group of national actors. The differences in interests between those actors delay the establishment of the scheme. Furthermore, solving the differences by finding the lowest common denominator implies that the labelling criteria are unlikely to be strict.

Even worse, the same arguments apply for the regular revision of the schemes. To maintain the same level, that is, to support the environmental pioneers of an industry branch, the criteria which have to be fulfilled to receive a label must be strengthened at regular intervals. International schemes which are based on co-decision procedures of actors from a number of countries and which have to reflect the interests of a large number of groups will find it very difficult to maintain this dynamic process.

This possibly constitutes a problem for national environmental policies. An international scheme which does not deliver the environmental policy results that it is supposed to do but which instead replaces an efficient national/regional scheme, can seriously hamper environmental policy objectives. To overcome this problem, close cooperation of the various parties is needed while developing the international labelling scheme. Additionally, appropriate structures and procedures are necessary; for example, a certain degree of autonomy on the part of the scheme operators and clear rules for decision making.

Free trade

A fourth aspect to be taken into consideration when talking about the implications of international ecolabel schemes for tourism is the relationship between free trade and ecolabels (Kahlenborn *et al.*, 2000). So far, tourism ecolabels have been of marginal importance to the development of the tourism market. For that reason, the labels were never challenged by the advocates of free trade. That is likely to change. As soon as the first schemes have a major impact on the market, the question will arise of whether they are compatible with free trade. To the extent to which the schemes are covered by the World Trade Organization (WTO) free trade agreements (especially GATS), the question will then be solved by the WTO dispute settlement body. WTO members can take other signing parties of the WTO agreements before this body if they feel that rules have been violated. If ecolabelling programmes are to be successfully defended in front of the WTO dispute bodies, they must be consistent with these agreements. If not, the WTO could ultimately serve as the biggest hurdle to effective ecolabelling programmes in the international marketplace (Piotrowski and Kratz, 1999; compare also Ward, 1997).

This threat is not yet real. The General Agreement on Trade in Services (GATS), which applies to the tourism sector, does not include regulations on ecolabelling. However, with a new trade round starting soon, the legal basis is likely to change. Taking past trends into account and looking at the position of some WTO member states, regulations concerning tourism ecolabelling might be included in GATS II.

At first glance, this does not present an obstacle to international schemes. In contrast with national schemes, which risk being biased towards domestic industry standards, both intentionally and unintentionally, international schemes will normally avoid domestic bias. For example a domestic bias of a labelling scheme might start with the definition of the product/service category. Thus, regions or states which promote golf might introduce labels for environmentally friendly golf courses. Those labels would, however, exclude by definition other more environmentally friendly outdoor leisure activities prevailing in other regions. Additionally, international schemes avoid unequal treatment by using easy application procedures. National schemes can function as a 'so-called' technical barrier to trade, even if they are open to applications from abroad, because of the additional difficulties faced by the foreign service providers in submitting their products/services for approval by the national ecolabelling programmes (Piotrowski and Kratz, 1999).

However, the requirements which might be imposed upon ecolabelling schemes go far beyond the issues mentioned above. The International Organization for Standardization (ISO), a worldwide association of some 100 national standards bodies, has already adopted the ISO Standard 14020 on General Principles for All Environmental Labels and Declarations. Principles 7 and 9 have been especially contentious. The former prohibits environmental labels which create 'unnecessary' obstacles to trade. A note accompanying the principle explains that the guideline will be subject to all WTO rules, including its dispute procedures. The latter requires that the labelling process be open to all interested parties and that 'reasonable efforts' be made in order to achieve a consensus, which in this context means an absence of serious and sustained opposition (Piotrowski and Kratz, 1999). The ISO standards for ecolabelling, might be used as the standard for future WTO rules.

To allow for effective international ecolabelling schemes, environmental policy makers will have to make sure that the WTO agreements leave ample space for such schemes during the 'Millennium Round'. Otherwise, every scheme with a real impact on the market might be dismantled later by WTO rulings as has happened in the past few years to a number of environmental policy initiatives.

Environmental Benefits of International Schemes

The enumeration of direct and indirect implications of international tourism ecolabelling schemes should not omit several distinctly positive consequences of such schemes for the implementation of environmental policy objectives.

More transparency and clarity

As was stated at the beginning, international schemes can solve the current chaos of regional and national tourism ecolabels by substituting them. More transparency and more clarity of the labelling market will raise public trust in the schemes. Equally, as more service providers begin to use these labels, levels of public awareness and trust will increase. The importance of ecolabels in the decision-making process of tourists will thus increase.

Positive impact on the behaviour of the industry

Furthermore, the international schemes will probably attract more tourism companies and therefore have more impact on the behaviour of the industry itself. As the lack of interest in tourism ecolabels has been a strong impediment for companies to adopt these labels, more interest on the part of tourists will augment the interest of the companies. In the best case scenario, this could lead to an upward spiral of more customer and company interest in ecolabelling. A widespread, effective tourism ecolabelling scheme which develops along such lines could obviously lend strong support to national and international environmental policy.

New markets

Another important advantage of international tourism ecolabel schemes is that they can serve to stimulate environmental awareness in national tourism markets which have not yet developed much sensitivity to environmental issues. International schemes which are well known to international tourists can be introduced even in countries with low demand from domestic tourism for ecolabelling schemes. After the introduction of the international scheme, national tourists might get interested in the labels as well. Subsequently, even tourism companies which focus on the domestic market might possibly raise their environmental standards and apply for an ecolabel.

International ecolabelling schemes can also be introduced in small countries with very small tourism markets. In cases where the development of a national ecolabel is inappropriate and the adoption of a scheme from neighbouring countries is not feasible, an international label can be a good alternative. Similarly, an international ecolabelling scheme constitutes an important alternative for countries in which the tourism industry and environmental policy actors have not yet developed efficient structures and in which the preconditions for developing a national/regional tourism ecolabel do not exist. Such countries can save much time and money by relying on internationally approved schemes.

Efficiency

Finally, international tourism ecolabelling schemes may prove more difficult to set up as has been mentioned before. However, by replacing national/regional schemes, they also replace the contorting negotiating procedures which always accompany the introduction or revision of these schemes. They, therefore, save resources (time and money) and can speed up the process of introducing ecolabelling schemes in the tourism industry in many countries.

Conclusions

Much has been said in this chapter about international ecolabelling schemes for the tourism sector, but still much more would have to be added for a complete picture. However, it was not the objective of this chapter to answer all questions surrounding international tourism ecolabelling schemes. The goal was simply to shed some light on an issue which has received little consideration in the past. Moreover, the objective was to demonstrate that we have probably only seen the tip of the iceberg of what international ecolabelling schemes in tourism will be in future. Additionally, the environmental policy implications of the likely shift from national to international schemes have been highlighted.

Very few international schemes currently exist. Furthermore, most are not organized by actors which have the power to make these schemes successful. Most importantly, public authorities which have been of vital importance for the development of strong ecolabelling schemes in many European countries are only now beginning to give real support to international programmes.

With a rather poor past behind them, international ecolabelling schemes can still expect to have a bright future. For a number of reasons, including changes in the tourism sector and the advent of globalization, international ecolabelling schemes are likely to become much more prevalent. In the near future, we should expect the 'market share' of international schemes to rise quickly. The development of international schemes will bring about new risks and new opportunities for environmental policy. Overall, however, the opportunities probably outweigh the risks. It is important that environmental policy makers react and take advantage of these chances while at the same time minimizing the risks. More specifically, several recommendations for national environmental policy-makers can be made:

- Policy-makers should take an active role in setting up new international ecolabelling schemes. This will prevent industry-driven, less environmentally efficient schemes from acquiring a central position. Thus, they should give support to well-thought out initiatives for introducing such schemes, especially in areas where no such schemes or no efficient schemes currently exist. Furthermore, national policy-makers should consider mutual recognition of national (and regional) schemes. Furthermore, they should take into consideration the option of extending a scheme in a second step instead of introducing new national and regional schemes in a first step (Kahlenborn, 1999).
- The greater market reach of international ecolabelling schemes makes the misuse of such labels likely. Environmental

policy-makers should consider how to counteract such moves, for example by introducing international minimum standards for ecolabels.

- Research must be carried out to overcome the structural obstacles for international schemes. In particular, the question of how to adapt such schemes to different regional environmental preconditions needs to be investigated. National environmental policy-makers should finance such research.
- With free trade agreements interfering more and more with ecolabelling efforts, environmental policy-makers might do better to introduce safeguards into future international agreements. Such safeguards should protect effective ecolabelling schemes from being forced by the WTO to apply inadequate criteria. The safeguards should also ensure that further growth of the schemes is not hampered.
- While setting up international schemes, national environmental policy-makers have to make sure that the institutional framework of such schemes is effective. International schemes which are not autonomous will find it difficult to produce convincing outcomes. The autonomy of international labelling bodies obviously results in a diminishing role for national authorities. That is the price which they have to pay and which they have to accept.

References

DWIF – Deutsches Wirtschaftswissenschaftliches Institut für Fremdenverkehr (1998) *Fachtagung 'Umweltkennzeichnungen im Tourismus'. Dokumentation der Beiträge, 29 October 1998, Ludwig-Maximilians-University Munich*. DWIF, Munich.

Earth Negotiations Bulletin (1999) CSD-7 highlights Tuesday, 27 April 1999. *Earth Negotiation Bulletin* 129, 28 April, 1.

ENDS, Environmental Data Services (1996) ISO under fire over environmental standards. *ENDS Report* 260, 3–4.

EWWE, Environment Watch Western Europe (1996a) EU members unhappy at draft ISO ecolabel standard. *EWWE* 7, 5 April, 1–3.

EWWE, Environment Watch Western Europe (1996b) ISO ecolabelling principles on track to become global standard. *EWWE* 14, 19 July, 9–10.

Hamele, H. (1996) *Das Buch der Sieben Siegel. Umweltauszeichnungen im Tourismus. Internationaler Überblick und Entwicklungen*. German Federal Environment Ministry, Berlin.

Kahlenborn, W. (1999) Der Blaue Tourismus-Engel ist noch flügellahm. *fvw International* 5, 142.

Kahlenborn, W., Kraack, M. and Carius, A. (1999) *Tourismus- und Umweltpolitik*. Springer, Heidelberg.

Kahlenborn, W., Imbusch, K. and Turmann, A. (2000) *Umweltschutz und Tourismus. Deutsche Tourismusaußenpolitik zwischen GATS und CSD.* Libri, Hamburg.

Piotrowski, R. and Kratz, S. (1999) Eco-labelling in a globalised economy. *Internationale Politik und Gesellschaft* 4, 29–43.

UNEP, United Nations Environmental Programme (1999) Tourism and the environment: enemies or allies? *UNEP Press Release* 4 February 1999. UNEP, Nairobi.

Ward, H. (1997) Trade and environment issues in voluntary ecolabelling and life cycle analysis. *RECIEL* 2, 139–147.

Chapter 16

Conclusions: a Strategic Analysis of Tourism Ecolabels

XAVIER FONT

Introduction

This book has reviewed the role of ecolabelling in marketing tourism and recreation products claiming to be environmentally friendly; how these labels have appeared; the role they aim to fulfil; how they have developed and common pitfalls; examples of labels and current initiatives from different countries; and the reasoning behind different national and subsectoral approaches to certification and ecolabelling. The review has been kept to tourism-specific certification, and therefore not covered general systems such as ISO and EMAS which have substantial literature dedicated to them. This book has purposely not covered the technical aspects of environmental criteria and their measurement and monitoring, since this was considered beyond the scope of the book.

The growing number of labels suggests three arguments: (i) labels are easy to create; (ii) the labels are generally immature; and (iii) labels are a commonly accepted method to improve practice. Throughout this book, contributors have emphasized that currently there are too many tourism ecolabels, which are not clear to the potential tourist, are run at a small scale, generally by organizations with limited environmental management expertise and under pressure to increase the number of labelled organizations year after year. Labels are generally not self-financing and most of them have been developed in the last few years; soon funding bodies will start asking for a certain degree of self-financing from these operations, and ecolabels will need to justify their expenditure. Therefore how can an ecolabel justify its presence in the market? We can assess their effectiveness against:

- *The funding body's objectives*. Although generally we do not know if labels are aimed more at consumers or regulators.

- *The ecolabel's development.* This is generally understood as an increase in applications and certifications.
- *The market share of certified products.* In general this is not used, since the ratio is very low and shows the weaknesses of labelling, and also because it is difficult to tell how many companies there are in some tourism subsectors.
- *Consumer awareness of the ecolabel.* Generally expensive to assess, and in most cases research carried out on behalf of the ecolabelling agency, which raises questions regarding its reliability.
- *Influence on consumer decision making.* We do not know if consumers pay any attention to ecolabels, although Chapters 4 and 5 have put into perspective the value and use of environmental values within the decision-making spectrum.
- *Ability to influence industry's performance.* This depends on the ability of the label to prove that applicants made improvements in order to gain the label, instead of being awarded for work already done in the past.

Development Strategies for Tourism Ecolabels

Some of these are harder to assess than others, but in general labels will aim to continue operating in the future. For this reason this concluding chapter concentrates on modelling possible strategies for tourism ecolabels to develop their presence and impact in the tourism industry (see Table 16.1).

Market penetration

Market penetration is likely to be the most straightforward of methods, and certainly one used by most labels in the near future due to the newness of ecolabels in tourism. The traditional approach taken by ecolabel awarding bodies is to penetrate the market by increasing the market share of companies applying. The potential consumer will only be able to trust an ecolabel if they cannot find the same environmental quality from a non-certified product (see Chapter 2). Also the larger the market share, the more impact the label will have in the industry, to almost become a trading standard. Probably only one label in tourism has reached a large market share, the Blue Flag for beaches, thanks to its European approach and the fact that tourists place high value on health and safety issues related to bathing water quality. Three strategies are suggested here to increase the market share of the label: reviewing the certification criteria, enhancing the label's image and reducing the application costs.

Table 16.1. Development strategies for tourism ecolabels.

Product	Market	
	Same	New
Same	• Review certification criteria • Enhance the label's brand image • Reduce application costs	• Target new countries • Target new sectors
New	• Reposition from ecolabels to quality labels • Provide ancillary services • Act as distribution channel for certified products	• Joint marketing by keeping the chain of custody • Merge with other labels • Take over labels with funding difficulties

Review certification criteria

The criteria for most ecolabels are based on a list developed by experts on issues that are important to that particular industry, at the time of assessment. Although there seems to be a trend towards some actual, hard, substantive criteria, at least in some of the hotel labels, criteria are not always transportable across countries and situations. This limits the expansion of ecolabels and raises criticisms (see for example, Chapter 9).

At the same time, environmental concerns and proposed management solutions have been developed in parallel, with some efforts in recent years to introduce environmental management to the corporate board through initiatives such as the EU Eco-management and Auditing scheme (EMAS) and the ISO 14001 standards. The next few years will see the extrapolation of systems developed for large companies to small and medium-sized enterprises (SMEs) and from manufacturing to the service industries. This process will only be successful if systems are adapted and simplified to the needs and abilities of other industries, otherwise most tourism companies will find the implementation of environmental management systems a burdensome and costly exercise. Yet the adaptation of total quality management (TQM) and environmental management systems (EMS) should ensure that quality and environmental recognition systems are based on strict criteria and open verification. In the tourism industry, the key example is the work done by the World Travel and Tourism Council (WTTC) and SGS on the Green Globe Agenda 21 label.

The advantage of taking a management approach to certification criteria is that this makes them more flexible, adaptable to local conditions and forces the company's management to draw up their own environmental agenda (Font and Tribe, 2001). The EMS approach can be used in conjunction with the benchmarking of best practice (Zairi, 1994; CREM, 2000; see Chapter 10) within each sector of the tourism and hospitality industry, providing models and examples to follow which can be incorporated into the manuals for potential candidates.

Enhance the label's brand image
From a marketing point of view, ecolabels can be compared to brands in aspects like image creation and promotion. The tourism industry is undergoing a process of standardization and internationalization of products wherever and whenever economies of scale and markets allow (Vellas and Bécherel, 1999). Yet the tourism industry is characterized by small players operating fairly independently, raising the issue of quality assurance prior to consumption of tourism services. The promoters of ecolabels may want to take a more aggressive marketing approach to raising the profile of their label's image, aiming to position it as a trademark of environmental quality recognized by the public. Seeking high profile fundraisers and label endorsement from recognized large players in the industry will increase exposure and therefore awareness.

Reduce application costs
A third method that can be used by ecolabelling schemes to encourage further applications is to reduce the application costs. This may be useful as a short-term method to penetrate a market and to gain first-time applicants, but it should be discouraged as a long term method, particulary because the cost of applications is already subsidized in most labels.

Market development

Two main options will be reviewed in the development of new markets: the penetration of new countries and the targeting of complementary subsectors within the tourism industry.

Target new countries
Most tourism ecolabels are at national or sub-national level, with a small number of newer international initiatives. Some of these labels actively market themselves by emphasizing their geographical boundaries (e.g. Urlaub auf Biohöfen in Deutschland and the Scottish Golf Course Wildlife Initiative), and in doing so they define the scope of the label, and also limit their possibility of geographical expansion.

In the short to medium term international labels may well expand into countries where no labelling systems are available nationally. As an example, a recent report commissioned by the Jamaican Hotel and Tourist Association recommended to the organization and its members the Green Globe Agenda 21 certification over other programmes, due to recognition, applicability, cost and access to certifiers (Hagler Bailly, 1999). Some of the labels in tourism have already been devised with an international scope in mind. Those that have not, and aim to move into new markets, will have to be aware of the difficulties in the internationalization of brands (Usunier, 2000).

Target new sectors
For those labels with a geographical boundary, the market development option will be to target new sectors that are compatible. The Blue Flag has expanded its scope by including marinas as well as its more recognized work on certifying beaches. Another example is the National Ecotourism Accreditation Programme (NEAP), currently moving towards certifying adventure tourism, as well as ecotourism packages. Ecolabels for projects have a greater possibility to expand in this way, for example the Tourfor award was researched on forest tourism and recreation sites, yet in some countries there would not be a critical mass to make it feasible. This process can potentially blur the differences between labels, entering in direct competition, and force alliances.

Product development

The suggestions under this section denote possible extensions to the current ecolabels, or additions to complement them. Inevitably these product developments will make the ecolabel appealing to new markets, but the main emphasis is placed on the development of the products first.

Reposition from ecolabels to quality labels
Environmental impacts are not the only concern of tourism companies, and some would advocate that labels of quality based only on environmental issues do not reflect the industry responsibilities, nor the destination requirements. From a resource-based approach, socio-cultural impacts and stakeholder involvement should be included to ensure a more complete picture. Chapter 14 already suggests grouping environmental and social considerations under one heading.

From a market-based approach, product and service quality would be paramount, which suggests the development of ecolabels' certification criteria by including quality management issues. Yet this has its dangers, since in doing so, they will enter into direct competition with a wider range of general management awards and labels, the best known of them being the ISO 9000 family. Total quality management (TQM) systems, in their infancy 10 years ago, have become widespread practice and the measurement of performance has become part of business management for large corporations (Neely, 1999). TQM models do consider environmental issues (Grandzol and Gershon, 1998), but the value allocated to the 'externalities' of business management, such as social and environmental issues, is low. A review of nine national quality awards showed that only 5% of the average weight of their criteria was placed on social and environmental issues together, justified by the fact that general management awards are 'customer oriented, results-driven with a strong focus on people performance and satisfaction', and the environment and society do not 'contribute directly to organizational performance' (Puay *et al.*, 1998: 33). This could be taken as a warning of the lower relative value of the environment against other priorities held by corporate boards and the average customer.

Provide ancillary services

Ecolabels in the past have passively recognized good environmental performance, and the majority of applicants expected recognition for a good past record. The provision of ancillary services can strengthen the value of applying, since it may attract companies that aim to improve their performance by following a structured approach to environmental management, and therefore increase the number of applicants by diversifying the products on offer.

Ancillary services that can be provided vary, but in general they can be grouped into two categories. First, know-how related services such as company-specific training, short courses on aspects of environmental management, information sharing services, consultancy, provision of help-desks and so on. Second, services made possible through the economies of scale achieved by clusters of companies. A membership system for awarded companies can raise the level of empowerment and engagement of applicants. The ecolabelling organization can then become a purchasing unit to gain critical mass, as well as the lobbying voice for companies, for example in claiming preferential use of government or NGO-owned land, such as the case of NEAP members claiming preferential use of Australian national parks.

Act as distribution channel for certified products

Tourism ecolabels have a relatively low market exposure, due to the considerably lower promotional budget an ecolabel has compared with large tourism and hospitality corporations. Market awareness of labels is low, and even if the market is aware and willing to buy green, ecolabelled products need to be made more readily available. Ecolabels need to provide convenience as well as verification; this involves taking a proactive approach to marketing the values of the ecolabel, by becoming a distribution channel of green tourism products.

Using ecolabels as a distribution channel can work in two directions. From the point of view of the market, channel acceptance and support for green innovations is paramount to facilitating sales (Wong *et al.*, 1996). The endorsement of a reputable organization not only through an ecolabel, but also by coordinating and facilitating tourism sales, will facilitate the purchase of green products, and create consumer awareness and confidence. The standardization of products offered by the organizations certified will determine the feasibility of such a proposal, but this could be feasible for labels targeting hotels, camp sites and ecotourism packages. Second, by selling direct, ecolabels can increase their appeal to prospective applicants, and therefore increase their presence in the market place, as well as generate extra revenue from the sales commission.

Diversification

Finally, there are three suggestions in this section which relate to major changes to the ecolabels or the way in which they are managed, usually arising from closer links to other labels. Although it could be argued that these are not a diversification in itself but a product development, the complexity in shifting the focus from one label to merging two of them, plus the issues in managing criteria, verification and applicants from two labels, justifies placing them under the diversification category. The concept of chain of custody is also discussed here due to the change in philosophy that it requires on behalf of ecolabel organizers.

Joint marketing by keeping the chain of custody
The immaturity of the tourism ecolabels means that most of them are marketing themselves independently, despite usually standing for similar principles. In other industries, with a larger percentage of the providers being certified, the current trend is to look for chains of custody in certification. By chains of custody it is meant that companies buy from and sell to other certified companies. For example, hotels certified as being environmentally friendly will buy whenever possible from providers that are also certified (and therefore will look for Forest Stewardship Council (FSC) timber, Soil Association vegetables, and ISO 14001 certified appliances) and will sell primarily to companies that will make good use of their products (certified distribution systems).

Encouraging chains of custody is not entirely a novelty to tourism; for example the Pan-Parks certification requires national parks to ensure that tourism providers in their vicinity adhere to the park's conservation principles. A second example is the work by the tour operator TUI in encouraging hotels in their brochures to improve their environmental performance and recognizing them via the 'TUI Environmental Champion'. The concept of keeping the chain of custody among tourism providers will help in the implementation of environmental management in those sectors of the industry where the environment would play a small part in the tourist's choice criteria. This is, therefore, a huge knock-on effect on the industry as a whole, although the economies of scale may prevent its development.

From a marketing point of view, the advantage of introducing chains of custody in the certification criteria means that labels can promote each other, therefore increasing exposure, strengthening their position and reaching new markets. From a management point of view, it means that each label does not have to reinvent a new set of criteria to set out rules on providers and purchasers, but instead link criteria across labels. This can be a first step towards the merging of two or more labels, as seen below. Chains of custody will help the certification of tourism businesses that tourists would not consider as having to improve their environmental performance, or where environmental issues are low on the consumer's decision making priorities, and therefore companies have less incentive to 'green their act'. For example most tourism ecolabels target accommodation and destinations, yet the tourism system (Inskeep, 1991; Gunn, 1994) includes many other services that will be part of the package. The transport industry, catering, management of destination infrastructures and tourist services at the destination are low on the ecolabelling agenda.

Merge with other labels

Part of the process of streamlining tourism labels will be merging some of them. Two types of mergers will be considered here, first a merger of branding, where two awarding bodies are still run independently but they both use a single label brand. This is the result of joining forces between two institutions, partnership agreements and similar arrangements (see for example Green Globe with the Danish Green Key). Issues here will be the comparability of criteria and verification methods, and the brand to promote themselves under. Second, a merger of awarding bodies, usually involving a large label taking over the applicants and expertise of a smaller one, rebranding their work under the umbrella of the larger scheme after a period of joint branding.

Mergers are more likely to happen among labels within one country (see the Austrian and Upper-Austrian case), or labels that were already planned as international labels (Green Globe and PATA Green Leaf). International ecolabels depend on the credibility and weight of the international endorsing body. National organizations will usually have more exposure within their country, and therefore more opportunities to be recognized by the consumer.

There is also the tenuous possibility for ecolabels to merge with other methods to recognize quality and to be integrated with them. For example, an ecolabel may influence the inclusion of environmental elements in the grading of hotels, and be part of the criteria for land management to achieve certain status as protected areas, yet these links are not likely to take place in the near future, and in any case they would generally mean that the ecolabel would be taken over which, by and large, is not what the funding bodies want.

Take over labels with funding difficulties

The need for streamlining labels is most evident in Europe (see Chapter 12), where there are several labels competing for the same market, and one tourism company can opt to apply for three or four labels. And yet at a global scale there is no evidence of whether international labels will take over national or sub-national ones. The reasons for the internationalization of labels are strong (see Chapter 15), although the power of national bodies organizing labels will make it difficult for the latter to be superseded. This may change in the next few years, since the majority of tourism and hospitality labels have been operating for less than 10 years, and in the near future funding bodies will start asking for financial independence, at least partially. This will force some weaker labels out of the market, and will give the opportunity chance to stronger players to take over their member's list. Also there have been several awards and label proposals that did not go beyond the development stage due to funding difficulties, despite proposing and having been tested in very useful subsectors of the tourism industry, and for those labels that were run for projects only (see Chapter 13) to be integrated into mainstream programmes.

Branding issues will also become problematic in the takeover of labels, and may require expensive repositioning campaigns. One of the strongest European labels, the Blue Flag, has a strong enough image that it could be expanded into the certification of other sectors, and is currently certifying marinas as well as beaches. Recent conversations with the team developing the Tourfor award suggested the possibility that the Foundation for Environmental Education in Europe (organizing the Blue Flag and endorsing the Clefs Vertes) may take forward the Tourfor award and pilot it in several European countries. Although the Blue Flag brand has a much higher awareness, introducing the applicants of the Tourfor award (tourism and recreation in forests) under the umbrella of the Blue Flag may take some time to explain to potential tourists, and may cause confusion. Rebranding may be seen as worthwhile if several smaller brands are brought together under one new initiative.

Conclusions

Green marketing is here to stay, for as long as it is seen as a method to gain competitive advantage. The present ecolabels certify current good environmental performance; few applicants make efforts to meet these criteria as having or not having an ecolabel is not the key to the subsistence of their business. Therefore the current ecolabels do not ensure a more sustainable tourism industry, just the recognition of past good practice. Improving performance is the only method to green the whole tourism industry, and ecolabel organizers will have to become more proactive to make ecolabels a necessary element to trade in tourism. Other industries, such as forest management, have managed to put pressure on key distribution channels for timber products, forcing timber producers to change their production systems, yet this process has caused endless arguments and international conflicts. The variety of tourism distribution channels and the importance of direct purchasing would make such a top-down approach in feasible, yet there is a lesson to be learned from the Forest Stewardship Council experience (see Murphy and Bendell, 1997).

The need for high environmental standards will not fade, but environmental issues will stop being a source of competitive advantage (Menon and Menon, 1997). The maturity of some international ecolabels should give an instrument to the discerning tourist to purchase green, to the point that more companies see the advantage of working to green principles, and these become standard practice. And yet as more companies reach some environmental thresholds, consumers may start to place more importance on other values. Also as the criteria set by ecolabels become common practice, these will be introduced into legislation and expected from the tourism industry. This will mean that today's environmental considerations will stop being an element of differentiation between tourism operators, and environmental claims may well give way to other marketing plots. In the meantime, tourism ecolabels will be developed and others will cease to trade, the majority will remain at a sub-national level, and hopefully some will grow to international recognition. This chapter has interpreted the findings from the previous chapters by suggesting strategic development choices for tourism ecolabels in a generic format that can be applied to the majority of schemes reviewed in this book and presented in the directory of labels.

References

CREM (2000) *Kick-off Document FEMATOUR Project (Feasibility and Market Study for a European Eco-label for Tourist Accommodations).* Consultancy and Research for Environmental Management (CREM), Amsterdam.

Font, X. and Tribe, J. (2001) Promoting green tourism: the future of environmental awards. *International Journal of Tourism Research* 3(1), 1–13.

Grandzol, J. and Gershon, M. (1998) A survey instrument for standardising TQM modelling research. *International Journal of Quality Science* 3(1), 80–105.

Gunn, C.-A. (1994) *Tourism Planning: Basics, Concepts, Cases*, 3rd edn. Taylor & Francis, New York.

Hagler Bailly (1999) *Assessment of Voluntary Environmental Rating and Certification Programs: Environmental Audits for Sustainable Tourism.* Hagler Bailly (consultants), Arlington, Virginia.

Inskeep, E. (1991) *Tourism Planning: an Integrated and Sustainable Approach.* Van Nostrand Reinhold, New York.

Menon, A. and Menon, A. (1997) Enviropreneurial marketing strategy: the emergence of corporate environmentalism as market strategy. *Journal of Marketing* 61(1), 51–67.

Murphy, D.F. and Bendell, J. (1997) *In the Company of Partners: Business, Environmental Groups and Sustainable Development post-Rio.* The Policy Press, Bristol, UK.

Neely, A. (1999) The performance measurement revolution: why now and what next? *International Journal of Operations and Production Management* 19(2), 205–228.

Puay, S., Tan, K., Xie, M. and Goh, T. (1998) A comparative study of nine national quality awards. *The TQM Magazine* 10(1), 30–39.

Usunier, J.C. (2000) *Marketing across Cultures*, 3rd edn. Pearson Education, Harlow, UK.

Vellas, F. and Bécherel, L. (eds) (1999) *The International Marketing of Travel and Tourism: a Strategic Approach.* McMillan, London.

Wong, V., Turner, W. and Stoneman, P. (1996) Marketing strategies and market prospects for environmentally-friendly consumer products. *British Journal of Management* 7(3), 263–281.

Zairi, M. (1994) Benchmarking: the best tool for measuring competitiveness. *Benchmarking for Quality Management and Technology* 1(1), 11–24.

Austrian Ecolabel For Tourism Organizations
(Österreichisches Umweltzeichen für Tourismusbetriebe)
Austria

Otto Fichtl, Ecolabel Officer, Austrian Consumer Association (VKI)

The Austrian Eco-label for Tourism awards companies providing catering facilities and accommodation for their efforts in environmental
management and social responsibility. This joint project of the Federal
Ministry of Economic Affairs and Labour and the Federal Ministry for
Agriculture and Forestry, the Environment and Water Management
represents a national instrument aiming at promoting quality and
environmental awareness in the Austrian tourism and leisure industry.

The idea of creating a nation-wide environmental prize for companies operating in tourism has existed since as early as 1991 (at the same
time as the introduction of the environmental prize for products). This
went back to the initiative by the Minister for the Environment at that
time, Mrs Feldgrill-Zankel. In 1994 the Austrian Consumer Association, which is also the competent body for the criteria development for
the Austrian ecolabelling scheme for products, was commissioned to
produce a catalogue of criteria, based on a study by the OeAR regional
planning association.

Because of a great number of ecolabels of different qualities for
tourism companies in some provinces and many regions of Austria, one
aim of the Austrian Eco-label for Tourism was to create a nation-wide
identical, comparable guideline. For that reason the already existing
regional ecolabels were involved in the course of development as well
as representatives of tourism and environment, representatives from all
nine Austrian provinces and the chambers of commerce. The criteria

© CAB *International* 2001. *Tourism Ecolabelling*
(eds X. Font and R.C. Buckley)

document for issuing environmental awards for tourism companies was passed in October 1996. By January 2000, 86 tourism companies had been certified, steadily increasing over the previous 3 years (8 in 1997, 32 in 1998, 48 in 1999). These 86 companies are a variety of hotels, B&Bs, training centres, youth hostels, restaurants, camping sites, alpine mountain huts, private rooms and farmhouse holidays, together providing more than 7000 bed spaces.

The criteria catalogue examines each environmental issue on which the business has an impact. This comprehensive view of all areas of the tourism companies should guarantee that only the best companies with ecological management can be awarded. The system differentiates between mandatory criteria, which must be fulfilled and target criteria with different significance at which a certain number of points has to be reached (rating of 60%). Ecologically innovative initiatives can bring additional points. The issues are:

- *Procurement and avoidance of waste*, in food and in the kitchen overall (avoiding the purchase of over-packaged goods) in cleaning and hygiene (environmentally sound detergents and cleaning agents), in equipment and furnishing (natural decoration for the tables), in the office and reception area (use of recycled paper or chlorine-free paper for writing and copying purposes and brochures).
- *Waste recycling and disposal*, for example drawing up a waste concept and arrangements for separated waste collections.
- *Energy management*, for example drawing up an energy concept in order to identify energy-saving opportunities.
- *Water/waste water*, for example water-saving washing machines and dishwashers.
- *Outside area/construction work*, for example no use of de-icing salt; no pesticides; no mineral fertilizer; and unsealed car parks.
- *Air/noise*, for example use of propellant-free sprays, no-smoking zones.
- *Transport*, for example pick-up service or discounts for guests who use public transport; bicycles for hire.
- *Social criteria/information for guests and staff*, for example the criteria catalogue must be available for guests, and there will be staff training and motivation.

The criteria are not static but are revised every 3 years on the basis of increasing environmental, technical and statutory developments as well as the experiences of the audits, those companies already awarded and of consultants. The first updating of the criteria document was finished in October 1998.

Both Ministries, the Austrian Consumer Association (Verein für Konsumenteninformation, VKI) and the administration to the technical bureau Hauer commission the auditing process. These organizations distribute information material. Applicants for the Austrian Eco-label for Tourism place their request together with necessary documents (waste concept and the energy concept) at the Austrian Consumer Association. The VKI assigns verifiers, who check the agreement with the criteria document on site. After having been audited successfully a certificate is presented to the grantees by the two responsible ministers in the context of an honorary meeting. This certificate entitles the grantees to use the Austrian Eco-label for Tourism for marketing for a period of 3 years. A follow-up test is necessary after that time. In order to ensure that the criteria are maintained during this period, the grantees have to deliver a letter of intent annually. Additionally spot tests are executed.

The two ministries support the organizational and administrative costs and most of the marketing costs. Likewise, the (further) training of the examiners and advisers, the technical work for the revision of the criteria and the work for the creation of an information package, which should offer support to the grantees for the implementation of the criteria (checklists, product information), are financed by the ministries. The grantees have to pay for the use of the label for the 3-year period. The following three categories of fees were established: category 1, ATS 4500 (approx. US$/€327) hotels, inns, holiday villages, apartments; category 2; ATS 2250 (approx. US$/€163) B&Bs, guesthouses, youth hostels, holiday homes, restaurants, camping sites, alpine mountain huts; and category 3, ATS 750 (approx. US$/€54) farmhouse holidays and private rooms with up to ten beds). In addition to these fees, the companies have to take over the auditing costs (between ATS 2000 and 3000 (approx. US$/€150–220) depending on the categories). Consulting costs (if needed) are to be taken over by the applicants; here some provinces of the Federal Republic or the chambers of commerce offer generous supports. As well as the above-mentioned support and the publication of a quarterly information letter, the following marketing measures are financed by the Federal Ministries: publication of a catalogue of the grantees; advertisements and articles in professional journals; cooperation with tour operators; presentations at trade fairs; and a homepage.

If a tourism company involved is checked for its environmentally friendly operation, positive effects on the environment can be targeted as well as monetary savings. Ecological management can also result in a qualitative increase in the structure of goods and services offered. At the same time it can contribute to an improvement in the environmental situation by reducing pollution. Reductions in water and energy consumption, washing and cleaning agents, and waste will also provide the company with a direct economic advantage. The Eco-label also creates and maintains a competitive advantage for the tourism establishments. It is a means for advertising and also for improving the image of the companies. The substantial motives of a tourism company to apply for the Eco-label are benefits regarding their own marketing as well as a general improvement in their image. In addition to the savings achieved, there is the conviction that this programme can bring tourism and environmental protection in agreement.

For tourists the Eco-label is an orientation aid. It provides objective environmental information and the nation-wide standard of the Austrian Eco-label for Tourism guarantees the high quality of the label. Although enquiries prove that a large number of guests consider environmental questions during the planning of their holiday, the Eco-label should be regarded only as an additional benefit of marketing. It should be pointed out that any ecolabel stands, not only for the protection of the environment, but also for a high standard of quality.

Some of the targets of the Austrian Eco-label have already been reached (although some only partially). These include:

- to raise awareness of environmental issues in the Austrian tourism and leisure industry;
- to demonstrate that environmental management is a quality element in tourism;
- to show that environmental management makes good business sense;
- to offer guidance for interested tourists;
- to present an additional marketing instrument for the tourism companies; and
- to improve the environmental situation.

Nevertheless, it will be important in the future to increase the level of awareness of the label further, as much among the guests as among the tourism industry.

Bed & Bike: bicycle-friendly guest operations (Bett & Bike: Fahrradfreundliche Gastbetriebe) Germany

http://www.eco-tip.org/Eco-labels/ecolabels.htm and http://www.fa-tourismus.adfc.de/faf7gb.htm

Although not planned as an ecolabel, this quality label has many of the characteristics of ecolabels, since it encourages environmental transport. It was launched in 1997 by the ADFC-Bundesverband (the National Association of the German Cycling Club), Bremen. ADFC recognized that cycle-borne guests were forming a growing proportion of customers for the catering and hotel trades and far from being seen as the 'poor man's holiday', cyclists are now found to be the 'new middle class', that is, middle-ranking and senior white-collar workers, teachers and civil servants who, although are seeking varying accommodation requirements, for example from a campsite to a five-star hotel, also have certain expectations, for example, greater supplies, as they can only carry a small amount of luggage.

The award targets the following groups in Germany: accommodation, food and beverage retailers, and campsites. In order to qualify for an award, applicants must fulfil all of the minimum criteria and at least two criteria from the list of additional options. The minimum criteria for accommodation providers are: acceptance of cycling guests (also for one night only), a lockable room, drying facilities, breakfast or cooking facilities, cycling maps, cycle repair sets, and information on bicycle repair workshops. Additional options include: advice on environmental means of arrival and departure by public transport, pick-up and drop-off services for cycling guests, possibilities for bicycle hire, important spare parts, a reservation service for booking overnight stays in other bicycle-friendly establishments, lunch bags, etc.

Food and beverage retailers are required to at least have bicycle parking facilities, drinks appropriate for cyclists, warm meals during opening times, cycling maps, bicycle repair kits, and information on bicycle repair workshops. Additional options include regional cuisine, organic food, drying facilities, etc.

Campsites are required to have separate camping areas for cyclists and non-motorized guests, a grassy area for tents, drying facilities, no additional costs for acceptance of bicycles, cycling maps, bicycle repair kits and information on bicycle repair workshops. Additional options include facilities for leaving bicycles, cooking facilities, shopping facilities, important spare parts, tents for hire, etc.

An application can be made at any time by filling in an ADFC Questionnaire. A one-off fee of DM 240 (approx. US$/€120) and an annual participation fee of DM 50 (approx. US$/€25) is applicable. The award is made on the basis of the information provided by applicants; however, random spot checks are carried out. The awards are valid for 1 year and prolongation is possible, although it can also be discontinued if an operator does not conform to the minimum criteria. After expiry of the contract, the operator is obliged to return the plaque to the ADFC.

There are currently approximately 2300 bicycle-friendly tourism businesses. It is felt that acceptance in the national/regional ADFC Bed & Bike Guidebook is proving to be positive for the awarded establishments. This publication can also be accessed via the Internet. The ADFC offers advertising products such as flags, stickers and bicycle repair kits for bicycle-friendly tourism businesses.

Biosphere Hotels, Spain

Pilar Guillen, Biosphere Hotels Officer, Asolan

Biosphere Hotels is a private and independent certification system, aiming to give public recognition to management, service and environmental quality of those hotels complying with the Responsible Standard System. This system was created to direct and improve global hotel quality, on a voluntary basis, and is promoted and directed by the Responsible Tourism Institute, a non-profit organization whose aim is to support tourist management models engaged in quality and environmental responsibility. Biosphere Hotels has been operating in Lanzarote (Canary Islands, Spain) since 1997. The initiative was launched by ASOLAN and has been backed by the MaB Committee of UNESCO. The Responsible Quality System was designed for every area, region or territory objectively complying with the sustainable development requests established by the Rio Conference Declaration. 'Biosphere Reserves' are among these areas, although currently this has only been piloted in the Canary Islands. The general objectives are:

- to promote the adoption of sustainable conduct in the tourist industry;
- to provide a basis for the continuous improvement of this conducts;
- to establish cooperation systems by means of management and coordination models;
- to supply a label certifying the responsible engagement of the establishment; and
- to provide tourists with a reference for a better choice and the possibility of environmental engagement in their tourist experience.

The criteria on which the standard is based can be divided into four groups: (i) resource economy and management efficiency of resources; (ii) environmental adaptation and minimization of impacts; (iii) sustainability; and (iv) environmental quality. The criteria involve examining the promotion, licensing and publication of the environmental and ecological quality of these hotels, such as: water and energy saving, waste avoidance and waste separation, transport, prevention measures, environment, heritage, responsible tourism, information and awareness promotion.

Applicants are from those resorts attached to the Biosphere Reserves. The Biosphere Hotels audit involves three stages. During a first review, the establishment will put itself before the standard requirements, in order to plan the completion of the responsible tourism system, with guidance and support of the Responsible Tourism Institute (ITR) staff. This is followed by an auto-evaluation audit, an internal audit carried out by the establishment itself, with help from the ITR, to verify whether the establishment meets the required standards before applying for the conformity evaluation to obtain the Biosphere Hotels' Label. This is then followed by the formal audit, at which stage successful companies will receive the ecolabel. Once awarded the label, the establishment must carry on complying with the required standards; this will be reviewed via annual follow-up inspections. If the audit result is negative, the ITR will inform the establishment in order to overcome the digression from the standard, and will subsequently grant the label. In June 2000, 15 establishments were promoted as being certified (from nine in 1997). Steps have been made to extend the label outside Lanzarote to other biosphere reserves, although no results have been reported to date.

The Blue Flag Campaign, Europe

Finn Bolding Thomsen, Blue Flag Coordinator

The Blue Flag Campaign is an EC-funded programme to certify the quality of beaches and marinas, mostly for the quality of bathing water. It is run by the Foundation for Environmental Education in Europe (FEEE) and operated at national level by satellite offices from FEEE. The main partners are the European Commission, United Nations Environment Programme, World Tourism Organization, the International Life Saving Federation, and other institutions at national level.

The Campaign started in France in 1985 and expanded into an European programme in 1987, when 244 beaches and 208 marinas in ten countries were awarded. In 1999, this number had risen to 1821 beaches and 619 marinas, in 21 countries: Belgium, Bulgaria, Croatia, Cyprus, Denmark, Estonia, Finland, France, Germany, Greece, Ireland, Italy, Latvia, The Netherlands, Norway, Portugal, Slovenia, Spain, Sweden, Turkey and the United Kingdom. Several organizations and authorities outside Europe have made applications to FEEE requesting cooperation on spreading the Blue Flag Campaign to non-European countries. FEEE is currently exploring the possibility of extending the Campaign to Southeast Asia, the Caribbean, southern Africa, Canada and the United States.

The award is currently based on 27 criteria for beaches and 16 criteria for marinas, covering four aspects of management: water quality, environmental education and information, environmental management, and safety and services. Some criteria are imperative, whereas others are guideline criteria. Some of the criteria require compliance with health and safety legislation, others encourage proactive visitor management. The applicant will be the management unit responsible for the site; in the case of beaches it will be the municipality or council, whereas for marinas it will be their owner, either the public or private sector. Criteria are verified through site visits throughout the summer season and at times before the season, carried out by the national organization with Blue Flag coordination. The bathing water quality data are controlled by the national environmental protection agency. If some of the criteria are not fulfilled during the season or the conditions change, the Blue Flag will be withdrawn. The Flag is awarded per summer season, in practical terms this is 1 year.

Criteria are set by FEEE and regularly updated; these have been reviewed and a number of changes have been implemented from 2000: guideline criteria have been made imperative, new criteria have been set up, and there is an increased focus on waste water treatment and Agenda 21 activities. The criteria will increasingly need to take the situation in the destination into consideration. A further revision of criteria was planned for 2000, and new marina criteria will take effect from 2002. For both beaches and marinas there will, in future, be changes in the criteria, moving towards an environmental management system, where more emphasis is placed on the management of the individual beach or marina at all levels and the need for continuous improvement.

The Campaign requires a considerable amount of resources. In the European coordination office there are two full-time and three part-time staff, and there are between one and three people at national level, depending on the number of applications. The funding of the campaign is from a combination of sponsorship and fees, although this varies across countries, since fees vary according to local conditions: in Denmark, the fee per beach or marina is DKK 4000 (approx. US$/€530), in Finland: FIM 700 (approx. US$/€115), and in Greece Drs 22,000 (approx. US$/€60); in some countries applicants do not pay fees.

Since the Blue Flag Campaign was established internationally in 1987, it has gained wide recognition within the tourism sector as well as with tourists, and it has become one of the elements of promotion of tourist destinations and choice for tour operators and tourists alike. The European Commission has also acknowledged the invaluable role that the Blue Flag has played in the successful implementation of the European Bathing Water Directive, and the better implementation of national legislation. The Blue Flag Campaign is playing a particularly important role in the new Central and Eastern European countries joining the project. The interest and support by the national environmental authorities can be visually demonstrated through subsequent investments and improvements in environmental infrastructure such as sewage treatment plants and waste management. The Blue

Flag, furthermore, appeals to environmental organizations in the new democracies as a very tangible tool for raising environmental awareness. Thirdly, it is identified by new countries in the Campaign as a tool to integrate the developing tourism sector with the environment. Lastly, in new participant countries the Campaign results in greater collection and dissemination of environmental information. The Foundation for Environmental Education in Europe will be looking to consolidate the position of the Blue Flag scheme in Europe and to disseminate good practice beyond.

Blue Swallow (Blaue Schwalbe) Europe

http://www.eco-tip.org/Ecolabels/ecolabels.htm and http://www.eco-tour.org/info/w_10057_en.html

Blue Swallow was established in Europe in 1990. It is a private initiative in collaboration with experts and representatives of associations. The main cost is for advertising in the magazine *Verträglich Reisen*. The initiative targets the following groups: spa hotels, hotels, holiday departments and seminar centres in Germany, Austria, Switzerland, Italy, Sweden and Finland. The criterion involves assessing if the food and drink, transport/traffic, energy, water, waste, cleaning products and gardens are sustainable. It also involves analysing whether trains or buses can reach the establishment from Germany, Austria or Switzerland.

In order to apply for the 'Blue Swallow' ecolabel, applicants have to comply with a checklist regarding the criteria mentioned. If successful, the award period is 1 year. Control of the ecolabel is attained in writing and partly through visits. The awarded establishments must sign a contract with a minimum of criteria. Between 1990 and 1998 approximately 120 enterprises (including many which have won several times) won the award. In 1998, 78 enterprises were awarded it and in 1999, this number increased to 107. The grantee receives support services such as publicity, as the award is publicized through the publication *Verträglich Reisen* which has approximately 120,000 copies in circulation. In addition to this, there is an active benefit to grantees as they are involved in a presentation of enterprises at 12 fairs in Germany, Austria and Switzerland on a joint stand or press service. Since 1994 the environmental seal has received less attention. The magazine *Verträglich Reisen* as a main product serves as a forum for enterprises, operators and initiatives. *Verträglich Reisen* offer joint stands for tour operators and tourism regions as well as medium services.

British Airways Tourism for Tomorrow Awards, Worldwide

Maxine Kibble, Environment branch, British Airways

British Airways is an industry organization which operates the 'Tourism for Tomorrow' Awards. The label was launched in 1992 and targets the following sectors of the tourism industry; accommodation, tour operators, leisure facilities, environmental experience, national parks and protected areas, mass tourism and the built environment. There is just one full-time member of staff and one student working on the scheme, which is funded through industry sponsorship. The geographical scope of the labelling scheme is international. In 1999 114 applications were received for the labelling scheme and of these there were seven winners and 15 highly commended. Since the labelling scheme was introduced in 1992, the numbers of applicants have doubled, although the number of applicants being awarded the label has remained the same.

In order to meet the criteria for the ecolabel, the applicant must complete an application form, include a brief description of the project with a 1500-word maximum document describing how the project will meet one or more of a number of objectives established by British Airways, supply six 35 mm colour slides or photographs and ensure that the entry form is signed by an appropriate officer of the organization. British Airways and judges establish the criteria. The label is awarded for 1 year; the labelling criteria have evolved since the inception of the scheme because they are now judged by categories, not regions. The criteria are reviewed and updated each year. The ecolabels specify priority action areas as being national parks and protected areas.

As the winners of the ecolabels are flown to London for the awards night, they could gain a lot of publicity on the radio (national and regional) and in national newspapers; some are shown on the *Wish You Were Here* annual Tourism for Tomorrow TV programme. The labelling scheme will verify the information provided in the application form as at least one judge will know about the project first hand. Third-party verification is received before the ecolabel is awarded, as all entries require two independent references. The scheme recognizes and rewards grantees that have taken particularly noteworthy environmental action.

The award offers promotion via the radio, television and the *Green Travel Guide* newspaper. The media responses to the labelling scheme have been very positive, providing widespread publicity. British Airways claim that last year's winner, 'Chumbe Island Coral Park' is fully booked at present, suggesting that their tourists are showing preferences for ecolabelled services. The main reasons for tourism operators to apply for the ecolabel are prestige, status and recognition. In the future, British Airways plans for its award to be of a higher standard and to also encourage applicants from lesser-known countries.

Committed to Green, Europe

http://www.committedtogreen.org/

Committed to Green is a practical environmental management and accreditation programme for golf courses, further expanded to include other sports facilities and events, in Europe. The programme has been in operation since September 1997, EC President, Jacques Santer launched Committed to Green on behalf of the European Golf Association Ecology Unit. The programme is jointly sponsored by the European Commission (DG XI). Committed to Green has been run as an independent, non-profit foundation since March 2000, as a reorganization of the former European Golf Association Ecology Unit.

The criteria for Committed to Green revolve around the development and implementation of a simplified environmental management system (EMS) as its basic structure, with threshold criteria specific to golf courses. The programme has been developed in common with the Audubon Cooperative Sanctuary Programme in the USA, although the latter does not want to be identified as a label for green tourism or recreation.

Committed to Green operates as a staged system. The entry level recognition is based on commitment to an environmental approach, the intermediate level recognition is gained on introduction of an environmental management system, and the full, international, recognition is based on a complete, integrated environmental management programme, which has been independently verified. Committed to Green Europe handles the third level only, whereas the first two are managed at the national level by sport environment bodies. Criteria for Committed to Green are based on the following 12 sections, taken from the organization's web page. The guidelines are generic, and a subsequent matrix shows the relative weighting of each one of the 12 sections for specific sports, such as golf, football and athletics grounds.

1. *Environmental management planning*: adoption of environmental policy, review of environmental situation, implementation of environmental management system, specific environmental management targets.
2. *Nature conservation*: protection of flora, fauna and habitats (biodiversity), relation to designated protected areas.
3. *Landscape and cultural heritage*: relation between green surfaces and built components, visual/aesthetic integration into rural/

urban/land planning context, protection of archaeological/historical features.

4. *Water resource management*: source of water supply and alternatives (e.g. rainwater farming), use of treated waste water, conservation measures (e.g. turfgrass type, irrigation system design and utilization).

5. *Pollution control*: cultural and biological methods of sports field management instead of chemicals, management of type, application and storage of hazardous products, protection of ground and surface water quality, limitation on air emissions, noise and light pollution.

6. *Waste management*: reduce, reuse, recycle, waste disposal methods.

7. *Energy efficiency*: heating, lighting, air-conditioning, ventilation and other systems (e.g. irrigation, use of electric or petrol/diesel vehicles), green office policies.

8. *Transport*: policies to reduce private vehicle movements to and from site, links to public transport network, options for using less polluting vehicles/forms of transport.

9. *Purchasing policies*: safe and durable materials used for construction of facilities, selection of environmentally preferred equipment and materials.

10. *Education and the working environment*: staff training, health and safety.

11. *Communications and public awareness*: internal promotion of initiative, external communications and outreach programmes, public access to site.

12. *Environmental innovation*: use of new ideas, methods and technologies.

Committed to Green is still establishing its internal structures that will allow them to define environmental performance indicators and benchmark standards for recognition criteria, the assessment of candidate verification reports and the recommendation of awards. There are no joining fee costs at present, although it is understood this may need to change in the future. At present the organization acknowledges that it would be too onerous for each and every participating club to self-finance a fully independent environmental audit from external verifiers. Instead it is suggested that Committed to Green National Ecology Officers should be trained to carry out an appropriate environmental audit of applicants within their countries, with selective random spot checks from external verifiers. Independent verification will not be possible at this stage, and the focus will be on credible internal verification with input from experts.

The programme has been successful in raising awareness of environmental management issues. The success in engaging golf courses to join the programme will be more evident in the next 5 years; out of

5500 golf courses in Europe to date around 150 clubs have joined the initiative or its national counterparts, although levels of achievement are not specified. The first group of pilot sites that have applied for full recognition were planned for verification in autumn 2000. The imperfections of a first round of verification will allow for applicants to have few quantitative measurements, although criteria will be strengthened for the renewal 3 years later. Besides the work done on golf courses, one of the main challenges for Committed to Green in the future is to position itself as a basis for a general green label for sport in Europe.

Costa Rican Sustainable Tourism Certificate, Costa Rica

http://www.turismo-sostenible.co.cr/EN/home.shtml

The Certification in Sustainable Tourism Programme (CST) is a product of the Costa Rican Tourism Institute (ICT). This ecolabel is an institutional scheme introduced within the National Strategy for the Development of Sustainable Tourism, and is a part of the government's national and regional programme which seeks to manage development of Costa Rica in a sustainable manner. The main objective of the CST is

> to turn the concept of sustainability into something real, practical and necessary in the context of the country's tourist competitiveness, with the aim of improving the way in which the natural and social resources are utilized, to motivate the active participation of the local communities, and to support the competitiveness of the business sector.

CST is regulated by the Costa Rican National Accreditation Commission and consists of a scale of five levels of sustainable tourism achievement. This programme seeks to address the problem of some companies claiming to be behaving in a sustainable manner, when in actual fact they are not. This is achieved by providing reliable information on the companies that are really making progress in producing a sustainable tourist product.

Participation in the programme is entirely voluntary and is open to all hotels, inns, bed and breakfast services, and cabins in Costa Rica, without restriction on their location (near to the beach or the mountains, etc.) or their size. Joining the CST and the initial evaluation are at no cost to the companies. The only initial requirement is completion of an application form. CST was designed to provide an advantage to tourism sector businesses based on how much they comply with a sustainable model of natural, cultural and social resource management. In order to assess this, four fundamental aspects are evaluated:

1. *Physical–biological*: interaction between the company and its surrounding natural habitat.

2.   *Infrastructure and services*: management policies and the operational systems within the company and its infrastructure.

3.   *External clients*: interaction of the company with its clients in terms of how much it allows and invites the client to be an active contributor to the company's policies of sustainability.

4.   *Socio-economic environment*: interaction of the company with the local communities and the population in general.

For each of these aspects specific questions are asked to help evaluate how much the company complies with a series of standards previously established for the social, environmental and economics fields. Each of the questions refers to a factor of sustainability with which the firm should comply in order to qualify for the different stages or levels of achievement. The final rating will be assigned to the company in question according to the lowest level achieved in any of the four fields evaluated. To measure these levels, the CST programme uses a rating system on a scale of 0–5, in which each number indicates the relative position of the firm in terms of sustainability. Level 1 shows that the company has begun acting in a sustainable manner, and each level thereafter shows that the company is using more advanced sustainable measures.

The CST system is designed to include a number of incentives for the companies, which improve as the company receives a higher rating. Such incentives may include: international and national publicity and promotion, specifically designed for the CST; training for its personnel; and priority participation in various worldtourism fairs and events, etc.

The David Bellamy Conservation Award, United Kingdom

Gill Thirlwell, Projects Executive, BH&HPA

The British Holiday and Home Parks Association (BH&HPA) is the representative trade body of the parks industry in the UK, including holiday caravans, chalets, mobile homes, touring caravans, tents and all forms of self-catering accommodation. Some 80% of all licensed pitches are owned and operated by the Association's members. In 1995, Professor David Bellamy approached the BH&HPA regarding the possibility of launching an environmental audit for the parks industry to encourage sustainable tourism and raise awareness of good environmental management. The protection of the environment is a vital part of the industry and for many parks the immediate surroundings make up a major part of a park's attraction.

The Bellamy Award Scheme was established in 1996 as an acknowledgement to the industry for the many varied endeavours by park owners to protect and preserve the environment. Professor Bellamy and The Conservation Foundation, in conjunction with the BH&HPA, administer this environmental award for the industry which, despite being called an award, has most of the characteristics of an ecolabel in its own right. The scheme is funded by participation fees paid by parks entering the scheme together with sponsorship from the BH&HPA.

The Conservation Awards are launched annually early in the spring. All member parks are eligible to enter. The park owner initially completes a form outlining the basic structure of the park, what features it contains, types of plants/trees/wildlife etc., and environmental initiatives. An assessment is then carried out by a local branch of the Wildlife Trust, arranged by the Conservation Foundation. This assessment is undertaken in the first year of joining the scheme, and subsequently every fifth year, unless the park owner wishes to upgrade his or her park. (Parks attaining a Gold Award are inspected annually to maintain both the standard and the credibility of the awards.)

The public are also asked to play a part and pre-addressed postcards are distributed by the park to its customers. The postcards invite comments and suggestions by the public regarding the environmental credentials of the park and are returned directly to Professor Bellamy. The involvement of the public, while not always easy, is a very important part of the scheme; it encourages people and their children to involve themselves in their surroundings and take real pleasure in learning more about the environment that supports every one of us. Professor Bellamy places great importance on this particular aspect of the scheme, indeed, he is very interested and supportive of any initiatives that park owners may undertake that involve the local community. Being a good neighbour and contributing to the local community actively counts towards achieving an award. Some parks form an important part of their local community by allowing their neighbours to use the pub, club or shop, providing services that remote rural communities often lack. The Conservation Award judging is carried out in late summer by Professor Bellamy and parks receiving either a Gold, Silver or Bronze Award are presented with their certificates at the next BH&HPA Convention by Professor Bellamy himself.

Many park owners are pleasantly surprised in finding that they are already well on the road to achieving an award when they carry out their own environmental audit. Good park management will quite naturally include planting of native trees, shrubs and hedges, thereby sustaining habitats for local wildlife; recycling of waste where possible; use of recycled paper both in the office and on the park etc.; the avoidance of chemical fertilizers and pesticides; and use of environmentally kind cleaning agents. All these items are noted and make up a great part of the criteria of an award park. Some parks have achieved awards without making any changes to their regular park management.

The opportunities for enhancing and encouraging the environmental aspects of a park are limited only by the geography of the area and the imagination of the owner.

Each park is as varied as the surroundings in which it is located, and this is taken into consideration when the parks are assessed by the Wildlife Trusts. No park is penalized for not planting trees or shrubs if the ground on which it is located cannot sustain them, for example if the park is adjacent to wetlands, on cliff tops or next to the sea. Every park has the opportunity to protect and enhance its habitat in its own individual way. The awards simply encourage the best possible use of and support for the local environment, sustainability and to spread the green message to a wider public. As the public become increasingly aware of the importance of protecting the environment and encouraging wildlife, the value of the awards as a marketing and public relations tool becomes even greater.

The BH&HPA promote the award winning parks in a dedicated brochure, distributed at Tourist Information Centres throughout the UK. A rolling press release campaign is undertaken by the Association's PR agent, the brochure is also promoted at major exhibitions and used as a response piece to the many telephone enquiries. Individual members with awards are sent a press pack containing valuable advice about how to put together a constructive press release and capitalize on the asset they have achieved.

The award is recognized and acknowledged in both government and tourism circles and increases in popularity year by year. In 1999, 224 holiday, caravan and camping parks received an Award (including the commendations), whereas in 1997 it was 150 establishments and in 1996, 108 establishments awarded. At present over 350 parks have entered the 2000 awards, an increase of 227% since the launch year of 1996. All the applicants are from England, Scotland and Wales, with none from Northern Ireland to date. It is proving to be a vital self-regulated environmental audit for the parks industry, one which is doing much to promote and sustain tourism destinations in the UK.

Destination 21, Denmark

Bente Mortensen, Secretariat for Destination 21,
c/o The Danish Tourism Development Centre, Copenhagen, and
http://www.eco-tip.org/Eco-labels/ecolabels.htm

Destination 21 is a recently developed ecolabel (1999) in Denmark that awards tourism destinations with evidence of sustainable development. Between 1998 and 1999, a number of Danish tourism-related organizations worked to create the basis for the present association which was founded on 31 August 1999. These partners are the Danish Outdoor Council, The Destination 21 regions, Danish Camping Board, Danish Tourist Board, HORESTA, Confederation of Employees in Trade, Transport and Services (HTS), and Cooperation between Danish Tourist Trade. The Destination 21 label is financially supported by Ministry of Trade and Industry and The Green Job Programme and by member funding. The label is operated by the Destination 21 Association.

The label focuses on three aspects: ecological, economic and socio-cultural sustainability. The criteria are the reduction of resource consumption and waste production, reduction of transport nuisances, organic food production, promotion of product development in a sustainable direction, development of tourism's economic effect and impact on employment, local organization and coordination between prime stakeholders at the destination, stimulation and preservation of local culture, and operating within residents' tolerance threshold in terms of local tourism.

There are currently 21 pilot destinations in the South Funen Archipelago, Himmerland, Læso, Møn, Odsherred, Rømø, Rønne. The first awards were given in summer 2000. Application procedures will probably be based on a qualification period leading to fulfilment of some minimum targets supplemented by goals and indicators that depict sustainable development in different areas. The marketing of the award is being prepared, with a website under construction and promotional material to be developed before the end of 2000.

Eco-dynamic Enterprise (Entreprise Éco-dynamique), Belgium

http://www.eco-tip.org/Ecolabels/ecolabels.htm

This ecolabel was launched in May 1999 by IBGE, the Brussels region Department for the Environment and Energy, 'Voluntary Companies Actions' department. Partners of this ecolabelling project are various organizations in Brussels, public and private, including the regional Department for the Economy and Employment, The Chamber of Commerce and Industry, the Union of Businesses, the regional agency responsible for waste collection, the Society for the Promotion of Economic Development, and the Organization for the Promotion of Technological Innovation. Its objectives are to continue improvement in the environmental performance of the organization and the integration of environmental management principles.

Applicants for the ecolabel can be any type of organization with an operational site in Brussels-Capital region (e.g. private companies, including hotels and conference centres, public bodies, non-commercial organizations). The year 2000 will be the first year of awards.

This progressive ecolabel exists at three levels (1, 2 or 3 star level). In the first stage, a steering committee uniting representatives of professional federations, universities and associations was created to form a consultation structure. They developed a questionnaire to send to a number of companies. The second stage is the act of applying for the label. This entails the signing of a charter by the highest level of management in the organization. The applicants then have a maximum of 3 months to submit a first report assessing, among other things, their environmental performance, and a maximum of 2 years to submit their application file. For each of these two documents, the applicants receive a specimen to guide their work and assist them with the content of the report, assessing, among other things, their environmental performance level. At the time they submit their application file, the applicants must be able to attest that they conform to environmental legislation.

To obtain the label, enterprises have to respect the 92 criteria with general wording, making them suitable for different applicant profiles. There are four groups of criteria:

- Eco-management practices by environmental field (management practices, technological choices and behaviour aimed at improving environmental performance in eight fields: energy, air, water, waste, mobility, noise, soil, green and undeveloped areas).
- General eco-management practices: human, financial, communication and organizational resources allocated to the environment.
- Quality of the environmental analysis work required for the application file.
- Quality of the environmental programme drawn up for the application file. There are no mandatory criteria.

The applicants receive the criteria together with a checklist, called 'Catalogue of practical eco-management measures', which may assist them in reviewing their environmental performance.

The last stage is the evaluation. After the receipt and analysis of the application file a verification visit will take place with a view to understanding better certain points in the application file, according to the actual site of the organization. The jury comprises different socio-economic constituents from Brussels, representatives of various interest groups: professional federations, public institutions, environmental organizations and consumers. Then, a summary report is drawn up, accompanied by a recommendation on whether or not the label should be awarded. This report is addressed to a jury, to whom the decision falls, in the end, on awarding the label.

First awards of the ecolabelling will be during 2000. In February 2000 there were 70 applicants for the label; 15% of which were hotels and a conference centre. The applicant hotels, of 3, 4 or 5 star rating, included both small (e.g. 22 rooms) and large (e.g. 280 rooms) facilities. Some of them belong to large international chains. A new application file must be submitted every 2 years. The organizations that are awarded eco-labels will be able to use the 'Eco-dynamic company' logo on certain communication media defined in consultation with the Department (IBGE). Furthermore, the IBGE and its public partners will take the necessary steps to organize an official promotion for the eco-label winners and inform the media of the results of the label awards.

Ecolabel for the Luxembourg Tourism Organizations (Ecolabel für Luxemburger Tourismusbetriebe), Luxembourg

Michael Böhm, Environmental Counsellor and Project Manager, Stiftung Oeko-Fonds

This ecolabel, aimed at the tourism enterprises in Luxembourg, is an initiative of the Ministry of Tourism. Its goal is to promote and valorize hotels, rented holiday accommodations and campsites that pay particular attention to the environment. The Öko-Fonds Foundation was put in charge of the application of the project as well as the implementation of a consulting and counselling programme. The project receives subsidies from three ministries and covers the whole country of the Grand-Duchy of Luxembourg (approx. 700 accommodation providers). The project began at the end of 1996, after having seen that there was a strong need within the national tourism industry, as well as tourists. There are four main phases:

- In the first stage, a steering committee uniting important representatives of the Luxembourg tourism branch was created. An inventory allowed the analysis of results obtained from a questionnaire sent to a representative number of accommodations and campsites.
- Phase 2 was the organization of an Environment and Tourism competition: determination of the criteria to meet (from the results of the analysis) to be nominated, first selection of the candidates and verification of the criteria on-site. Thirty-one enterprises were awarded a prize in 1997.
- Phase 3 (1998–1999) led to the ecolabel concept, by the establishment of a complete set of criteria, determined in collaboration with the partners of the steering committee. This concept was inspired

by existing ecolabels in other countries. Parallel to this, training for hotel and campsite managers, ecological management consulting and energy audits were conducted. The label was attributed for the first time in May and October 1999 to 16 enterprises. In May 2000, five new enterprises followed and the next inspections took place in May 2001.

- The fourth phase, starting from summer 2000, is consolidation and marketing. It includes the search for new candidates as well as the organization of specific workshops, excursions, daily seminars and pilot-projects. For the marketing of the newly awarded companies, a marketing brochure was published in January 2000 by the 16 enterprises in collaboration with the National Tourist Office (ONT). Nature protection on campsites is the priority action area in 2000. Other specific actions will follow.

To obtain the label, enterprises have to respect the 100 criteria catalogue, which includes compulsory criteria and optional criteria. The accommodations receive help *in situ* from counsellors of the Öko-Fonds Foundation and an energy consultancy firm. The candidates receive an 'EcoLabel-Info-Tipp' every month, with practical tips on ecological products. This counselling programme is financially covered by subsidies from the Ministry of Environment. The Ministry of Energy gives subsidies to accommodation providers willing to undertake an energy check.

These criteria are reviewed every 2 years, following evolution in the environmental sector (further information and details about the criteria in German and French language: http://www.emweltzenter.lu/emweltzenter/oekofonds/ecolabel/virstellung.htm). The update of the criteria is made by the Öko-Fonds Foundation in collaboration with the steering committee. The label is valid for 2 years; after this period of time, the enterprises have to apply for a new evaluation. The inspection of the accommodations is assured by an independent auditing commission. This third-party verification is executed by two environmental auditors who verify, by a site visit, the information provided by the enterprise. Until now, there have been no registration fees. The labelled accommodation provider must engage to give access to the criteria catalogue on request of the guests.

A future challenge is to adapt the ecolabel criteria to the existing quality criteria in Luxembourg's natural parks. The idea is to enlarge the existing set of environmental criteria to other economic branches related directly or indirectly to tourism (craft, agriculture, etc.).

Eco-Snail of the North Sea Island of Borkum (Umweltschnecke Nordseeinsel Borkum), Germany

http://www.eco-tour.org/info/w_10073_en.html and http://www.eco-tip.org/Ecolabels/ecolabels.htm

Eco-Snail of the North Sea Island of Borkum is an action and environmental label that was established in 1990. It works in cooperation with resort administration, authorities, Borkumriff Feuerschiff (fireship), Borkumer Zeitung (local newspaper), Vereinigte Lichtspiele (cinemas), and Borkum retail and wholesale trade. Between 1990 and 1993, DM 500,000 (approx. US$/€250,000) were spent on a waste avoidance pilot project phase, of which three-fifths of the costs were covered by the Ministry for the Environment and one-fifth each by town of Borkum and 'Landkreis' Leer. The costs for follow-up from 1994 onwards are to be covered by the budget of the town of Borkum.

Applicants for the label include enterprises, administration and private households. Eco-snail of the North Sea Island of Borkum produce a 'Catalogue of Criteria' with 47 points for waste avoidance and a 'Catalogue of Recommendations' for purchasing supplies and for hotels. Applications involve a PR-campaign on 'waste-avoidance' in newspapers, on the radio and television, in cinemas, on publicity posters, through special events, exhibitions and brochures. In order to keep the ecolabel, grantees must recognize and abide to the 'Catalogue of Criteria' and the implementation of the 'Catalogue of Recommendations'.

There have been a number of effects from the application of the label. In 1999, 111 accommodation enterprises were allowed to use the Action and Environment ecolabel to advertise the environmental and social commitment of their enterprises. The label was also used in the Accommodation Guide, the result of which was a clear improvement in the image of the accommodations listed. Through implementing the label there has also been a significant reduction in the quantities of waste produced. The ecolabel has led to the development of the '10 Theories to Optimize Pollutant Reduction, Waste Management and Protection of Resources'.

Since the introduction of this ecolabel the main development has been with 'Dosenschwur' (Pledge of Tin Cans) which involves voluntary abandonment by the industry of selling drinks in cans. In addition, there has been a gradual reduction in the use of products that cannot be recycled and an increase in the use of regional, ecological products. The difficulty of running a scheme of this type is the manpower requirements to ensure continuity.

Ecotel Certification, Worldwide

http://www.hvsecoservices.com/ecotelcollection.htm

In 1994, HVS Eco Services established the ECOTEL® Certification, with the cooperation of hospitality and environmental experts, including hospitality consultants and the Rocky Mountain Institute. Since then over 1000 hotels, resorts, and inns have applied for the certification, yet only 39 hotels and accommodation facilities worldwide have been awarded the ECOTEL® certification, as it requires such high levels of environmental accomplishment. HVS Eco Services is a consulting group that helps hotel companies design and implement environmental programmes that enhance value. The company was started by Steve Rushmore, founder and president of parent company HVS International, to help hotel companies turn environmental liabilities into opportunities. The first certified hotel was the New York Vista, which re-opened in 1994 after having been closed since the 1991 terrorist bombing attack at the World Trade Center in Manhattan's financial district. Since then, Eco Services has received numerous awards and accolades and has been covered in the media hundreds of times. Many hoteliers consider the ECOTEL® Certification to be the industry's most stringent and most credible.

All members of the ECOTEL collection are included in HVS's global marketing programme and assisted in marketing efforts by Leora Lanz, direct of the HVS's Marketing and Communications department. Marketing programmes are custom designed for each member hotel to help announce the hotel's certification in a manner which will affect occupancy and rate (the two main components of the hotel value equation). Memberscan expand their marketing effort through the ECOTEL website and the special eco-awards application programme administered by HVS Eco Services.

The ECOTEL® inspection is based on five separate inspections each with a three-tiered numerical scoring system. The five inspections correspond with the five globe awards: Environmental Commitment; Solid waste management; Energy efficiency; Water conservation; and Employee environmental education and community involvement. Within each globe inspection there are three levels of criteria and scoring: primary, secondary and tertiary scores. All hotels applying for certification must satisfy all of the primary criteria before an inspection will be scheduled. The hotel must submit a form of an application describing how the primary criteria are achieved, and include descriptions of other environmental efforts and programmes that are in place at the hotel.

Once it is evident that all of the primary criteria have been satisfied, inspections are scheduled to ascertain the accommodation facility's score according to the secondary criteria. Inspections – both guided by hotel staff and unannounced – are completed throughout the accommodation facility to determine whether the environmental programmes that the hotel reports to have in place are actually part of the day-to-day operations. Each department or functional area of the hotel (i.e. main restaurant kitchen, banquet kitchen, room service kitchen, front desk and office area, executive office areas, etc.) is inspected and scored individually. A percentage score is calculated for each department inspection, and each department must score above a certain level to be awarded the certification. If any department scores below that level, but above a minimum threshold, the tertiary criteria can boost that department's score in order that the hotel may achieve the award.

The tertiary criteria are most easily described as a bonus system. The hotel receives bonus points for environmental programmes discovered in operation that are not part of the primary criteria, and are considered to be above ordinary levels of environmental responsibility. An example of a programme that would earn tertiary points in the solid waste management category comes from a hotel in Latin America that collects cigarette butts and soaks them in solution to draw out chemicals before the butts are disposed of; these chemicals are then used as pest-repellent for the fruits and vegetables grown on-site.

Based on the hotel's NRS score in each category, the accommodation facility will receive from zero to five ECOTEL® Globes, corresponding to each of the five cornerstones. Hotels that achieve the globes qualify as ECOTEL®-certified hotels for a period of 2 years, but must agree to re-inspections (announced or unannounced) at any time during that period. If the hotel falls short of achieving certified status, the HVS International inspection team will prepare an action plan to help management make the changes necessary and prepare for re-inspection. There are only three hotels in the world which currently hold all five Globes: The Benjamin in New York City, and the Arco Iris and Lapa Rios in Costa Rica.

Ecotourism Symbol Alcudia (Distintivo Ecoturístico Alcudia), Spain

Magdalena Truyols, Tourism Officer, Alcudia Council

The municipality of Alcudia, in Mallorca (Spain) has developed a programme to improve the environmental performance of local tourism-related services. The Council decided to adopt a non-interventionist approach to promoting environmental values among tourism companies, and therefore considered the development of an ecolabel as the most appropriate tool. The objectives of this ecolabel are:

- to achieve the active participation and engagement of tourism entrepreneurs in the project of environmental awareness 'Alcudia: ecotourism municipality';
- to achieve a multiplier effect across the totality of hotels and tourism establishments in the municipality;
- to stimulate participation from tourism companies which act only with financial purposes to also participate, through the promotional benefits and profile raising from the ecolabel;
- to negotiate the inclusion of the ecolabel in tour operator's catalogues.

The programme has been in operation since 1994, run by the local government with six part-time members of staff employed by the municipality with responsibilities for tourism, biology and engineering. There is a locally based committee that manages the ecolabel, which has published a set of criteria. The applicants will:

- have undertaken a course in tourism and the environment;
- reduce waste and introduce selective waste disposal;
- use recycled materials and ecological products;
- save on electrical consumption;
- save on water consumption;
- improve sewage disposal;
- reduce noise pollution;
- garden areas surrounding the site (40% of the land area);
- act with environmental consideration;
- promote customer education;
- protect local culture and language;
- design and decorate buildings in keeping with local styles;
- promote regional menus.

Based on these criteria, an environmental audit has been developed, which will be carried out at least once a year, covering: use of water and energy; noise; transport; and waste; with 164 separate topics. Applicants will pay 15,000 pesetas (approx. US$/€90). Verification will take place through a site visit and the inspection of documented evidence (a list of documents that may be required is provided beforehand). Establishments obtain the certificate for 1 year, after which they have to reapply. Criteria are set to a higher standard on a yearly basis, but for repeat applications it will only be necessary to present additional information.

After 5 years in operation, only 16 establishments are certified (there are 74 tourism accommodation providers). The first 4 years saw a very low ratio of certifications to applications, which illustrates the strictness of the label, but at the same time limits the potential growth of the label. With a critical mass of the local hotels accredited, the

Ecotourism Symbol has successfully engaged tour operators in giving preferential consideration to those local hotels that are certified.

The Emblem of Guarantee of Environmental Quality (El distintiu de qualitat ambiental), Spain

Francesc Abad Nadales, Environmental Officer, Catalan Agency of Environmental Quality

The Emblem of guarantee of environmental quality is a generic environmental label for manufactured products as well as services for companies in Catalonia (north-east Spain). This label is run by the Catalan government, and the environmental criteria for each specific product category are published as legislation by the regional government in their official journal. The product categories and the criteria are evaluated by the Environmental Quality Council formed by a variety of government agencies, NGOs, trade union and industry representatives.

The application procedure and the generic criteria are to date mostly geared towards the certification of products (for example, the application needs to be accompanied by samples of the product and laboratory tests of the product). The Emblem requires independent verification of environmental claims, and the submission of documentation for a desk review. The verification process will be a combination of site visit and desk research, based on documented evidence provided by the organization. Fees depend on the company's turnover. A company with a turnover under €300,000 will pay €240, if the turnover is over €3 million, the fees are €1800, plus a baseline cost for the administration of €375. The Environmental Authority has granted a subvention to help motivate small and medium-sized enterprises in tourism to apply for the Emblem or ISO by subsidizing the verification (over €2000). The award will be for a maximum period of 3 years.

The criteria for campsites were published in December 1998, and for youth hostels and hotels, in June 2000. To date 25 companies have been awarded, yet only one of them, a campsite, relates to the tourism industry. Between 15 and 20 campsites aim to achieve the emblem by the end of 2000, and five of them had begun the certification procedure in June 2000. The applicant must comply with the current environmental legislation, as well as all compulsory criteria outlined and a proportion of optional criteria (at least 60 optional criteria points). These criteria are set in eight categories, scored from 1 to 9. In the case of criteria for hotels, those establishments that do not have indoor swimming pools or air conditioning will need only 52 optional criteria points, and when they have neither, they need only 44 points. Newly built establishments will need 70 points. Criteria for hotels are as follows:

1. *Waste management.* Basic criteria are selective waste collection of main products, identification of selective waste containers and customer information. Optional criteria include selective waste on a broader range of products and composting.

2. *Water saving.* Basic criteria include monthly maintenance of facilities, customer information, and appropriate signage on water-saving tips. Optional criteria include quantitative control of water, regulation of water consumption of showers, taps and toilets. Hotels will be encouraged to identify and implement other systems to save water, although these are not specified.

3. *Swimming pool.* Open air swimming pools will not be heated, and indoor pools will be kept within thresholds for water and air temperature and humidity. Signage regarding reasons for these measures will be placed in changing areas. Optional criteria relate to the use of chemical products, and the use of a thermal blanket to cover the water when the pool is not in use. Pools will be heated with renewable energy sources when possible. The heating system will meet a variety of standards in relation to energy consumption.

4. *Energy saving and efficiency.* Lighting saving measures should be implemented, especially in those areas with continuous lighting requirements. Hot water pipes need to have lagging, heating devices need to meet minimum energy efficiency thresholds. Air conditioning facilities require thermostats in all rooms, with measures to avoid direct sun in the rooms. Customer information should be provided on check in, including practical tips. Signage required. Optional criteria include quantitative control of efficiency, increased insulation, higher measures of saving on lighting, saving on hot water, and higher efficiency on air conditioning than the standard threshold. Extra points are available for the introduction of other measures not listed here.

5. *Purchasing.* Environmental criteria should be set for providers, such as for refrigerators and freezers. Optional criteria include minimization of packaging, use of recyclable bottles and cups when alternatives are available, and purchasing of ecolabelled products when possible.

6. *Environmentally friendly landscape architecture.* Basic criteria are the construction of the building in materials, colours and style in keeping with the area and which do not cause an adverse visual impact.

7. *Noise.* Basic criteria are meeting the local legislation on noise pollution.

8. *Environmental education.* Basic criteria include: customer entertainment amenities should meet environmental standards, environmental leaflets will be given on check in, public transport should be made available and information provided, staff will receive environmental training, local environmental information will be provided for customers. Optional criteria include: the establishment will run yearly courses on environmental savings, and customer entertainment will include environmental education.

Environment Squirrel (Umwelteichhörnchen), Germany

ADAC, Coordination Environmental Questions and
www.eco-tip.org/Eco-labels/ecolabels.htm

This ecolabel was launched in 1993 focusing on motorway service stations and later, in 1996, the scheme was extended to include holiday villages, holiday parks and centres across Germany. The scheme was initiated by the German Automobile Club (ADAC) and is operated with partners such as the Federal Ministry for the Environment, the Protestant and Catholic Association and a working Group for Family Holidays.

The criteria for the award cover the following areas: refuse, water and waste water, waste, and energy. Additional criteria of landscape and traffic apply for the holiday villages, parks and centres. Applications can be made at any time through the completion of a questionnaire and applications are then evaluated by means of a points system. Inspections can be made at irregular intervals without prior warning. Award winning businesses receive a certificate. The following list shows those applicants who have been successful since the scheme began:

- 1994: motorway service stations: Renchtal-West A5 (Pilot station), Weinstraße West, Weinstraße Ost, Wonnegau West, Remscheid Ost.
- 1995: Würzburg-Nord, Herford West, Herford Ost.
- 1997: Aachener Land-Süd.
- 1999: one motorway service station.

No holiday centres won the award in 1999. It is to be decided by 2002 whether to continue with the Environment Squirrel award scheme.

Environmental Quality Mark for Alpine Club Mountain Huts (Umweltgütesiegel auf Alpenvereinshütten), Germany

DAV, Deutscher Alpenverein e.V.,
http://www.eco-tour.org/info/w_10078_en.html and
http://www.eco-tip.org/Ecolabels/ecolabels.htm

The Environmental Quality Mark for Alpine Club Mountain Huts is awarded to establishments that meet a range of criteria. These include maintaining the beauty and natural environment of the mountain landscape and observing all the provisions of Federal and Land laws. However, most importantly, applicants must ensure that all new investments in supply and disposal systems are to be adapted to the most up-to-date technology, the mountain hut host must ensure that the hut's rules and regulations as well as a note of the Alpine Club ideology are clearly displayed and there must be an evaluation of measures with regard to criteria such as energy supply, water, waste-water, waste avoidance, air, hut management and hut environment, noise, and information for visitors concerning the previously mentioned points.

The Environmental Quality Mark is awarded to ideal mountain huts in such a way that both the owners and the hosts are responsible for its management. The owners because they are responsible for setting up an environmentally sound infrastructure with regard to supply and disposal systems, and the hosts because they are responsible for best possible use and maintenance of the environmental systems. Although the departments and hut tenants are motivated strongly by the award of the Environmental Quality Seal, the department owning the hut applies for the award of the Environmental Quality Mark. An independent jury decides if the establishment has met all of the criteria and therefore if it should be awarded the label, once the label has been given to an establishment the jury may withdraw the Quality Mark if these criteria are no longer met. The jury is obliged to check the huts every year.

The first Quality Mark was awarded in 1997, when six enterprises were awarded, in 1998 seven mountain huts were awarded and in 1999 four mountain huts were awarded with the prize. Establishments can apply for the award every year. Mountain huts may apply on a permanent basis, although prizes are always awarded within the framework of the General Meeting.

Environmental Seal of Quality Tyrol and South-Tyrol (Umweltsiegel Tirol & Süd-Tirol), Austria and Italy

http://www.dilly.at/1Root/Marketingverbund/104748/ Homepage/f_homepage...2.html

The Environmental Seal of Quality was established in Tyrol in 1994 and South Tyrol in 1995. The label was the decision of the Landes-regierung Tyrol (Government of State/Land of Tyrol) and was developed by a specially formed working group from different disciplines. The concept was adopted by the Südtirol Tourismus Werbung (South Tyrolean Tourism Public Relations Agency) in 1994. In Tyrol, the ecolabel works in cooperation with Wirtschaftskammer and

Landwirschaftskammer (Tyrol Chambers of Commerce and Agriculture), and Privatzimmerverband (association of private commercial accommodation providers). In South Tyrol it works in cooperation with the Südtirol Tourismus Werbung (South Tyrolean Public Relations Agency for Tourism) and Südtiroler Hotelier- und Gaststättenverband (South Tyrolean Hotel and Restaurant Association).

The ecolabel has been awarded to a number of companies, such as hotels, inns, holiday apartments, farms and campsites, throughout Tyrol and South Tyrol. In Tyrol 143 establishments and in South Tyrol 86 have been awarded the ecolabel. Such establishments try to give visitors an unforgettable holiday and allow them to spend time with nature. By awarding these establishments with the Environmental Seal of Quality they are considered to be responsible and eco-friendly operators. Only those accommodation providers who follow strict implementation guidelines are given this award.

In order to receive the award, the establishments must fulfil a catalogue of around 100 criteria. There is an independent body of experts who examine every single one of the applicants, making sure they meet the criteria and stick to an ecological way of running their establishment. The label is awarded for a 1-year period. The Environmental Seal of Quality is awarded to establishments in North Tyrol that take their responsibility for Tyrol's nature seriously. For some time the Tyrolean Environmental Seal of Quality of the Tirolwerbung and Südtirol Tourismus Werbung have been cooperating with a number of establishments in South Tyrol to be able to offer a healthy environment as well as traditional Tyrolean hospitality. To be awarded with the ecolabel certain criteria must be met, the most important of which are:

- cooperation with a local farmer who provides produce from animal-friendly and environmentally friendly farming;
- reducing waste by strict waste separation and recycling, starting in the guests' rooms and involving the guests;
- using biodegradable detergents;
- using water and energy-saving facilities;
- no single-portion-packs, whether in catering or in the sanitary area;
- establishing no-smoking areas.

Other criteria involve issues concerning use of local products, cooperation with the 'Twin'-farmer, managing waste, water and sewage, energy, air, soil, transport, noise and information for guests and staff.

The ecolabels are awarded at an award ceremony, with the award being made by the Lands/States of Tyrol and South Tyrol. An advantage of the award to grantees is that they receive advertising through the label in different brochures, electronic information systems and the Internet.

Environmentally Conscious Hotel and Restaurant Businesses in Bavaria (Umweltbewußter Hotel- und Gaststättenbetrieb in Bayern), Germany

Bayerisches Staatsministerium für Landesentwicklung und Umweltfragen, Munich

The scheme was developed in Bavaria in 1991 by the Bavarian State Government under the leadership of the Environment Ministry together with three partners: the Bavarian Hotel and Restaurant Association, the Bavarian Tourist Association (BTV), and a working group of the Bavarian Trade and Industry Chamber. The scheme went through some changes in 1997. The costs to develop the scheme were funded by the Environment Minister, and since 1993 the costs of operating the competition have been met by all partners.

The criteria for application are detailed and comprehensive, covering the following areas: avoidance, use and disposal of waste; energy and water saving; procurement; building; interior facilities; exterior facilities; transport/traffic; and information for employees and guests. The award is given for a period of 3 years and operates on a points system. Establishments undergo continuous evaluation and inspection. The awarding body verifies the quality of all applications through certified environmental inspections, before awarding the prize and with each renewal extension.

Approximately 1000 competitors took part in the competition between 1993 and 1994. Around 100 gold and silver awards were presented in the 1993/1994 competition, with around 500 acknowledgements. In 1997 104 gold and silver awards were presented, but the number fell to approximately 50 hotels and restaurants in 1999.

Environmentally Friendly Campsites – Lever (Umweltfreundliche Campingplätze – Lever), Germany

Peter Hambrinker, Gerhard Jakubowski, Kommunikations- und Konfliktberatung, Arendsburg

The Lever camping competition is operated by the washing powder and detergent manufacturers, Lever and takes place once a year. The competition was introduced in 1996 and between 1996 and 1998, 87 campsites from Germany took part in the competition.

The main focus of the scheme lies with the sparing and protection of water. Applicants are tested on the environmental standards of the following areas: traffic; water and waste water; energy; waste and materials; the care of green spaces; environmental education; and others. In order to enter, applicants must answer a set of questions covering the areas above. Applicants must answer questions, for example, regarding whether their campsites are completely or partially car-free zones and whether they provide car parks and whether a cycle path is provided. The competition also investigates how sanitized the water is on site, whether they re-use rain water and whether they keep control of the amount of water that is used. In terms of energy, the sites are tested on whether they use solar energy, and how much energy is used to heat the water and communal facilities and what equipment is used to heat these facilities. The application questionnaire also focuses on the provisions made for the collection of waste materials, and how much plant life there is around the campsite.

Lever produces three environment maps for the areas of Brandenburg (Berlin), Schleswig-Holstein and Mecklenburg-Vorpommern. Winners of the Lever Camping Competition not only receive prize money but have their names published in the media. Prize money ranges from DM 4000 (approx. US$/€2000) for first place to DM 500 (approx. US$/€500) for third place with additional prizes of 50 washing machines and Lever leisure time environment maps to the sum of DM 5000 (approx. US$/€2500).

The European Charter for Sustainable Tourism in Protected Areas, Europe

Laure Sagaert, Tourism Officer, Parcs Naturels Régionaux de France

The European Charter for Sustainable Tourism in Protected Areas is a charter that involves the commitment of Parks' authorities, local tourist providers and tour operators. The Charter is a response to the global priorities expressed in the recommendations of Agenda 21, adapted at the Earth Summit in Rio in 1992. It is also a contribution to the 5th community action plan for sustainable development, a priority action under the World Conservation Union (IUCN) Parks for Life programme. The charter follows the principles stated by the World Charter for Sustainable Development in Lanzarote in 1995.

The Charter gives assertion to the willingness of Parks' authorities and representatives of the tourism sector to promote tourism that is in keeping with the principles of sustainable development. It can be used to develop quality tourism in response to the environmental, economic, social and ethical aspects of the areas concerned, and of their inhabitants. The Charter's objective is to implement concrete action plans based on a close relationship between the local people and tourism professionals. Its ambition is also for the areas and enterprises

to be distinguished at European level, so that visitors to protected areas
are guaranteed a level of service which is in keeping with the wealth
and special features of these areas in the long term.

In order to subscribe to the Charter, applicants must produce a
sustainable tourism development strategy and commit themselves to
an agreed action plan for the area and the tourism business. Signing
the Charter means taking a strategic approach to sustainable tourism
development. Signatories must abide by the principles of sustainable
tourism. These include working for a better contribution from tourism
to the conservation and enhancement of their heritage, as well as
adopting principles of customer care and fair pricing.

The Charter pays particular attention to protected areas and enterprises that voluntarily adhere to the principles of sustainable tourism.
The delegated protected areas need to adapt a long-term strategy and
action plan produced in partnership with tourism professionals and
local residents. The providers of tourist services produce a plan that
will help in meeting local objectives. In particular, they must manage
the environment with respect, enhance the value of its natural and
cultural heritage, and make their customers sensitive to environmental
protection. Tour operators are responsible for providing information to
visitors and making them environmentally aware, selecting suppliers
who are environmentally aware and respecting local communities
when marketing tourism products.

Positive assessment and regular review of the strategies pursued
by its applicants shape the Charter. These must be able to measure
the progress of the enterprises towards sustainable development and
to review the relevance and effectiveness of actions taken. Applicants'
commitment to the areas and their progress towards sustainable
tourism development will distinguish them from other applicants.

The Environmentally Oriented Hotel and Guest House (Der umweltorientierte Hotel- und Gaststättenbetrieb), Germany

DEHOGA (German Hotel and Restaurants Association) Germany and http://www.eco-tip.org/Eco-labels/ecolabels.htm

This ecolabel was developed in 1993 by the German Hotel & Restaurants Association (DEHOGA). The competition is held by the regional
member associations (Hessen, Baden-Württemberg, Schleswig-Holstein,
North-Rhine-Westphalia, Mecklenburg-Vorpommern). Partners are the
Chambers of Trade and industry, regional Tourists' Associations,
Gewerbeamt, and Landesministerien, although this differs from region
to region.

The DEHOGA developed a 40-Point-Catalogue in their Manual: *How to Run an Environmentally-oriented Enterprise* which is very helpful for preparation for the competition. Some regional associations offer advisory services, seminars and additional information on environmental protection in the hotels and restaurants sector. In the Manual all criteria (e.g. water, waste, avoidance and separation of waste, energy, air, climate, local environment, regional products) are listed with general explanations and case studies. A partial expansion of the Basic Criteria depends on the individual Federal states.

The competition is open to any licensed food retailer and accommodation business in Germany (e.g. hotels, guest houses, restaurants and camp sites). The evaluation of the application form is according to a points system. The businesses are visited before the label is awarded. The inspection is made by an Examining Committee (representatives of the member associations in cooperation with other organizations); this is followed by a self-evaluation by guests and staff. The award-winning businesses are obliged to exhibit the 40 criteria and the award plaque (credibility and transparency). After a period of 3 years the award documents are no longer publicly exhibited and a new application must be made. Until the end of 1997, via the regional associations, a total of approximately 900 businesses had received the award nationally; for example in 1999, 97 businesses were awarded in Baden-Württemberg, 10 in North-Rhine-Westfalia and 70 in Schleswig-Holstein, although the future of the competition beyond 2000 is uncertain in the last region.

Marketing measures carried out by DEHOGA are: publicity via printed media (press), and an indication in the relevant accommodation guides. A future challenge is that analogous to the hotel classification, any interested entrepreneurs may also compete in the environmental competition at any time.

European Prize for Tourism and the Environment, Europe

http://www.eco-tour.org/info/w_10082_de.html

The European Prize for Tourism and the Environment has been in existence since 1995; the last prize was awarded in January 1996. The Prize was developed by a Committee of the European Commission and is implemented in 17 European countries. It works in cooperation with the National Ministries of Tourism and Environment.

The prize targets tourism areas, regions and destinations with at least 500 beds and at least 2500 inhabitants. Prizes are awarded to those applicants who have elaborated and successfully implemented environmentally friendly programmes to promote tourism. Cultural and social aspects are also considered. Applicants should provide proof of particular commitment to:

- economic and imaginative uses of natural resources;
- innovative measures to preserve natural areas and nature conservation;
- initiatives to reduce/minimize environmental damage (noise, pollution, waste);
- restoration of old buildings and damaged environments;
- new building measures: ecological building design and integration into the landscape;
- information and education programmes for experts working in the tourism and environmental fields;
- effective cooperation at all levels (national, regional, local);
- visitor management; and
- environmental education campaigns to include the local communities and visitors in both global and in-detailed planning.

Modification of criteria and selection procedure is only possible after the first award has been evaluated. The ecolabels are awarded for a period of 2 years. The relevant national tourism authority coordinates and implements the award. There is no standardized publicity procedure as each award is publicized differently, these are partly decided through PR-agencies commissioned by national Steering Committees supervised by the relevant ministries. The successful applicants are selected at national (member state) level by Steering Committees. Currently, up to five candidates per country comply with the criteria in the European Commission (national quotas), which is approximately 60 candidates. The final selection is made by the committee of the European Commission Directorate General in collaboration with DG XI (Environment) and advisers. At this stage the number of candidates is reduced to approximately 25, after which a jury procedure is set in motion, this involves one main prize and several special prizes. Prizes should be prestigious such as a trophy, or have considerable media presence, and the possibility of future sponsoring for integrated measures for the award-winning destinations or regions.

In 1995, the 1st Prize was awarded to the Town of Kinsale, Ireland; the finalists were Cévennes National Park (France), the Weissensee Region (Austria) and Peak District National Park (UK). Special Prizes were awarded to Colbitz Letzlinger Heide (Germany), Oscos Eo (Spain), Pöijönne Lake District (Finland), British Waterways (UK), Historic Centre of Corfu and Vido Island (Greece), Veluwe Mobility Plan (The Netherlands), Açores (Portugal) and Ponte de Lima (Portugal).

Gîtes Panda, France

http://members.tripod.co.uk/catalyst_maps/fivedit_panda.html and http://www.eco-tip.org/Eco-labels/ecolabels.htm

A Gîte Panda is an accommodation classified by Gîtes de France (quality B&B accommodation), set in a Regional or National Nature Park, which has been granted the World Wide Fund for Nature (WWF) France label. Gîtes Panda was developed by Gîtes de France, WWF and the Federation of the Regional Nature Parks of France (PNRF). The costs are carried by all partners according to the organization generating the expenditure.

Objectives of this ecolabel are to favour good-quality, environmentally friendly tourism, to maintain and diversify rural and agricultural activities, to help visitors to discover and appreciate nature through guidance and conditions favourable to nature observation. The criteria are:

- they must offer the possibility of spending a stay in a high-quality nature area;
- they must have specific observation and information equipment, which enable the observation of nature;
- they must be administered by owners (or responsible persons) who strive for environmental protection.

They must also comply with one of the two following statements: (i) be located on a property of interest for discovering nature, on which a walking and watching circuit (nature trail) is reserved for gîte guests' use; the circuit may contain small watching posts; and (ii) be located in direct proximity to a footpath or area open to the public in a quality nature environment of interest for discovering nature.

The applicant should have a moral commitment that its general behaviour conforms to environmental requirements. The owners (or responsible person) should commit themselves to respect the recommendations, in order to assess the natural wealth of the protected area. Behaviour such as complaints of the owner with regards to the presence of animals (e.g. beavers) on his or her area, are not compatible with the concept. The owner must also provide a minimum amount of information about the most important discoveries to be made in the area. The customers receive a 'discovery suitcase', which contains general information about the park, books on flora and fauna and observation material made available to them.

National and Natural parks pre-select accommodation providers that are likely to meet the requirements. Assessors from WWF and PNRF carry out inspection visits to the applicants as part of the verification process. Costs of the assessors reach approximately

FF 150,000 (approx. US$/€22,000) and travel expenses for the assessors reach approximately FF 50.000 (approx. US$/€7600). The costs to the parks and of the Gîtes have not yet been estimated. These costs fall particularly on the advisory personnel, brochures and advertising.

The Gîtes Panda is an example of a well-established programme within France, which shows the revaluation of tourism service organizations. It deals with the genuine assessment of action programmes in order to develop sustainable tourism. The first Gîtes Panda were accredited in 1989 in the Brenne Regional Nature Park. By 1997 there were 224 Gîtes Panda in 25 Regional Nature Parks and two National Parks. The sixth edition of the guide for 2000 is 240 pages long, and includes 250 rural accommodation sites, including small hotels, in 31 natural parks and three national parks.

Green Globe 21 Standard For Travel and Tourism, Worldwide

Margot Sallows, Manager, Environmental Services, Green Globe

Green Globe is a global environment and certification programme for the travel and tourism industry. It works with consumers, companies and communities to create a sustainable industry through the implementation of Agenda 21. Green Globe was established in 1994 by the World Travel and Tourism Council with the aim of turning the principles of Agenda 21 into practical, low-cost action for the travel and tourism industry. In 1999 Green Globe became an independent company with a board of directors drawn from key travel and tourism companies and establishments.

Green Globe is a truly global company with representation worldwide. It has formal relationships with over 30 international industry associations, and in 2000 created partnerships in the Asia/Pacific region and the Caribbean with the Co-Operative Research Center for Sustainable Tourism in Australia, as well as the Caribbean Alliance for Sustainable Tourism (CAST). In addition it has joined forces with several national ecolabelling programmes such as the Danish Green Key, and the Pacific Asia Travel Association's Green Leaf.

The principle objective of the Green Globe Standard is to promote environmentally sustainable development in the travel and tourism industry. It provides travel and tourism companies or organizations of any sector, size or location with a framework for achieving year-on-year improvement in relevant key performance areas, resulting in overall improvement in environmental performance. Achieving Green Globe Certification involves the development and implementation of an environmental management system. The Green Globe Standard, which was initially launched in 1998, provides a generic set of requirements supported by guidance material on how to apply the issues to specific sectors of the travel and tourism industry. The Standard has been developed as a practical tool that is applicable and relevant to the needs of a service industry such as tourism.

Green Globe's vision is to become the Travel and Tourism industry's premier global ecolabel, and the brand that represents the established hallmark of environmental best practice. In June 2000 over 100 businesses were registered as working towards Green Globe certification globally, with 135 businesses having already achieved it.

The criteria outlined in the Green Globe Standard are based on Agenda 21 principles and include:

1. Energy efficiency, conservation and management;
2. Management of fresh water resources;
3. Ecosystem conservation and management;
4. Management of social and cultural issues;
5. Land-use planning and management;
6. Air quality protection and noise control;
7. Waste water management;
8. Waste minimization, reuse and recycling; and
9. Storage and use of hazardous substances.

The significance of a company's impact will depend on its sector, size and location. Companies are required to establish the significance of impacts and determine an appropriate level of action through consultation with key stakeholders including staff, customers, communities and suppliers of products and services.

Companies have a 12-month period from committing to achieve the Green Globe Standard to when they are assessed by an independent assessor, and then awarded the Green Globe Certification. After this, there is an annual surveillance visit to monitor compliance and ensure continuous improvement. Should a company not meet the requirements of the standard following a corrective action period then the Green Globe Certificate will be withdrawn. Green Globe has prepared a series of short sector guides to assist companies in achieving certification to the Green Globe Standard. The guides help companies to understand the requirements of the Standard and the local and global environmental impacts of typical activities in that sector. They also provide examples of measures taken by companies to satisfy the requirements.

Green Globe can provide consultancy services to businesses to develop the environmental management system, however an independent third party undertakes the final assessment against the standard. In addition, Green Globe has an established website, which links businesses to relevant best practice information. There is a bi-monthly newsletter that is circulated to all those businesses with the Green Globe Certificate, as well as those working towards it and other interested parties. This newsletter (available electronically and hard copy) provides case study material and highlights what businesses are achieving around the world as part of the certification programme.

The fee payable to register into the Green Globe programme is variable, depending on the size and location of a company. Green Globe uses the World Bank classification of developed, less developed and developing countries to set its fees at 100%, 75% and 60% of the full fee, respectively. In addition to this registration fee, there is an assessment fee charged for the final assessment and issue of the certificate. Any consultancy work undertaken by Green Globe carries an additional cost, which is dependent on the size and complexity of the work involved. Certification to the Green Globe Standard helps companies to protect local and global environmental quality, conserve local heritage, improve local living conditions and contribute to the local economy, reduce negative exposure to environmental legislation and regulations and improve relations with the regulators, attract a new breed of consumer looking for products and services with better environmental profiles, encourage existing customers to return, motivate employees and improve relations with local communities.

Companies that have been certified to the Green Globe Standard are entitled to use the special Green Globe 'tick' brand to promote their environmental achievements. Green Globe will support these companies in obtaining maximum publicity for their success and will market their products to a global audience increasingly exposed to the Green Globe brand. There has been considerable media coverage of the Green Globe brand in 2000. The certification programme was praised for its independent assessment approach in the June edition of the *Geographical Magazine*, and will be included in a forthcoming edition of *Conde Naste Traveler*. Specific industry publications such as *Travel Weekly* have also praised the programme.

Climate change has been identified as one of the main environmental problems facing our society. While it is recognized that tree planting to neutralize carbon emissions created by travel-related activity is only a very small part of the path towards sustainable development, it is symbolic, practical and relatively inexpensive. Hence, Green Globe has linked up with Future Forests for a campaign to raise awareness of the importance of sustainable development, global climate change and the role of new and old growth forests in offsetting emissions of carbon dioxide, a greenhouse gas. By calculating emissions used and the number of trees needed to be planted to offset them, companies and individuals can become carbon neutral.

Green Globe is the first globally applicable scheme that recognized environmental performance specific to the travel and tourism industry, utilizing the environmental management system and third party, independent verification approach. The take-up rate has been relatively high, especially considering that the concept of environmental certification in any industry is relatively new, and has only been operational since 1996.

The challenge for the future is to get more consumers to make a proactive choice to preferentially use travel and tourism businesses that have made a public declaration of their commitment to sustainable tourism development through implementing an environmental management system and participation in the Green Globe Certification programme. In addition, Green Globe has commenced the development of procedures on how to apply the Green Globe Standard to entire tourism destinations. This will involve developing a series of environmental indicators against which performance will also be measured. By the time this book goes to press this programme will be active.

Green Hand – We Do Something for the Environment (Grüne Hand – Wir tun etwas für die Umwelt), Austria

http://www.eco-tour.org/info/w_10084_de.html

This scheme was launched in 1991 in Saalbach-Hinterglemm (Austria) and was the initiative of an accommodation operator. The local authority finances the implementation of the scheme and advertising is financed by the Tourist Association (FVV). Criteria for the scheme cover the following areas: service, cuisine, room service, office, hospitality, personnel/staff, energy and external measures. Criteria are amended yearly. For example, new criteria were developed for 1996/1997 through the environmentally sensitive operator initiative, the state waste and environmental consultancy and the environmental committee of the local authority.

Applicants must fill out an assessment sheet and the scheme is measured on a points system. Site visits for verification are carried out yearly (unannounced) by a third party, on the advice of the local authority. The award presentations take place once a year. The label and its logo are publicized via press releases and leaflets, and prize winners' lists can be found in the tourist information centres. Over 100 applicants took part in the competition between 1991 and 1993. Around 60 organizations were awarded the Green Hand in both 1994 and 1995.

The scheme has proved to help in the reduction of waste and energy costs, promotion of sustainable farming and the expansion of the local recycling depot.

Green Hotels Association, Worldwide

http://www.greenhotels.com

The management of 'green' hotels are interested in implementing plans that save water and energy and reduce solid waste. Such hotels can be brought together through the Green Hotels Association®. The Green Hotels Association encourages, promotes and supports the 'greening' of the accommodation industry. Green Hotels is designed to devote itself to researching ways in which hotels can reduce water and energy consumption. Hotel managers, chief engineers and executive housekeepers rarely have the time to spend on such research; however, many are interested in it and therefore they can become a member of Green Hotels to implement ideas from them. On joining, members receive a comprehensive list of suggestions and ideas on how to reduce the hotel's impact on our environment.

One idea suggested by the Green Hotels Association® is to offer visitors to the hotel a 'towel rack hanger' and a 'sheet changing card', which ask guests to consider using their linens more than once. These are now found in thousands of hotel guest bathrooms, and are helping these hotels to save 5% on utilities and at least 70% of guests will probably participate.

The Green Hotels Association® produces a 'catalogue of environmental products for the accommodation industry' wherein the best choices of water and energy saving products are advertised. The catalogue includes suggestions such as a toilet-tank fill diverter to help save water consumption that can save about 3 l of water per flush. This is invisible to the guest, does not affect the flush in any way, and costs less than US$1. Another idea offered by the Green Hotels Association® is to introduce hair and skin care dispensers, which will help to save money. Hotels can also offer guests shampoo and soap at the push of a button.

There are a number of benefits to hotels from joining the Green Hotels Association®. Such benefits include the *Membership Conservation Guidelines and Ideas*; a bi-monthly newsletter packed with practical ideas; heavy media publicity; and an Internet listing and public identification as a Green Hotel via pole and front desk flags. Hotels can join for as little as US$50 and the ecolabel welcomes worldwide membership.

The Green Key (Den Groenne Noegle), Northern Europe

Torben Kaas, senior consultant, Horesta

The Green key Ecolabel was launched in 1994 and targets hotels, youth hostels, camping sites and holiday homes. In the near future it will also target restaurants, visitor attractions and conference facilities.

The operator is a partnership of the industry, the workers union, the Danish Outdoor Council (NGO), the Danish Tourism Council and the Environmental Protection Agency (EPA) and the scheme is funded through registration fees. The label operates independently and the main secretarial services are provided by HORESTA (Association of the Hotel, Restaurant and Tourism Industry in Denmark). The Green Key is also supported by The Danish Tourist Board, The Outdoor Council, Danhostel (Danish Youth Hostels), Danish Tourist Associations and Danish Tourist Offices, The Danish Union of the Catering Trade, The Danish Camping Board, The Association of Danish Summerhouse Accommodation Companies and The Ministry of Environment. There are two full-time positions, as well as many people involved on a part-time basis. No volunteers are involved.

To date The Green Key has operated in Denmark only, however, in spring 2000 the Green Key joined forces with Green Globe 21. The agreement now expands the scope of the Green Key to the five Nordic countries (Denmark, Iceland, Finland, Norway and Sweden), the Baltic countries (Estonia, Latvia and Lithuania), and Poland. The Green Key will within the next year or two be present in all of these countries and was recently made available in Greenland.

The motivation for the launch of the scheme was that the industry sensed a need for a serious label and thus formed a label on its own initiative. It was formed according to the Nordic tradition, without government interference, but with representation of all interested parties (NGOs, industry, unions, tourism council and the EPA as an observer).

Each year every establishment holding the Green Key has to reapply for the Key. The Green Key is held by around 110 establishments and this number is increasing. There is no limit to the number of applicants, or to the number of companies being certified. Due to the new agreement with Green Globe 21 and plans for expanding into eight new countries, it is expected to at least double that number by 2001.

Criteria for environmental management and specific criteria for a number of environmental impacts are put into 54 specific demands to be met. The criteria are divided into three categories: compulsory criteria, phased compulsory criteria and advanced criteria. In order for the application to be accepted, all the compulsory criteria must be fulfilled. All of the phased compulsory criteria must be fulfilled according to an agreed plan of action; the advanced criteria can be regarded as recommendations and are supposed to serve as a new inspiration for the future development of the companys' environmental concern. The criteria are established by a steering group with representation by all the organizations supporting the Green Key. The criteria cover the following areas: energy; water; waste; food management; indoor climate; belonging to parks and park areas; green activities; and administration.

When the application form has been submitted then the business will be contacted in order to arrange an inspection visit. The control visit will be carried out by The Green Key's secretariat or a person that has been appointed by the secretariat. At the inspection visit it will be observed whether all criteria have been met. If so, the application will be processed at the next executive committee meeting. If the criteria are not met then the business will be informed of the shortcomings. In this case another inspection visit is required which will be paid for by the business. If it is revealed by the ongoing verification that the business fails to fulfil some of the criteria then the business can be deprived of The Green Key.

The day-to-day work of the label is carried out by HORESTA, The Camping Council or The Holiday Homes Association depending on the type of the establishment. At present HORESTA accounts for 104 of 106 establishments holding the Green Key. Interested establishments acquire the application form and fill it in. If questions arise, they contact HORESTA to clarify them.

The criteria have been through a number of adjustments and one major revision. Environmental management principles were brought into the label at the revision and technical requirements were brought up to date. Besides this, the criteria are adjusted to new segments (i.e. restaurants, campsites, visitor attractions, etc.) as they are adopted; when the label enters new countries the criteria are adjusted to local energy supply systems and waste management systems. The label is awarded for 1 year. The criteria on environmental management ensure that the most important impacts for specific sites are dealt with.

The Green Key offers a number of services for its members, including: site visits, consultations, a telephone response service, website, various marketing materials (CD-ROM), courses on environmental work and meetings between Green Key establishments with external speakers. Some of these services are free, others have to be paid for by the businesses. Services such as site visits, consultations, telephone services and marketing material are covered by the application fee.

All establishments are visited by applying once every year. The verification is made by the relevant secretariat (HORESTA, Camping Council or Holiday Homes Association). When entering the label, the steering group will look into the application and the verification report. Otherwise, the steering group brings about a number of mystery visits to the Green Key establishments each year. The label has an element of environmental management (demands on policy, targets and action plans). The policy must contain an obligation to continuous improvement. This is mirrored in targets and action plans, which are controlled thoroughly by control visits.

A CD-ROM with promotional material and standard press releases is offered as promotional support and the label is promoted in the relevant media. The agreement with Green Globe 21 offers worldwide exposure. The Green Key is widely recognized as a serious label by the media in Denmark.

It has been proven that Green Key establishments use about 25% less energy and 30% less water than non-Green Key establishments. This is an important reason to join the Key. Secondly, a large number of hotel managers show concern for the environment and want to do their bit. Many hotels also see the Green Key as something in line with their business philosophy (ethics, good management, etc.).

From the applicants' point of view, the single most important reason for the label's success is that the criteria are formed by a steering group representing all interests and that the label is run by the same steering group as opposed to being run by the government or another uninvolved party. From the market point of view, a large number of tourists have asked for green accommodation services, particularly in the German and Nordic markets. The main challenges faced with developing and implementing the scheme have been to make balanced criteria that on the one hand mirror the seriousness of the single environmental impacts and, on the other hand, do not favour some establishments over others. The next challenge is to encourage willingness to pay extra for a 'Green Key Bednight', which at present is not great. Future plans of the scheme include bringing in restaurants, conference halls and visitor attractions and working together with Green Globe 21 to penetrate the Nordic, Baltic and Polish markets.

Green Keys (Les Clefs Vertes), France

http://www.ifrance.com/clefsvertes/

Les Clefs Vertes is a programme for environmental improvement among camping, caravanning and bungalow sites. It was first conceived in Denmark in 1996 by the Foundation for Environmental Education in Europe (FEEE), but not implemented until 1999 by the French office. It is currently run in partnership with the French Federation of Naturism (FFN).

Thirty-eight criteria, in five groups, are divided into compulsory, medium-term compulsory and ideal. The groups are: (i) environmental information; (ii) waste management; (iii) energy management; (iv) water management; (v) land use. A manual is produced to help sites in their application and general environmental management.

In order to achieve the recognition, applicants need to complete a questionnaire and return it to FEEE before the end of March, demonstrating how they meet the compulsory criteria, establishing a calendar to implement the medium-term criteria, and satisfying a minimum of half of the ideal criteria that apply to the site (there are criteria that only apply to sites with a capacity over 200 pitches). The questionnaire is then fed through a verification system, involving control procedures and a decision taken by a jury. The fee for sites for their application and verification is approximately €225, according to Ecotrans.

Out of 69 candidates, 49 campsites were awarded in 2000 (from 42 the previous year), concentrated in 35 departments and 16 regions, the majority of them in the south of France. Awardees have the right to use the Clefs Vertes logo for 1 year.

FEEE carries out a considerable amount of promotion of this scheme. The awardees are included in the guides *Susse France Camping Caravaning* and *des Vacances Ecologiques*, as well as in the Clefs Vertes Internet page, fairs, press and conferences. Les Clefs Vertes aims to broaden the base of its label by including hostels and holiday centres, and by ensuring that the campsites are promoted in camping guides outside France.

Green Tourism Business Scheme, United Kingdom

Jonathan Proctor, environmental auditor, Shetland Environmental Agency Ltd

The Green Tourism Business Scheme (GTBS) is an environmental recognition system in operation in Scotland since 1998, with an English pilot in South Hams District Council (a council known for developing the Green Audit Kit) and South West Tourism. GTBS is run by the Shetland Environmental Agency Ltd (SEA Ltd), in partnership with the Scottish Tourist Board, Highlands and Islands Enterprise and financed by the Scottish Enterprise. This label targets accommodation providers, catering facilities, leisure facilities, visitor attractions and holiday caravan parks.

The Scheme has three levels. The Bronze award is given for basic environmental good practice; the Silver award for examples of significant good practice and performance improvements; and the Gold for significant good practice, monitoring and supplier screening.

Achieving the Gold award puts the company in a good position to apply for ISO 14001. There is a considerable incremental requirement from one level to the other, the Bronze level requiring minimum commitment to environmental principles.

The Scheme is reported to be a success. In 1999 there were 97 Bronze, 74 Silver, and 25 Gold awards. Only four applicants did not achieve Bronze. There is considerable interest from hotel groups to join: Ecotrans reports that all Scottish British Trust Hotels have joined at Bronze level, Scottish Youth Hostels Association has joined as a group and it plans to have 58 Gold Members by 2001. The award is held for a 2-year cycle, and the verification process takes place every 2 years by an experienced environmental auditor. The Scheme is funded through government sponsorship and subscriptions. Companies pay £50 (approx. US$/€76) to join at Bronze, £100 (approx. US$/€152) for Silver and £150 (approx. US$/€228) for Gold. These fees are payable every 2 years. Applicants only have to pay for specialist and time-consuming additional work, for example design advice for new buildings.

Criteria for application comprise over 120 elements, and these are updated every 2 years. These are divided into ten sections, taking into account regional environmental differences, and considering the diversity of tourist businesses. The Scheme is based on an environmental management system approach, where the business is encouraged to identify its own priorities and to prepare a programme to achieve its own environmental targets. Criteria groups are listed below, taken from the Scheme's documentation:

1. *Compulsory measures.* To ensure applicants meet minimal standards, legal compliance, basic tidiness and cleanliness, and having a member of staff with environmental responsibilities.
2. *Waste.* Focus on waste minimization. Reduction through bulk purchase and return schemes, reuse through refilling bottles, rechargeable batteries, paper, and recycling in bottle banks, and for soaps and cooking oil.
3. *Energy.* Focus on energy efficiency, through low energy appliances and 1000 watt kettles, through low-energy lights and dimmer switches, through thermostatic radiator valves and timeclocks, and through draughtsealing main doors, and using instant hot water systems.
4. *Water.* Focus on water savings, by reusing water in recirculation in modern/commercial dishwashers, grey water recirculation units, general good practice by avoiding leaks and dripping taps, use of economy cycle on washing machines, and water minimization through flow regulators, waterbutts, urinal controllers and the reduction of flush toilets.

5. *Transport.* Focus on public transport, cycling and walking, by providing information on public transport and walking/pedestrian routes, bike hire information, cycle racks and secure bike storage, and encouraging staff car share and electric/LPG vehicles.

6. *Green products.* Focus on purchasing green products and supplier screening through supplier screening of green correspondence, using recycled products such as office paper, toilet paper, recycled plastic containers or bags, and printer cartridges; focusing on food products through buying local food and drink, organic or 'home grown' produce and membership of the Natural Cook; and buying eco sensitive products such as phosphate/chlorine free products and pump action sprays.

7. *Training and monitoring.* Focus on raising staff awareness through environmental issues in staff induction and training, feedback between staff on environmental issues, staff 'green' notice board, staff suggestion box; focus on environmental monitoring such as energy monitoring, waste monitoring, water consumption meter readings, transport monitoring and environmental feedback through visitor responses.

8. *Communication.* Focus on communication of environmental practices to guests through contracts or joint ventures with other members, involvement in green community projects, taking bookings on e-mail or a website, and having a towel agreement.

9. *Wildlife and landscape.* Focus on measures to support local wild plants and animals, such as planting native species, establishing a wildlife area, putting up a bird or bat box, helping support a wildlife initiative or providing information on local nature reserves or wildlife parks.

10. *Bonus section.* This section allows for any examples of innovation or particularly good practice not covered by other sections.

The Scheme has developed a web page to promote itself and companies awarded. Applicants also have a telephone support line to help them in undertaking measures; consultations; and a newsletter. They are also allowed to use the logo in their advertising and the Scottish Tourist Board publications. The Scottish Tourist Board Occupancy Annual Report 1999 figures show that hotels and guest houses awarded with the Green Tourism Business Scheme award have an average of 6% higher occupancy rate, and smaller establishments such as bed and breakfast and self-catering establishments have a 10% higher rate. This possibly reflects that individual tourists choose green rather than larger, more corporate hospitality which may have more business customers. The press has been positive towards the scheme, although it is too early to make conclusions. The main challenges are to secure future funding, to expand from Scotland to the whole of the United Kingdom, to help other national organizations in Europe to develop similar systems, and to set up a green purchase scheme online.

Holiday Villages in Austria (Dorfurlaub in Österreich), Austria

http://www.eco-tour.org/info/w_10066_en.html

Dorfurlaub in Österreich (Holiday Villages in Austria) began in 1991 as an innovative attempt to encourage environmentally compatible tourism reflecting the true character of Austrian villages. This scheme is designed to make better use of capacity and charge higher prices for this kind of sustainable tourism, which attracts visitors seeking recreational value, outstanding environmental quality and attractive scenery.

Membership of the Association is awarded to villages which meet a range of specified criteria, ranging from village character, building construction, the proportion of residents to holidaymakers, to the entire eco-structure of the community. Membership totals 24 villages at present, with another 50 on the waiting list. The association doubles as a cooperative marketing initiative with the villages uniting to produce their own brochures and advertising. Acting as a self-regulatory body, the association also vets newcomers. A newcomer must satisfy wide-ranging criteria:

- *The village character*: quality of village setting, e.g. typical of the region; sympathetic blending of commercial, industrial, residential, and tourist buildings and facilities into the landscape. The buildings will be a maximum of three floors high. There has to be a good architectural balance between old and new buildings.
- *Ecological minimum standards and load thresholds*: the land-scapes will be natural and typical of the region, in proximity to a variety of protected landscape areas. There will be strict quality restrictions in the use of fertilizers. Motorways will be at least 3 km away and there is a maximum limit on through roads of 3000–4000 vehicles per day to meet air quality and noise criteria. There will be no noise or emissions from industrial zones. There will be good access to public transport and alternative transport options, e.g. cycle tracks. There will be facilities for reuse and recycling. The village will have a good network of farm produce for shops and hotels. The village will have a farming community emphasis, with a choice of farmhouses for farm holidays, visits and farm shops selling direct to the public. Tourist facilities will be environmentally compatible, welcoming to locals and cater for children.
- *Social and tourism minimum standards and load thresholds*: the population will have a maximum of 1500 inhabitants, with a maximum of 25% second homeowners. The proportion of inhabitants to guests beds should ideally be 1 : 1, with mixed accommodation

structures in preference to large hotels; there should be voluntary measures to limit the size of businesses. There should be an active village community life (societies, active folklore, tradition and customs; involvement of local community in planning and in providing for tourists). The village will have a tourism information office and at least the minimum tourist requirements, such as easy access to natural tourist amenities such as hiking paths; minimum guest bed requirement is 100 beds.

Irschen is one of the founder villages of the association and is typical of the membership. All development has to be contained within the present confines of the village and the surrounding landscape has to be compatible. There is positive discrimination in the awarding of contracts to local businesses with control exerted over the materials and techniques used. All houses are fitted with water-saving devices in the toilets and washing machines, and 80% of water heating comes from solar panels. All homes and hotels have to use thermal glass and meet very high insulation standards. Parking places around public buildings have to be at least 80 m away and all hotels pick up guests from the railway station free of charge and have cycle hire facilities. All street lights are automatically turned off at midnight.

Dorfurlaub in Österreich forecasts that the network of green villages will spread throughout the country, benefiting tourists and residents alike.

Horizons, Canada

Ian McGilp, Product Development Branch, Tourism Saskatchewan

During April 2000, a new ecotourism accreditation system was introduced in the Province of Saskatchewan (Canada). The name 'Horizons' was selected to symbolize the system. Accreditation is an initiative of the Ecotourism Society of Saskatchewan, and the Saskatchewan Tourism Authority (Tourism Saskatchewan). The programme has been developed over an 8-year period of extensive research, consultation, planning and application in the field. Criteria have been designed for ecotourism product suppliers in the categories of attractions, accommodation, and guided tours. It provides an assurance that products and services will be delivered with a commitment to the environment and ecological processes, and a commitment to providing quality experiences.

The 'Horizons' programme is operated by the Ecotourism Society, which is a non-governmental organization with a membership of nature-based attractions, tourism businesses, educators, ecological consultants, and conservation organizations. The Society has an elected 12 member volunteer board of directors and two appointed advisers, one of whom represents Tourism Saskatchewan. Tourism Saskatchewan is an industry–government partnership responsible for tourism marketing and product development, membership and visitor services, and tourism education and training. Limited human resource, administrative, and logistical support is provided to the Society by Tourism Saskatchewan. Programme development and implementation costs to date have been funded by memberships, and support from Tourism Saskatchewan. In-kind support from business operators and educational institutions has also helped considerably.

The geographical scope of the programme is the province of Saskatchewan, an area of approximately 65 million ha^2 including portions of Canada's Prairie, Boreal Plain, Boreal Shield and Taiga Shield ecozones.

The 'Horizons' programme was launched in response to the need to identify and promote genuine ecotourism operations and best practices in this growing sector of the industry. It was felt that by branding or labelling through accreditation, business opportunities available to these operations could be expanded, while ensuring the conservation of the natural resources upon which they depend. Accreditation is granted to operations that follow the principles of ecotourism in Saskatchewan, and meet the assessment criteria described in a two-part application and confidential evaluation report. Participation in the programme is voluntary. Here is how the system works:

The applicant completes part one of the application – answering a series of questions – and returns it, along with copies of all promotional material that would be provided to a prospective customer. The applicant also starts work on completing a considerably more detailed evaluation report, part two of the process. The Ecotourism Society reviews the part one material, and assigns three directors to visit the applicant and complete part two of the application. The applicant must provide detailed maps identifying various landforms, sensitive areas, vegetation types, nesting areas, itineraries, aboriginal spiritual areas and sacred sites, and locations being used by other industries such as forest harvesting, oil and gas exploration and development, trapping and cattle grazing. It is during this part that site tours and facilities inspections take place. The purpose of this mapping is to ensure that the applicant has a thorough and appreciative knowledge of their areas and is fully cognizant of the needs of other users of these natural resources. Many of the areas identified are specifically to be avoided at certain times of the year. Area sensitivity, group size, visitor profiles and impact, and impact assessment and restoration measures are all included in this process. Relevant information is then verified with references and land managers.

Assuming the reports of the committee and references are favourable, accreditation in one or two or all three categories (as the case may be) is then awarded by a vote of the Board of Directors of the Ecotourism Society. It is granted for a 1-year term. Annual renewal has not required a further in-depth review since these operations are usually visited by members of the Society and Tourism Saskatchewan when they are in the area on other business or perhaps on holiday.

Support services provided jointly by the Society and by Tourism Saskatchewan include the following: assistance in completing the accreditation process, business consulting advice, a quarterly newsletter, monthly meetings in different locations, an annual meeting/conference, networking opportunities, regional workshops, representation in land-use planning processes, use of the logo on promotional material, and marketing assistance including Internet listing on two websites and identification in tourism publications, recommendations with respect to site development and management, construction techniques, and best practices information.

Applicants pay a Can$100 (approx. US$/€70) fee for accreditation, and a Can$50 (approx. US$/€35) annual renewal fee. It has generally been the case that accommodation and meals are also provided to the accreditation team, and Tourism Saskatchewan has covered transportation. The process usually takes less than 8 weeks to complete when areas can be properly accessed and inspected. Delays occur due to freeze-up and break-up of ice when travel by canoe, motor boat or floatplane is required. The Society's directors and advisers are thoroughly familiar with the province's landscapes and resources.

Commencing in 2001, the Tourism Saskatchewan literature series will use the logo to identify listings and advertisements placed in its publications by accredited ecotourism operations. They will also be identified on the Tourism Saskatchewan website, and the Ecotourism Society website. Businesses report that interest in ecotourism experiences is steadily increasing. They believe that consumer recognition of the accreditation logo will give them a competitive advantage over other businesses. Accordingly, they want to be part of the network of accredited operations. The challenges being faced in implementing the 'Horizons' programme are:

- securing adequate public and private sector financial support for the Ecotourism Society and its volunteer board of directors (accreditation costs exceed the Can$100 fee);
- maintaining the commitment of human resources and expertise currently provided by Tourism Saskatchewan;
- successfully integrating the needs of the ecotourism sector with those of other industries competing for access to Saskatchewan's natural resources.

The major achievement of the 'Horizons' programme is that it has given the ecotourism sector a clearly recognizable, heightened profile in the marketplace. It has further enabled the sector to become a more significant component of the tourism industry in Saskatchewan. The programme is proving successful because of the integrity and wisdom of the people behind its development and implementation. The support of Tourism Saskatchewan in both of these activities has been instrumental and essential. The 'Horizons' programme will continue to evolve and improve in response to the ideals it seeks to address.

IH&RA Environmental Award, Worldwide

http://www.eco-tip.org/Eco-labels/ecolabels.htm

The International Hotel and Resort Association (IH&RA) Environmental Award has been in operation, under different names and forms, since 1990. It was developed in cooperation with IHEI (International Hotels Environment Initiative) and in partnership with the United Nations Environment Programme with particular reference to technology, industry and economics. The funding of the award is through sponsorship provided by American Express.

The award is focused towards the restaurant and accommodation sector of the tourism industry. It is awarded to hospitality professionals who provide exceptional examples of leadership in planning and carrying out environmental actions especially in the area of sustainable development, and who have shown a personal commitment to continuously improving environmental performance and staff awareness over the last few years and who also show personal initiatives for continuously improving the environment in the future. Award winners must also show a commitment to bringing the benefits of tourism to the local community, to communicating the importance of environmental awareness and involving staff members. Successful operators will also reflect an ability to communicate environmental performance to guests, staff and the wider hospitality industry.

The closing date for applicants is August. The Award is given to members of the IHA (national associations in the Hotel and Restaurants sector), which produce environmental protection programmes or complex action programmes in environmental protection for its members. The annual Award is given under a different motto each year: (1991, Energy Savers; 1993, Pollution Solutions; 1995, Green Hotelier). The evaluation of the award involves a maximum of 25 points, which are broken down as follows: planning aids carry a maximum of 10 points, implementation of the plan a maximum of 10 points and the case study/report a maximum of 5 points.

The Independent and Corporate winners will each receive US$2500, an engraved plaque and trophy, publicity in IH&RA newsletters, HOTELS magazine and the international trade press, and an invitation to the IH&RA Annual Congress. There are winners in three categories: Young Hoteliers Award winners, Young Restaurateurs Award winners and Environmental Award winners and runners-up). In 1999, there were four winners of the Young Hoteliers/Restaurateurs Award, two Environmental Award winners and three prizes given to runners up (names of companies not available). The following is a list of earlier environmental actions and the winners of the award for such action:

- 1991: Energy Savers (Ramada International Hotels and Resorts);
- 1992: Conserve and Preserve (The Laguna Beach Resort, Thailand);
- 1993: Pollution Solutions (Inter Continental Hotel, Miami);
- 1994: Environment Matters (Royal Dutch Horeca, Netherlands);
- 1995: Corporate Green Hotelier of the year (J.-M. Leclercq), Independent Green Hotelier (I. Aston, Derwentwater Hotel, Cumbria, UK);
- 1996: Corporate Green Hotelier (A. Checkley, Canadian Pacific Hotels), Independent Green Hotelier (P. McAlpine, Phuket Yacht Club, Thailand);
- 1997: Welcome group Park Sheraton Hotel and Towers, Madras; Conference Centre, Stockholm;
- 1998: Inter-Continental Hotel Sydney; Club Alda, Turkey.

International Environmental Award (Internationale Umweltauszeichnung), Worldwide

Ute Quintar, Environment Department, Deutscher Reisebüro und Reiseveranstalter Verband

The German Travel Agents and Tour Operators Association (DRV) operates the International Environment Award, an international prize for 'Tourism and the Environment', which recognizes achievements for outstanding conservation projects and has been awarded annually since 1987. The award targets a number of sectors of the tourism industry including the overall destination, accommodation, catering facilities, tour operators, leisure facilities and all other 'tourism and the environment' projects. The award is made to individuals, groups, organizations, companies and communities who have achieved a notable success in protecting or improving the environment – the countryside, the animal and plant world, the ground, water and air, as well as humans and their culture – and who, at the same time, have supported tourism. Applications from projects and activities which have the following objectives are considered:

- protection of the natural habitat to enable its environmentally safe use for tourism;
- promotion of environmental awareness and conservation activities in the destination countries, in the tourism industry, and among the tourists themselves;
- development of practical concepts in order to ensure a sustainable tourism;
- creation of effective conditions and prerequisites for an environmentally safe tourism;
- to minimize environmental stress or to re-create destroyed elements of the environment, in tourist regions.

Measures designed to improve the infrastructure, such as drainage systems, waste disposal sites and sewage plants, or the establishment of nature conservation projects which are only partly related to tourism are normally excluded. Projects taking into consideration both environmental and cultural aspects are more likely to be awarded. The winner of the award will not necessarily be the largest or most expensive project, but that which makes an effective, exemplary and innovative contribution to furthering environmentally safe tourism. It is most important for the jury to see the success so far achieved and how a successful control is carried through.

The criteria that the applicant must meet in order for the ecolabel to be received, are that the applicant must send, in German or English, a short description of the project or activity including details of the contact name and address, a detailed description of the project with photographs, any literature which provides evidence of the importance of the project or activity for tourism and the environment, and the name of the person who is authorized to receive the award. The criteria are established by the DRV International Environment Award Jury, which is also responsible for verifying the information in the application. The award is not awarded for a certain period of time but is a long-term prize. The selection of grantees may involve a site visit depending upon the nature of the application in question. The ecolabel does not specify priority action areas. The applicants that are successful and receive an award will have a report in the leading German trade papers, which will generate major publicity, resulting in German and international contacts.

There are a number of part-time members who work on the award scheme, along with a number of jury members. The award scheme does not require third-party verification before the ecolabel is awarded. Depending on the project, the award scheme may recognize the continued environmental improvement by grantees; however, it does not recognize and reward grantees who have taken particular environmental action. The media response to the award scheme has been positive with a number of reports in the German travel media. Although there is no evidence to show that the tourists are showing preference to ecolabelled services, the DRV thinks it might motivate tourists to book. The DRV claims that it is the first industry organization granting an environment award. The major achievements of the scheme are that it has increased awareness of the link between tourism and the environment. The DRV believes that the main reason for the success of the award scheme is that it has been continuously implementing the award scheme for many years.

Publicity for the event and the award-winning project is usually generated through reports in the leading German trade papers with further representation at the ITB (Internationale Tourismusbörse), an international trade fair in Berlin resulting in many German and international contacts. There is also the possibility of support from the DRV for the prize-winner to attend a Conservation Congress or to undertake further education on the topic of tourism-related environmental protection. The number of applications for the prize varies from 10 to 70 and the number of applicants being awarded the label will always remain at one per year. In 1999, 14 projects applied and one applicant was awarded the prize.

Kiskeya Alternative Tourism Sustainability Certification Programme, Dominican Republic/Haiti

Yacine Khelladi, Coordinator, Kiskeya Alternative

The Kiskeya Alternative Tourism Sustainability certification programme is an ecolabel to certify good practice in tourism, currently under development in the Dominican Republic and Haiti. It is being developed by Kiskeya Alternative, a non-governmental organization, with two volunteers to design and pilot the labelling scheme.

The project targets the following sectors of the tourism industry: the overall destination, accommodation, tour operators, leisure facilities, community services, tours and excursions. The label will be launched in order to meet the following objectives:

• To have a tool to be sure to integrate in our project only partners (tourism operators) that meet minimal levels of sustainability on the environmental, social and cultural aspects (unfortunately in the Dominican Republic and Haiti any tour can be labelled as 'ecotourism').

- To develop and continue the process in collaboration with other institutions (environmental National Government Organizations, academic, official) to build real and complete tools for establishing a National Certification Programme, which would be a powerful marketing tool (as a social quality guarantee and for differentiating 'products').
- To establish mechanisms for permanently monitoring our integrated partners on their activities' sustainability and 'product quality'.

Currently Kiskeya Alternative is conducting a 'Tourism Sustainability Identification Questionnaire'. The benchmarking process is to conduct the questionnaire on five projects and it is planned to apply it to around 25 elements that are combined in the five ecotours. Further plans are for it to develop in the Dominican Republic. The next step in the process for Kiskeya Alternative is to present the preliminary work and results to several institutions (environmental NGOs, academics, official tourism institutions and specialized bodies) in both the Dominican Republic and Haiti and propose regular work to create a real certification tool; this will then be sanctioned by all those institutions.

The selection of the grantees involves a site visit. The ecolabel may specify priority action areas and this is currently in progress. Kiskeya Alternative plans to provide support services to grantees by creating a Caribbean Tourism Sustainability Certification, Consulting and Assistance Network. This is a project proposal that aims to:

- create and/or reinforce any links between researchers and institutions that develop activities in this area;
- extend the 'Tourism Sustainability Certification' and 'Service Quality Label' to a regional level; and
- propose consulting services for helping tourism initiatives to enhance their level of sustainability (social, cultural, environ-mental, economic) and to create mechanisms to make regional providers meet tourism projects in need of solutions to their sustainability problems.

These support services are provided by site visits, consultations, the Kiskeya Alternative website, electronic information exchange and by having access to the database. At present, grantees do not have to pay for these support services; however, it is uncertain if this will change in the future. It is also not determined yet which services will be covered by subscription/application fees and which will be available at an additional cost.

The labelling scheme will verify the information in the application form through site visits. It is not yet determined if third party verifica-tion will be required before the ecolabel is awarded or if the labelling scheme will recognize continued environmental improvement by grantees. However, the scheme will recognize and reward grantees that have taken particularly noteworthy environmental action, there will also be procedures implemented to ensure that the criteria are maintained during the life span of the label. The main challenge that Kiskeya Alternative may face in developing and implementing the labelling scheme is the financial costs of the labelling process.

Landscape of the Year (Landschaft des Jahres), Europe

Manfred Pils, Secretary General, International Friends of Nature

The Landscape of the Year is a competition that awards a European region for its transboundary, ecologically valuable or endangered landscape. The award is not targeted directly to tourist destinations, although the regions awarded have tourism potential, or an established tourism industry. The award has been organized by the International Friends of Nature in a formal way since 1989, first yearly and currently every 2 years. The event takes place at the International Presidents' Conference of the Nature Friends Federations.

As a logical consequence of the principles embraced by the Friends of Nature and of their movement's history the idea was taken beyond the concept of gentle tourism and extended into an overall concept for sustainable, regional development. The ecological, social and economic dimensions of a given region must be integrated and the people living in the 'Landscape of the Year' must be given the opportunity to shape their living and working environment (following bottom-up principles). This is why dialogue and the involvement of the local population, of organized interest groups and initiatives in the regions concerned are vital to the projects.

The principal aim pursued with every 'Landscape of the Year' project is the sustainable development of the region selected. The 'Landscape of the Year' project is intended to provide the framework for a proactive approach to the problems of a given region, for developing viable strategies for sustainable development together with the local population and for initiating suitable projects whose effect will still be felt when the 'Landscape of the Year' project has long been concluded. To achieve this aim the Friends of Nature have chosen a three-pronged approach, seeking to strike a balance between the implementation of practical projects, the organization of events and hands-on activities for participants as well as political consciousness building and lobbying at regional, national and international level. The model regions are to be presented throughout Europe and awareness of the problems of the regions and their populations is to be raised.

In cooperation with local communities, organizations, associations and political representatives, workshops and other events are to be organized in the model regions with a view to picturing the perspectives of sustainable development and pointing the way to the future. The information media of the Friends of Nature are employed in networking important activities within the regions.

Ecological travel programmes offered by the Friends of Nature federations provide opportunities to get in touch with the regions and, at the same time, encourage the development of alternative tourism. Model projects are implemented in the regions together with interested regional bodies and groups. These projects are designed to create 'eco-jobs' and in this way to sustain the economic viability of the regions. The criteria for the selection of Landscapes of the Year are divided into positive and negative criteria. Positive criteria are the perception of national borders as an incentive to solving common problems, rather than as a barrier, the positive role played by the ecological importance of the region, the manageable size of the region (usually three or four districts), and the presence of potential, regional support bodies. Negative criteria would be the designation of the area as a national park or biosphere reserve, since this would already fulfil some of the functions of this award, and excessive mass tourism in the region, to avoid the misuse of the Landscape of the Year designation.

Previous landscapes of the year were Lake Constance (Austria, Switzerland, Germany) in 1989, Neusiedler Lake (Austria, Hungary) in 1990, the Eifel-Ardennes region (Belgium, Germany, France, Luxembourg) in 1991/1992, the Oder delta (Germany, Poland) in 1993/1994, the Alps (Austria, Switzerland, Germany, France, Italy, Slovenia) in 1995/1996, the river Maas (France, Belgium, The Netherlands) in 1997/1998 and the 'Bohemian Forest' (Austria, Czech Republic, Germany) in 1999/2000.

Model Campsites in Germany (Vorbildliche Campingplätze in Deutschland), Germany

Nicole Habrich, DTV

The Model Campsites in Germany competition is organized by the German Tourism Association (DTV), with support from the Ministry for Food, Agriculture and Forestry; the Ministry for Family, Senior Citizens, Women and Children and the Ministry for the Environment, Nature Protection and Nuclear Plant Safety. The competition was launched in 1993 and winners are announced around October each year.

Invitations to participate in the competition are sent to the owners of approximately 5800 campsites across Germany, in the form of a manual. The award operates on a two tier level, first selecting winners for each federal state; these then compete at national level. The number of possible winners within each federal state depends on the total number of campsites within the state. For example if one state has between three and 20 campsites, two winners are allowed and if a state has over 40 campsites, four winners can proceed to the next stage. A total of 32 campsites are chosen from different federal states in Germany. These winners of the regional campsite competitions are then put forward to the national competition where gold, silver and bronze awards are presented.

The main aim of the competition is to promote the camping tourism sector and to achieve attractive campsites across Germany, which offer high-quality services and consider the needs of their guests and the environment alike. It is felt that campsites which can achieve these goals will also stand a better chance in international competitions. The economic importance of camping is recognized in Germany and it is felt that a competition such as this will help to secure and further develop campsites, therefore putting the sector in a good market position.

The requirements of the competitions are put together in a document written by the well-known Institute BTE-Tourism Management and Regional Development, Hanover. The assessment criteria for the competition cover a wide range of areas, which are measured on a points system. These include:

- How the campsite fits in with the area and the landscape and how ecological it is. Applicants can score up to 25 points by covering criteria such as how they have dealt with the natural surroundings through the development of the campsite and the implementation of environmental technology. This section also focuses on the accessibility and communal usage of infrastructural facilities belonging to the community.
- Structure and design of the campsites. The functionality and target group breakdown of the campsite is examined, as well as how the site considers the tourist and social requirements; for example with specific children's areas and sports facilities. The land usage is also examined, that is, whether it is damaging to the natural surroundings and how the campsite deals with the supply of energy and recycling of waste. The usefulness of signposting provided for visitors is also looked at.
- Target-group orientated facilities and equipment. The supply of visitor facilities such as drinking water, shops and cooking facilities are examined here along with the supply and use of

camping vans and whether special plots are provided for motor caravans. This section also looks into the provisions that are made for disabled visitors.

- Organization, care and marketing of campsite. This section of the criteria investigates such areas as the cleanliness of the site and its facilities, the structure of the site (including price structures and in-house entertainment facilities) and the provision of tourist information and target group offers.

In order to enter the competition, applicants have to provide written and visual material such as building plans and aerial photographs of the campsite in order to support the above criteria. Information regarding how the site was used before the development of the campsite and what developments are planned for the future is also requested.

Nature and Ecotourism Accreditation Programme, Australia

Meaghan Newson and Alice Crabtree, Ecotourism Association of Australia

The Nature and Ecotourism Accreditation Programme (NEAP) is a world first. It is an industry-developed and driven initiative in response to the need to identify, encourage and reward operators of genuine nature tourism and ecotourism products in Australia. It is designed to provide industry, protected area managers and consumers with an assurance that an accredited nature tourism or ecotourism product has passed a stringent and independent assessment of its compliance with current best practice standards. NEAP has been developed to provide a number of benefits to operators, consumers, protected area managers, and host communities. For example, NEAP:

- provides consumers with a recognized means to identify genuine nature tourism and ecotourism product, thus allowing them to make informed choices in selecting ethical product;
- provides operators with a means to determine the degree to which they practise ecologically sustainable tourism, and to continually improve their environmental performance;
- contributes to the achievement of economic sustainability for operators, by providing them with competitive advantage in marketing their product (for example, accredited operators gain access to discounted advertising in some industry publications, NEAP logo inclusion in product guides and cooperative marketing opportunities);
- assists protected area managers in identifying and rewarding operators who meet required standards;

- provides host communities with the means to identify genuine nature tourism and ecotourism product, and assists them in determining an appropriate mix of tourism product for their region.

NEAP is a joint initiative of Australia's top ecotourism industry body, the Ecotourism Association of Australia, and the Australian Tourism Operators Network. The programme was developed by a team of specialists in ecotourism, minimal impact practices, protected area management, licensing systems, environmental auditing and management of accreditation programmes. A panel of industry experts, consisting of two members from each partner organization and an independent chair, oversees the management of the programme. A team of assessors reviews accreditation applications, which are then forwarded to the panel for a final decision. A transparent appeals system and review programme is in place for operators wishing to have the decision on their application re-examined. NEAP operates as an entirely self-funding programme, with administration, assessment and auditing costs covered by application and annual fees paid by accredited operators.

Three types of tourism product may be accredited under NEAP: tours, attractions (including parks), and accommodation. To achieve accreditation, the product must meet the principles of eligibility outlined in the table below. Each of these principles is reflected in assessment criteria that establish three categories of accreditation: Nature Tourism, Ecotourism and Advanced Ecotourism. Operators of

The nature tourism or ecotourism product:	Nature tourism	Ecotourism	Advanced ecotourism
Focuses on directly and personally experiencing nature	✓	✓	✓
Provides opportunities to experience nature in ways that lead to greater understanding, appreciation and enjoyment	Optional	Mandatory but not necessarily core to experience	Core element of experience
Represents best practice for environmentally sustainable tourism	✓	✓	✓
Positively contributes to the conservation of natural areas		✓	✓
Provides constructive ongoing contributions to local communities		✓	✓
Is sensitive to and involves different cultures, especially indigenous cultures		✓	✓
Consistently meets customer expectations	✓	✓	✓
Is marketed accurately and leads to realistic expectations	✓	✓	✓

a product that achieves accreditation are eligible to display the distinctive NEAP 'tick' logo on their marketing material, thus providing consumers with a ready means of identification.

NEAP was originally launched in 1996 as the National Ecotourism Accreditation Programme. This first edition of the programme encompassed two categories of accreditation: Ecotourism and Advanced Ecotourism. Over 260 ecotourism products were accredited under NEAP Edition I. Collectively, these products represent the diverse nature of the Australian ecotourism industry, ranging from single person operations running small group tours, to large-scale ecotourism resorts with the capacity to cater for several hundred guests.

Integral to the scheme is a continuous improvement programme. The first comprehensive review of the criteria was conducted during 1999, and the second edition of the programme was launched in early 2000. Following extensive consultation with protected area managers from around Australia, the decision was taken early in the redevelopment process to expand the programme to include a third category of accreditation: Nature Tourism. This new category of accreditation was introduced in recognition of the need for *all* tourism in protected areas, not just ecotourism, to be ecologically sustainable.

The expansion of NEAP has increased its relevance to industry in two main ways. Firstly, it provides a readily utilized means for protected area managers to recognize and reward licence applicants who comply with best practice standards. For example, at the time of writing, two Australian protected area management agencies are providing NEAP accredited operators with extended tenure, and it is likely that other agencies will provide similar benefits in the near future. Secondly, the expanded programme allows responsible nature tourism operators, who may not have the desire include the wider range of criteria applicable to ecotourism as part of their product, to none the less be recognized as providers of quality tourism experiences. Such operators would include those who operate sustainable adventure tourism products that leave few opportunities for interpretation, or those who gain a greater marketing advantage from targeting their product towards the broader nature-based tourism market. The other major improvements included in NEAP Edition II were:

- an increased emphasis on the interpretation criteria to distinguish between categories of accreditation, particularly between Ecotourism Accreditation and Advanced Ecotourism Accreditation;
- the comprehensive review and redrafting of all of the NEAP Edition I accreditation criteria, including an increase in stringency in the criteria needed to achieve Advanced Accreditation;

- an improved introduction section, with a comprehensive background to the programme and a clearer application procedure,
  drawn from 3 years' experience of managing NEAP Edition I; and
- an expanded appendix section that provides operators with a glossary, information on innovative best practice and interpretation,
  suggested reading and a comprehensive list of industry contacts.

A key feature of NEAP is that it recognizes that nature tourism and
ecotourism accreditation alone do not encompass all of the dimensions
of ecologically sustainable tourism. Rather than duplicate existing
criteria in other accreditation schemes, strategic alliances have been
established between NEAP and programmes dealing with business
accreditation and guide certification. These linkages are designed to
encourage operators to implement best practice standards across all
aspects of their businesses. For example, operators already accredited
under the 'Better Business' accreditation programme receive a discount
on their NEAP application fees. Additionally, by the launch of NEAP
Edition III, it is expected that an operator must ensure that at least their
head guide is eligible for certification under the Nature and Ecotour
Guide Certification Programme in order for their product to achieve
Advanced Accreditation.

One of the reasons for NEAP's continued success is that it provides
a practical, measurable process for assessing the sustainability of
nature tourism and ecotourism product. Rather than requiring
participating operators to simply sign off on a voluntary code of practice, the programme obliges them to demonstrate that they actually
have best practice management in place before they can be accredited.
However, as the first part of the application process is based upon
self-assessment, NEAP also provides a non-threatening means for
operators to determine the extent to which they comply with the
standard. Thus, it is essentially an educational tool for ecotourism
operators.

Natural Products Hohe Tauern National Park (Naturprodukt Nationalpark Hohe Tauern), Austria

Helmut Haslinger, ARGE National Park Region Manager

The ARGE National Park region Hohe Tauern was established in 1994.
The aim of the ARGE National Park is 'to have careful sustainable
management in this sensitive but ecologically still intact nature area
and to have the implementation of joint marketing measures for

products from the National Park region, especially in the commercial areas agriculture, trade, and tourism'. Certain natural products of the national park region come from a sensitive, yet ecologically intact, nature space. As an increasing number of consumers demand such products there is a danger of them being destroyed and so they need to be marketed as a specialist product to a smaller number of consumers.

This label is broader than other environmental labels, since it covers a variety of regional quality issues. The key aims of the label are to encourage progress in the following three subsectors:

- Natural products of the National Park region Hohe Tauern: these include bio-agriculture, location in the National Park and green-land management. The quality assurance check for this area involves a bio-check and personal knowledge.
- Restaurant operators of the National Park: these involve bio-product use and cooperation with the national park administration. The quality assurance check for this is to test families, conduct a goods application query and conduct training courses.
- Handicrafts of the National Park: this is a non-standard assignment and involves assessing the location in the National Park region, ecologically oriented philosophy of the enterprise and endorsement of the National Park aims. There are non-standard checks to assure quality.

To achieve the above objectives, the park encourages tourism operators to meet certain criteria, such as:

- the use of local and high value natural products from controlled producers;
- an economy based on recycling and sustainable use;
- traceability of natural products from farmer to customer;
- waste avoidance and transport reduction to a minimum;
- working with up-to-date and environment-orientated energy supply;
- positive evaluation of biological husbandry methods, contributions to nature conservation as well as efforts to preserve breeds of domestic livestock.

There are 24 partner organizations. The award of the regional mark 'Partner Organization', makes use of advertising advantages; membership of the ARGE National Park Region Hohe Tauern is in each case limited to 1 year. The advantages of cooperating with the ARGE National Park include a thrice-yearly newspaper with news, subscriptions, meeting notes and histories, a weekly column in the regional press and the participation in regional and seasonal speciality days.

The Nordic Ecolabelling of Hotels, Scandinavia

**Tanja Annila, Technical Assistant, Finnish Standards Association and
Herbert Hamele, Ecotrans**

The Nordic Ministry Council operates SFS – Ecolabelling, a generic ecolabel with specific criteria for product groups based on an environmental management system approach. The Nordic Ecolabelling of Hotels is the resulting label for one specific product group, operational since 1999. This product group includes any form of temporary accommodation, and also restaurants, conference facilities and swimming pools, when linked to accommodation provision. SFS operates across the Scandinavian countries (Denmark, Sweden, Iceland, Norway, Finland) with verification bodies in each country. Thirteen full-time members of staff work on the SFS scheme, which is funded through registration fees and Government sponsorship.

In the first year of operation two hotels in Sweden and one in Norway were awarded with the ecolabel. The label for hotels is very recent and therefore there has not been time to establish if the number of hotels receiving the award has increased. It is clear that there is an increase in the number of hotels interested in applying for it soon.

A number of criteria must be met for the Ecolabel to be awarded; these include criteria concerning energy, water, chemicals, waste management, transportation and management systems. A Nordic expert group establishes the criteria; the group includes experts from environmental and travelling organizations, and representatives from hotel chains. Due to new knowledge and production methods the criteria must be updated regularly. The period of validity of each set of criteria is 2–3 years. New revised criteria are presented at least 6 months before the expiry date. A handling fee is paid upon submission of a complete application. The turnover value of the actual product determines the additional annual fee.

Applicants apply for an ecolabel through an application form, and the Nordic expert group researches further information about the hotel; the final stage of the process is a visit by the Nordic expert group. If the applicant is successful, the ecolabels are awarded for a period of 3 years, after which the criteria will be reviewed and updated. After receiving the ecolabel, the hotel will receive support services such as site visits, consultations, a telephone response service, websites, electronic information exchange and publications (manual, diskette version and hard copies). The application fee covers these services. There are application costs and annual costs, which differ slightly across countries. In Finland the application fee is FIM 4000 (€672) and an annual fee of 0.4% of half the annual turnover of the accommodation business.

The criteria are based on evaluation of the environmental impacts during the actual products' life cycle. Based on a thorough examination, the criteria set requirements towards a number of factors considered environmentally harmful. Upon application all products found to meet the requirements of the criteria are awarded the environmental label. Accommodation services and their ancillary services offer scope for savings in energy and water and minimizing chemicals used for washing, cleaning and other applications. Waste processing is managed indirectly by minimizing overall quantities of materials purchased and by means of sorting at source. Purchases of raw materials and consumer durables are characterized both by a minimization of purchases of disposable articles and encouragement of the selection of environmentally friendly and ecolabelled alternatives.

Furniture, fixtures and fittings have a longer useful life and in their case the requirements are activated only when purchases take place. Criteria relating to transport take the form of requirements imposed on subcontractors, the establishment's own cars and solutions involving the transport requirements of guests. The requirements are expressed in the form of four key figures, each of which has three different levels, depending on the scope and size of the establishment. In the case of energy the key figure ranges from 250 to 300 kWh m^{-2}. In the case of water consumption the key figure ranges from 200 to 300 l per guest night. For active content of chemical technical substances the key figure lies between 25 and 35 g per guest night. For quantity of unsorted waste the key figure lies between 0.5 and 1.5 kg per guest night.

In addition, the establishment must fulfil a number of obligatory measures such as: CFCs must not be used; washing agents must be ecolabelled; reactive chlorine compounds must not be used for cleaning; waste must be sorted at source into at least four categories; PVC must not be purchased for furnishings, fixtures and fitting; and no brominated flame retardant agents may be present in textiles that are purchased. Furthermore, the establishment must fulfil 65% of the total of the scored criteria and 45% of the points for the various environmental aspects (energy, water, etc.). Here, points are awarded for, for example, heat recovery, low-energy light bulbs, renewable electricity, toilets and showers with low water consumption, chemical-free cleaning methods, dispensers for soap and shampoo, the option of sorting at source in guest rooms, ecolabelled consumer articles, organic food on the buffet, ecolabelled textiles, renewable fuel for the establishment's own fleet of vehicle and shared transportation. Finally the establishment must have a documented environmental programme including a number of specific measures described in the document. These include procedures to ensure maintenance of equipment, control of energy and water losses, personnel training and communication with guests.

After receiving an ecolabel, the hotel will be monitored during the site visits where, for example, the environmental management procedures are checked and it is verified that the suppliers of the hotel are using products/services that are acceptable. Such measurements must be documented. In addition, the criteria are reviewed and tightened periodically, so that the applicants have to improve their actions. When applying for the ecolabel, applicants must have an environment programme such as an action plan in place, which must include the hotel's environmental targets along with a timetable of actions. This action plan is also monitored. The labelling scheme ensures that the criteria are maintained during their 'life span' through site visits, telephone calls and by checking the marketing criteria; however, the scheme does not reward grantees who have taken particularly noteworthy environmental action during this time.

The scheme offers grantees promotional and public relations support, including: marketing campaigns, press conferences, articles and announcements in its web pages. The media response to the scheme has been very positive and there has been a lot of interest in the label. There are some students and tourists showing preferences to ecolabelled services. The main reasons for tourism operators to apply for an ecolabel include image, cost, and to be seen as a pioneer and model to the rest of the accommodation sector. The main difficulty involved in developing and implementing a labelling scheme for hotels is that because hotels are very different from each other, there needs to be a number of varying actions included in the criteria. The major achievement of the scheme is that it informs people about the environmental impacts of tourism. The main reason for the success of the ecolabels is that customers demand an ecolabel. In the future, marketing will continue and more services will be taken into the ecolabel system.

PAN Parks, Europe

http://www.panparks.com/

PAN (Protected Area Network) Parks is a new initiative developed by the World Wide Fund for Nature, various protected area authorities and the Molecaten Group. Nature conservation organizations, travel agencies, the business community and several local partners have united their resources to form a network of nature reserves in Europe. PAN Parks mission is to balance nature conservation and tourism in Europe's protected areas. In order to meet this mission, PAN Parks must follow the following principles:

- PAN Parks are protected areas important for wildlife, ecosystems and natural or seminatural landscapes that are representative of Europe's natural heritage. These parks are large enough to maintain vital ecological processes and a viable population of threatened species.
- PAN Parks management maintains and restores ecological processes and biodiversity in natural ecosystems.
- Visitors are welcomed to PAN Parks and are offered good information, services, facilities and the opportunity to experience the natural features of the area, while respecting the nature conservation objectives.
- Relevant partners in the PAN Parks region aim at achieving a synergy between nature conservation and sustainable tourism development by developing a sustainable tourism development strategy, committing to it, and jointly taking responsibility in its implementation.

To become a PAN Park, applicants must follow the following ten steps:

1. Take part in the PAN Parks self-assessment.
2. Send back the self-assessment questionnaire.
3. Working report on the results of self-assessment will be compiled.
4. Evaluation of self-assessment by PAN Parks European Management Organization.
5. Finalization of PAN Parks Principles and Criteria by PAN Parks European Management Organization.
6. PAN Parks European Management Organization will judge/review the result of the self-assessment.
7. Protected areas receive the results of self-assessment.
8. Protected Area management decides whether or not to apply for PAN Parks certification.
9. Final verification by an independent organization.
10. PAN Parks certificate awarded by the PAN Parks European Management Organization.

In order to guarantee the quality of the PAN product for visitors, every park and partner that displays the PAN Parks logo must undertake independent verification. Between December 1999 and March 2000, 17 protected areas, most of them National Parks, from 14 European countries participated in the 'self-assessment'. The final responsibility to approve the Principles and Criteria document lies with the PAN Parks Supervisory Board.

The main principle is to elaborate strict quality standards, applicable to different types of nature and administration of protected areas in Europe. The challenge is balancing nature conservation and tourism. PAN Parks aims to ensure that the protected areas and the visitors are managed so that flora and fauna are not endangered but also so that tourists can visit the Parks. To achieve this, a management plan must be implemented and should be supported by relevant research and monitoring. The criteria concerning visitor management need to ensure that visitors to PAN Parks are satisfied with their visit. The PAN Parks logo is only awarded to Parks that offer nature-based activities and also allow visitors to observe nature without causing a disturbance to it. A suitable network trail is also a necessity.

Tourism, accommodation and other commercial partners wishing to use the PAN Parks trademark and logo must truly support nature conservation, for example, by ensuring that a certain share of profits that tourism brings to the region return to the 'green magnet'; this could then be used for investments in the protected area and its management. In addition to this, the park must ensure that the tourism generated from the park must bring long-term benefits and jobs to the host community of the protected area.

Q-Plus – Kleinwalsertal (Quality Plus – Kleinwalsertal), Austria

Kleinwalsertal-Tourismus, Hirschegg and http://www.eco-tip.org/Ecolabels/ecolabels.htm

Through a further development into a label for quality tourism, the Q-Plus-Kleinwalsertal superseded the previous Kleinwalsertal environmental label (the Silver Thistle). The region of the Kleinwalsertal has been an international pioneer for environmental labels in tourism. In the last few months the Walser have been thinking about how they can improve their services to their customers and have consequently developed the idea of Q-Plus. A wide range of organizations have all committed themselves to the scheme, large and small, in order to further meet the needs and wishes of their customers as much as possible.

Participants include hotels, guest areas and restaurants, guest houses, holiday flats, private accommodation, trade and industry, mountain railways and lifts, public transport, shopping outlets, the Alps and lodges (mountain huts), divers, agriculture, ski- and snowboarding schools, and Kleinwalsertal tourism/events in the Kleinwalsertal. The aims of this label are improving the quality of services offered by all service providers (tourism and non-tourism); the improvement of the overall quality of the tourism offered; the noticeable effects for the local community and visitors.

These enterprises have to respect the 27 mandatory criteria for all businesses; additional mandatory criteria tailored to each target group (environment and quality criteria such as water, waste, energy, mode of arrival and departure, etc.); and optional criteria tailored to each target group (contact with people, non-smoking rooms, food). There is an open explanation of the measures required to fulfil the criteria. The inspection of the accommodations is assured by the group 'Q-Plus' as well as by visitors.

The label is valid for 1 year. After this period of time, the enterprises have to apply for a new evaluation. The label was attributed in 1999 to around 148 businesses, of which 111 were accommodation providers, including hotels, pensions, guesthouses and private accommodation.

Scottish Golf Course Wildlife Initiative, Scotland

Jonathan Smith, Ecology Scottish Golf Course Wildlife Adviser, and http://www.scottishgolf.com/sgu/services/10.htm

The Scottish Golf Course Wildlife Group (SGCWG) developed their Environmental Award as a method of recognition of good environmental management practice in golf courses. This is one method to encourage more clubs to join the initiative and for those already implementing environmental management plans and pro-environmental projects to receive acknowledgement. The label was launched in 1996.

The criteria applicants need to achieve in each category are similar to those for the Committed to Green Awards, and the Committed to Green Foundation is consulted prior to making a full award. The award given here would be equivalent to the Committed to Green award, since this body would validate its equivalence, and the SGCWG Environmental Award in fact will match with the Committed to Green recognition and include its logo. Criteria are broken down into six categories, and criteria for each category are broken down into three levels: the basic requirements that apply to every club, achievements beyond the requirements that will be site specific, and future plans. Only a simplified version of the basic requirement criteria is included here:

1. *Environmental planning*: write an environmental policy, complete an environmental review, produce a site layout plan, produce a written environmental management plan, compile a register of relevant legislation and check compliance, and put in place monitoring, recording and review systems.

2. *Communications, education and the workplace*: communicate environmental issues, actions and plans to staff, club members and visitors, store an environmental dossier, and post information regarding activities. Education includes staff training, and keeping a register of accidents, an emergency incident plan and staff training log.

3. *Nature conservation*: baseline surveys of flora, fauna and habitats with descriptions, mapping and evaluations, specific mention of key species, and statutory designation of the area.

4. *Landscape and cultural heritage*: identify landscape classification and statutory designation within and around the site, carry out a landscape and heritage assessment.

5. *Turf and water management*: document the turfgrass management programme, annual fertilizer and pesticide usage, annual log of disease occurences and pest outbreaks, definition of tolerance thresholds for specified pests and diseases, and compliance with product legislation.

6. *Waste management and energy efficiency*: policy of waste minimization at source, register of hazardous products kept on site and managed in accordance with legal requirements, clear accident protocol, provision for waste separation, policy for dealing with grass clippings, quantification of solid and hazardous waste produced annually.

The award has been planned on a grading system, to allow recognition for gradual progression, while allowing clubs to be involved from an early stage. In this way a club can begin with one category or environmental issue and focus their efforts on that particular issue. Once they have met the criteria for this category they get an Environmental Award Certificate, recognizing achievements on one particular issue. It is expected that dealing with one issue at a time will allow clubs to engage in the process, while the more issues that are met, the more holistic the management approach and the more embedded environmental issues will be in the club's management. When all issues are covered, and the club can prove that environmental management is holistic and proactive, the club receives a Certificate of Environmental Excellence.

Applicants do not have to pay for the services provided. The SGCWG is funded through a government agency, two private sector organizations and one trust, and the certification is part of the services provided by the initiative. The organizers of the award provide a variety of support services, such as site visits and consultations, a telephone response service, website, electronic information exchange, the publication of manuals, seminars, conferences and greenkeeping training.

In 2000, 33 golf courses were awarded with the SGCWG Environmental Award, although it is estimated that over 70 courses would be eligible for recognition for certain categories of their management. Four sites were close to receiving a Certificate of Environmental Excellence (none granted by June 2000). Also, 40 courses have environmental management plans in place and another 30 are on their way, which will increase the number of sites aiming for full certification. Applications have increased twofold since the inception of the scheme. The initiative is highly regarded in Scotland for its benefit to the perception of golf. The organizers plan to increase the number of courses applying for certification, although they also recognize the challenges this poses on limited resources.

Seaside Award

Jose Stanton, Tidy Britain Group

The Seaside Awards recognize clean, well-managed beaches in the UK, set standards of coastal management and provide information for the general public. Introduced in 1992 by Tidy Britain Group, the Seaside Awards were designed to compliment the existing Blue Flag Campaign which was already well-established throughout Europe.

Both Seaside Award and Blue Flag beaches must fulfil various strict criteria, one of which is bathing water quality monitored according to the Bathing Water Directive EC/76/160. The Blue Flag requires the higher guideline, or recommended, standard while the Seaside Awards, which focus more on the land-based management of beaches, require compliance with the legal minimum, or mandatory, standard. The sophisticated level of infrastructure and management required at a Blue Flag beach means that only resort beaches, with guideline water, are eligible. The Seaside Awards provide information about a wider range of beaches as they encompass both resort and rural beaches with consistently good management.

A Seaside Award resort beach must fulfil 29 criteria and ensure proper safety and first aid provision, access and facilities for disabled visitors, clean and well-maintained facilities, dog control and hygiene and a range of public information. A Seaside Award rural beach, which has more limited facilities, must meet 13 criteria including cleanliness, safety with the provision of life-saving equipment and be checked regularly. Both resort and rural beaches are required to display the bathing water quality results for the current season and well as the previous 5 years.

The awards set standards of good practice and, as the UK beaches improve, more are becoming eligible for consideration for an award. In 1992 there were 92 Seaside Awards; in 2000 there were 272 with approximately 90% of coastal local authorities now involved. Since the introduction of the awards independent research has shown a marked improvement to our busier beaches. Between 1993 and 1998 there was an 11–14% increase in the provision of first aid, information, lifesaving equipment, dog refuse bins, supervisors or lifeguards on the UK resort beaches.

The high profile of the campaign makes it an ideal tool to change visitors environmental behaviour. In 1998 Tidy Britain Group conducted an Attitude and Awareness Study of Litter and Environmental Issues in which it discovered that 23% of respondents were aware of the Seaside Awards. Together with the Blue Flag, the Seaside Awards is one of the first ecolabels to combine the environment with tourism. Environmental labelling is an effective market-based instrument, capable of reducing negative impacts of tourism whilst at the same time improving the environmental quality of tourism destinations.

The Seaside Awards succeed in four main areas:

1. Raising environmental awareness of the main stakeholders in tourism – industry, local authorities and consumers.
2. Involvement in environmental activities of small and medium sized enterprises.
3. Improving the environmental performance of the tourism sector in deliberately targeted areas where improvement is most needed.
4. Providing environmental information for consumers, thus helping them make an informed choice.

Administration
The Tidy Britain Group, which administers both the Seaside Awards and the Blue Flag in the UK, is an independent charity, working for the improvement of local environments. The beach awards are two of the campaigns and programmes administered through the eleven regional and national offices throughout the UK. The regional offices form part of the network of assessors which review the beaches each year before the beach operator submits detailed applications in the autumn. As well as a good performance during the season a beach has to provide evidence of the environmental initiatives it promotes. In December, a national jury convenes and studies each application to verify the information provided. The results are then announced in March with the Seaside Awards being presented at the annual Beach Management Conference. The jury also submits its recommendations to FEEE for those beaches which should also be considered for a Blue Flag and these are announced in June.

The Beach Management Programme
Because the award criteria are now often interpreted as the norm, this year TBG introduced a Beach Management Programme to assist those beaches which are seeking to improve. It will encourage further sustainable development of existing award beaches and help those which have yet to address some of the more basic issues. The Programme will not only allow the dissemination of best practice but will enable the assessment of the environmental impact that the increasing number of

visitors has on our coast. Each beach operator will eventually develop an integrated Beach Management System including the management of sustainability issues through Local Agenda 21 and involving all beach stakeholders and organizations with an interest in the management of their section of the coast. As each beach operator has its own unique structure the management system will operate with, rather than against, the grain of existing arrangements and practices. In accordance with the principles of 'best value', the revised approach will allow for improved economies of scale and more efficient allocation of resources. It is based upon, and compatible with, the principles of established management systems including the ISO 9000 series, BS EN ISO 14001 and the EU's Eco-Management and Audit Scheme (EMAS).

As a partner to the Programme, a beach operator will be able to send a representative to the annual Beach Management Conference. The Conference, which is held at a different coastal location each year, provides an opportunity for local authorities, beach operators and interested organizations to discuss and share information about a variety of coastal issues. The 2001 Conference will be held in Torbay in March, and will focus on managing different beach users and the conflicts that can result.

The annual Seaside Awards continue to increase communications between local authorities and beach operators and together continue to work to benefit tourism throughout the UK.

SmartVoyager, Ecuador

Chris Wille, Director Conservation Agriculture Programme, Rainforest Alliance

Responding to eco-minded tourists who want to visit the Galapagos Islands without damaging the world-famous park, an Ecuadorian conservation group and the Rainforest Alliance began a programme to give a 'green seal of approval' to tour boats that tread lightly on the vibrant but fragile ecosystem. The SmartVoyager® certification programme aims to minimize the impact of tour boats in the Galapagos Islands. Each year, 60,000 visitors travel from island to island on specially equipped tour boats, which also serve as floating hotels.

The programme was designed by the Corporación de Conservación y Desarrollo (CCD), an Ecuadorian non-profit organization with experience in ecotourism and ecolabels. Working with scientists, conservation experts, tour operators and others, CCD developed standards for the maintenance and operation of the tour boats. Tour companies that wish to participate invite a team of specialists aboard their boats to evaluate the vessels according to the guidelines.

The Rainforest Alliance, an international non-profit conservation group based in New York, has extensive experience in ecolabel programmes and certification. The group created SmartWood, the first certification programme for well-managed forestry, and ECO-OK, the first certification programme for well-managed commercial, tropical farms. The Rainforest Alliance and CCD collaborate on the certification of banana and cocoa farms in Ecuador as members of the Conservation Agriculture Network, a coalition of grassroots environmental groups in Latin America. The tour boat certification programme is also guided by an advisory committee comprising the Ecuadorian Minister of Tourism, scientists, park officials and representatives of the tourism industry. The International Galapagos Tour Operators Association, representing the companies that manage tourism in the islands, supports the programme by distributing information to the tour operators and the tourists themselves.

The standards cover potential sources of pollution, such as wastewater and fuels, and set rules for the management of everything from docks to the small craft that ferry visitors ashore. Procurement and supply management guidelines are designed to minimize the chances of introducing alien wildlife species to the area. The standards require good living conditions and advanced training for the boat crew and guides. Passengers must be given maximum opportunity to appreciate the beauty of the islands and close encounters with wildlife while leaving no trace of their visit. During their development, the standards were discussed with park officials, guides, scientists and major tour operators

Once the tour operator brings a boat into compliance with the standards, the craft is 'certified' and allowed to display the SmartVoyager seal of approval. This seal gives Galapagos visitors the assurance that they are travelling with an operator which cares about the conservation of the islands and has taken every measure to ensure that passengers enjoy a safe, educational and thrilling adventure without harming wildlife or the unique environment. Travellers are encouraged to ask if their tour operator is enrolled in the SmartVoyager programme.

The Galapagos archipelago, located 960 km (597 miles) west of mainland Ecuador, is a world-renowned biodiversity hotspot and one of the best places on Earth to see evolution in action. The islands enchant visitors with their stark beauty and abundant wildlife, including sea lions, seals, blue-footed boobies and the famous giant tortoises. Tourists contribute millions of dollars to Ecuador's treasury, a powerful incentive for the government to protect the islands. However, tourism is also a threat. Even though all the islands and the waters around them are a national park, land continues to be cleared for farming and tourism-related development. The biggest threat is the introduction of exotic species by people, disrupting the delicate web of life on the islands and devastating the defenseless native species and habitats. Overfishing in the marine park is another major threat. Most of the fishing is illegal and the catch is sold to foreign markets. Tour boats could actually help to reduce this threat by serving as the eyes and ears of park authorities.

Principles of Certification require the company to have a management policy that includes compliance with national legislation and international agreements, as well as the SmartVoyager standards. The tourist operation must support and promote conservation of the Galapagos National Park and the Galapagos Marine Reserve. The tourist operation must prevent or mitigate and compensate for any environmental damage done to the Galapagos Island and Marine Reserve and prevent the introduction of species from the continent to the islands and the dispersal of species between islands. The tourist operation must elevate the socioeconomic welfare and quality of life of the workers and their families. All personnel involved with the tourist operation must receive environmental education and training. The company must make a commitment to the welfare and socioeconomic development of the Galapagos Islands community.

Boat operators must plan and control the consumption, supply and storage of materials taking into consideration the well-being of tourists, workers, local communities and conservation of natural ecosystems. Boats must follow a waste-management plan, including reduction, reuse, recycling, and adequate final treatment and disposal of all wastes. Tourists must be guided in their involvement in protecting natural resources and local cultures, in accordance with these standards to avoid impacts and collaborate with the island conservation programmes. The tourist operation must guarantee the safety of all involved individuals. The tourist operation activities must be planned, monitored and evaluated, taking into consideration technical, economic, social and environmental factors.

After 2 years of development, the programme was launched in May 2000. The standards were tested on several boats, and the first SmartVoyager certifications were expected before the end of 2000. CCD has six scientists with experience in certification who will conduct the audits. The group can also call on experts in local agencies, within the industry itself, the park service, research institutions and the Rainforest Alliance. Boat operators will pay for audits and the use of the ecolabel. Programme managers hope that these fees will eventually cover the costs of the initiative. Most boats operating in the Galapagos are expected to join the programme. The criteria will be revised annually in an open, transparent, inclusive and documented process. Certification contracts are for 1 year; boats must be inspected at least annually. SmartVoyager auditors can guide boat operators to a variety of expert sources of information and technical services.

Tourfor, Europe

Xavier Font, Leeds Metropolitan University

Tourfor is the working title for a proposed ecolabel for tourism in forest areas (and by extension, outdoor recreation) in Europe. This project is based on a partnership between the European Commission LIFE (L'Instrument Financier pour l'Environnement) programme and Buckinghamshire Chilterns University College (UK) with support from North Karelia Polytechnic in Finland and Estacao Florestal Nacional in Portugal (LIFE96ENV/UK/000413). The label has been planned for accommodation and recreation management units in partially forested areas. The proposal purposely targeted a subsector of the tourism and recreation industry with high potential for tourism development, high environmental value and limited economic returns from its traditional revenue-generating activities (i.e. timber production).

The Tourfor ecolabel criteria are based on the implementation of environmental management systems (EMS) by the management of the sites applying for the label. This places the onus on the management of the site to take responsibility for defining its own agenda in a way that it can be managed and that is appropriate to local conditions and resources. An EMS will require the site to write a policy, prepare a site review and identify impacts, prioritize them, prepare a programme and carry it out, keep records of actions taken and measurements of impacts after actions, and finally monitor the system. The approach of this label makes it partially compatible with EMAS and ISO 14001.

A manual has been developed and published, and this has been piloted in the UK, Finland and Portugal. Several prizes were given in an event at the Millennium Dome (Greenwich, London) in January 2000 to the managers of sites demonstrating achievements towards some or all the elements of an EMS. These have been written as case studies of good practice, showing how an EMS can be adapted to both large and small operations with formal and informal recreation and tourism activities.

The proposal was submitted to the European Commission in January 2000, with the recommendation to pilot the results from Tourfor into an ecolabel under the auspices of the Foundation for Environmental Education in Europe.

TUI Environment Initiatives, Worldwide

Mechtild Latussek Environmental Management TUI Group and http://www.tui-environment.com

Touristik Union International (TUI) is the largest tour operator in Europe (5 million tourists per year), and is an outstanding example in environmental management applied to business practice. TUI does not have its own ecolabel logo, because for a tour operator it is problematical to undertake any self promotion about environmental quality in this way. However, the work done on environmental purchasing policies is worth mentioning in this context.

TUI has incorporated environmental criteria as part of its environmental purchasing policy, based on the assessment of providers against environmental checklists. TUI holiday brochures provide the customer with the results from environmental surveys so they can choose those with sound environmental management. In the description of the hotel clients find additional remarks about hotels with an outstanding engagement in environmental management and activities compared with other hotels in the region. In 1999, 200 hotels out of 10,000 contracting partners of TUI all over the world were selected to be advertised as hotels with environmentally sound hotel management. Some environmental measures and activities by the hotel are mentioned as examples and as proof for the customer. Since 1997 the company also recognizes outstanding environmental performance and customer satisfaction in five hotels per year with the 'TUI Environmental Champion'.

There are environmental checklists for destinations, accommodation providers and transportation. The TUI environmental checklist for hotels, clubs and holiday apartments includes:

1. *Hotel management*: sewage treatment, waste disposal, water supply and water-saving measures, energy supply and energy-saving measures, consumption numbers, purchasing and provision, food goods and beverages department health and hygiene, and training of employees.
2. *Architecture and building materials.*
3. *Noise protection.*
4. *Green spaces.*
5. *Pool area.*
6. *Location and immediate surroundings.*
7. *Quality of the sea near the hotel.*
8. *Quality of the beaches near the hotel.*
9. *Environmental information and offers.*
10. *Environmental activities.*

Although this is not an ecolabel, since it does not give hotels recognition outside the TUI brochures, for all intents and purposes it is operated with the rigour and methodology of an ecolabel. Furthermore, the environmental practices in purchasing green products and assessing environmental issues among the suppliers, together with their crucial purchasing power, mean that other companies and tourists value environmental statements made by TUI. This is printed in 30 million tourist brochures, a much larger marketing campaign than any ecolabel can run in the foreseeable future, and this becomes the strength of their work.

Besides their environmental purchasing policy programme, TUI operates the 'TUI International Environment Award', an annual award recognizing projects that have an outstanding contribution to the environment in tourism destinations used by TUI. This award can be given to individuals, organizations and companies active in environmental protection and tourism, and a cash prize of up to DM 20,000 (approx. US$/€10,000).

Addresses of Ecolabelling Bodies

Austrian ecolabel for tourism organizations (Das Österreichisches Umweltzeichen für Tourismusbetriebe), 'Umweltberatung – Gesellschaft für ökologische Projektabwicklung, Bildung und', Forschung mbH, Mariahilferstraße 89/29, A-1060 Wien, Austria. Phone: 43-1 5877393, fax: 43-1 587739318

Bed & Bike: bicycle-friendly guest operations (Bett & Bike: Fahrradfreundliche Gastbetriebe), ADFC-Bundesverband, Postfach 107747, 28077 Bremen, Germany. Phone: 49-421 346290, fax: 49-421 3462950, www.fa-tourismus.adfc.de/bettbike.htm

Biosphere Hotels, ASOLAN-Asociación Insular de Empresas y Apartamentos de Lanzarote, Burgao 3, E-35510 Puerto del Carmen, Lanzarote, Canary Islands, Spain. Phone: 34-34285/3627, fax: 34-34285/3646, www.biohotel.com, e-mail: mpguillen@asolan. com

The Blue Flag Campaign, The Danish Outdoor Council (on behalf of FEEE), Scandiagade 13, 2450 Kopenhagen SV, Denmark. Phone: 45-33790079, fax: 45-33790179, www.blueflag.org

Blue Swallow (Blaue Schwalbe), Verträglich Reisen, PF 40 19 03, D-80719 München, Germany. Phone: 49-89 3080128, fax: 49-89 3080118

British Airways Tourism for Tomorrow Awards, British Airways plc/ Tourism for Tomorrow Award, PO Box 365, UB7 OGB, UK; Waterside (HBBG), Harmondsworth, West Drayton, UK. Phone: 44-181 7385816, fax: 44-181 7389850

Bundesumweltzeichen für Tourismusbetriebe, Ooe Umweltakademie, Stockhofstrabe 32, A-4020 Linz, Austria. Phone: 43-732 7720 4418, e-mail: johanna.lang@ooe.gv.at

Certification of lodges, Eco-tourism Society of Kenya (ESOK), ESOK Secretariat, Tack International, PO Box 55922, Nairobi, Kenya. Phone: 254-2 228776/7/8/9/, fax: 254-2331897/21336, e-mail: tack@form-net.com

Committed to Green, Committed to Green Foundation, 51 South Street, Dorking, Surrey RH4 2JX, UK. Phone: 44-1306 743 288, fax: 44-1306 742 496, http://www.committedtogreen.org/, e-mail: admin@committedtogreen.org

Competition for environmentally friendly campsites in Germany (Wettbewerb Umweltfreundliche Campingplätze in Deutschland), Deutscher Hotel- und Gaststättenverband (DEHOGA), Kronprinzenstr. 46, D-53173 Bonn, Germany. Phone: 44-228 820080, fax: 44-228 8200846, www.dehoga.de

Costa Rican Sustainable Tourism Certificate, Costa Rican Tourism Institute, PO Box 777-1000, San Jose, Costa Rica. Phone: 506-223 1733 x 328, fax: 506 223 5107, www.turismo-sostenible.co.cr/EN/index-en.shtml, e-mail: info@turismo-sostenible.co.cr

The David Bellamy Conservation Award, BH&HPA, British Holiday and Home Parks Association, 1 Kesington Gore, London SW7 2AR, UK. Phone: 44-1452526911, fax: 44-1452508508, www.ukparks.com

Destination 21, Grønt uddannelsescenter i, Vestsjælland, 'Bakkedraget 22, Hjembæk, 4450', Jyderup, Denmark. Phone: 45-59 26 86 70, fax: 45-59 26 27 29, www.eco-net.dk/Blad/nr35/andre.html#7, e-mail: groencenter@get2net.dk

DRV International Environment Award, Deutscher Reisebüro-Verband e.V. (DRV), Ms Ute Quintar, Mannheimmer Str. 15, Frankfurt/Main 60329, Germany. Phone: 49-69 27 3907-22

Eco-dynamic Enterprise (Entreprise éco-dynamique), Institut Bruxellois pour la Gestion de l'Environnement, Département éco-comportement et éco-management, Gulledelle 100, 1200 Bruxelles, Belgium. Fax: www.ibgebim.be/FR/, e-mail: mge@ibgebim.be

Eco-Ibex (Eco-Grischun) in Graubünden, Verein Ökomarkt Graubünden, Geschäftsstelle Altes Schulhaus, CH-7215 Fanas, Switzerland. Phone: 41-81 330 30 20, fax: 41-81 330 30 24

Ecolabel for the Luxembourg Tourism Organizations (Ecolabel für Luxemburger Tourismusbetriebe), Stiftung ÖKO-FONDS, 6, Rue Vauban, L-2663, Luxembourg. Phone: 352-42 44 84, fax: 352-42 22 42, www.emweltzenter.lu/emweltzenter/oekofonds/ecolabel/virstellung.htm, e-mail: emweltberodung@emweltzenter.lu

Eco-Snail of the North Sea Island of Borkum (Umweltschnecke Nordseeinsel Borkum), Stadt Borkum, Postfach 2060, D-26746 Borkum, Germany. Phone: 49-49223030, fax: 49-49223200

Ecotel Certification, HVS International, 372 Willis Avenue, Mineola, New York 11501, USA. Phone: 1-516 248-8828 x 238, fax: 1-516 742-3059, www.hvsecoservices.com/ECOTEL.htm, e-mail: cbalfe@hvsinternational.com

Ecotourism Symbol Alcudia (Distintivo Ecoturistico de Alcudia), Municipio de Alcudia, C/Albellons 2, E-07400 Alcudia, Mallorca, Spain. Phone: 34-971 548071, fax: 34-971 546515

The Emblem of Guarantee of Environmental Quality (El distintiu de qualitat ambiental), Medi Ambient, Avda. Diagonal 523–525, 08029

Barcelona, Spain. Phone: 34-934 445100, fax: 34-934 197630, www.gencat.es/mediamb, e-mail: wsia@correu.gencat.es

Environment Squirrel (Umwelteichhörnchen), Allgemeiner Deutscher Automobilclub (ADAC), Am Westpark 8, D-81373 München, Germany. Phone: 49-89 76766407, fax: 49-89 7608300, www.adac.de

Environmental quality label of holiday houses (Umweltgütezeichen für Ferienhäuser), Møns Turistbureau, Storegade 2, 4780 Stege, Denmark. Phone: 45-55 814411, fax: 45-55 814846, www.moen-touristbureau.dk

Environmental Quality Mark for Alpine Club Mountain Huts (Umweltgütesiegel auf Alpenvereinshütten) Deutscher Alpenverein e.V., Postfach 500 220, 80972 München, Germany. Phone: 49-89 14003-0, fax: 49-89 1400311

Environmental Seal of Quality Tirol and South-Tirol (Umweltsiegel Tyrol & South-Tyrol), Tirol Werbung, Maria-Theresienstraße 55, A-6010 Innsbruck, Austria. Phone: 43-512 5320 0, fax: 43-512 5320150, www.tiscover.com/oeko-

Environmentally conscious hotels and guest houses, Bavaria (Umweltbewußter Hotel- und Gaststättenbetrieb, Bayern), Bayerisches Staatsministerium für Landesentwicklung und, Umweltfragen, Rosenkavalierplatz 2, D-81925 München, Germany. Phone: 49-89 92142353, fax: 49-89 92142471, www.bayern.de/stmlu

Environmentally Friendly Campsites – Lever (Umweltfreundliche Campingplätze – Lever), Kommunikations- und Konfliktberatung Gerhard Jakubowski, Große Straße 22, Ahrensburg 22926, Peter Hambrinker, Germany. Phone: 49-4102 51268-69, fax: 49-4102 56255, e-mail: g.jakubowski@t-online.de

Environmentally friendly guest houses (Umweltfreundliches Gastgewerbe), Tourismusverband Mecklenburg-Vorpommern e.V., Platz der Freundschaft 1, D-18059 Rostock, Germany. Phone: 49-381 4030500, fax: 49-381 4030555

The environmentally oriented hotel and guest house (Der umweltorientierte Hotel- und Gaststättenbetrieb), Schleswig-Holstein & Hessen, DEHOGA Schleswig-Holstein, Hamburger Chaussee 349, D-24113 Kiel, Germany. Phone: 49-431 651866, fax: 49-431 651868, www.dehoga.com

The European Charter for Sustainable Tourism in Protected Areas, Federation Des Parcs Naturels Régionaux de France, 4, rue de Stockholme, F-75008, Paris, France. Phone: 33-1 44 90 86 20, fax: 33-1 45 22 70 78, e-mail: svautier@parcs-naturels-regionaux.tm.fr

European Prize for Tourism and the Environment, European Commission, DG XXIII, Tourism Unit, 80, rue d'Arlon (2/28), B-1040 Brüssel, Belgium. Fax: 32-2 2961377

The Farmer of Liechtenstein (LandWirt Liechtenstein), Herr Andreas Gerner, Gewerbe- und Wirtschaftskammer, Zollstraße 23, FL-9494 Schaan, Liechtenstein

Gîtes Panda, La Chaume, 36380 Rosnay, France. Phone: 33-254378203, fax: 33-254 377744

Green Alliance (Alianza Verde), Conservation International Foundation, 2501 M Street, NW, Suite 200, Washington, DC 20037, USA. Phone: 1-202 429-5660, fax: 1-202 887-0193, www.conservation.org/

Green Globe 21, Green Globe 21, 30 Grosvenor Gardens, London SW1W ODH, UK. Phone: 44-20 77304428, fax: 44-20 77305515, www.greenglobe21.com

Green hand – we do something for the environment (Grüne Hand – Wir tun etwas für die Umwelt), Gemeinde Saalbach, c/o C. Deutinger, Hotel Birkenhof, Haldweg 312, A-5754 Saalbach-Hinterglemm, Austria. Phone: 43-6541 6257, fax: 43-6541 8482

Green Hotels, Green Hotels, PO Box 420212, Houston, TX 77242-0212, USA. Phone: 1-713-789 8889, fax: 1-713-789 9786, www.greenhotels.com/, e-mail: info@greenhotels.com

The Green Key (Den Groenne Noegle), HORESTA (Danish Hotel, Restaurant and Tourism Employers Association), Vodroffsvej 46, Fredriksberg C, DK-1900 Kopenhagen, Denmark. Phone: 45-31356088, fax: 45-31351510, www.dengroennenoegle.dk/, e-mail: kaas@horesta.dk

Green Keys (Les Clefs Vertes), FEEE, Fondation pour L'Education a l'Environnement en Europe, 6, avenue du Maine, 75015 Paris, France. Phone: 33-145 49 40 50, fax: 33-145 49 27 69, www.ifrance.com/clefsvertes/acceng.htm

Green Leaf, Green Leaf Foundation, c/o Thai Hotels Association, 203-209 Ratchdamnoen Klang Avenue, Bowornivet, Bangkok 10200, Thailand

Green Palms (Grüne Palme), GEO SAISON, 20444 Hamburg, Germany. Phone: 49-40 37033690

Green Tourism Business Scheme, SEA Ltd, 28 Glasgow Road, Perth PH2 ONX, UK. Phone: 44-1738 632162, fax: 44-1738 622268, www.greentourism.org.uk/, e-mail: john@green-business.com

Grüne Bäumchen, ADAC Reise GmbH, Leonhard-Moll-Bogen 1-3, D-81373 München, Germany. Phone: 49-89 7676 6779, fax: 49-89 76766155, www.adac.de

Holiday Villages in Austria (Dorfurlaub in Österreich), Verein Dorfurlaub in Österreich, Unterwollaninger Str. 53, A-9500 Villach, Austria. Phone: 43-4242 257531, fax: 43-4242 257581

Holidays in bio-farms in Germany (Urlaub auf Biohöfen in Deutschland), ECEAT Deutschland, Postfach 11 02 43, 19002 Schwerin, Germany. Phone: 49-385 562918, fax: 49-385 562922

Horizons, Tourism Saskatchewan, 101-230 22nd St East, Saskatoon, Saskatchewan S7K 0E9, Canada. Phone: 1-800-331-1529, fax: 1-306 933 5900, www.ecotourism.sk.ca/, e-mail: hnaj@sk.sympatico.ca

IH&RA Environmental Award, International Hotel and Restaurant Association, 251, rue du Faubourg St. Martin, F-75010 Paris, France. Phone: 33-1 44899407, fax: 33-1 10367330

International Environmental Award (Internationale Umweltauszeich-nung), Deutscher Reisebüro und Reiseveranstalter Verband (DRV), Mannheimer Str. 15, D-60329 Frankfurt a.M., Germany. Phone: 49-69 2739070, fax: 49-69 236647, www.drv.de/navigation/verband5.html, e-mail: info@drv.de

Kiskeya Alternative Tourism Sustainability certification program, Kalalu-Danza, PO Box 109-Z, Zona Colonial, Santo Domingo, Dominican Republic. Phone: 1809 537 8977, fax: 1809 221 4219, www.kiskeya-alternative.org, e-mail: kad@kiskeya-alternative.org

Landscape of the Year (Landschaft des Jahres), NFI Naturfreunde Internationale, Diefenbachgasse 36, A-1150 Wien, Austria. Phone: 43-1 8923877, fax: 43-1 8129789, www.nfi.at

Millieubarometer, Recron, Postbus 666, NL-6800 AR Arnkern, The Netherlands. Phone: 31-152 127690, e-mail: info@recron.nl

Model campsites in Germany (Vorbildliche Campingplätze in Deutschland), Deutscher Tourismusverband (DTV), Bertha-von-Suttner-Platz, 53111 Bonn, Germany. Phone: 49-02289 852215, fax: 49-0228 698722, www.DeutscherTourismusverband.de, e-mail: DeutscherTourismusverband@t-online.de

National Award for Environmentally-friendly Tourism Resorts, Deutscher Fremdenverkehrsverband e.V., Bertha-von-Suttner-Platz 13, D-53111 Bonn, Germany. Phone: 49-228 985220, fax: 49-228 698722

National Ecotourism Accreditation Program, Ecotourism Association of Australia, GPO Box 268, Brisbane 4001, Queensland, Australia. Phone: 61-7 3229 5550, fax: 61-7 3229 5255, www.ecotourism.org.au, e-mail: mail@ecotourism.org.au

Natural Products Hohe Tauern National Park (Naturprodukt Nationalpark Hohe Tauern), ARGE Nationalparkregion Hohe Tauern, Saalfeldnerstr. 7, A-5700 Zell am See, Austria. Phone: 43-6542 7239326, fax: 43-6542 7239330

The Nordic Ecolabeling of Hotels, SFS-Ecolabelling, PB 116, 00241 Helsingfors, Finland. Phone: 358-9 1499331, fax: 358-9 14993320, www.svanen.nu/nordic/Swanindex.htm

Ökto-Pikto Camping, ADAC Verlag GmbH, Am Westpark 8, 81373 München, Germany. Phone: 49-89 76762836, fax: 49-89 76762836, www.adac.de

PAN Parks, WWF International, Avenue du Mont-Blanc, 1196 Gland, Switzerland. Phone: 41-22 3649426, fax: 41-22 3643239, www.panparks.com/

Q-Plus-Kleinwalsertal, Kleinwalsertal – Tourismus, Im Walserhaus, 87568 Hirschegg, Austria. Phone: 43-551 751140, fax: 43-5517 511421, www.tiscover.com/kleinwalsertal

Quality Mountain, Monique Paccolat, Rue de l`Avenir 11, Postfach 654, CH-1951 Sitten, Switzerland. Phone: 41-27 3222727, fax: 41-27 3225727, e-mail: montagne-plus@bluewin.ch

Raiffeisen-Förderungspreis, Naturforum Weissensee, A-9762 Weissensee, Austria. Phone: 43-4713-22200, fax: 43-4713 222044

Regionalmarke Biosphärenreservat Schorfheide-Chorin, Kultur-landschaft Uckermark e.V., Kirchstrasse 11, 16278 Greiffenberg, Germany Phone: 49-33334 86990, fax: 49-33334 86715

Scottish Golf Course Wildlife Initiative, Scottish Golf Course Wildlife Group, The Stables, Dalkeith Country Park, Midlothian, EH22 2NA, UK. Phone: 44-131 660 9480, www.scottishgolf.com/environment, e-mail: scotgolf.wildlife@virgin.net

Seaside Award, Seaside Award Office, Tidy Britain Group, Seymour House, 5 Chalk Hill House, 19 Rosary Road, Norwich NR1 1SZ, UK. Phone: 44-1603 766076, fax: 44 1603 760 580, www.tidybritain.org.uk, e-mail: joses@tidybritain.org.uk

Smart Voyager, Rainforest Alliance, 65 Bleecker Street, New York, NY 10012, USA. Phone: 1-212 677 1900, www.rainforest-alliance.org, e-mail: smartvoyager@ra.org

TAT-Orte – Municipalities in the ecological competition (TAT-Orte – Gemeinden im ökologischen Wettbewerb), Deutsches Institut für Urbanistik, Arbeitsbereich Umwelt, Straße des 17 Juni 112, D-10623 Berlin, Germany. Phone: 49-30 39001 244, fax: 49-30 39001241, www.difu.de/tatorte/navigation/

The best choice for the environment (Die beste Wahl für die Umwelt), Collegium Touristicum Corinthian (CTC), Aichelburg-Labiastr. 43, A-9020 Klagenfurt, Austria. Phone: 43-463 591813, fax: 43-463 5548810

Thüringen Gastlichkeit, Thüringer Hotel- und Gaststättenverband e.V., Geschäftsstelle Suhl, Würzburger Strasse 3, D-98529 Suhl, Germany. Phone: 49-3681 309304, fax: 49-3681 309305

Top Team NaTour: Federal Competition for Children and Youth Travel (TopTeamNaTour: Bundeswettbewerb Kinder- und Jugendreisen), AG Jugendreisen mit Einsicht, Bad Meinberger Str. 1, D-32760 Detmold, Germany. Phone: 49-5231 993633, fax: 49-5231 993666, www.topteamnatour.de

Tourfor, Buckinghamshire Chilterns University College, Kingshill Road, High Wycombe, Buckinghamshire, HP13 5BB, UK. Phone: 44 1494 605163, fax: 44-1494 465 432, www.tourfor.com, e-mail: jtribe01@bcuc.ac.uk

TUI Environment Initiatives, TUI, Department of Environment, Karl-Wiechert-Allee 23, D-30625, Hannover, Germany. www.tui-environment.com/english/r/re0.htm

We run an environmentally oriented operation (Wir führen einen umwelt-freundlichen Betrieb), Hotel- und Gaststättenverband Baden-Württemberg, Goethestr. 4, D-88214 Ravensburg, Germany. Phone: 49-751 31708, fax: 49-751 26098, www.hogabw.de

Wettbewerb Gemeinsam – ontour, Die NaturFreunde Bundesgruppe, Postfach 60 04 41, 70304 Stuttgart, Germany. Phone: 49-711 4095418, fax: 49-711 409544

Index

DATE DUE

NOV 2 8 2003